Home in the World

AMARTYA SEN

Home in the World
A Memoir

Liveright Publishing Corporation

A Division of W. W. Norton & Company
Celebrating a Century of Independent Publishing

To *Emma*

All rights reserved
Printed in the United States of America
First published as a Liveright paperback 2023

For information about permission to reproduce selections from this book, write to
Permissions, Liveright Publishing Corporation, a division of W. W. Norton & Company, Inc.,
500 Fifth Avenue, New York, NY 10110

For information about special discounts for bulk purchases, please contact
W. W. Norton Special Sales at specialsales@wwnorton.com or 800-233-4830

Manufacturing by Lakeside Book Company

Library of Congress Cataloging-in-Publication Data

Names: Sen, Amartya, 1933– author.
Title: Home in the world : a memoir / Amartya Sen.
Description: First American edition. | New York, NY : Liveright Publishing Corporation, a division of
W. W. Norton & Company, 2022. | Includes bibliographical references.
Identifiers: LCCN 2021048968 | ISBN 9781324091615 (hardcover) | ISBN 9781324091622 (epub)
Subjects: LCSH: Sen, Amartya, 1933– | Economists—India—Biography.
Classification: LCC HB126.I43 S487 2022 | DDC 330.092 [B]—dc23/eng/20211115
LC record available at https://lccn.loc.gov/2021048968

ISBN 978-1-324-09292-6 pbk.

Liveright Publishing Corporation, 500 Fifth Avenue, New York, N.Y. 10110
www.wwnorton.com

W. W. Norton & Company Ltd., 15 Carlisle Street, London W1D 3BS

1 2 3 4 5 6 7 8 9 0

Contents

Acknowledgements   vii

A Note on the Spelling of Sanskrit Words   ix

Preface   xi

PART ONE

1 Dhaka and Mandalay   3

2 The Rivers of Bengal   19

3 School Without Walls   35

4 The Company of Grandparents   57

5 A World of Arguments   79

6 The Presence of the Past   93

PART TWO

7 The Last Famine   113

8 Bengal and the Idea of Bangladesh   122

9 Resistance and Division   138

10 Britain and India   155

PART THREE

11 The Urbanity of Calcutta   173

12 College Street   190

13 What to Make of Marx   207

14 An Early Battle   223

15 To England   239

CONTENTS

PART FOUR

16 The Gates of Trinity   255
17 Friends and Circles   264
18 What Economics?   282
19 Where is Europe?   295
20 Conversation and Politics   308
21 Between Cambridge and Calcutta   326
22 Dobb, Sraffa and Robertson   342
23 American Encounters   357
24 Cambridge Re-examined   368

PART FIVE

25 Persuasion and Cooperation   385
26 Near and Far   395

Notes   409
Name Index   426
Subject Index   443

Acknowledgements

'Fond Memory brings the light / Of other days around me,' wrote Thomas Moore, in the sadness of what he describes as a 'stilly night'. He recalls the friends who had to 'fall', and 'the smiles, the tears / Of boyhood's years', and also talks about his sense of being 'deserted' by all. The recollection of memories can certainly be a sad exercise, evidently even for a young man of twenty-six, as Moore was at the time he wrote the poem. And yet remembering the past – even from long ago – can also be enjoyable, bringing one back to happy events, engaging reflections and challenging dilemmas.

Remembering, however, is not the same thing as writing a memoir. The latter has to be aimed mostly at other people. The self-indulgence of what is called in Sanskrit *smriticharan* ('the grazing of one's own memory') may not interest others at all, who may nevertheless be curious about what actually happened and how the experiences and thoughts of another person can be understood – and shared. In assisting me to move from my memory to a written memoir and in making sure that what I have tried to say does not lack clarity and cogency, Stuart Proffitt has been astonishingly helpful. I am hugely indebted to him for what he has done for the book.

At a critical stage of planning this book, I also received excellent advice from Lynn Nesbit, and also from Robert Weil. I am grateful to them both. In talking about the book while it was being written, I have benefited from points raised by my children, Antara, Nandana, Indrani and Kabir, and also by my cousins Ratnamala and Miradi. I have also received good suggestions from Rehman Sobhan, Rounaq Jahan, Paul Simm, Victoria Gray and Sugata Bose. A long public conversation I had some time ago with Tim Besley and Angus Deaton, partly on my work, for a report to the Annual Review of Economics, has been very helpful to me in writing some parts of this book, and I am grateful to them both.

Kumar Rana and Aditya Balasubramanian read large parts of the manuscript of the book at different stages of my writing, and their careful comments have been tremendously useful for me. The book was written over nearly a decade, and most of the writing happened – mostly during the summers – at the Hotel Le Dune in Sabaudia, Italy, and at Trinity College, Cambridge. For their help in coordinating my efforts, I am very grateful to Inga Huld Markan, Chie Ri and Arabinda Nandy.

I greatly appreciate the assistance of a number of people at Penguin Books whose help has been critically important for the production of this book, including Jane Robertson, Richard Duguid, Alice Skinner, Sandra Fuller, Matt Hutchinson, Ania Gordon and Coralie Bickford-Smith.

Finally, my wife Emma Rothschild, to whom the book is dedicated, read the entire manuscript and made numerous valuable suggestions, commenting on almost every page. It is not easy to express my appreciation of this adequately.

A Note on the Spelling of Sanskrit Words

I have abstained from using diacritical marks in spelling Sanskrit words (except where I quote other writers) since they can be discouraging to non-specialist readers because of their complication. They can also be a bit confusing to those whose main alphabetic experience has been through English. For example, it is hard to persuade a diacritical amateur that *calk* is a good way of making people invoke the object that goes with a blackboard (called 'chalk' in English). I have tried instead to spell Sanskrit words with letters that approximate to their English pronunciation. With some indulgence, this can be made to work, but it is not perfect.

Preface

One of the earliest memories from my childhood is being awakened by the loud hoot of a ship. I was nearly three years old. The sound made me sit up with some anxiety, but my parents reassured me that all was well and that we were sailing from Calcutta to Rangoon through the Bay of Bengal. My father, who taught Chemistry at Dhaka University in what is now Bangladesh, was about to begin three years' teaching in Mandalay as a visiting professor. When the hoot woke me, our ship had just completed the hundred-mile journey from Calcutta to the sea on the Ganges (in those days Calcutta was still serving as a port for quite big ships). My father explained to me that we were now going to be on the open sea until we arrived in Rangoon in a couple of days. I did not, of course, know what a sea journey would be like, nor anything about the different ways that people travelled from one place to another. But I did experience a sense of adventure, and an exciting feeling that something serious was happening to me which had never happened before. The deep blue waters of the Bay of Bengal looked as if they had been conjured from Aladdin's lamp.

Nearly all my earliest memories came from Burma, where we stayed for a little over three years. Some of what I remember was clearly real, such as the beautiful palace in Mandalay, with a charming moat around it, the striking views from the banks of the Irrawaddy River and the presence of shapely pagodas wherever we went. But my memories of the elegance of Mandalay may not match the accounts some others give of a very dusty city, and the striking beauty of our typical Burmese house was, I expect, exaggerated by my love for it. The fact is, I could not have been happier.

I travelled from my earliest days. After my childhood in Burma, I went back to Dhaka, but then moved again fairly soon to live and study in Santiniketan, where Rabindranath Tagore, the visionary poet, had established his experimental school. He was a great influence on me and my family. The title of this memoir is inspired by his book *The Home and the World*, and reflects his influence.

After ten engaging years at Tagore's school in Santiniketan, I went to Calcutta to begin my college education. I had some excellent teachers and great classmates there, and the work of the college was well supplemented by a coffee house next door in which wonderfully engaging discussions and debates often occurred. From there I went to Cambridge, England, which started with another captivating boat journey, this time from Bombay to London. Both Cambridge and my college, Trinity, drew me into their splendid old history.

Then came a year spent teaching at MIT in Cambridge, Massachusetts, and at Stanford in California. I made brief attempts to put down roots in various places before returning to India (via Lahore and Karachi in Pakistan) to teach at Delhi University, offering courses in economics, philosophy, game theory, mathematical logic, and – a relatively new subject – social choice theory. The recollection of the first three decades of my life ends with happy days as a dedicated young teacher, with the anticipation of a new – and a more mature – stage of my life.

As I found my feet in Delhi, I had time to think a little about my earlier years, filled with a wide range of experiences. I decided that there were two quite different ways of thinking about the civilizations of the world. One approach takes the 'fragmentary' perspective and sees a variety of features as manifestations of quite distinct civilizations. This approach, with the additional feature of hostility between the fragments, has come much into vogue recently, threatening a lasting 'clash of civilizations'.

The other approach is 'inclusive', and concentrates on looking for different manifestations of ultimately one civilization – perhaps we should call it a world civilization – which generates different flowers through an interrelated life of roots and branches. This book is not, of course, an investigation of the nature of civilization, but, as the reader will see, its sympathies are with an inclusive rather than a fragmentary understanding of what the world offers.

From the Crusades in the Middle Ages to the Nazi invasions in the last century, from communal clashes to battles between religious politics, there have been tussles between varying convictions, and yet there have also been forces for unity working against the clashes. We can see, if we look, how understanding can spread from one group to another and from one country to the next. As we move around we cannot escape clues to broader and more integrative stories. Our ability to learn from each other must not be underestimated.

Being in reflective human company can be an enormously constructive experience. At the end of the tenth century and the beginning of the eleventh, the Iranian mathematician Al-Biruni, who spent many years in India, remarked in his book *Tarikh al-Hind* that learning about each other contributes both to knowledge and to peace. He presents a wonderful account of mathematics, astronomy, sociology, philosophy and medicine in India a thousand years ago, and also shows how human knowledge expands through friendship. Al-Biruni's fondness for Indians contributed to his interest and expertise in Indian mathematics and science. This fondness did not, however, prevent him from teasing them a little. Indian mathematics is very good, Al-Biruni says, but the most unusual gift Indian intellectuals have is something quite different: it is their ability to talk eloquently on subjects about which they know absolutely nothing.

Would I be proud of that gift if I had it? I don't know, but perhaps I should begin by talking about things I do know. This memoir is a small attempt to do just that, or at least to talk about things I have experienced, whether or not I actually know them.

PART ONE

I

Dhaka and Mandalay

I

'Where do you consider to be your home?' I was asked by a BBC inter-viewer in London, as we were getting ready for the recording. He was looking at some kind of biography about me. 'You have just moved from one Cambridge to another – and from Harvard to Trinity; you have lived in England for decades but you are still an Indian citizen, with – I presume – a passport full of visas. So, where's your home?' This was in 1998, just after I had rejoined Trinity College as Master (which was the occasion for the interview). 'I feel very much at home here right now,' I said, explaining that I had had a long association with Trinity, having been an undergraduate, a research student, a research fellow and then a teacher there. But I added that I also felt much at home in our old house near Harvard Square at the other Cambridge, and I very much feel at home in India, particularly at our little house in Santini-ketan where I grew up and to which I love going back regularly.

'So,' said the man from the BBC, 'you have no concept of home!' 'On the contrary,' I said, 'I have more than one welcoming home, but I don't share your idea that a home has to be exclusive.' The BBC interviewer looked completely unconvinced.

I have experienced similar defeats in my attempts to respond to other searches for unique identification. 'What is your favourite food?' they asked. There can be many answers to that question, but I gener-ally choose to mumble something like *tagliolini con vongole* or Szechuan duck, and of course *ilish mach* – what the English in India used to call 'hilsha fish', taking liberty with aspirates. But, I went on to explain, it has to be cooked in proper Dhaka style with ground

3

mustard. This kind of reply did not satisfy the questioners, who asked: 'But which is *really* your favourite food?'

'I love them all,' I said, 'but I would not like to live on any one of them as my only food.' My interlocutors did not generally accept that they had obtained from me a reasonable answer to a good question. However, if I was lucky, I did get a polite nod in the discussion of food – but never, ever when it came to something as serious as 'home'. 'Surely, you must have some particular place where you are *really at home*?'

2

Why one place? Perhaps I relax too easily. In traditional Bengali, the question 'where is your home?' has a precise meaning – something very different from the one that the English question literally conveys. Home – '*ghar*' or '*baḍi*' – is where your family came from, looking back a few generations, even if you and your immediate ancestors have lived somewhere else. This usage has some following all over the subcontinent and, when used in conversations in English, the idea is sometimes translated into the kind of graphic imagery that Indian English has made its own: 'Where do you *hail* from?' Your 'home' may be at a place from which your ancestors could have hailed heartily a few generations ago, even though you yourself may not have been there at all.

My family was living in the city of Dhaka when I was born, though I was not in fact born there. This was in the late autumn of 1933, which, I would learn later, was a year of terrible loss of home and lives in Europe. Sixty thousand professionals – authors, artists, scientists, musicians, actors and painters – emigrated from Germany, mostly to other countries in Europe and to America. A few – usually Jewish – went to India as well. Dhaka, which is now a lively, sprawling and somewhat bewildering city and the energizing capital of Bangladesh, was then a quieter and smaller place, where life always seemed to move gracefully and slowly. We lived in the old, historic part of the city called Wari, not far from Ramna, the campus of Dhaka University, where my father, Ashutosh Sen, taught chemistry. This is all 'old Dhaka' – modern Dhaka extends tens of miles beyond it.

My parents were very happy in Dhaka. So was I and my sister

Manju was too – she was four years younger than me. The house was built by my paternal grandfather, Sharada Prasad Sen, who was a judge in the Dhaka courts. My uncle, Jitendra Prasad Sen, the elder brother of my father, was rarely there, as he was posted to different places in Bengal as a civil servant, but his arrivals at our joint family home (particularly with his daughter Miradi, who was about the same age as me) in Dhaka over the holidays were the beginning of intensely enjoyable periods in my young life. We also had other cousins living in Dhaka (Chinikaka, Chotokaka, Mejda, Babua and others); Manju and I were rather spoilt by the care and attention we got from them.

My roaming uncle's eldest son (he was called Basu but I called him Dadamani) studied in Dhaka University and lived with us. He was an immense source of wisdom and amusement for me. He looked for engaging films for children to take me to, and through his initiative I came to know what I took to be 'the real world', as portrayed in fantastical films such as *The Thief of Baghdad*.

My early memories include going to my father's laboratory, and the huge excitement of seeing that one liquid mixed with another in a test tube could generate something altogether different and unexpected. My father's assistant, Karim, used to show me these absorbing experiments – and I thought his demonstrations were always wonderful.

Those memories came back to me when, at the age of twelve, I first read, with my proudly acquired Sanskrit, the theory of the chemical basis of life according to the Indian materialist school, the Lokayata, which had flourished in India from the sixth century BC: 'from these material elements alone, when transformed into the body, intelligence is produced, just as the inebriating power is developed from the mixing of certain ingredients; and when these are destroyed, intelligence at once perishes also.' I found the analogy very sad – I wanted more in my life than chemistry, and did not at all like the 'at once perishes' bit. Later, when I grew older and thought about many different theories of life, my earliest memory of the laboratory at Dhaka University and Karim's demonstrations retained a lively and haunting presence.

I knew I belonged to Dhaka, but like many urban Bengalis I too saw my home as the village from which the family had moved to the city, in my case two generations earlier. My home village, the ancestral home of my father's family, is a tiny one called Matto, in a district called Manikganj. It is not all that far from the city of Dhaka, but when I was a child it used to take the best part of a day to get there – travelling mostly on boats through a network of rivers. These days you can drive from Dhaka to Matto in a few hours on reasonably good roads. We used to go there once a year, just for a few weeks each time, and I would then feel totally relaxed, thinking that I was back home. There were other boys and girls to play with in Matto who also came in festival times from the far-flung towns where they lived. We had good seasonal friendships, and said goodbye for a year when the time for our urban return arrived.

3

The name of our house in old Dhaka, 'Jagat Kutir', meant 'the cottage of the world'. This partly reflected my grandfather's scepticism of national-ism, though my family would generate quite a few nationalists fighting the British Raj (more on that later). The name also celebrated the mem-ory of his beloved late wife, my paternal grandmother, who was called Jagatlakkhi (sometimes written as Jagatlakshmi, as in Sanskrit). She had died well before I was born. The memory of Jagatlakkhi's much admired wisdom influenced our lives in many ways, and I still practise her rem-edy for hiccups – slowly drinking a glass of cold water with a couple of spoons of sugar stirred in. This, incidentally, is a much pleasanter way of overcoming hiccups than by choking yourself out of breath.

While my father taught at Dhaka University, his father, Sharada Prasad Sen, the judge, was also closely associated with the university, helping with its legal and financial management. People were coming and going all the time, to and from our Dhaka home. These visitors told me about all kinds of things they did in different places. Some of those places were not very far away (they certainly included Calcutta and Delhi, but also Bombay, Hong Kong and Kuala Lumpur), but in my childhood imagination they covered the entire earth. I loved sit-ting next to the fragrant champa tree in the veranda upstairs, listening to the exciting tales of travel and adventure, which I hoped some day would come my way as well.

When my mother, Amita, married, there was no need for her to change her last name, because my maternal grandfather, a well-known scholar in Sanskrit and Indian philosophy, was called Kshiti Mohan Sen. My mother's maiden surname being the same as my father's surname causes problems for me even today for identity checks, when the guardians of secure communication ask me for my mother's maiden name ('no, no, I said her *maiden* name!').

Kshiti Mohan taught in Santiniketan, in what is now West Bengal in India, in an educational institution named Visva-Bharati – a name that invoked the objective of uniting the world (*Visva*) with all the articulated wisdom (*Bharati*) it could offer. It was centred around a distinguished school, but also had facilities for advanced research, which were quite widely known. Visva-Bharati had been established in 1901 by the poet Rabindranath Tagore. Kshiti Mohan was not only something of a lieutenant to Tagore, helping him to give shape to Visva-Bharati as an educational institution, but he also contributed greatly to its academic standing because of his extraordinary reputation as a scholar and his much-admired books – written in Sanskrit, Bengali, Hindi and Gujarati.

My mother's family were all very close to Rabindranath. My mother, Amita, was a skilled stage dancer in a new style that Tagore had helped to devise – a style that would now be called 'modern dance' (and would have appeared extremely modern then). She played the lead female part in several of Tagore's dance dramas in Calcutta, at a time when women from 'good families' did not appear on the stage. Nor did they learn judo, as my mother did at the Santiniketan School. It says something about Tagore's school that this opportunity was offered to girl students as well as boys a hundred years ago.

When my parents' marriage was being arranged, my father was very impressed, I was told, by the fact that Amita was one of the first middle-class women to appear on stage in a dancing role, in a highly literate play. He had newspaper cuttings containing both great praise of Amita's artistic performance and conservative criticism of the inappropriateness of a woman's appearance on a public stage. Amita's daring, in addition to her dancing talents, played a role in my father's rapid response when the marriage was proposed. Indeed, this was the one hint of volition which both my parents were later keen to emphasize in their arranged marriage. They were also fond of talking about the fact that they had gone out to a film together on their own (though, I guess, this would have been very much a part of the 'arrangement'). But the newspaper reports of my mother's performance in dance dramas, written and directed by Tagore, were, my father told me, quite central to the story.

When I was born, Rabindranath persuaded my mother that it was boring to stick to well-used names and he proposed a new name for me. Amartya, by inference, means immortal in Sanskrit: 'Martya', which comes from *mrityu* (one of the several Sanskrit words for 'death'), is the name for earth where people die, and 'Amartya' is someone from a place where people do not die – presumably heaven. I have had to explain this grandiose meaning of the name to many people, but I preferred its more literal – and perhaps more spooky – meaning: 'unearthly'.

There is an old custom, common in Bengal, whereby the first child is born at the mother's family home, not at her new – married – one. I suppose the origin of the custom reflected a lack of trust on the part of the mother's parents in the ability of the in-laws to take sufficiently good care of their daughter during childbirth. Following this custom, I came from Dhaka to Santiniketan to be born, still in my mother's womb, and went back to Dhaka when I was two months old.

Santiniketan (which means 'the abode of peace' in Bengali) gave me another home, as well as Dhaka. This was initially at my grandparents' house, provided by the school – a little thatched cottage, austere but elegant, in a part of Santiniketan called 'Gurupalli' (teachers' village). Then in 1941 my parents built a small house of their own in another part of the town called 'Sripalli'. The newly built small house was named 'Pratichi', which indicated – in Sanskrit – that it was at the western end. My grandparents then built a home of their own, just next door to our new house, intending to leave the official quarters of the school at some stage.

I was particularly close to my maternal grandmother, Kiranbala, my '*didima*', who was a talented painter on pottery and also highly skilled as a midwife, assisting all births in the medically primitive Santiniketan, including that of her own grandchildren. Kiranbala had very considerable medical knowledge she had carefully acquired over the years. I remember listening to her intently when she explained to me how much difference to safety – and indeed to the chances of survival – is made even by very simple informed care, such as adequate and intelligent use of antiseptics, which were so often neglected in those days in home births. Among many other things, I learned from her a great deal about the unnecessarily high death rates in India both of mothers and of children during delivery. Later, when maternal mortality and child morbidity became a part of my own research interests, I would often think of my long chats with Didima, sitting next to her in the kitchen on a cane-made *mora*. I developed a great admiration for her scientific attitude in every action she undertook.

4

I loved both Dhaka and Santiniketan when I was growing up, but my earliest memories were not of either place. Those were from Burma, where I went with my parents just before my third birthday. We arrived in 1936, and stayed until 1939, while my father had a three-year visiting professorship at the Mandalay Agricultural College, on leave from Dhaka University. I was very excited about the travel, but leaving Didima was not easy. I was told afterwards that when we first sailed from Calcutta to Rangoon and I saw the receding figure of Didima on the quay, I desperately tried to stop the big ship from continuing to move, with loud protests. Happily, the separation was not eternal and we came back each year for holidays in Dhaka and Santiniketan. Like me, my sister Manju was born in Santiniketan, in my maternal grandparents' home. She then spent the first year and a half of her life in Burma. In 1939 we all came back to the quiet beauty of Wari in old Dhaka, combined with regular visits to Santiniketan.

By the time our Burmese days were coming to an end, I was nearly six and my memory had begun to store things. I was happy in Mandalay, and remember many of my early experiences and thrills. The Burmese festivals were particularly wonderful, the bazaars were always humming with intriguing activities, and our wooden home, in the common Mandalay style, was infinitely explorable. I was excited to see something new – and often very colourful – every day as I went out with my parents or my nanny, and learned the Burmese words for nearly everything I saw.

There was also the excitement of seeing new places as I travelled across Burma with my parents – to Rangoon, Pegu, Pagan, even distant Bhamo. I could sense that these were places with a lot of history – great pagodas and buildings that looked like palaces, as indeed some of them were. I loved the view of Maymyo, about twenty-five miles away, from our home at the eastern end of Mandalay, and also much enjoyed the weekend trips to Maymyo to see family friends.

George Orwell, a seasoned Burma dweller, wrote of the enticing journey from Mandalay to Maymyo which would fascinate me when I read it later on.

> Mentally you are still in Mandalay when the train stops at Maymyo, four thousand feet above sea-level. But in stepping out of the carriage you step into a different hemisphere. Suddenly you are breathing cool sweet air that might be that of England, and all around you are green grass, bracken, fir-trees, and hill-women with pink cheeks selling baskets of strawberries.

We used to travel between Mandalay and Maymyo by car, with my father driving and stopping frequently to show me interesting sights. On one night journey we saw – a great excitement for me – a large leopard sitting on the side of the road downhill, its eyeballs shining in the headlights of the car.

On our trips on the river, on boats up the Irrawaddy, the landscape around us changed constantly. Our walks on the banks of the river gave me some understanding of the land and its inhabitants – including varying clusters of people from different tribes, with varying ethnicity, in striking attires. Burma offered an endless variety of exciting experiences and sights, and this is where the world revealed itself to me. I could not compare what I was seeing with anything elsewhere, but the earth did seem beautiful in my young eyes.

5

Because of its many pagodas and palaces, Mandalay is often known as 'the Golden City'. Rudyard Kipling, who had never actually been there, romanticized it in his elegant poem 'Mandalay', though my father told me that what he describes raises questions of physical feasibility. I left those challenges to geographers and decided to be thrilled by my imagining of 'the dawn comes up like thunder outer China 'crost the Bay'.

George Orwell – Eric Arthur Blair – who spent many years in Mandalay, arriving in 1922 to work in the police academy, found it 'dusty and intolerably hot' and generally 'rather a disagreeable town'. It looked very different to me. My memory is of a very agreeable place, with eye-catching buildings, beautiful gardens, intriguing streets, the old royal palace and its moat. Above all, the Burmese seemed to me to be extremely warm, constantly smiling and very likeable.

Since my father had a Ph.D. and was known generally as 'Dr Sen', we had a fairly regular flow of self-selected visitors dropping by to seek 'medical advice from Dr Sen'. My father, of course, knew no medicine (even though he told me that 'we belong to the medical caste – the *vaidyas* – but that was many generations ago'). He nevertheless did what he could to help the seekers of medical attention to receive care from the public hospitals in Mandalay – there were a few that delivered free advice and a modicum of attention, though not much actual medicine.

It can still be hard to get medical attention in today's Burma, unlike in some other countries in the region such as Thailand (which now has a great system of public health care). This is so for the ethnic Burmese in that dysfunctional state, but even more so for the ethnic minorities who actively seek their rights against the regime. The military move them around by means of systematic persecution, and stable arrangements for medical services can be very rare indeed. Yet when medical services do come their way, for example from a group of committed 'backpack medics' from Johns Hopkins Medical School in America, who try to help by going into dangerous territories at great risk to themselves (between 1998 and 2005, six people from one group of medics from Johns Hopkins were actually killed), the Karens, for example, seek health care with great eagerness and are quick to respond to medical advice offered to them.

6

I remember the sense of joy in returning to Mandalay when we had been away – returning to our wooden home on the campus of the Agricultural College at the eastern edge of the town, with its captivating view of the Maymyo hills. How I loved to watch the sun rise behind those hills from our wide veranda! Mandalay had definitely become my home – like old Dhaka, like Matto in Manikganj, like Santiniketan.

Burma, however, was more to me, even then, than just the country of my first memories. I learnt a bit of Burmese and could chat in a halting way. The Burmese nanny who looked after me – and later on my sister Manju too – knew some Bengali words and also spoke a little English – rather more, I suppose, than I did at that time. She was, I thought, breathtakingly lovely. Later on, when I was around twelve, I asked my mother whether she was really gorgeous, and my mother said that she was indeed 'very pretty' – a description that did not seem to me to do adequate justice to her beauty.

But beauty was not the only impressive thing about my nanny (I only wish I could recall her name). She advised everyone in the family what to do. I remember my mother often seeking her counsel, and it was she who once skilfully informed my parents, as they were returning from being out, that, though they would be surprised by the fresh paint on the living-room walls, my drawings really showed extraordinary artistic talent. The crisis of my misbehaviour was thus diffused, and I sometimes wish I could have done more with the artistic talent that she had seen in me.

Women are very prominent in Burma. They are in charge of many of the economic activities and have a strong voice in family decisions. In that respect, Burma is like sub-Saharan Africa and also South East Asia, but very unlike most parts of India, or what is now Pakistan, or West Asia. The importance of women was a strong memory from my childhood recollections of Burma. I didn't think of it as a particularly distinguishing feature at the age of five or six, but later on, when I examined other traditions, my Burmese memories served as a standard against which to compare things elsewhere. They may even perhaps have influenced my attitude to gender-related issues and helped me to think about the agency of women, which would later become one of the subjects of my research.

7

These early memories were among the reasons that Burma still remains a country of great interest to me. This admiration was further enhanced by my coming to know Aung San Suu Kyi, a remarkable woman who led the country with much courage and vision to resist the rule of the military which had seized power in a violent takeover in 1962. I knew Suu Kyi well as a fearless leader, and I felt very fortunate in knowing such a remarkable and brave person, who tolerated awful harassment and prolonged incarceration to fight for the cause of democracy in Burma. I also had the opportunity to come to know her dedicated husband, Michael Aris, a great scholar of Asia, particularly of Tibet and Bhutan.

Michael was effectively excluded from Burma by the military, but from his home in Oxford, where he was a Fellow of St John's College, he did whatever he could to help Suu Kyi – and to work for Burma. In 1991, Michael came to visit Harvard immediately after the award of the Nobel Peace Prize to Suu Kyi had been announced. I was very happy to join him in the celebrations that followed. The sad times came later in 1999, when Michael was dying from metastasized cancer. I was then in England at Trinity College, Cambridge. I feared the worst one morning in late March 1999 when he called to tell me that, even though I would have heard that he was dying, this could not be happening since he had much work to do in looking after 'my Suu and my Burma'. I could see very clearly his sense of crisis and how his mind was working. About two days later I received a message from Oxford that Michael had just died. It was the 27th of March, which was also his birthday. Suu lost not only her loving partner, but also the most constant source of dedicated support and advice she had.

Suu Kyi eventually won a victory over the military in 2010 when she was granted a highly constrained but still substantial role in the political leadership of the country. However, her problems went on increasing, as did those of others in Burma whose misfortunes she perhaps could not – certainly did not – relieve.

Indeed, something went terribly wrong in Suu Kyi's leadership, reflected particularly in her unwillingness to help a vulnerable minority community in Burma: the Rohingyas, a Bengali-speaking Muslim minority group. Her treatment of other minority groups, of which Burma has many, was not exemplary either. Terrible barbarities committed against the Rohingya community by the military and also by intolerant Buddhist activists have not – at least so far – moved her to do anything substantial to help the victims.

If there is a puzzle about Suu Kyi, there is a greater enigma that is even harder to understand, which is particularly disturbing for me: that the Burmese, whose kindness impressed me so much as a young boy, seem to have turned brutally hostile to the Rohingyas, who have had to endure barbarities, torture and murder in an organized pogrom. Aside from being hugely saddened by these events, I also had to question whether my memory of the natural kindness and the outstanding warmth of the Burmese had all been an illusion. But other observers also had an impression similar to mine of the warm and kindly Burmese. A friend – a dedicated backpack medic from Johns Hopkins, Adam Richards – who worked hard to help those Burmese without health care has written: they are 'constantly laughing, constantly singing and smiling. To see their dedication and their humor, in the face of all this adversity is truly inspiring.' These and other accounts chime well with the inexperienced and primitive admiration for the Burmese that I had developed as a young boy.

This inevitably makes me ask the question: what has changed? I can only speculate. What seems to have made the critical difference is the intense propaganda against the Muslim Rohingyas that the military has systematically carried out over recent years. The gentle Burmese my family and I knew have been trained to become violent haters, and in that conversion the military has played a critically influential role – by poisoning people's minds and using well-organized racist propaganda and strong-armed bigotry to induce torturing and killing.

There is, in fact, a global lesson here in the possibility of transforming a gentle population. The power of such propaganda can be seen not just in Burma, but in many countries in the world today. What is happening in Burma (or Myanmar, as it is now called, a name championed by the military) is, of course, particularly barbaric, but the effectiveness of agitations against particular minority groups can be seen in many countries in the world – for example against immigrants in Hungary, or the gay community in Poland, or against Gypsies nearly everywhere in Europe. There is a lesson here which is peculiarly important today in formerly secular India: the religious extremists have been very dedicated – even through governmental policy – in undermining inter-community relations and in threatening the human rights of Muslim minorities.

The Burmese military had harboured an animus against the Rohingyas for a long time, and various legal and civic moves were taken against them even in the 1980s and earlier. But the huge battle against this community peaked later. A particularly severe attack was launched in 2012, with government propaganda urging Buddhist men in Rakhine – where the Rohingyas mostly lived – to defend their 'race and religion'. The military won that propaganda war without serious opposition. This helped them to occupy a strong ground, viciously mistreating the Rohingyas and ultimately preparing to expel them – with the support of remoulded public opinion, using carefully cultivated vilification.

The early days of the propaganda battle would have been a possible time for Suu Kyi to fight against this subversion, and she could have also resisted the concocted story, championed by the military, that the Rohingyas had moved from Bangladesh to Burma, rather than recognizing that in the division of South Asia by the departing British, Rakhine (part of the old Arakan), the area in which the Rohingyas had been living for a very long time, was given to the newly independent Burma. But Suu Kyi remained oddly passive during the period when the military was deliberately distorting the image of the Rohingyas and inciting others to violence against them. It seemed that she did not try to counter the propaganda by the military early enough, when she could have mobilized her political party and her allies as she had done many times before, defending Burmese values – on behalf of the democracy movement. She chose not to fight against the vilification of this minority group, when she could have waged an effective resistance. And after that it was too late.

Within a few years, government propaganda had successfully transformed public opinion so radically against the Rohingyas that anyone standing up for them would face strong opposition from a large proportion of the Buddhist Burmese people. Indeed, by then, defending Rohingyas had become politically dangerous. The military had made sure of that. Suu Kyi's leadership of Burma would have been severely called into question if she had chosen to fight for the Rohingyas once the propaganda battle had been lost. I accept – even as an old admirer of the Burmese people – that Suu Kyi and the national political leadership cannot be freed from responsibility for the social disaster that the Rohingyas faced (and continue to face), but when and how the process became irresistible demands a fuller analysis than they tend to receive.

If there are lessons here, they are not only those of ethics and morality, but also those of political wisdom and of pragmatic practical reasoning. As selective hatred emerges, as it is clearly doing in many countries in the world today from Europe to India, timing and practicality become increasingly relevant. The huge attempts made by human societies to draw closer to each other after the Second World War, which I encountered so strongly in my own experiences, seem today to be in danger of being replaced by terrible manifestations of intolerance, of which Burma provides a most distressing example. Many other countries are also developing similar risks today.

8

While I had some home lessons when we were in Burma, my primary education began seriously only after we returned to Dhaka – at St Gregory's School in Lakshmi bazaar, not very far from our home. It is a missionary school run by a foundation based in America, but, since we could not easily follow what I now think must have been the American English of the white-skinned teachers, there was a rumour among the children – for reasons that I cannot remember – that they came from Belgium. St Gregory's was academically very distinguished, and Brother Jude, the headmaster, was keen not only to provide excellent education, but also to make sure that in the final examinations across the region Gregorians would outshine students from everywhere else. As the school's 125th anniversary publication noted in 2007, recollecting those early days: 'Our boys took the First to the Tenth places time and again.' Some Gregorians became great scholars and lawyers as well as political leaders (presidents of Bangladesh among them). As Kamal Hossain, the first Foreign Minister of independent Bangladesh, has noted, the academic performance of the school was related to the dedication of the teachers to do whatever they could to help the students, being always available outside classes as well as being exceptionally dedicated during them.

The high performance and the strong disciplinary culture of St

Gregory's did not, alas, suit me. I found it quite stifling, and did not want to 'shine', to use Brother Jude's favourite word. Much later on, when I visited Dhaka shortly after the Nobel award in December 1998, the headmaster of St Gregory's put on a special celebration for me. He mentioned that to inspire the current students he had fished out my exam papers from storage, but was 'discouraged when I saw that your performance ranked 33rd in a class of 37'. Then he added kindly, 'I suppose you became a good student only after you left St Gregory's.' The headmaster was not mistaken – I became what would count as a good student only when no one cared whether I was a good student or not.

During my years of schooling in Dhaka, I went to Santiniketan intermittently but regularly. Initially, there was no thought that I might actually move there to study. However, soon after the Japanese military occupied Burma in 1941, my parents sent me off to live with my grandparents and study at the school there. My father wanted me to go on studying at St Gregory's, which was a much better school in terms of the usual criteria of academic excellence. But he became increasingly convinced that, while the Japanese military would bomb Calcutta and Dhaka, no Japanese bomber would take any interest in remote Santiniketan.

My father was right about the possibility of the Japanese attacks. Both Calcutta and Dhaka had regular defence drills during those war years, with screaming sirens. On one occasion, when I was staying in Calcutta with some family friends for a short holiday, the Japanese bombed the dock area of the city five times during one week in December 1942. One evening, while pretending to be fast asleep in my bed, I managed to go out on to the veranda of the third-floor apartment where I could see some glow of fire at a distance. It was, in fact, at quite some distance, but to a child it was very exciting. Unlike Calcutta, Dhaka luckily was not bombed.

It was as a result of my father's wartime logic that I ended up at the remarkably progressive school in Santiniketan, which I loved immediately. Their priorities were relaxed and less academic than St Gregory's, and they combined learning about India's own traditions with many opportunities to learn about other countries too and their cultures right across the world. The emphasis at the Santiniketan School was on fostering curiosity rather than competitive excellence; indeed, interest in grades and examination performance was severely discouraged. I greatly enjoyed exploring Santiniketan's open-shelved and welcoming library with stacks of books about places all around the world, and I absolutely loved not having to perform well.

The tide of the war turned not long after I went to Santiniketan. The Japanese retreated, but I would not agree to retreat from my new school – I loved it. Santiniketan, my fleeting birthplace, was rapidly becoming my long-term home. But of course I went to Dhaka regularly where my father continued to teach, and where my family lived very happily, including my younger sister Manju who stayed on with our parents. Being in Santiniketan for the school terms and Dhaka for long holidays seemed an ideal combination to me. My cousins, especially Miradi (Mira Sen, later Mira Ray), made the vacations such fun.

All this changed with the partition of the country in 1947. The communal riots and terrible bloodshed generated continuous sadness. It also meant that we had to move. Dhaka became the capital of a newly born East Pakistan, and my family's home base had to shift to Santiniketan. I loved Santiniketan, but I greatly missed Dhaka – and Jagat Kutir. The protruding champa tree that made the veranda upstairs so fragrant was no longer a part of my life. I wondered where my old friends in Dhaka were, and who was playing with them now, and what was happening to the jackfruits and mangoes from our garden. I had lost a world. The loss of Dhaka could not be obliterated by the fulfilment – great as it was – of being in Santiniketan. Enjoying a new life, I was rapidly discovering, does not exclude intensely missing the old.

2

The Rivers of Bengal

I

Dhaka is not far from the mighty river Padda, the bigger of the two branches of the celebrated Ganga – 'the Ganges' for the anglophone. Ganga splits into two as it enters Bengal, past the ancient cities of northern India, including Benares and Patna. The Padda (whose name is the Bengali form of the Sanskrit *Padma*, meaning 'lotus') saunters gracefully south-east before it ends up in the Bay of Bengal. The other branch, Bhagirathi, moves more directly south, past the city of Calcutta, to join the Bay after a much shorter journey. Somehow the minor branch has managed to keep the old name 'Ganga', used interchangeably with Bhagirathi (as well as Hooghly, a comparatively recent name). Both Bhagirathi and Padda are much celebrated in old Bengali literature and there has been a certain amount of rivalry about their respective charisma. As a young boy from Dhaka, I remember telling my friends in Calcutta that they had been fobbed off with an inferior stream, devoid of the grandness of lotus-like Padda.

The division of Ganga's water had a more serious – and intensely political – aspect, which would come to prominence later when the Government of India built a large dam on the river, the Farakka Barrage, in 1970 to divert more water into the Bhagirathi to invigorate it. One of the main objects was the clearing of the silt that had gradually choked the port of Calcutta. The barrage did not succeed in clearing the silt, but it did manage to generate understandable hostility in east Bengal. All that political strife was far off when I was a child, but the sense of rivalry about water was already strong.

My boasting about the Padda was in fact not well grounded, since

Dhaka is not actually on the river, and if it had been at some stage (as some people believe), the Padda had moved away many centuries ago. It is one of the remarkable features of the soft alluvial soil of Bengal that the rivers flowing through it change their course often – over historical, rather than geological, time. Dhaka is actually still on a relatively minor river called the Budiganga (meaning, 'elderly Ganga'), a frank admission of its geriatric nature. The magnificent Padda is easily reachable by a short journey from Dhaka. It becomes even more spectacular as it moves away from the city, collecting water from its tributaries, and especially after it joins up with another large subcontinental river, the Brahmaputra, which in this part of Bengal is also called Jamuna (thereby confusing north Indians, since there is a more famous Jamuna further north on whose banks Delhi and Agra – and the Taj Mahal – can be found). A little further down, Padda joins another river, the Meghna, which then gives its name to the gigantic confluence. I still remember my thrill when I first stood next to this amazingly majestic river without being able to see its other bank. I asked my father, 'Is it really a river? Is its water salty? Are there sharks here?'

Our lives in east Bengal, which is now Bangladesh, were woven around these rivers. When we went from Dhaka to Calcutta, either to visit 'the great city' or on the way to Santiniketan, we would take a short train ride from Dhaka to Narayanganj, and then a long boat journey on a steamer on the Padda. After a feast of changing views on the banks, we would arrive at the river junction of Goalando, from where we could take a train straight to Calcutta.

These steamer rides on the Padda always enchanted me. We would see the constantly varying Bengali landscape, animated by busy villages, where children, who seemed never to be in school, looked at us on the boat as passing entertainment. My instinctive anxiety about these children missing school was not much relieved by my father telling me that most Indian children did not have schools to go to. He assured me that this must change after independence, but that seemed to me to be a long way off. I was unaware then that things would not change fast enough even after independence, nor, of course, that expanding school education – in India and elsewhere – would become one of the major commitments of my life.

Those steamer rides also gave me an introduction to the world of engineering. The engine room of the boat must have been hopelessly primitive by modern standards, but I was always excited when my father got the permission of the captain to take me there (we went every time) to observe the steel rods moving up and down and side to side, with clearly visible rotatory movements of the wheels, combined with the distinctive aroma of engine oil and grease. I much enjoyed being in a world of continuous activity – a contrast from the smooth and slow-moving view from the deck. I now realize this was one of my early attempts to understand how complicated things such as a ship's engines work.

2

The boat journey to and from Goalando was only a part of my child-hood experience of rivers. Seasonal holidays in eastern Bengal tended to be very watery affairs. I mentioned earlier how the journey from Dhaka to Matto in Manikganj involved short stretches of water but took a long time to negotiate. It was the same when I went with my parents and my sister Manju to the ancestral home of my mother's family in Sonarang in Bikrampur, close to Dhaka in east Bengal, which also involved long boat rides through the rivers. My maternal grand-parents travelled regularly from Santiniketan in western Bengal to Sonarang, their 'real home', far away from their actual residence and work.

When I was nearly nine, I was told by my father that he was arran-ging for us to live on a mobile houseboat (with a small engine) for a month during the summer vacation and to travel through a network of rivers. I thought one of the great moments of my life was arriving, and indeed it was. Those days in a slow-moving boat proved to be just as thrilling as I had expected. We went first along the Padda, but then on other rivers too, from the charmingly tame Dhaleshwari to the magnificent Meghna. It was altogether breathtaking. There were plants not only at the edges of the water, but also under the surface, stranger than anything I had ever seen. The birds that circled over-head or rested on the boat constantly caught my eye, and I could show off to Manju, then five, by identifying the names of some of them. The continuous sound of water moved around us – so different from our quiet garden in Dhaka. On a windy day the waves would splash noisily on the sides of the boat.

The fish included species that I had never encountered before, and my father, who seemed to know all about them, tried to help me identify their distinguishing features. There were small fish-eating river dolphins too – the Bengali name for them is '*shushuk*' (the biological name is *platanista gangetica*) – that were black and shiny and came to the surface to breathe, and then took very long dips. I enjoyed their dynamism and elegance from a distance, but was not anxious to get too close, fearing that they might confuse my toes with some unknown fish.

The 'flyin'-fishes' that had so fascinated Rudyard Kipling in Burma were plentiful in the Padda and Meghna too, and quite enchanting. My parents had brought with them many books of poetry, in both English and Bengali. I read a lot of poetry during our river holiday, including (again) Kipling's poem 'Mandalay'. I liked it still and was so glad to be reminded of Mandalay, but I was puzzled about where this Englishman saw his jumping varieties of fish. Writing the poem in Moulmein, which my father reminded me we had visited in our Burmese days, far from Mandalay itself, Kipling had placed these elegant creatures right 'on the road to Mandalay'.

On the road? How is that possible? I remember wondering as I went to sleep whether to this Englishman the Irrawaddy would have looked like a road, or did he mean that the river was next to some road – a road I could not recall? Before I could resolve this urgent problem, I fell asleep. I was with Kipling at the other end of the night as well, when the 'dawn comes up like thunder'. I was then ready to banish my night-time worries and welcome another day running around the boat with my eyes and ears open, and swimming carefully in the water around us.

The banks of the rivers were full of villages – some prosperous, others rather stricken, and some on what looked like precariously receding land at the edge of the water. I asked my mother whether they were as perilous as they looked. She told me they were. In fact, they were even more dangerous than they appeared: what seemed like solid ground around the banks could start to give way before the shifting river consumed the land. The rivers of Bengal, which are one of the main sources of the traditional prosperity of the region, are also an unpredictable hazard for human life and security. Thoughts about the challenges of living around course-shifting rivers took root in my mind, and the intimate combination of beauty and danger would continue to fascinate me. But at the time I was gripped by the physical grandeur of the rivers and the excitement of life on them. This dual attitude to rivers, I would gradually come to understand, is innate in the minds of many people in east Bengal.

Bengal's enthralment with the creative beauty of its normally quiet rivers is matched only by its fascination with the destructive splendour of the rivers in rage, and both are reflected in the carefully crafted evocative names that its rivers were typically given. There are nicely attractive names – such as Mayurakkhi or, more formally, Mayurakshi ('eyes of a peacock'), Rupnarayan ('divine beauty'), Madhumati ('sweet as honey'), Ichamati ('the fulfilment of our desires'), as well as the familiar Padda ('lotus-like'). The destructive side of the often-flooding and ever-shifting rivers is also captured in names, celebrating their prowess in drowning towns and villages, such as in another of Padda's names – Kirtinasha ('the destroyer of human achievements'). When I moved from St Gregory's School in Dhaka to the Santiniketan School, I also moved from being next to – or close to – Kirtinasha to being proximate to Ajay ('the invincible'), a quiet river through much of the year which tended to swell unimaginably in the monsoon season, submerging a great many towns and villages in the neighbourhood. This ambivalent nature of a river is a captivating analogy for the struggle for a secure role in society – a society that can both help and decimate the human beings relying on it.

3

As we moved from the smaller rivers to the larger ones in our riverboat, the colour of the water changed from off-white to blue. Dhaleshwari takes its name from its fair beauty (*dhal* – an uncommon word – is a kind of a pale colour, with *dholo* contrasting with *kalo*, black), whereas Meghna is as darkly beautiful as a monsoon cloud (*megh*). The water around us captured our attention in all kinds of ways. I had devoured Rabindranath Tagore's long poem 'Nadee' (the main Bengali word for 'river' – though there are many others), which describes the people and their lives all around a river, probably the Ganga, as it flows from its mountainous origin in the Himalayas, through varying human settlements, all the way to the ocean. Reading this poem, I felt at last that I understood what a river really was, and why people made so much fuss about them.

Looking through the maps with which my father always travelled, I made a gigantic discovery that I felt should have featured in our geography class but didn't – the fact that the Ganga and the Brahmaputra, flowing in totally different directions, both originate in the same lake, the Manas Sarovar ('mind-generated lake'), high up in the Himalayas (and much eulogized in Sanskrit literature). After two very long journeys by distantly separated routes, the two rivers join up in Bengal – far away from their origin. While the Ganga runs south of the Himalayas, through the plain of north India, passing by well-populated ancient cities from Rishikesh, Kanpur and Benares (Varanasi) to Patna, the Brahmaputra in contrast stays north of the plain and of the Himalayas for thousands of miles before it joins the Ganga (after turning right to cross the flattening Himalayas) – like a meeting of long-lost friends. To this realization add the definition, which I had just learned at school, of an island as a land mass surrounded by water. Ergo, I decided, with the pedantry of a child, the biggest island in the subcontinent is not Sri Lanka (then called Ceylon), as we had been told, but the huge land mass trapped between the Ganga, the Brahmaputra and the lake, Manas Sarovar.

I would not have dared to air my new 'discovery' at St Gregory's in Dhaka, but in the more relaxed atmosphere of Santiniketan I was happy to unleash it in our geography class. Even though our geography teacher was quite willing to let me try out my new answer to the question 'What is the biggest island in the Indian subcontinent?', he was dogmatic in denying the force of my breakthrough, as were my fellow students. 'That is not what is called an island,' I was told. 'Why not?' I asked, 'just remember the definition of an island – a land mass surrounded by water!' My detractors then unleashed a hitherto unstated codicil to the old definition, that the water surrounding the land mass had to be of seas or oceans, not rivers or lakes. But I was not going to give up. Since we had been told a few weeks earlier about the island in the middle of the river Seine in Paris, I insisted that we must now reclassify that island as something else ('maybe a crocodile,' I suggested, to the annoyance of everybody around me). I did not win the argument, and Ceylon remained the largest island in the subcontinent, but I did acquire the reputation – undeserved, I thought – for missing the obvious by concentrating too much on the obscure, and for using bizarre reasoning.

4

More seriously, the importance of rivers for the prosperity of the surrounding economy and society came into our discussions in Santiniketan a fair amount. Rabindranath saw the connection clearly enough, and talked about it in his essays as well as poems. What I did not know then was the significance that was attached to the role of rivers by pioneering economists who celebrated the constructive role of trade and commerce. That connection – extending my understanding of the positive role of rivers from my days in Santiniketan School – became a matter of particular interest to me when I was later a student at Presidency College in Calcutta. It was there that I read the analyses of Adam Smith on the place of rivers in the development of the market economy. Smith saw Bengal in the eighteenth century as very prosperous economically, which he linked not only to the skills of local trained workers but also (very much) to the opportunities arising from rivers and navigation.

Smith even attempted a sketchy history of ancient civilizations in terms of the navigational opportunities they enjoyed. He talked particularly about 'those great inlets, such as the Baltic and Adriatic seas in Europe, the Mediterranean and Euxine seas in both Europe and Asia, and the gulphs of Arabia, Persia, India, Bengal, and Siam, in Asia, to carry maritime commerce into the interior parts of that great continent.' While the role of the Nile in the civilization of northern

Africa fell into this general pattern of Smith's analysis, he attributed the backwardness of much of the rest – including 'inland parts of Africa' – to the absence of other navigational opportunities: 'the great rivers of Africa are at too great a distance from one another to give occasion to any considerable inland navigation'.

Smith saw the same cause of the historical backwardness of economies in that part of 'Asia which lies any considerable way north of the Euxine and Caspian seas, the ancient Scythia, the modern Tartary and Siberia': 'The sea of Tartary is the frozen ocean which admits of no navigation, and though some of the greatest rivers in the world run through that country, they are at too great a distance from one another to carry commerce and communication through the greater part of it.' As I read Smith's theory of human progress and eulogy to the economic power of rivers late into the night in my room in the YMCA hostel in Calcutta, I was more and more tempted to link the celebration of rivers in Bengali culture, which had so impressed me in my childhood days, with their constructive role in the prosperity of the region.

Even though he had never seen them, Smith understood how the rivers that crisscross Bengal had been important in the practical lives as well as in the imagination of the people of Bengal. The rivers and settlements around them were central over thousands of years for trade and commerce, feeding the domestic economy, and many of them were also known abroad and served in the pursuit of global trade and exploration. It was from this region, from a port near the ancient city of Tamralipta, that in AD 401 the Chinese traveller and Buddhist scholar Faxian took one of the regular ships and sailed to Sri Lanka, then to Java, and finally back to China, after spending ten years in India. He had come first to India from China by the northern land route, via Afghanistan and central Asia, and stayed mostly in Pataliputra (now Patna) up the Ganga. Faxian's *A Record of Buddhistic Kingdoms*, written in Nanjing after he returned to China, which happens to be the oldest travel book in the Chinese language, tells in some detail what he saw in different regions of India.

In the seventh century, a highly talented and enterprising student from China, Yi Jing, came to India via Sri Vijaya (what is now Sumatra), where over the course of a year he learned his Sanskrit before coming to Tamralipta in Bengal. From there he went up the river to what is now Bihar to study at the ancient university of Nalanda – a global centre for higher learning which flourished between the early fifth and the late twelfth centuries. His book presents the first comparative account of Chinese and Indian medicine and public health practices.

By the end of the seventeenth century, the mouth of the Ganges near today's Calcutta was the point of export for many Indian products, particularly cotton textiles made in Bengal, which were well known in the wider world, including Europe, but also for commodities obtained further north (such as saltpetre from Patna), which were sent down the Ganges to be shipped out. The lucrative trade and commerce of the region was, of course, the reason why foreign trading firms originally came there. These included the East India Company, which would go on to establish what would become Britain's Indian empire. The English, established in Calcutta, were not alone in seeking trade with – and through – Bengal. There were also French, Portuguese, Dutch, Prussian, Danish and other European trading companies, all operating in Bengal.

Trade within east Bengal was more difficult in the early years, because of navigational problems. There is some evidence that the trading prospects improved as the original flow of the Ganges (through Hooghly, past what is now Calcutta) decreased because of silting, and the flow of water eastwards into what is now Bangladesh increased over time. Given the nature of the soil and persistent sedimentation, Ganga has had a tendency to spill out of its riverbed while journeying to the east, generating new distributaries such as Bhairab, Mathabhanga, Garai-Madhumati and others. When the larger Padma emerged in the late sixteenth century and linked directly to Ganga, it became the main branch of old Ganga carrying the bulk of its water to east Bengal. This change had the immediate effect of linking the economy of east Bengal to subcontinental as well as global markets and led to a rapid expansion of economic activities in the east, reflected also in the fast-rising revenue collection from eastern Bengal for the Mughal treasury.

Looking abroad, Ptolemy in the second century talked about this region in some detail and identified accurately 'the five mouths of the

Ganges' that took the water to the Bay of Bengal. While it is hard to pinpoint the exact locations of the prosperous and lively towns that Ptolemy describes, his discussion of the trade and commerce of the area seems plausible enough; it is also broadly confirmed by other early authors such as Virgil and Pliny the Elder. And, more than a millennium later, Adam Smith clearly recognized the economic importance of the region close to what is now contemporary Calcutta.

5

The fascination with rivers in Bengali literature goes back to the early days when Bengali emerged as a language, with a serious grammar, around the tenth century, differing greatly (though descending from) Sanskrit. It had a close connection with a popular version of classical Sanskrit called 'Prakrit'. The old Bengali tales were very involved with rivers. For example, the much read and critically admired *Manasha-mangal Kavya*, dating from the late fifteenth century, is set almost entirely on the river Ganga-Bhagirathi and tells of the adventures, and ultimate defeat, of the merchant Chand, who revolted against the ruling cult of Manasha, the snake goddess, only to die in the process. It also makes an excellent play.

I was disappointed as a child by *Manashamangal*, since I wanted Chand, the defiant merchant, to triumph over the nasty snake goddess. I remember also being generally frustrated by the power of supernatural entities in popular stories and dramas and hoped they would be vanquished. That would happen occasionally, but any satisfaction I then had was extensively undermined when I went to the United States later in life and noticed the vigour and popularity of supernatural agents on American television, especially on cable TV late in the evening. You start watching, trustfully, what looks like a crime-and-detection story, but when the cornered villain opens her shapely mouth, there emanates a ten-foot-long tongue – which is apparently no surprise to the trained American audience. As the plot develops further, many physical norms are overturned. The hold of the supernatural in fiction in the scientifically most advanced country in the world is a remarkable feature of the popular American imagination – where a hundred

*Manashamangal*s, without their literary merits, pop out of television stories nightly.

River-based literature in ancient Bengali varies greatly in concentration and themes. I was particularly thrilled when I read the early Bengali ruminations of Buddhist Sahajiya thought in the ancient *Charjapad* (*Caryapad* in Sanskrit). They date from between the tenth and twelfth centuries and are among the earliest of identifiably Bengali writings. They are good to read both for literary reasons (though you need some practice to see clearly how the old words correspond to their modern Bengali versions) and for historical interest for what they tell us about the lives and priorities of these dedicated Buddhists. The author, Siddhacharja ('Siddhacharya') Bhusuku, expresses his sense of victory in verse, reporting cheerfully that he has been robbed of his wealth ('good riddance') on the river Padda and that he has also married a woman from a very low caste and is now 'a true Bengali'. Siddhacharja puts it thus:

> I have steered the thunder-boat along the course of Padda.
> The pirates have robbed me of my misery.
> Bhusuku, today you have become a true 'Bangalee'
> Having taken a Chandal woman as your wife.

Detachment from property and a Buddhist defiance of caste – Chandals had been categorized among the lowest – clearly fitted into Bhusuku's idea of being a proud egalitarian Bengali.

Between the tenth and twelfth centuries, being a 'Bangalee' (or 'Vangali', as it is spelt in *Charjapad*) did not, however, mean exactly what being a 'Bengali' means now – that sense was yet to evolve. Rather, a 'Vangali' in the tenth century meant coming from a specific sub-region of Bengal, then called Vanga, which was entirely in what is now Bangladesh – geographically what has been called 'east Bengal' for a very long time. Old Banga, or Vanga, included what are now the districts of Dhaka and Faridpur. Coming from Dhaka, I was both a Bengali in the modern sense and a 'Bangali' (or 'Vangali') in the classical description. I felt some closeness to Bhusuku for this reason, but also for his Buddhism – in my schooldays I was fascinated by Buddha's ideas. Alas, my attempt to interest my school friends in Bhusuku's thousand-year-old thoughts was a complete failure. The one exception was my Chinese classmate in Santiniketan, Tan Lee, but even then I could not be sure whether he listened to my chatter out of loyalty to me or because of his genuine interest in the subject.

6

Over the centuries there has been a substantial contrast between east Bengalees (known in western Bengal as 'Bangal', which also meant being totally naive) and western Bengalees (called by their detractors from the east 'Ghoti', which literally meant a handleless mug). This division has no particular connection with the political division of Bengal in 1947 between what then became East Pakistan – and is now Bangladesh – and what remained in India as the state of West Bengal. The political partition in 1947 was almost entirely on religious lines, whereas the cultural division between Bangals and Ghotis predated it by a long time and was completely unrelated to religious boundaries. As it happens, a majority of Bangals were Muslim and a majority of Ghotis Hindu, but the Ghoti–Bangal rivalry had little to do with that religious division.

There was a general historical divide between west and east Bengal. Much of east Bengal, as I just mentioned, came from the ancient kingdom of Vanga, whereas the western part of Bengal corresponded substantially to the kingdom of Gaur, far to the west, which succeeded the earlier kingdoms of Rarh and Suhma. Siddhacharja Bhusuku clearly hints that social practices differed in distinct parts of early Bengal. Certainly, the Bengali accent varies from region to region, and, even though there is some uniformity in formal speech, the local accents are widely different. Even the words commonly chosen by Bangals and Ghotis for very basic ideas could, in some cases, be quite different. For example, while people reared in West Bengal around Calcutta, or Santiniketan, would say 'bolbo' – meaning 'I would say' – we in the east tended to say 'kaibo' or 'kaimu'. When I first came to Santiniketan from Dhaka, I slipped into regional speech often, and at the beginning my classmates were unaccountably amused by my speech and insisted on calling me Kaibo. That became something of a nickname for me, and the Ghotis laughed with rustic joy whenever they repeated it. After about two years the capacity of my Ghoti friends to continue being amused by an alternative choice of words was eventually exhausted.

How much real difference did these regional contrasts within Bengal make? There was a lot of innocuous banter between the two groups, especially in Calcutta, the capital city of pre-Partition Bengal, where Ghotis and Bangals intermingled. Perhaps the one subject in which that division was really serious was in football (or soccer, to distinguish it from the furious game that is played in America). The old Calcutta team Mohan Bagan was largely supported by Ghotis, and a newer team, called East Bengal, drew its support from Bangals. Religious differences did not figure in this at all: there was a separate team, also a high performer, called Mohammedan Sporting, though it had Hindu players as well. The games between Mohan Bagan and East Bengal could bring together huge crowds – and still do. Many people in Calcutta clearly thought that the game was the most important event in the yearly calendar and its outcome a matter of life and death. Given my origins in Dhaka, I was of course a supporter of East Bengal. Though I went to see a game only once, at the age of ten, I kept an interest, through the media, in the outcome of their momentous encounters. I received an undeserved reward when, fifty-five years later, in 1999, the East Bengal Club made me a life member, for my 'constant loyalty and support'.

The results of the Mohan Bagan v. East Bengal games had some evident economic consequences, including on the relative prices of different types of fish in Calcutta. Since most Ghotis like best a fish called 'rui' and Bangals from the east typically have deep loyalty to 'ilish', rui would tend to shoot up in price if Mohan Bagan won, leading to celebratory dinners by westerners; similarly, the price of *ilish* would leap up if East Bengal defeated Mohan Bagan. I did not know that I might someday specialize in economics (I was quite strongly hooked at that time on mathematics and physics, with only Sanskrit as a possible rival), but the elementary economics of a price rise due to a sudden hike in demand was immediately interesting. I even speculated on a primitive theory that this volatility should not in general be present, if the result of the game was firmly predictable. With predictability, the retail fish-sellers would increase the supply of the right kind of fish – anticipating the actual soccer result, and so the demand for the 'right kind of fish' would not really exceed the already expanded supply, and the price need not be hiked up. It was clear that the observed phenomena of the respective peaking in the price of rui or ilish depended on the unpredictability of the football results (namely, victories respectively of Mohan Bagan or East Bengal).

There was, I must admit, some little fun in working out exactly what assumptions are needed for the prices to be stationary, or volatile. But I also came to a second conclusion. If economics really consisted of sorting out problems of this kind, it is likely to give us – I told myself – a bit of analytical fun, but most likely quite useless fun. I am glad that this scepticism did not deter me when the time came to decide to do economics as a first-year undergraduate. Adam Smith's speculation, I could happily note, on the relation between the presence of navigable rivers and the flourishing of civilizations offered more substance to think about.

7

Given the traditionally river-centred life of the Bengalis, it is quite natural that social and cultural issues are frequently given some kind of a river-based analogy. The river supports human life, sustains it, destroys it and can kill it. The society that has grown up around it can do the same to individual human beings.

In a remarkable Bengali novel published in 1945, called *Nadi O Nari* ('River and Women'), the noted Bengali novelist and political essayist Humayun Kabir presented a far-reaching account of the way the relationship between rivers and people influences Bengali life. As another leading Bengali writer, Buddhadeb Bose, commented in a review in a Bengali journal, *Chaturanga*, in Kabir's deeply engaging story the mighty river Padda is 'vigorous during the monsoon, quietly beautiful in post-monsoon autumn, frightening in the evenings of summer storms, a terrifying source of unexpected deaths, a powerful benefactor of good human life – and also a decimator of every valuable thing when torrents of rain come after a period of drought'.

The novel, which was translated into English shortly after it appeared in Bengali (with a gender change in the title to *Men and Rivers*), tells the story of struggling landless families trying to live on the land created and destroyed by a shifting river. The families are Muslim, as was Humayun Kabir, but their struggle is a shared predicament of river-dependent Bengalis irrespective of their religious denomination. 'We are men of the river. We are peasants. We build our homes on sand and the water washes them away. We build again and again, and we till the earth and bring the golden harvest out of the waste land.' *Nadi O Nari* was a much-read – and much-discussed – book when I was in high school, and the issues it raised received widespread attention. It was a moving story of family life facing both the benefaction and the wrath of a mighty river.

There was, however, another aspect of Kabir's novel which generated huge interest. Aside from capturing the shared problems of precariously placed Bengalis, it told the story of a Muslim family in a way that was at odds with the Muslim separatism which had suddenly become a very strong force in India over those years. Humayun Kabir, as a Muslim political leader, had firmly rejected separatism, and indeed stayed on in India after Partition as a leading intellectual and powerful secular activist. He also helped the President of the Indian National Congress, Maulana Abul Kalam Azad, write his famous account of the non-violent struggle for the independence of India, *India Wins Freedom*.

Nadi O Nari was written in the 1940s 'at a critical moment in the lives of Bengali Muslims', but it was also a time 'with much promise', as Zafar Ahmad Rashed, another Bengali literary critic, explained the dilemma that Kabir chose to address. Many Muslim political leaders were then involved in cultivating religion-based politics, well reflected in 'the Lahore Declaration for an independent home land' for Muslims. But 'there was a real dilemma here that we saw develop, including debates about the language of communication and a culture that had to transcend the special demands of "Muslim culture" – and related thoughts – and be firmly located in the indigenous culture of the soil.'

A similar conflict was strongly present in the political and cultural deliberations of many Bengali Hindus. Communal violence, which emerged suddenly and expanded rapidly, was a newly powerful political force that had gripped Bengal in the years preceding Independence and Partition, and it caused much bloodshed in the 1940s. Even as schoolchildren we could not escape a feeling of anxiety and a very deep concern. We did not quite know how this venom had suddenly become so widespread, and we fervently wished the world would move on from the madness, wondering whether there was anything we could do to help. The river's indifference to religion-based separateness, both in creation and in destruction, was a reminder of the shared predicament of all people, irrespective of communal divides. That was perhaps the important message from the river captured in *Nadi O Nari*.

3

School Without Walls

I

Rabindranath Tagore died in August 1941. I was then still at St Gregory's School in Dhaka. The headmaster gave us the tragic news in a hastily called school assembly, and declared a suspension of teaching for the day. As I went home, I wondered why the likeable bearded man I knew as a family friend, and who I went to see with my grandparents or my mother whenever I was in Santiniketan, was so important for the world. I knew that Rabindranath was a much admired poet (I could even recite a few of his poems), but it was not obvious to me why he was thought to be so momentous a person. I was then seven, and had no idea how radically Tagore would influence my thinking in years to come.

When I reached home, my mother was lying on a sofa and crying, and I gathered that my father would be returning early from his work at the university. My three-year-old sister, Manju, was puzzled by what was going on, and I explained to her that someone very great and dear to us had just died. 'Gone away?' she asked (not quite sure what death meant). 'Yes,' I said. 'He will come back,' she said. I remembered her words when Manju died very suddenly seventy years later, in February 2011, from a short illness.

Everyone around us seemed overcome with grief on that muggy day in August 1941, including relations, servants and friends – there was an eruption of mourning. Our expert cook, a devout Muslim, who used to supply us with magnificent smoked *ilish mach* (hilsha fish), came to express his anguish and sympathy. He too was full of tears, he told us, because he loved Tagore's songs. But I suppose he came mainly to comfort us, knowing that my family, especially my mother, was very close to Rabindranath.

Tagore did indeed have a large presence in my life from my infancy. My mother Amita had not only studied at his school in Santiniketan, but (as mentioned earlier) had appeared regularly in leading parts in his dance dramas, directed by Rabindranath himself and performed in Calcutta. My maternal grandfather, Kshiti Mohan, taught and researched over decades in Santiniketan and they were close collaborators. Rabindranath would often draw on Kshiti Mohan's knowledge of the Indian classics and on his exceptional expertise in rural poetic compositions set in north India and also in Bengal. Rabindranath's last speech, a thundering oration in Bengali entitled 'Shabhytar Shankat' ('Crisis in Civilization'), was read out by Kshiti Mohan at a large public meeting in Santiniketan in April 1941, when Tagore was too weak to read it himself. This was a very insightful speech and, young as I was, I was greatly moved and challenged by it. Rabindranath was at that time depressed by the war, upset by the West's continued colonial behaviour, distressed by the barbarities of the Nazis and by the violence of the Japanese occupation forces, revolted by the emerging communal tensions within India, and deeply worried about the future of the world in general.

I too was deeply saddened by Rabindranath's death, especially as its implications sank in. I liked him greatly as a benign elderly person who seemed to enjoy talking with me, but I was also full of curiosity about what I was now being told about the importance of his ideas and the power of his creativity. I became determined to learn more about the much-admired man to whom I had not paid as much attention as I felt I should have done. My dedicated pursuit of Tagore's thoughts thus began just after his death and has given me a lifetime of rewarding engagement. In particular, his overarching emphasis on freedom and reasoning made me think seriously about those issues, which became increasingly important to me as I grew older. The role of education in enhancing individual freedom and social progress was among the subjects on which I found his ideas especially insightful and persuasive.

2

My mother was very keen that I should study at Santiniketan, as she had, and – perhaps paradoxically – Tagore's passing made her even more determined. My father was not entirely convinced, and in any case did not much like the idea of my moving away from the family in Dhaka to stay with my maternal grandparents in Santiniketan. But, as I mentioned earlier, with the war getting closer to India, my father did acknowledge the greater safety of being in Santiniketan. That was the clinching reason for my move. When the Japanese retreated, I refused to leave the school I had, by then, come to love.

In October 1941, within a couple of months of Tagore's death, I left for Santiniketan and received a huge welcome from my grandparents at my 'homecoming' (as my grandmother described it). They still lived in the thatched cottage where I was born in November 1933. On my first evening there, I sat on a low stool in the kitchen, as Didima cooked, catching up with both the news of the family and, of course, gossip, the significance of which was becoming increasingly clear in my nearly eight-year-old mind. I felt very grown up. In fact, between the ages of seven and nine my world of ideas and understanding was expanding with a rapidity that thrilled me.

3

I arrived in Santiniketan towards the end of the annual autumnal holiday (the Puja vacation), before teaching had resumed. I had time to look around the campus before classes began, and I inspected the school grounds, especially the playing fields. My maternal cousin Baren (I called him Barenda – 'da' being a shortened form of 'dada' or elder brother) introduced me to the captain of a cricket team of similarly aged children who were practising on the playing field. My first attempt at a game with them was a disaster. When the captain bowled to me to test my batting skill, the ball I hit struck him hard on his nose, which led to quite a lot of bleeding. While nursing his injury, I heard the captain tell Barenda, 'Your brother can certainly join my team, but tell him to aim at the boundary, not at the bowler's nose.' I promised to do so and celebrated my entry into the life of my new school.

Santiniketan was fun in a way I had never imagined a school could be. There was so much freedom in deciding what to do, so many intellectually curious classmates to chat with, so many friendly teachers to approach and ask questions unrelated to the curriculum, and – most importantly – so little enforced discipline and a complete absence of harsh punishment.

Prohibition of physical punishment was a rule on which Rabindranath was insistent. My grandfather, Kshiti Mohan, explained to me why that was a really important contrast between 'our school and all the other schools in the country' and why it made a big difference to education, especially in cultivating the children's motivation to learn. It is not only, he said, that beating a helpless child is a barbaric act which we should learn to abhor, but also that a student should be led to do the right thing through a reasoned understanding of what makes something right – not just to avoid pain and humiliation.

However, despite his devotion to those principles, there was an amusing story in circulation about a conflict my grandfather once had to face, on one of the rare occasions when he was assigned to teach young children. Apparently, in one of his classes for six-year-old children, one unruly and boisterous little boy went on placing his sandals, again and again, on the teacher's lectern. When Kshiti Mohan failed to dissuade this energetic child in a number of different ways, including giving reasoned explanations, he could not help saying that if the child went on like that, he would deserve a slap. The child replied brightly, 'Oh Kshiti-da, perhaps you haven't heard that Gurudev [Rabindranath] has ruled that no student can be physically punished on the soil of Santiniketan?' The story goes that Kshiti Mohan then lifted the boy up by the collar of his shirt and asked him to confirm that he was no longer on the soil of Santiniketan. After an agreement on that point – and a mild token slap – the sandal-wielder was restored to the soil of Santiniketan.

4

Classes in Santiniketan were unusual. They were held outdoors, except for those requiring a laboratory, or if it was raining. We sat on the ground – we carried small mats to sit on – underneath a preassigned tree, while the teacher faced us from a seat made of cement, with a blackboard or a lectern next to him.

One of our teachers, Nityananda Binod Goswami (whom we used to call Gosainji), who was a great teacher of Bengali language and literature, and also of Sanskrit, explained to us that Rabindranath disliked barriers in every sphere of living. Having classes outside, unrestricted by walls, was a symbol of this, Gosainji suggested. At a broader level, Rabindranath did not like our thoughts being incarcerated within our own communities – religious or otherwise – or being moulded by our nationality (he was fiercely critical of nationalism). And despite his love of the Bengali language and literature, he did not like being imprisoned within a single literary tradition either, which could lead not only to a kind of bookish patriotism, but also to the neglect of learning from the rest of the world.

Gosainji also noted that Rabindranath particularly welcomed a student's ability, which could be cultivated, to concentrate on work even when the outside world was within sight and hearing. Being able to learn in this way, he believed, indicated a commitment to avoid sequestering education from human life. This was quite a theory, and we, the classmates, discussed it from time to time. Even though some of us entertained deep scepticism about it, we thought the experience of outdoor schooling was exceptionally pleasant. There would be an excellent case for outdoor schooling, we decided, even in the absence of any positive pedagogic gain from it. We also agreed that, while we might sometimes have problems keeping up in classes, this could not be because we were not surrounded by walls. Later in life, when friends have commented on my ability to work while sitting in a loud and chaotic railway station, or standing in a huddle at an airport gate, I sometimes think about Gosainji's words about the immunity from easy distraction that outdoor schooling offered us.

5

Holding classes outdoors was only one of the ways Santiniketan differed from other schools around us. It was, of course, a progressive, co-educational school, with an immensely broad and inclusive curriculum, including substantial immersion in the cultures of different parts of Asia and Africa.

Academically, it was not particularly exacting – often we did not have any examinations at all, and little store was set by the results when we did. It could not, by the usual academic standards, compete with some of the better schools in Calcutta or Dhaka; it certainly could not hold a candle to St Gregory's. But there was something remarkable about the ease with which class discussions could move from traditional Indian literature to contemporary as well as classical Western thought, and then to China, or Japan, or Africa, or Latin America. The school's celebration of diversity was also in sharp contrast to the cultural conservatism that was strongly present, if only implicitly, in school education in India in general.

The cultural breadth of Tagore's vision of the contemporary world had close parallels with that of the great film director Satyajit Ray, who had studied at Santiniketan and would later make several outstanding films based on Tagore's stories. (He arrived the year before me, though he was a dozen years older.) Ray's assessment of Santiniketan School, written in 1991, would have greatly pleased Rabindranath:

> I consider the three years I spent in Santiniketan as the most fruitful of my life . . . Santiniketan opened my eyes for the first time to the splendours of Indian and Far Eastern art. Until then I was completely under the sway of Western art, music and literature. Santiniketan made me the combined product of East and West that I am.

Rabindranath was well served by members of his close circle in helping to advance the causes he stood for. As well as Kshiti Mohan, Santiniketan was full of very talented people with diverse interests, with convictions similar to – and clearly influenced by – Rabindranath. The teachers' salaries were tiny, even in Indian terms, and they had gathered there simply because they were inspired by him and shared his goals. The group included many excellent teachers and researchers, of whom several were from abroad, such as Sylvain Lévi, Charles Andrews, William Pearson, Tan Yun-Shan and Leonard Elmhirst, among others.

There was also Nandalal Bose, one of India's leading painters and an outstanding teacher of the fine arts, under whose direction and leadership Santiniketan developed its justly famous school of fine arts, Kala Bhavan, where a number of talented artists (such as Binodbehari Mukhopadhyay and Ramkinkar Baij) flourished. It was here that

Satyajit Ray received some of the teaching that transformed his ideas and art. He would later comment: 'I do not think my *Pather Panchali* would have been possible if I had not done my years of apprenticeship in Santiniketan. It was there, sitting at the feet of "Master-Mashai" [Nandalal Bose] that I learned how to look at nature and how to feel the rhythms inherent in nature.'

6

Santiniketan is located next to an old market town, Bolpur, which has flourished for about five hundred years. It is also a dozen or so miles from Kenduli, where a great Indian poet, Jayadeva, was supposed to have been born and grew up in the twelfth century. The *Jayadeb mela* (the 'fair for Jayadeva') is still held in Kenduli, as it has been every year for many centuries, and I remember being fascinated as a child to see the annual gathering of rural singers and village poets there, along with small traders selling cooking pots and inexpensive clothing. Given the traditional interest in mathematics in India, I was not surprised to see little booklets of mathematical puzzles being sold next to loudly coloured storybooks of pictures, derived from the Indian epics, and an array of kitchen utensils.

It was in 1863 that the landlord of Raipur estate, Sitikanta Sinha, gave a plot of land to Rabindranath's father Debendranath, who was a well-known scholar and a leader of the 'Brahmo Samaj', a modern religious group with a strong Unitarian influence. The original purpose of this gift was to find Debendranath a place of retreat, for reflection and meditation. The Sinhas were established landlords in Bengal, and there was even a Lord Sinha in the upper house of Parliament in London. Debendranath did not do much with the land that had been given to him, and in the early years of the twentieth century Rabindranath decided to use it for his new school. Thus in 1901 was born this new academic entity called Visva Bharati for the pursuit of world knowledge (*visva* – or *vishwa* – is a Sanskrit word for the world, rather like *jagat* in the name of my home in Dhaka, Jagat Kutir). It was going to be an Indian school with a commitment to pursue the best of the knowledge in the world, no matter where it came from.

Rabindranath's decision to create a new kind of school in Santiniketan was greatly influenced by his dissatisfaction with his own schooldays. He had passionately disliked the places he was sent to, and as a drop-out – he was afterwards educated at home with the help of tutors – he viewed the standard Indian schools with horror. Already in his childhood he had formed serious views on precisely what was wrong with the schools he knew in the Calcutta of his day, despite some of them having excellent academic reputations. When Tagore established his own school he was determined to make it radically different.

Sometimes a complete outsider can see more clearly – and explain more pithily – what is so special about an innovative institution than those who are immersed in it. The special qualities of the Santiniketan School were caught with clarity by Joe Marshall, a perceptive American visitor, educated at Harvard, who visited Santiniketan in August 1914, two decades before I was born:

> The principle of his method of teaching is that the individual must be absolutely free and happy in an environment where all is at peace and where the forces of nature are all in evidence; then there must be art, music, poetry, and learning in all its branches in the persons of the teachers; lessons are regular but not compulsory, the classes are held under the trees with the boys sitting at the feet of the teacher, and each student with his different talents and temperament is naturally drawn to the subjects for which he has aptitude and ability.

Joe Marshall also commented on Tagore's focus on freedom, even for schoolchildren. This identifies an aspect of Rabindranath's thought that standard accounts, especially those presented by his 'sponsors' in the Western world such as W. B. Yeats and Ezra Pound, missed comprehensively, a subject to which I will return. But, as I noted at the beginning of this chapter, the idea that the exercise of freedom has to be developed alongside the capacity to reason became increasingly clear to me as my education in Santiniketan proceeded. If you have freedom, you will have reason to exercise it – even doing nothing would be a kind of exercise. It is the training to make use of the freedom to reason (rather than fearing it, as rote learners are taught to do) that seemed, as my school years proceeded, to be one of the things

Tagore was most strongly trying to advance through his unusual school. The exceptional importance of that combination – freedom and reason – has remained with me all my life.

7

My earliest teachers at Santiniketan included Gosainji, whom I have already described, but also Tanayendra Nath Ghosh (we called him Tanayda), who taught us English language and literature with great skill and enthusiasm. My first encounter with Shakespeare – I think it was *Hamlet* – occurred under his wonderful guidance, and I can still remember the sense of excitement that it generated. I followed up what we were reading in class with further readings in the evenings, helped by an older cousin, Buddha Ray. I loved the dark drama of *Macbeth*, but was very disturbed by the terrible sadness of *King Lear*. My geography teacher, Kashinathda, was very friendly and talkative, and he made his subject – and anything else we discussed – immensely engaging. Critical scrutiny of the past came very elegantly from our history teacher Uma, who would visit me some years later at Trinity College and tell me several things about the College's past that I did not know.

My mathematics teacher, Jagabandhuda, was extraordinarily skilled but remarkably unassuming. Initially, he was worried that I wanted to study things outside our limited syllabus and that I would neglect what we were meant to do. Some of the standard topics of school mathematics did not, however, interest me at all ('I think I can work out where a projectile would land, but I cannot get excited about this calculation,' I told him rather pompously one day). I was determined instead to think about the nature and foundations of mathematical reasoning. Rabindranath's arguments in favour of freedom and reasoning encouraged me to try to do what I really wanted to do, even though Rabindranath himself had little personal interest in mathematics.

Jagabandhuda eventually gave in to my persistence. My first suspicion, that he was resisting because he did not know much maths outside the syllabus, proved to be wholly unfounded. Often, when I suggested a relatively unusual way of tackling a well-known problem in maths, he would suggest yet another line of thinking, which motivated me to try to outdo the novelty of his reasoning with something of my own. There were many months when I went every day to his home after school hours to talk – he seemed to have endless time for me and his wife was very tolerant of this intrusion into their family life (and often made tea for us to 'keep you two going'). I was tremendously encouraged by the way Jagabandhuda would look up books and articles to show me lines of reasoning I had not been aware of until then.

Later in life, when I became involved in systematically studying the foundations of mathematics (this was after I moved to Trinity College in Cambridge in 1953), I would discover that some of the reasoning Jagabandhuda had been trying to teach me drew on classic works on the subject. I would think of those formative days when, many decades later, I taught courses on 'Reasoning through Mathematical Models' and 'Axiomatic Reasoning' at Harvard, jointly with two very fine mathematician colleagues, Barry Mazur (who is an outstanding pure mathematician) and Eric Maskin (who is also an exceptional economic theorist). By then I could not, alas, go to see Jagabandhuda to thank him, since he died not long after retiring.

The teacher with whom I had most contact was Lalit Majumdar. He was not only a brilliant teacher of literature, but also a real ally in helping some of us school activists to run night classes for unschooled children in the neighbouring tribal villages. Along with his likeable brother Mohitda, who also taught at the school, Lalitda was a central figure at Santiniketan. The presence of these two brothers was a great gift to us. On one occasion – I would have been about twelve – I was due to go on a school excursion for a week, with tents, utensils and all kind of paraphernalia, to the old site of the fifth-century Nalanda university in the neighbouring province of Bihar, but I was unable to join the party because of some minor illness. I was hugely pleased when Mohitda dropped by a couple of days later and said, 'Why don't we both go and catch up with the explorers?' I was not deprived, as a result, of the fun and knowledge I got from camping near Nalanda, and I also came to know Mohitda, a fine teacher, much better during our long train journey from Santiniketan.

Lalitda was no less enthusiastic than me and my classmates in our juvenile attempts at running a night school for tribal children near Santiniketan. He kept our accounts in order and helped us to run these unsheltered schools. It was also his duty to warn us when we were in danger of neglecting our own studies as a result. Running night classes was a hugely creative experience, and we were pleased at our substantial achievements. There were children from our neighbouring villages who learned to read, write and count without having been to any other school. I cannot express adequately how much we benefited from Lalitda's gentle and wise guidance. He went on to lead a healthy and very active life well into his mid-nineties.

8

So far I have been recollecting subjects with which I was reasonably comfortable, but I should also say a few words about those in which I had no skill whatever. One of them was carpentry, and while my classmates made small boats, managing to bend wooden planks in the required way, I could not progress beyond making a primitive soapholder, and even that was not an object of beauty. Another was singing, which was very important in the Santiniketan curriculum. I loved – and continue to love – listening to music, including good singing, but I myself could not sing at all. My music teacher – a wonderful singer whom we called Mohordi (her real name was Kanika Bandopadhyay) – did not accept that I was simply deficient and initially refused to excuse me from the classes. She told me, 'Everyone has a talent for singing, it is just a matter of practice.'

Encouraged by Mohordi's theory, I did some quite serious practice. I was sure about my efforts, but wondered what I was achieving. After a month or so of practice, Mohordi tested my performance again and then, with defeat writ large on her face, told me 'Amartya, you need not come to the music classes.' Santiniketan produced many wonderful singers over the decades, including a large number of specialists in Rabindra Sangeet (Tagore songs), including Shanti Deb Ghosh, Nilima Sen, Shailaja Mujumdar, Suchitra Mitra and Rezwana Choudhury (Bannya) from Bangladesh, among many others. I remain very glad that it is possible to enjoy music without having to produce it oneself.

Santiniketan was also generous in leaving a lot of time for sports. The favourite game for the boys was football (soccer), in which I had no skill, and I was no magician with the hockey stick either. But I could play badminton with pass-grade skill and my record in cricket was close to adequate. I was a tolerable batsman, but not a bowler, and I was quite hopeless at fielding. I became, however, a champion in the sack race which used to appear in sports competitions partly to provide some fun, but also to give unathletic students like me something to do on a sports day. My success in the sack race was mainly the result of a theory I developed that it is hopeless to try to proceed by jumping forward (you will always fall), but you can with some stability shuffle forward with your toes in the two corners of the sack with little danger of falling. Since on the day of India's independence, 15 August 1947, the only sport offered in the celebrations was the sack race, I had the extraordinary experience of emerging as the sports champion on that momentous day. That prize was the peak of my athletic glory.

After independence there was an opportunity for me to reveal another inaptitude. The government had set up a National Cadet Corp (NCC) for voluntary military training for civilians, a post-independence version of the old University Officers' Training Corp (UOTC). We were asked whether we would like to join a little unit at Santiniketan, as a part of the Regiment of the 'Rajput Rifles'. This led to a debate among Santiniketan students about whether we should participate, and the consensus was, why not see what the training offered and what we might learn from it? If it was of no use (and no less importantly, if it was just too boring), we could abandon it. If, on the other hand, it proved helpful and taught us some useful things, we could continue.

The big decision, of course, was whether, given the strong commitment to non-violence in the social climate of Santiniketan, there would be some kind of violation of our shared ethics in receiving military training at all. However, since none of us thought that the military forces of the country should be disbanded – even Gandhiji had not advocated that – the possibility seemed remote. So most of us decided to sign up, and I suddenly found myself putting on odd clothing and handling unfamiliar objects in between classes in physics and mathematics. We had our meetings mostly over the weekends, but also in our free hours during weekdays.

My military life was, I suppose predictably, a dismal failure. It was not so much that I was incapable of doing the things they asked us to do (which were not difficult), but that it was very hard to listen to the lectures from the officers commanding us. Not long after we had joined, we were given a lecture entitled 'The Bullet' by the Subadar Major (the Indian equivalent of sergeant major – the same initials helped in the recycling of old badges and brass tags from the British Indian army). The Subadar Major told us that the bullet accelerates after leaving the rifle and then, after a while, it starts to slow down, and that it is best to hit the object to be struck when the bullet is travelling at its maximum speed. At that point, I found myself raising my hand and offering some Newtonian mechanics, telling our Subadar Major that the bullet could not possibly accelerate after leaving the rifle since there is no new force to make it gain velocity.

The Subadar looked at me and said, 'Are you saying I am wrong?' I wanted to give the only possible answer to the question – namely, yes – but that seemed unwise. I also thought that in fairness I should concede that the bullet *could* possibly accelerate if its rotatory movement could somehow be converted into a linear forward movement. But – I had to add – I could not see how that would occur. The Subadar responded by giving me an angry glance and saying, 'Rotatory movement? Is that what you are saying?' Before I could clear up that muddled point, he ordered me to raise my arms above my head, with the unloaded rifle held high, and run around the field five times.

If that was an inauspicious beginning, the ending wasn't good either. Eighteen of us had written a letter of protest to the same Subadar Major complaining that we were having too much drill and too little rifle practice. He called us to his home and explained that any letter signed by more than one person is considered by the military to be a mutiny. 'So,' he said, 'I have two options. Either you can withdraw the letter and I will tear it up, or I shall have to send you all to be court-martialled.' Fifteen of the group of eighteen immediately withdrew their names. (One of them explained to me later that this was because he had been told that being court-martialled meant being summarily tried and shot.) Three of us did not budge. We were told by the Subadar Major that he

47

would report us to the higher authorities, but would dismiss us immediately without honour and without waiting for the official punishment
to be communicated. I have not yet heard from the higher authorities,
but that was the end of my military career.

9

Aside from our teachers, we learned a lot from visitors to Santiniketan who came to speak to us on a wide variety of subjects. One
unusual visitor was General Chiang Kai-shek, who came in February
1942 when he was visiting Calcutta as a part of the Allied war efforts.
His oration to us, lasting about half an hour and delivered to us in
Mandarin, was made completely impenetrable by the eccentric decision of the Santiniketan authorities not to provide any translation.

I had moved from Dhaka to Santiniketan only a few months earlier,
and had begun to think about world issues with as much seriousness
as my eight-year-old mind could accommodate. At Chiang Kai-shek's
lecture I was initially impressed that all the children listened to the
untranslated Chinese with apparently rapt attention. But before long
there was a rather embarrassing hum, which grew louder and then
turned into an eruption of conversations. Along with some other students, I had been asked to tea with the Chinese visitors (or, more
exactly, to hang around while the visitors had tea with the school
authorities) and I remember how Madame Chiang, who spoke English
fluently, kept up the pretence that she had not perceived any problem
with the audience at all. She also wanted to make clear that the General was not upset there was no translation, about which the school
authorities were now apologizing. I did not, of course, believe what
she said out of simple politeness, but I did think that she was exceptionally gracious – as well as stunningly good-looking.

Another great occasion for us all was the visit of Mahatma Gandhi in
December 1945 – this was four years after Rabindranath's death. In his
speech, he expressed some worry about the future of Santiniketan in the
absence of its inspired founder, and, even as a twelve year old, I could see
the reasons for his concern. When he was asked in a meeting in Santiniketan what he thought of the school's focus on music, Gandhiji dropped

the politeness and expressed his doubts about it. He spoke about life being itself a kind of music, so that music did not have to be formally separated from life. I remember thinking that Rabindranath would have disputed whether they were making any such separation. But I liked the fact that Gandhiji said something unusual, since the school was full of people repeating the same 'great ideas', about which I was beginning to grumble. The *Visva-Bharati News* reported Gandhiji as saying: 'The music of life is in danger of being lost in the music of the voice.' I liked the challenge there to the official thinking.

I went to see Gandhiji with an autograph book. Since he would sign such a book only in exchange for a five-rupee donation – a fairly small sum by any worldly standard – to his fund to fight the inequities of the caste system, I had to come up with the money. Luckily, I had saved some of my pocket money. I went and made my contribution – Gandhiji was reading some handwritten notes, sitting in the living room in the guest house. He thanked me for the donation, but before signing my autograph book told me with a laugh that my fight against the caste system had just begun. I liked his laughter and enjoyed the remark as much as he did. The signature itself was unadorned – just his name in Devanagari (the common script of Sanskrit and modern Hindi), and only his initials and surname.

I didn't want to leave just yet – hoping to talk with him a little more – and so Gandhiji asked me whether I was ever critical of things I saw around me. I cheered up at the opportunity of sharing my concerns about the world with one of the greatest persons alive and said yes. Our discussion was going very well, I thought, but, just as I was asking him about his dispute with Rabindranath on the Bihar earthquake (I shall return to that subject in Chapter 5), one of his minders came along and told me that I would have to continue the conversation at another time. With a warm smile, Gandhiji waved me goodbye as I left, and got back to the notes he was reading.

I was also particularly interested to hear Eleanor Roosevelt, when she came to Santiniketan in 1952, just after I had started studying at Presidency College in Calcutta. I went back to attend her lecture. The Universal Declaration of Human Rights, sponsored by Mrs Roosevelt and adopted by the United Nations in 1948, used to ring in my ears in those days – indeed, it still does. What she said was a model of humanity and clear-headedness in a very murky world. She also talked about why there was so much to be done – to be 'done by each of us'. That too has remained with me. I was sad I could not get beyond the admiring crowd that surrounded her and did not get the chance to talk with her personally.

One regular visitor who particularly influenced my literary interests was Syed Mujtaba Ali. Syed-da was a superb writer and also a family friend, being very close both to my parents and my grandparents. My mother absolutely adored him. I had started reading some of his writings. His essays were very witty and thought-provoking and I decided that his was the best Bengali I had ever read. I used to hang around while he chatted with older people, just to listen to him. I was immensely impressed not only by his scholarship and liberal wisdom, but also by the way he knew that, for any idea conveyed by a Bengali word, there were many other Bengali words which meant something very similar but not exactly the same. The richness of his language showed a level of discernment that was altogether exceptional and was an inspiration for me.

I would be reminded of Syed-da's intense interest in the choice of words when I arrived in England and joined Trinity College as a student and saw how judiciously Piero Sraffa – a brilliantly original, philosophically inclined economist – chose his words in English, though he was Italian by birth. I thought that Bernard Shaw might have been right when he said, in *Pygmalion*, that a foreigner, carefully using non-native English, could sometimes make better use of the wealth of the language than native speakers; writers such as Joseph Conrad and Vladimir Nabokov bear him out. However, Shaw's point could not apply to Mujtaba Ali, since Syed-da was very much a native Bengali. It was really a matter, I decided, of how much you cared about saying things well. Good language is a product of discerning love.

10

When I look back at my student days, I am thrilled that I had such wonderful classmates and friends whose constant company I could enjoy. My first close friend in Santiniketan was Tan Lee, who was born in Shanghai, China, in 1934. His father, Professor Tan Yun-Shan, was a wonderful scholar who was deeply interested in the history of both China and India, and in particular their interconnections over two millennia.

He and Tagore had first met in 1927 in Singapore, when Tagore was on a trip with friends (including my grandfather, Kshiti Mohan) to visit other Asian countries. Tagore was immensely impressed by Tan and invited him to visit Santiniketan, which he did the following year. Professor Tan was then persuaded by Tagore's persistent pleading to move to Santiniketan and take the lead in founding an institute of Chinese studies in India – a dream Tagore had entertained for a long time. It would be based on the higher educational part of Visva-Bharati University, much like the institution for studying Sanskrit and ancient India led by my grandfather and another great Sanskritist, Bidhu Shekhar Shastri (with whom my grandfather got on tremendously well, though their academic emphases were quite different). Professor Tan worked very hard in founding Cheena Bhavan (including obtaining gifts of funds and books), and the development went through several stages, beginning with the establishment of the Sino-Indian Cultural Society in Nanjing in 1933, just before Tan Lee was born. Cheena Bhavan, which was established in 1936, rapidly became a much-admired centre for Chinese studies in India.

When I moved to Santiniketan School from St Gregory's in Dhaka, both Tan Lee and his sister Tan Wen were already studying there. Tan Lee served as a guide to Santiniketan for me, explaining what happened where. The Tan family had become remarkably 'Indian' with admirable speed, the children speaking Bengali fluently; a later-born sister, Chameli, would go on to become a famous teacher of Bengali at Delhi University. An older and extremely scholarly brother, Tan Chung, who stayed longer in China, would eventually also move to India and become Professor of Chinese studies, also at Delhi University. The Tan family became hugely important to me, as Tan Lee was such a close friend; I also liked his siblings and was in their home for hours at a time. I loved talking with the Tan parents too, and I often felt that these conversations were opening up a door that took me straight and deep into China. Tan Lee, who died suddenly in 2017, was certainly my longest-standing friend.

Another very close friend, from much the same time, is Amit Mitra, whose father, Haridas Mitra, also taught at Santiniketan. In addition to Amit's academic accomplishments (he studied engineering in Calcutta after Santiniketan), Amit was also an excellent singer. He lives now in Pune, directing an institute of Rabindra Sangeet ('songs of Tagore'), in addition to his engineering work. Amit was, like Tan Lee, a source of much strength for me, and I could always rely on sympathy from both of them if something went wrong. Since I plunged early into public speaking at various assemblies of students (usually on literary, social and political subjects), there were certainly bad days – sometimes made more intense by the loud scorn of those who disagreed with me. The lesson that the presence of close friends vastly expands one's ability to take adverse criticism came to me powerfully and early.

I I

Among the girls in my class, Manjula Datta, Jaya Mukherjee and Bithi Dhar outshone the rest with their intelligence and liveliness – though there were others who were impressive as well. Santiniketan being the kind of school it was, the brilliance of the girls received proper attention, and also, since grades were seen as ultimately unimportant, the evaluation tended to stretch well beyond exam marks (to the extent that such marks were given at all). I remember being amused by the remark of one teacher, commenting on Manjula's stellar exam performance: 'You know, she is really quite original, even though her grades are very good.'

The deceptive nature of what is revealed by exam grades is a much simpler issue to understand than the tendency of a group of students to systematically undersell their performance, no matter how measured. I had the impression that these girls were a lot more intelligent and talented than they liked others to think. Gender inequality has been a subject of interest to me throughout my life, and I wondered whether the gender bias in the culture (which was undeniable, despite the attempts at its suppression in Santiniketan) was encouraging girls to claim less, thus allowing boys to enjoy being 'better', making them happier and less competitive. I didn't manage to sort out the answers to all my questions, but I did wonder whether a psychology of modesty could be one of the factors contributing to the strong gender bias against women in India. The disadvantages of Indian women compared with men have so many different features that it would be hard to be sure of all the constitutive causes, but I think this psychological factor demands a fuller investigation even today. The distortions it produces are of course not by any means confined to India.

12

Among the initiatives that some of us took in school was a literary magazine that was launched by Alokeranjan Dasgupta, Madhusudan Kundu and me – we were all close friends as we entered our teens. We raised a tiny amount of money to pay the bills for printing the magazine; divided the work of writing essays, poems and stories amongst us (Aloke was already writing very fine poems, and would become, later in life, a much-celebrated poet); and we invited others in the school to submit their literary attempts. The magazine was called *Sphulinga*, which means a spark – a title that had Leninist ancestry (Lenin's journal was called *Iskra*, with the same meaning) though our magazine was, in fact, quite deliberately non-political. There was no congruence of political ideas among the editors. The magazine was greeted kindly and even praised for a while, but, after a little over a year, *Sphulinga* lost its power and disappeared in the way sparks do.

Tan Lee and I then started a different kind of venture – a magazine of political cartoons. This too was a short-lived success. The hand-drawn magazine, placed in the reading room of the general library, initially seemed to be much in demand, which pleased us. We chose to reverse our names – 'by Eelnat and Aytrama' the credit line read – not so much to hide our identities (which were of course instantly known) but to indicate that not everything we said was meant to be literal or straightforward. Among other concerns, we expressed frustration that things were changing so slowly in bringing more political and economic justice to independent India (we were perhaps being a little unfair to the government of India, since this was only two years after independence). A cartoon I had drawn for the magazine was of Jawaharlal Nehru with a very bright face – a man evidently full of great ideas – but no hands to do anything at all. One of our teachers – I think it was Kashinathda – remarked that we were 'just too impatient'. He was probably right, even though patience in the decades that followed in India has not been well rewarded either. My advocacy of impatience, which, rightly or wrongly, became a central theme in my writings, was, I suppose, already beginning to take shape in those early days.

I was very lucky with my classmates and do not doubt that my personality would have been quite different but for the warm and creative relations with my close friends. My schooldays were made memorable and influential by the friendships I had with – in addition to those already recalled – Sadhan, Shib, Chitta, Chaltu, Bheltu and later Mrinal (who became one of my closest friends), Prabuddha, Dipankar and Mansoor; and, among the girls, Manjula, Jaya, Bithi, Tapati, Shanta and others. My memories of Santiniketan are so bound up with them that a fair account of what I remember would involve little biographies of each one.

I sometimes think that so much has been written in literature about love and so little about friendship that there is a real need to redress the balance, without trying to redefine friendship under some kind of a broadened umbrella of love when they are not really the same thing at all. I was immensely happy, therefore, that a more recent friend, Vikram Seth, chose to speak about friendship and poetry when giving a lecture in memory of my late wife, Eva Colorni, at the London School of Economics in 2010. Eva would have loved Vikram's lecture – the subject of friendship greatly interested her, and Vikram's observations, particularly on the astonishing reach of friendships, were extremely insightful. What he said also took me far beyond what I had previously thought about friendship, even when helped by E. M. Forster – and also Ashok Rudra, who taught at Santiniketan and wrote a beautiful essay on friendship.

Aside from my immediate classmates, Santiniketan offered the engrossing opportunity of close relations with people who were several years older, but who seemed willing to talk with us almost without limit. They had interests and talents of many different kinds. Amit-da wrote fabulously funny things (poems, plays, essays); Biswajit-da knew about books I had not even heard of; Bhulu-da could sing beautifully – and lead others to sing in a way that would transform a group into a community; Mantu-da showed why genuine curiosity about others can be the basis of real affection; Sunil-da showed the humanist side of Marxist thinking in a remarkably convincing way.

When I look back at my schooldays, I cannot help feeling that the many different pieces fitted together so well it would be easy to imagine they had been placed there as a kind of 'intelligent creation', a jigsaw puzzle that made a coherent whole. When things go so well, I can see why the temptation to believe in some kind of a superhuman agency in the world can be so strong. Caution comes, however, with reflection on how terribly badly the lives of many others – hundreds of millions – go when deprivations of various kinds are heaped on each other. So, despite my own good fortune, there is clearly no lesson here about any intelligent and kindly creator. That thought was often in my mind as I went through my extraordinarily happy schooldays.

13

Rabindranath devoted much of his life to advancing education in India and advocating it everywhere. Nothing absorbed as much of his time as the school he had established in Santiniketan and for which he was constantly raising money. There is a nice story – perhaps apocryphal, but certainly characteristic – about the way in which he told others about his Nobel Prize in Literature when it was announced in November 1913. Apparently, he learned about the Prize in a telegram that was delivered to him in a meeting of a school committee he was attending, which was discussing the challenging problem of how to finance a new set of drains that the school needed. His sharing of the news from Stockholm apparently took the eccentric form of saying, 'Money for the drains has just been found.' Whether or not the story was exactly true, the commitment that it conveys was entirely genuine and Rabindranath certainly did use the Nobel Prize money for improving facilities in Santiniketan.

This belief in reason and freedom underlaid Tagore's outlook on life in general and education in particular, leading him to insist that education in depth, and for all, is the most important element in the development of a country. In his assessment of Japan's remarkable economic development, for example, he highlighted the hugely constructive role of good school education – an analysis that would be echoed much later in the economic literature on development, including by the World Bank and the United Nations. Tagore argued, 'the imposing tower of misery which today rests on the heart of India has its sole foundation in the absence of education'. Even if we can think of qualifications to this judgement, it is not hard to see why he thought the transformative role of education was central to economic development and social change.

4

The Company of Grandparents

I

I have told how, within two years of returning from Burma, I was in Santiniketan, attending school there and living with my grandparents. Their cottage, where I had been born, was a modest but charming house provided by Visva Bharati, in a row of houses for teachers called Gurupalli ('the village of teachers'). It had a kitchen, a dining room and two bedrooms on either side of a small study, in which my grandfather could most often be found when he was at home (rather than working, as he often did, on the top floor of the Santiniketan library). Sometimes he liked to work on the veranda, sitting cross-legged on a small cotton carpet in front of a low-level writing desk on the floor.

I always admired Kshiti Mohan's ability to concentrate on his work while his grandchildren and their friends ran around him – both inside the house and out. I was the grandchild who lived most steadily with him and my grandmother, but other grandchildren would come and stay for months too. My mother's elder brother, Kankar (or Kshemendra), then unmarried, lived in Calcutta, working for a newspaper, the *Hindusthan Standard* (now defunct). He came often to Santiniketan, and I greatly enjoyed chatting with him, thrilled by his gentle humour.

My mother's two older sisters had, between them, eight children, and there was a floating crowd of cousins staying with us in the cottage in Gurupalli, especially over the vacations. I was particularly close to my 'cousin-brothers' Khokonda (Kalyan), Bacchuda (Somshankar) and Barenda (Barendra), and fond of my cousin-sisters too, especially Sunipa (Mejdi), but also Reba (Didi), Shyamali (Shejdi), Sushima

(Chordi), Ilina and Sumona. After her marriage, when Mejdi, my favourite cousin-sister, moved with her husband to rural Bihar where her father-in-law worked as a medical doctor, I would often go and spend a part of my summer vacation with her and her husband (Kalyan-da, with whom I used to have very enjoyable conversations) in the beautiful wilderness. From my childhood onwards, I have always loved being in rural Bihar.

There were also other cousins – Piyali and Dula – who could be found in their parents' home in Santiniketan during the school vacations, along with their brother Shami. I had some very pleasant times with them, and as we grew older I became even closer to Piyali and Dula. And there were still more cousins living mostly in Santiniketan, in particular Kajali, Gablu and Tuktuk, and their brothers Barenda (who I have mentioned already) and Bratin, providing me with excellent company. We often slept in each other's homes. Living with others, with shared bedrooms – and indeed beds – was a common feature of my life. The understanding that my sister Manju and I were a part of a large integrated family had made a strong impression on us.

The only bathroom in our house in Gurupalli was outdoors and, depending on how many of us were there at the same time, a certain amount of queuing was a regular part of our lives. There was no electricity, in contrast with our brightly lit house in Dhaka, but I got used to living in the light of kerosene lamps – and doing my studies by it as well. If in my subsequent life I have shown a strong urban preference, this could be because I felt I had done my stint of rural living already. I did enjoy village life, but gradually developed the conviction that there is something to be said for bookshops, coffee houses, cinemas, theatres, musical events and academic gatherings.

My grandfather would wake up every day at around 4 a.m., when it was quite dark and, after getting ready, would go out for a long walk. On mornings when I was up too (it is difficult to think now that in those days I used to be an early riser), he would try to make me familiar with the stars that shone in those early hours – he knew all of them by their Sanskrit names and some by their English names too. I loved accompanying him as the dawn broke and enjoyed knowing the names of the stars, but most importantly it gave me the wonderful opportunity to bombard him with questions. He told me a lot of funny stories about his own childhood, but we discussed serious subjects as well. A walk could become a class on such subjects as the dismal way India treated its pre-agricultural tribal population, usurping their land (he knew well the sad history of that process, including the failure of successive governments to build schools and hospitals for them). He told me that Ashoka, a great Buddhist emperor who ruled over much of India in the third century BC, expressed special concern about 'forest people' in the already urbanizing India, asserting that the tribal folk had their rights too, just like those who lived in the cities and towns.

2

I learned that Rabindranath, also an early riser, would sometimes visit my grandparents before dawn – without warning, counting on their early rising habits. This was, of course, well before I came to live in Gurupalli, indeed, mostly before I was even born. On one occasion, I learned from my grandmother, he arrived, without any warning, just before dawn on a day when – unusually – Kshiti Mohan was still sleeping.

So Rabindranath put his question to my grandmother (who was fortunately awake), in a quickly composed poem, using the fact that his name, Rabi, meant the sun, whereas Kshiti meant the earth. Translated from Bengali, it went:

> Dawn has come
> Rabi [the sun] has appeared
> At the door of Kshiti [the earth].
> Is it possible that the earth is not awake yet?

Didima said that she felt sad that she had to wake up the earth before Rabindranath's engaging poetry could proceed further. She was happy to see the two of them go off for a walk, but wished Rabindranath was still sitting on her porch completing his spontaneous composition.

3

In 1944 we moved to a new house that my grandparents had built at the western edge of Santiniketan, in Sripalli – no more than a quarter of a mile from the campus, in what was still a tiny town. Dadu and Didima's new house was, as I have mentioned earlier, next to a small house called Pratichi that my parents, still in Dhaka, had built in 1942. Sometime after we moved to Sripalli, I started sleeping and working next door in Pratichi, but continued to eat with my grandparents.

I became very attached to Pratichi, where I lived more or less alone, except for the company of a young servant, Joggeshwar, who stayed separately in his own apartment inside the compound of the house. Joggeshwar had come as a starving young boy from the neighbouring district of Dumka, looking for work and a little income, in the year of the Bengal famine of 1943. There was no particular need for a new servant in our family then, but there was a consensus on the necessity of doing something to help this fresh-faced Dumka boy, and so Joggeshwar was sheltered and fed first by my maternal aunt, Renu, and then by my mother. My mother gave him charge of the then uninhabited Pratichi – Joggeshwar told me that he loved 'having an entire house to himself'. By the time I moved with my grandparents from Gurupalli, I was ten and Joggeshwar was fifteen. And when, a couple of years later, I started sleeping in Pratichi, Joggeshwar was given the job of keeping an eye on me. My grandparents, next door, were of course really in charge.

Joggeshwar lived with and worked for us for nearly seventy years. He was very happy that the two public benefit trusts that I was able to set up, with the help of the Nobel money which came my way in 1998 – one in Bangladesh and another in India – aimed at improving elementary education, basic health care and gender equity, are called 'Pratichi Trusts'. 'I like the names very much,' Joggeshar told me with a huge smile.

In time Joggeshwar became the chief employee at our home, and moved with my parents to Delhi and Calcutta after my father resigned from his Dhaka University employment in 1945, shortly before the blood-soaked partition of India. When my father eventually retired from his job in New Delhi in 1964, they all settled in Pratichi – and by then the house had been extended. Arabinda Nandy, who used to help my mother with her literary work, particularly with the editing of a Bengali magazine (*Shreyashi*) which she had started, also took on the job of 'managing' the household as my mother grew older. After my father died in 1971, my mother continued to live in Pratichi. Those who were working for us – of tribal (*Santal*) origin – had by then almost become members of the family (Rani was the leader of the group). My mother eventually left us at the age of ninety-three in 2005. Before her death she gave me a firm command that none of the six servants working in Pratichi (including the two in charge of the garden) should be fired, and each should receive their full salary and complete medical coverage even after they retired. I have obeyed her instructions, and Pratichi still hums with life – especially after a 400-channel cable connection was installed to keep everyone entertained.

Since I am very fond of – and still much involved with – Pratichi, it is wonderful for me to see that, despite the human departures, the house is not much less vibrant today than in earlier days. One of the added benefits is the attachment of my children to Pratichi. This applies to both Antara and Nandana as well as the younger two – Indrani and Kabir – and it is wonderful that through the year they make elaborate plans to go there quite frequently. My mother would have been really happy about that. To return there myself, if only for a short while, as I now do about four times a year (except when COVID-19 rules supreme – as it does at the time of writing), feels like taking a dip in an old familiar river, even though I understand the philosophical warning that we cannot really dip in the same stream twice.

When I was a child, my meals with my grandparents next door often lasted a long time, mostly because I so much enjoyed talking with Dadu and Didima. There was an almost endless range of topics on which we had long conversations. At one stage (I think I must have been then about eleven), Kshiti Mohan, whose basic education was that of a Sanskritist, became very interested in finding out how evolution worked. He had read something – I think it was by J. B. S. Haldane – that made him understand natural selection for the first time and how even very small advantages in survival end up making one species dominant over another, given enough time. I remember helping him with the maths of growth at compound rates and the magic of exponential expansion entertained him more than I had anticipated.

However, then came a question that bothered him – and me too. While it is easy to see how the species that fit better in the world get to be dominant and outnumber the others, the competition is surely restricted to the collection of species that happen to be – for one reason or another – present. The question that engaged both my grandfather and me was: why were they there in the first place, enabling them to enter this competition for the fittest? Kshiti Mohan would not invoke God in explanation, for he did not think God worked in that kind of a competitive way, and I would not invoke God either, since I did not think that there was a God arranging horse races between the species. Kshiti Mohan said that he must understand the problem better, and so do some more reading. A few days later we had a tremendous discussion on mutation and its role in natural selection.

Kshiti Mohan was fascinated by the thought that something that could be taken to be largely accidental (namely, which species would come into existence through mutation) worked with systematic – and even predictable – results in terms of survival advantages (that is, which species, once in existence, would become dominant) to end up producing the orderly world that we find around us. I shared his fascination with the combination of causality and chance, and enjoyed the search; but there was also, for me, much fun in working with a person of gigantic academic achievement in other fields who, because of his unfamiliarity with genetic issues, was willing to enter into an intellectual collaboration with his eleven-year-old grandson.

4

In a kind of ideological comparison with ancient sites of learning much eulogized in the Upanishads and in the epics *Ramayana* and *Mahabharata*, Santiniketan was sometimes referred to as an 'ashram'. Schooling in India's old ashrams, we have been told, put particular emphasis on fostering curiosity rather than competitive excellence, and this was the focus in Santiniketan too. Any kind of concentration on examination performance and grades was, as I have mentioned, strongly discouraged. This prompted me to read many of Tagore's essays on education – not just his poems and stories, as I had done earlier.

Tagore liked discussing his educational ideas in the weekly assemblies that were regularly held on Wednesday mornings in term-time at Santiniketan. They took place in what was called 'Mandir', which can be literally translated from Sanskrit as a 'temple', but the assemblies were not ceremonies of any particular religion. The weekly Mandir served as a regular forum for discussion of issues of gravity that interested the whole Santiniketan community. With its brightly coloured glass walls and translucent blocks of many different tints, the physical structure of the Mandir had some similarity, I later thought, with an old Christian church. There were some non-denominational prayers, but mostly discussions – quite wordy – on religious as well as general subjects with a moral slant.

Rabindranath used to lead those events, with plenty of songs in between the spoken words. After his death, it became the duty of my grandfather, Kshiti Mohan, to lead the assembly and to make the weekly speech, as Rabindranath used to. I was not a student at Santiniketan School in Tagore's time, though I was taken to Mandir a few times as a child visitor from Dhaka. Didima loved telling a rather embarrassing story about me attending a Mandir session led by Rabindranath. I was about five, and I was strongly instructed before being taken to the Mandir not to utter a word when the events were taking place. 'You must be completely silent – everyone has to be,' said my grandmother. I promised I would be completely mute. But when we were in the Mandir, as soon as Tagore started giving his speech, I understand I broke the silence with a loud question, 'Why is that man there speaking, then?' Rabindranath, I am told, smiled gently, but did not offer any explanation to help me solve the mystery.

5

I enjoyed hearing my grandfather at the weekly Mandir, at least initially, but I found no particular attraction to a weekly religious – or at least semi-religious – discourse. By the time I was twelve, I told my grandfather that I did not want to come to the Mandir assemblies regularly, for I had work to do. 'And, I suppose,' he told me (but did not sound particularly hurt), 'you do not enjoy these discussions at the Mandir?' I was silent. He told me that this would be fine, but I would probably change my mind as I grew up. I told him that religion did not interest me at all and I had no religious convictions. He said, 'There is no case for having religious convictions until you are able to think seriously for yourself – it will come to you in a natural way, over time.'

Since religious convictions did not come to me at all as I grew older – my scepticism only seemed to mature with age – I told my grandfather, some years later, that he might have been wrong, that religion had not come to me over time, despite my persistent attempts to think about the difficult issues that religion tries to resolve. 'I was not mistaken,' replied my grandfather, 'you have addressed the religious question, and you have placed yourself, I can see, in the atheistic – the Lokayata – part of the Hindu spectrum!' He also gave me a long list of references to atheistic and agnostic treatises in ancient Sanskrit – including the discourses of Carvaka and Jabali in *Ramayana*, and the works of the Lokayata school in general. Kshiti Mohan also referred me to the fourteenth-century Sanskrit book *Sarvadarsana Samgraha* ('Collection of All Philosophies') by Madhavacharya, the first chapter of which is devoted to a sympathetic exposition of the atheistic philosophy of Lokayata. Given my enthusiasm for Sanskrit reading at that time, I went to work on it enthusiastically. Madhavacarya is one of the best authors I have ever read in the way he demonstrates the reach of reasoning, defending alternative philosophical positions in different chapters. The defence of atheism and materialism in the first chapter of his book is one of the best expositions of those perspectives I have ever read.

Kshiti Mohan also drew my attention to a prominent verse – the so-called 'Song of Creation' – in the *Rig Veda*, which is the most ancient of the Hindu classics (probably dating from around 1500 BC). The song of creation expresses deep doubts about any orthodox story of how the world was created:

> Who really knows? Who will here proclaim it? Whence was it produced? Whence is this creation? The gods came afterwards, with the creation of this universe. Who then knows whence it has arisen?
>
> Whence this creation has arisen – perhaps it formed itself, or perhaps it did not – the one who looks down on it, in the highest heaven, only he knows – or perhaps he does not know.

I was much struck by the thought that agnostic or even atheistic analyses could be included within the Hindu corpus of thought – despite some frustration too in recognizing that in this broad view there was no escape from religion, even for an atheist.

6

I could well understand why Tagore was so keen on getting my grandfather to come to Santiniketan and join him in the building of a new kind of educational institution. Rabindranath had heard about Kshiti Mohan from one of his distinguished colleagues, Kali Mohan Ghosh, who was already in Santiniketan, mainly to help Tagore with his work on village reform and rural reconstruction, in addition to contributing to education at Santiniketan School. What Tagore heard about Kshiti Mohan impressed him sufficiently to undertake a kind of a background check. He found out about my grandfather's scholarship as well as his liberal inclinations and deep involvement with the poorest people in the society, and became adamant that Kshiti Mohan must be persuaded to come to Santiniketan. Rabindranath wrote in his notes:

> Even though he is very well versed in the scriptures and classical religion writings, his priorities are entirely liberal. He claims that he gets this liberality from reading the scriptures themselves. He may be able to influence even those who want to use their narrow reading of the scriptures to reduce – and insult – Hinduism. At least, he would be able to help remove narrowness from the minds of our students.

'I have a great need of an ally,' Rabindranath pleaded with Kshiti Mohan in a letter dated 24 February 1908, adding (in response to his reluctance to move), 'I am not yet ready to abandon hope.' The salaries were very low at Santiniketan School and Kshiti Mohan had a large family, including not only his own children, but also the sons (Biren and Dhiren) of his deceased elder brother, Abanimohan. By 1907 Kshiti Mohan had obtained a good job in the native kingdom of Chamba, in the foothills of the Himalayas, as the principal teacher in the school there. He had the warm support of the king, Bhuri Singh (they got on very well together), and he did not want to abandon the regular salary that the job offered him. Tagore continued his pleading and said that he would make sure that Kshiti Mohan's remuneration would be adequate for him to meet his family obligations.

Ultimately, Tagore did persuade Kshiti Mohan to come to Santiniketan, where he spent more than fifty contented and productive years – being both influenced by Tagore's vision and influencing the poet's own ideas. They also became close friends. It was with Kshiti Mohan that Rabindranath shared his worries on the morning after the famous literary dinner in London on 27 June 1912, hosted by W. B. Yeats, which 'launched' him in Europe, that he was being championed for entirely the wrong reasons. I shall return to that episode in the next chapter.

7

Kshiti Mohan Sen's family came from the small town of Sonarang in the Bikrampur District of Dhaka, not very far from Manikganj where my paternal family originated. Kshiti Mohan's father, Bhubanmohan, was a traditional doctor in the Ayurvedic system, with a reasonably good practice, but moved to Benares after he retired, taking Kshiti Mohan with him. I never heard Kshiti Mohan talk about his father, and I believe their relationship was not very close. I formed the impression that Kshiti Mohan rather disapproved of – or at least was saddened by – something in his father, but despite several attempts I could never discover what that might have been.

Bhubanmohan was, however, proud of his son's academic accomplishments and celebrated the fact that he had excelled in his studies in Queen's College in Benares, from which he received his Master's degree (it was formally from Allahabad University, to which Queen's College was affiliated). But he spent much more time at the traditional centres of Sanskrit education, the 'Chatushpathis' that were still flourishing in Benares in his time, and would write later about the great achievements of that tradition in preserving and advancing classical education in India, and of the tragedy of their slow disappearance with the advent of modernity in the country. He also received the much-coveted title of 'Pundit' for his Sanskrit scholarship. As a rather conservative Hindu, Bhubanmohan would presumably have approved of his son's mastery of Sanskrit and of ancient Hindu literature, but the radical broadening of Kshiti Mohan's literary and religious interests would have alarmed him – if he had known about it.

In fact Bhubanmohan was afraid that Kshiti Mohan might turn 'Western' in his attitudes and convictions and he tried to do what he could to prevent that from happening. Kshiti Mohan's broadening was actually going in a different direction altogether, since he was increasingly being captivated by the beauty and power of the poetry and songs of the Muslim Sufis, along with the literature of the Hindu Bhakti movement. He learned Persian, and in this he had great help from his elder brother Abanimohan, who knew Persian well.

At the age of fourteen, Kshiti Mohan decided to join the pluralistic religious tradition of Kabir, the 'Kabir Panth' ('the path of Kabir'), which capaciously combined Hindu and Muslim religious ideas and generated wonderful poems that have been recited and sung over the centuries. While joining Kabir Panth was a formal act, its liberality allowed Kshiti Mohan to lead his own life, with its own reasoned priorities. Kabir was born in a Muslim family in the middle of the fifteenth century (the birth date is usually given as 1440, but this is hard to ascertain) and drew on both Muslim and Hindu ideas and literary traditions. It is easy to guess that Bhubanmohan would not have approved of this. Kshiti Mohan would write later about the irony of what was happening:

> To keep me in the conservative [Hindu] fold, various strict arrangements were made [for exclusion from Christian influence], but the God who governed my life would have been amused by this. Attempts to keep me traditional were certainly undermined, but the danger did not come from the English.

The priorities of Kshiti Mohan's life changed with his evolving convictions. Ten years before he went to Chamba in 1897, when he was just seventeen, he decided to travel across northern and western India to collect and compile the poems and songs of Kabir, Dadu and other similarly inclined proponents (sants) who pursued religion in their own way, with respect for both Muslim and Hindu thought. There were huge territories to visit, since the followers of Kabir and the other sants were spread across many provinces of India.

My son is named Kabir, partly because the ideas of the historical Kabir moved me – and also because his mother Eva Colorni liked the name. Kabir is, of course, a Muslim name, and Eva, who was Jewish, told me that 'It is just right that the son of a Hindu-origin father and a Jewish-origin mother should have a nice Muslim name.' While deeply engaged in studying Kabir and his tradition, Kshiti Mohan also became aware that even in his native Bengal, there was a rich and lively tradition of Hindu–Muslim interaction among the Bauls, who had a similarly capacious outlook, drawing on thoughts of both religions and attracting followers from both communities. So in 1897–8 he also began his search for the Bauls of Bengal, and for their songs and poems.

These travels, and Kshiti Mohan's determination to keep extensive records, absorbed a lot of his time. Syed Mujtaba Ali, the great Bengali writer and scholar, who was a close friend of the family and who worked with Kshiti Mohan, has pointed out that he studied and analysed the rural oral texts he was collecting with the 'scientific thoroughness' that classical scholars applied to ancient texts.

8

While his father, Bhubanmohan, does not seem to have approved of the broadening of his son's interests, Kshiti Mohan received firm support from his mother, Dayamayi, and it was with her that he had a close relationship. She had helped him to lead an independent life and to pursue his own priorities, combining classical Sanskrit studies with rural religious and literary traditions. She also supported him in his ceaseless travels through rural India in pursuit of poetry and folk songs. It was she, too, who encouraged him to take up Tagore's invitation – she had read some of Tagore's writings and been much moved by his vision and by his extraordinary ideas. Bhubanmohan would not have approved of the move to Santiniketan, I imagine, but I could not persuade my grandfather to talk about that: 'my mother was very supportive' is all he would say.

On one beautiful evening in Santiniketan, just around sunset, I remember Kshiti Mohan asked my mother (we were all sitting on the veranda): 'Do you remember my mother, your grandmother?' I would then have been twelve, my mother about thirty-three and Kshiti Mohan around sixty-five. My mother said that she had really been too young to remember her – she wished she could. Dadu said, 'Of course, of course, it was silly of me to ask.' And then he fell into silence. I was saddened to think that my ancient and wise grandfather had a longing to recollect his mother, who would have been well over a hundred by then, had she been alive. On that hauntingly graceful evening, it was hard for the twelve-year-old boy to resist melancholic thoughts about the tragedy of time passing.

9

If Kshiti Mohan's mother was very important to him, so, unsurprisingly, was his wife, my Didima. Kiran Bala was the eldest daughter of a very skilled and successful engineer, Madhusudan Sen. Her two brothers, Atul and Shebak, became engineers too, and I greatly enjoyed chatting not only with their children (Kanai, Piku and Nimai), but also with them despite the gap in our ages. We often stayed at Atuldada's elegant house in south Calcutta when we came to the big city from Dhaka. My first couple of conversations with Atuldada – I must have been six or seven at that time – took place when he was repairing his car. He was entirely underneath it, with various tools next to him, but I could only see his outstretched legs. I had never before had a conversation with a pair of legs, but the unseen face from underneath the car was very engaging and kept me amused and occupied for more than an hour.

That side of my extended family were all very interested in technical things. Atuldada worked for an engineering firm in Calcutta, and Shebakdada was in charge of Santiniketan's electric supply. Kiran Bala's younger sister Tuludi, who lived in Santiniketan as well, entertained me with mathematical brainteasers, and from my earliest childhood her visits to our home were a source of great joy to me.

Kiran Bala's marriage involved an economic downgrading since her father, Madhusudan, was significantly more prosperous than the cash-strapped Kshiti Mohan. But she managed the practicalities of their life with great efficiency – amidst considerable hardship – and it was amazing to me how cheerful she always was despite having so much to do. This included not just the cooking and looking after the home, but caring for grandchildren like me, all her midwifery and also taking care of her mentally affected youngest sister Indira, who had been brain damaged in early youth by some passing epidemic which left her permanently disabled. Indira lived with us and Kiran Bala looked after her throughout her life – for forty years or so – carefully bathing her every morning, taking care of her throughout the day and even trying to amuse her, to the extent that was possible. Didima's affection for people in difficulty was extraordinarily inspiring for me.

There were also animals – stray animals – which received her attention. Among them was a pariah dog – a mongrel with no fixed abode – which would come every day at the same time for food that Didima gave it. This was a regular event and, oddly enough, towards the end of my grandmother's life, the pariah dog helped her in quite a remarkable way. One day Didima, who was then ninety, fell down an open staircase attached to the veranda and lost consciousness, at a time when there was no one else at home. The dog arrived in search of its meal, saw Didima in that state and ran to my parents' home next door, where my mother happened to be sitting on the veranda (I was living in Delhi at that time, and heard the story from my mother). The dog went on barking at her, and making a gesture of running to Didima's house, and coming back and doing the same thing again and again. After a few attempts, the dog was successful in making Ma curious and worried, so she went to Didima's house and found her on the floor, lying at the bottom of the staircase. Didima survived – for another six years to the age of ninety-six – but the doctors said that the outcome that day could have been quite different had medical attention not come quickly. The pariah dog was clearly the hero of the day, but it is also a tale, almost a moral tale, of being rewarded for kindness – a kindness that Didima radiated plentifully.

Dadu was thoroughly dependent on Didima for nearly everything, and they had an extraordinarily close relationship. I remember so well that when Kshiti Mohan returned home from work, there would come his loud announcement from the edge of the compound, uttered even before entering the house: 'Kiran'. Kshiti Mohan was a great letter-writer, but perhaps it is not so well known that the vast majority of his letters were to his wife, with whom he felt compelled to share, it seems, every thought that he ever had whenever they were apart.

When Nandalal Bose, the great artist, accompanied him and Tagore in their eastern voyage to China and Japan in 1924, Nandalal was amused that Kshiti Mohan used most of his free time to write letters to Kiran Bala: it was his 'favourite activity'. Nandalal commented in his notes on their joint travels that Kiran Bala must have been kept very busy, reading the torrent of letters she received from her husband.

Kshiti Mohan's biographer, Pranati Mukhopadhyay, managed to get hold of some of the letters that he wrote to Kiran Bala, beginning with a letter of 29 June 1902, just after their marriage, when she was visiting her parents. Dadu explained how wonderfully happy he had become since marrying her. The first letter began with Kshiti Mohan saying: 'Had there been a thermometer for happiness, I could have explained to you how happy I am!' I recollected that line recently when thinking about the methods of measuring happiness that is engaging the attention of people as different in their professions as my friend the economist Richard Layard and the philanthropic monarch of Bhutan.

10

Rabindranath's determination to get my grandfather to join him at Santiniketan School was mainly related to Kshiti Mohan's classical scholarship and command over Sanskrit and Pali texts, an area in which he had exceptional expertise. Some of the books he wrote while working at the ashram became deeply influential in encouraging a more liberal reading of the classics than had been acceptable earlier. Many of the themes on which he chose to write reflected his analysis of the injustices in Indian society, such as inequities of caste and gender, which were often supported by distorted readings of classical and scriptural texts. He wanted to undermine these evils through a fuller reading of the ancient texts.

I sometimes argued with Kshiti Mohan, in my belief that he would have opposed these inequalities anyway, even if they really had scriptural backing. He would not deny that point, but told me that 'it does not change in any way the fact that these injustices get support from many people who are influenced by shoddy scholarship, with distorted reading and biased selection of ancient texts'. He had to correct these intellectual transgressions even when he agreed that mistaken interpretation was not all that was involved in the ongoing practices. His painstakingly researched books, such as *Jatibhed* ('Caste distinction'), showed how tenuous was the scriptural basis of the stratification of people in Hindu practice. *Prachin Bharate Nari* ('Women in ancient India') discussed how the freedoms often enjoyed by women in ancient India had been gradually denied to them in medieval and contemporary India. In *Bharater Sanskriti* ('The Cultural Traditions of India') he showed, among other things, how different types of sources were used in the ancient Hindu literature, cutting across divisions of religion, caste, class, gender and community. These writings drew heavily on his classical scholarship.

As Tagore had hoped, Kshiti Mohan also helped to soften the traditional austerity of old-fashioned Sanskrit studies in the ashram. What he may not have expected is the extent to which Kshiti Mohan would broaden Tagore's own understanding not only of the classical and scriptural literature, but also of folk religious ideas and, most importantly, of rural poetry and songs. These came from Kshiti Mohan's extensive studies of these traditions, beginning with Kabir and the collections he had been putting together since his teenage years. It was with the strong encouragement of Rabindranath that Kshiti Mohan started publishing collections and commentaries on Kabir, Dadu and other visionary rural poets.

As far as Kabir was concerned, Kshiti Mohan concentrated on the orally sustained versions of his poems, originating more than five hundred years ago, which had undergone sometimes considerable variations over the centuries in the hands of Kabir Panthi poets and singers. His four-volume compendium, with Bengali translations of Kabir's Hindi poems, was published in 1910–11, not long after he moved to the ashram. Tagore was much influenced not only by Kshiti Mohan's liberal and lenient interpretation of Hinduism, which emphasized its creative rather than destructive interactions with other

great religions, particularly Islam, but also by the way Kshiti Mohan
drew attention to the sophisticated thoughts of allegedly unsophisticated rural poets.

The remarkable simplicity and reach of this old but living poetry,
which stood as a major bridge between the Hindu Bhakti movement
and the Islamic Sufi tradition, moved Tagore greatly. He produced,
with the assistance of Evelyn Underhill, English translations of 'one
hundred poems of Kabir' taken from Kshiti Mohan's collection. These
were published in 1915, two years after Tagore received the Nobel
Prize in Literature. Ezra Pound was involved in another English translation of Kabir's poems, based again on Kshiti Mohan's collection.
Even though some of these translations were published, the fuller and
more ambitious work Pound had in mind was never completed and
released.

I I

Questions have been raised by certain critics about Kshiti Mohan's
version of Kabir's poems as they do not always tally with the exact
wording of some other versions, and this subject was provoking academic interest by the time I was finishing my schooling at Santiniketan.
I had seen Kshiti Mohan's comment on this in the Introduction to a
later book of his, on the poems of Dadu, another rural sant – from
the sixteenth century – who was a follower of Kabir and who, like
him, bridged Hindu and Muslim traditions. In that book, published in
1935, my grandfather referred to the ongoing criticism that in his collection of Kabir he did not confine himself to the printed versions of
Kabir's poems, entitled *Bijak*. He said in response that had these critics read the Introduction to his book on Kabir, they would have seen
his explanation that his chosen focus was to introduce the public to
the traditions that were still orally active among the rural masses in
India. He included many of the poems from *Bijak*, but he had chosen
to go well beyond them.

I felt drawn into the debate, and sensed that Kshiti Mohan must
have been moved, at least partly, by his worry about the dominance
of urban elites in the interpretation of Indian culture, a subject about

which we had frequent discussions around the dinner table. So I asked him about this. Kshiti Mohan agreed, but also told me that there was nothing surprising about the fact that there were variations between different versions of Kabir's poems. Kabir himself had not written down any of the poems and, as a compiler, Kshiti Mohan thought it was right to give precedence to the poems that were recited or sung in contemporary oral practice. Other collectors often preferred to use versions that had been written down at one time or another, presumably based on oral versions that had been current at an earlier time. The surprising thing in all these debates was not, he told me, the existence of different versions of poems by an oral poet who lived many centuries ago, since a multiplicity of versions is a common feature of traditional oral poetry, but the extent to which many compilers insisted on sticking only to 'frozen versions in print' (he said with a smile), 'rather than allowing room for the living traditions of continuing practice'. I found that Kshiti Mohan had, in fact, explained all this in some detail in the Introduction to his original collection of Kabir's verses in 1910–11:

> From my childhood the 'Sants' with whom I became familiar in Kashi [Benares] and other places of pilgrimage, included Kabir, and I heard his communications clearly. I proceeded later to collect all of Kabir's songs from different parts of India, including all the published versions of Kabir's songs ... From my different readings I chose those that accorded most with what were being sung by the practitioners and which they and I judged to be true to the tradition. I need hardly add that from the variety of advice I got, I had to choose [by using my judgement]. The sadhakas often articulate things that fit their own time. And the same poems have different versions that could be understood easily only at the time when they were composed. I had to take note of all these concerns in making my edited collection of Kabir's poems. Some day I hope to publish a full collection of all versions of Kabir's poems.

The important thing to notice here is not only that there were different versions of Kabir's songs that were simultaneously in circulation (so that any claim of the unique authenticity of one version over all others is futile), but also that Kshiti Mohan consistently gave priority to what still lived in the active tradition of recitation and singing among Kabir's followers, who often came from the lowest strata of Indian society, and which he himself had heard recited or sung by practitioners. In this, Kshiti Mohan had much in common with what have come to be called 'subaltern studies'. There are striking parallels between what I heard from Kshiti Mohan about the biased neglect in our elitist society and what the pioneering subaltern theorists, beginning with Ranajit Guha, would tell us about the traditional neglect in the lives and ideas of lowly placed people in society.

Kshiti Mohan's insistence on giving preference, whenever possible, to the living oral traditions of rural people, often from the poorest part of society, was something he saw as a literary duty, which included a sense of justice. But it was also, he argued, the best way of understanding the creativity of Kabir, Dadu and others, since they were oral poets themselves, trying to reflect the understanding of common people. This was a priority that appealed particularly to Rabindranath and, through him, to a number of intellectuals abroad. Romain Rolland, the French writer, for example, wrote to Tagore on 30 December 1923 that he was deeply impressed by Kshiti Mohan's work on 'that wonderful Dadu, whose personality attracts me'.

However, Tagore too would face criticism from the same quarter that showed impatience with Kshiti Mohan's folk selections. There was certainly an elitist tendency to keep access to Kabir confined to the urban, educated classes, and to dismiss the possibility that rural poets could have had the sophistication to say things as smart as Kshiti Mohan and Rabindranath claimed. This was also a matter of some contention in my schooldays, and some of us discussed the issues involved, particularly that of elitism and urban bias, and the exclusive preference so many elitist scholars displayed for the written word, rejecting the living tradition of oral poetry among rural people.

A great Hindi scholar, who taught at Santiniketan, Hazari Prasad Dwivedi, whom I was privileged to know well, took up cudgels in favour of Kshiti Mohan. In the process he affirmed his own belief in the sophistication of dedicated rural poets, no matter how much their creativity might be downgraded by the urban elite. Dwivedi was particularly critical of those who found it difficult to think that common people could have sophisticated thoughts: he called these critics 'mahatmas' – not, I should explain, out of respect. He rejected the diagnosis of inauthenticity of Kshiti Mohan's collection and particularly the laboured argument that those poems were too sophisticated to have come from lowly sants of rural India. In his own – definitive – Hindi book on Kabir, which was published in 1942, Dwivedi reproduced a hundred poems of Kabir directly from Kshiti Mohan's collection, which he described thus:

> *Kabir Ke Pad*, edited by Kshiti Mohan Sen, is a new type of work. He has collected the verses he has directly heard through the songs of the followers [of Kabir] ... the underlying messages carry the stamp of authenticity. Despite this, some 'mahatmas' guided by their own self-interest and self-indulgence have tried to diminish the depth and importance of [Kshiti Mohan's] book.

I 2

If one of the reasons for Kshiti Mohan's involvement in the oral poetry of Kabir, Dadu and the Bauls was his wish to do justice to India's wealth of folk literature, which was often neglected through elitist bias, another was his deep engagement in pursuing the long history of interactions between Hindu and Muslim traditions in India. He went on to write specifically on that subject in several treatises, most importantly in his widely acclaimed Bengali book, *Bharater Hindu-Mushalmaner Jukta Sadhana* ('The Joint Quests of Hindus and Muslims in India'), which came out in the late 1940s when Hindu–Muslim tensions and riots were rampant. It took a position defiantly contrary to organized incitement to violence towards other communities, but also against the intellectual priority given to separatist histories of Hindus and Muslims. The book provides a far-reaching account of how extensive and creative the interactions between Hindus and Muslims have actually been, especially among the common people. It also shows how much of India's rich history is missed if the great religions of India are perceived as isolated islands surrounded by unnavigable waters, or – worse – as islands of belligerent foes dedicated to attacking one another. I will return to my memories of those incitements and the 'theories' that went with them in a later chapter (Chapter 8).

It was Kshiti Mohan's understanding that – contrary to what many sectarian Hindu theorists claimed – Hinduism had been significantly enriched by the influence of Muslim culture and thought. This thesis, certainly heterodox, also found a strong expression in his English book on Hinduism, which was originally published by Penguin Books in 1961 and reprinted many times since then. When Kshiti Mohan told me in the early 1950s that he was preparing this book, which he wanted to be short and accessible to all, I have to confess I was surprised to hear it. The surprise was not because I doubted his formidable expertise on the subject, or his commanding knowledge of the huge corpus of Hindu literature, nor the great success of his many treatises, in Bengali and Hindi (and in Gujarati). But Kshiti Mohan's main education had been in the traditional Sanskrit centres of learning in Benares, and his knowledge of English was extremely limited. Why, I asked myself, had Penguin asked him to write a book in English?

My questions prompted Kshiti Mohan to give me his correspondence with Penguin, and it turned out that another scholar, Sarvepalli Radhakrishnan (earlier the Spalding Professor of Eastern Religions and Ethics at Oxford, and later the President of India), had suggested to Penguin that they should approach Kshiti Mohan, in view of his exceptional command over the subject. But Radhakrishnan had also told the publisher that they must arrange for a translator who could create an English version of what Sen would write in Bengali or Hindi – or perhaps Sanskrit. So Penguin asked Kshiti Mohan to find a translator, and he gave that task to a friend of his at Santiniketan, Dr Sisir Kumar Ghosh. In some ways Ghosh's translation was decent enough, but there were editorial as well as stylistic problems that made Penguin reluctant to go ahead with it, even though they had the text in their hands for many years. So the manuscript gathered dust in the editorial offices of Penguin Books (if Penguin indeed allows any dust to come into their offices), and when in the late 1950s (I was by then in Cambridge) I enquired what was going on, they promptly asked whether I would agree to take charge of the English rendering, based on the Bengali text. I asked my grandfather about this, who told me that he would welcome my involvement very much, but he also wanted to revise the text, partly because of the passage of time.

This is how I found myself – a godless social scientist – busily engaged in producing a book on Hinduism in English, based on Kshiti Mohan's splendid Bengali text. As the English rendering was proceeding, along with editing, under my grandfather's firm instructions, he died suddenly after a short illness in 1960 and I had to see the book through the press. When the book was published by Penguin the following year, I remember thinking that Kshiti Mohan would have been happy to see that all his instructions had, in fact, been carried out.

Of the various novel features of the book, the one I want to comment on briefly here is Kshiti Mohan's reading of Hindu traditions, in particular his assessment of the influence of Islamic thought, especially from the Sufi tradition, on Hindu thought. His emphasis on the constructive mutual influences between Hindu and Muslim traditions in India was relevant enough when the book was written, but it has become immensely more important over the decades, thanks to the championing of aggressive and insular interpretations of Hinduism in contemporary South Asian politics.

The book drew on what Rabindranath Tagore had seen as Kshiti Mohan's 'seemingly endless store of knowledge about Indian culture and religion'. He invoked a larger corpus of texts as well as oral literature in insisting that we must not ignore the receptive and pluralist features in the history of Indian religions, no matter how distant they might be from the intolerant and austere interpretations favoured by combative advocates on different sides of the divide. Kshiti Mohan pointed out that 'their passionate concern with the present has led many Indians to ignore these influences [of Islam], but an objective study of the evolution of Hindu tradition must take into account the creative influence of this great religion'.

When I had arrived in Santiniketan, still not quite eight, to live with my grandparents, I had, of course, no idea how engaging my life – at home with Dadu and Didima and at the school – would be. But the exhilaration I felt on my first night in October 1941, sitting on a low stool in the kitchen, chatting with my grandmother as she cooked, was not deceptive. It was an enthralling moment, with a hint of the magical years to come.

5

A World of Arguments

I

There was a huge earthquake in Bihar – not far from Santiniketan – at 2 p.m. on 15 January 1934. I was then a little over two months old, still in the home of my maternal grandparents where I had been born. At the time the earthquake struck, I was lying on what Bengalis call a *dolna* – a kind of a hammock – hanging from a tree just outside the house. When the waves of the earthquake hit Santiniketan there was a lot of shaking. We were not far from the epicentre of the earthquake. Didima went on a frantic search for me, not being quite sure where I had been left by my mother when she went out for a few minutes. And then Didima could hear guffaws of laughter coming from the *dolna*, as I was very happily waving my hands as it oscillated. Of course I remember none of this, but Didima told me later, 'Clearly, the earthquake gave you the best experience of your life.'

Benign as the scene was in Santiniketan, where there were no casualties, not far away was a gigantic tragedy. The earthquake, which measured 8.4 on the Richter scale, caused havoc in Bihar, flattening the districts of Muzaffarpur and Munger, killing about 30,000 people and ruining the lives of hundreds of thousands of others. While Tagore and others expressed their deeply felt grief and sympathy, and went actively into organizing relief activities, Mahatma Gandhi not only joined in those efforts, but also decided to make a statement identifying the earthquake as a punishment given to India by God for the sin of untouchability. Gandhiji was, of course, very deeply involved then in the fight against untouchability and decided to derive a powerful argument from this event in his all-out battle against the dreadful caste system. 'A man like me', Gandhiji said, 'cannot but believe the earthquake is a divine chastisement sent by God for our sins.' He added, 'For me there is a vital connection between the Bihar calamity and the untouchability campaign.'

Rabindranath was predictably furious. He was, of course, equally committed to the removal of untouchability and had joined Gandhiji wholeheartedly in the anti-untouchability movement, but he was appalled by Gandhiji's interpretation of a natural event that was causing intense suffering and death to hundreds of thousands of innocent people – including children and infants. He also hated the epistemology of seeing an earthquake as an ethical phenomenon. 'It is all the more unfortunate because this kind of unscientific view of a phenomenon is too readily accepted by a large section of our countrymen,' he lamented in a letter to Gandhi.

In the exchange that followed, Tagore expressed his dismay at the linking by Gandhiji of 'ethical principles with a cosmic phenomenon'. He also demanded to know, if Gandhi were right, how so many atrocities could have occurred in the past without precipitating any natural catastrophe:

> Though we cannot point out any period of human history that is free from iniquities of the darkest kind, we still find citadels of malevolence yet remain unshaken, that the factories that cruelly thrive upon abject poverty and the ignorance of the famished cultivators, or prison-houses in all parts of the world where a penal system is pursued, which most often is a special form of licensed criminality, still stand firm. It only shows that the law of gravitation does not in the least respond to the stupendous load of callousness that accumulates till the moral foundations of our society begins to show dangerous cracks and civilizations are undermined.

In his reply Gandhi reiterated his own belief that: 'To me the earthquake was no caprice of God, nor the result of the meeting of blind forces.'

Tagore would have readily agreed with Gandhiji, when the latter wrote to him, 'we have come upon perhaps a fundamental difference.' There was an unbridgeable difference between the two on science and ethics. Gandhiji's letter was dated 2 February 1934. On the same day, in an article in the journal *Harijan*, he asserted that he must refuse to be drawn into a rationalistic argument about his position: 'I am not affected by posers such as "why punishment for an age-old sin", or "why punishment to Bihar and not to the South [where the practice of untouchability had been much stronger]", or "why an earthquake and not some other kind of punishment". My answer is: I am not God.' When I read this *Harijan* essay some years later, I doubted that Gandhiji could really have stopped there, for surely he was also telling the world what was intended by God in that earthquake. He seemed to be distinguishing between different kinds of questions – some of which he could answer on behalf of God and others he had to leave to God. I spent some time thinking about how Gandhiji categorized the questions, wishing I could understand better how his mind worked.

While continuing to be out of tune with Gandhiji, Tagore would have sympathized with him deeply at the personal level, particularly because, as Gandhiji expressed in another letter to him, 'My remarks on the Bihar calamity were a good handle to beat me with.' Indeed, as criticism of Gandhiji grew louder and louder across India (among others, Jawaharlal Nehru issued a strong dissent), Tagore felt compelled to remind people how Gandhiji carried 'greatness with him'. But their attitudes to science and the permissibility of giving moral explanations for physical calamities – even in the service of the best causes – continued to divide them.

Another significant difference between the two was Gandhiji's advocacy of everyone using the *charka* – the primitive spinning wheel – thirty minutes a day. He saw spinning with the *charka* as one of the foundations of his alternative economics as well as a method of personal uplifting. Tagore disagreed sharply and thought little of Gandhiji's version of alternative economics. Instead he saw reasons to celebrate, with a few qualifications, the liberating role of modern technology in reducing human drudgery as well as poverty. He was also deeply sceptical of the argument that diligent spinning with a primitive machine elevates the mind. 'The *charka* does not require anyone to think,' he reminded Gandhiji. 'One simply turns the wheel of the antiquated invention endlessly, using the minimum of judgement and stamina.'

As I was growing up, the *charka* was becoming a huge symbol of the Indian approach to human progress, as interpreted by Gandhi. Encouraged by some of my Gandhian friends (I had many), I did try spinning a few times to find out what it was like. To say that I was bored by the seemingly endless turning of a wheel would be true, but not quite adequate, since I kept asking myself how someone as great as Gandhiji could attach such value to this extraordinarily mechanical, repetitive and thoroughly mindless activity. I also wondered how he could be so keen to make people undergo a drudgery that could be altogether avoided by making use of simple technical innovations. A modest technological change could make people more productive and more fulfilled and, to follow Rabindranath's argument, allow them more time for real thinking.

2

The controversies between two of the great leaders of India would come up again and again in our schooldays in Santiniketan. Underlying the debate on the earthquake were two major issues: first, the place of science in understanding natural phenomena and, second, the tactical use of scientific nonsense in helping a great cause. In addition to occasional discussions on these issues, I recollect vividly the sharp nature of the differences in reasoning among my classmates through long evenings when the school year at Santiniketan was coming to an end.

Rabindranath and Gandhiji had very different concerns in the arguments they tended to present to each other. Related to his suspicion of modern science, Gandhiji was in many ways quite hostile to modern medicine as well. At this time my friends and I were very involved in doing things in our primitive lab – simple things that introduced us to 'the laws of nature' – and we also read a lot about breakthroughs in science and medicine (one of which – the medical use of radiation – would save my life only a year after I left Santiniketan). To varying extents we all remained puzzled about the way Gandhiji's reasoning seemed to proceed, and saw ourselves very much on Tagore's side of this division. I thought I was batting for scientific reasoning – and that seemed important.

3

I must say, however, that the extent of unanimity at Santiniketan worried me, since it seemed like a predictably conformist attitude of
students trained in 'Tagore's school'. Fear of conformism is one reason why I was so pleased when Gandhiji said a few things against the
official thinking of Santiniketan when he visited our campus in 1945.
On the Gandhian advocacy of the *charka*, I wondered whether there
was some important connection that we were all missing.

It is indeed possible that we were, in our youthful way, being unfair to
Gandhiji – and Rabindranath might have been too. Performing the same
tasks that manual labourers constantly do may have had, for Gandhiji,
the virtue of acknowledging a togetherness with the underdogs of society, which could be important. The thought of togetherness – the
sentiment of being 'with' others less fortunate than us – can certainly
have a wide resonance. I was surprised – but also very interested – when
I found later (after I arrived at Trinity College, Cambridge) how deeply
preoccupied Ludwig Wittgenstein had been in wanting to follow the
lifestyle of manual labourers. He talked about this a lot, in particular
with his friend (and, later, my teacher) Piero Sraffa.

Wittgenstein's social beliefs combined a sentimental longing for the
arduous life of a hard-working manual labourer with the hope – more
than slightly eccentric – that a workers' revolution would lead to a
rejection of the 'adoration of science', which he saw as a corrupting
influence on contemporary life, and here too there was some similarity with Gandhi. A comparison between Wittgenstein and Gandhi
might look bizarre, especially given the former's involvement with
logic and the foundation of mathematics and the latter's spiritual priorities, yet there was something shared between the two. This first
struck me when I was reading some of Wittgenstein's papers in the
Wren Library at Trinity.

Later, too, I realized that my initial thought – that Gandhiji was just
confusing the demands of reasoned choice with some kind of unreasoned
romance of hypothetical closeness to the underdogs of society – was
much too naive. As I grew older, I began to think that there was much
more to the difference between the two leaders of thought in India,

and I was frustrated that I could not really pin down exactly what gave the Gandhian position the force it evidently had. Even though I continued to remain deeply sceptical of the sentimental priority that Gandhiji and Wittgenstein apparently shared, I began to allow serious doubts about my earlier belief that there was no argument on Gandhi's side at all.

4

When I was finishing my schooling at Santiniketan, the winds of change in India were strongly in the direction of left-wing politics. This was especially important in Bengal, before as well as after the partition of 1947. A significant component of the case for the left that so influenced Indian intellectuals was appreciation of the success of the Soviet Union in extending school education across its vast territory, including in several educationally backward Asian countries. And in Tagore's praise of the Soviet Union, its educational expansion played a big part.

Tagore visited the USSR in 1930 and was much impressed by its development efforts, especially by what he saw as a real commitment to eliminate poverty and economic inequality. What impressed him most, however, was the expansion of basic education across the old Russian Empire. In *Russiar Chithi* ('Letters from Russia'), published in Bengali in 1931, he chastised the British Indian government for its total failure in tackling widespread illiteracy in India, contrasting it with the Soviet Union's efforts to expand education for all:

> In stepping on the soil of Russia, the first thing that caught my eye was that in education, at any rate, the peasant and the working classes have made such enormous progress in these few years that nothing comparable has happened even to our highest classes in the course of the last hundred and fifty years . . . The people here are not at all afraid of giving complete education even to Turcomans of distant Asia; on the contrary, they are utterly in earnest about it.

The British rulers were so upset by this comparison that when the Bengali book was translated, in part, into English in 1934, it was immediately proscribed. There would not be any English version of the *Letters from Russia* until after the independence of India from Britain in 1947. I had the full Bengali book in my little study corner in Santiniketan, but my attempts to get a copy of the proscribed English version were not successful. The left, understandably, used Tagore's argument as an endorsement of Soviet policies on education and a strong indictment of the lamentable record of the Raj in public education – as indeed it was.

Tagore's endorsement of the Soviet Union had important qualifications. He gave it high marks for educational expansion, but a very low mark for political freedom. My maternal uncle, Kshemendra Mohan – known to us as Kankarmama – who was a socialist but fairly strongly anti-communist, told me that Tagore was upset that an interview he had given in Russia, criticizing the prohibition of dissent in the Soviet Union, was not published. I was not quite sure how Kankarmama knew about this, but when, much later, I looked into that history, it turned out that he was absolutely right. Indeed, as Krishna Dutta and Andrew Robinson discuss in their well-researched biography of Tagore, the visiting poet gave an interview to *Izvestia* in 1930, which they refused to publish. They did publish it eventually, nearly six decades later, in 1988, after much political change and the reforms of Mikhail Gorbachev.

However, the doubts and questions that Rabindranath expressed in the *Izvestia* interview found their way into the pages of the *Manchester Guardian* a couple of weeks after he gave it:

> I must ask you: Are you doing your ideal a service by arousing in the minds of those under your training anger, class-hatred, and revengefulness against those whom you consider to be your enemies? . . . Freedom of mind is needed for the reception of truth; terror hopelessly kills it . . . For the sake of humanity I hope you may never create a vicious force of violence, which will go on weaving an interminable chain of violence and cruelty . . . You have tried to destroy many of the other evils of [the czarist] period. Why not try to destroy this one also?

Tagore wanted education for all, but also the freedom to reason, to disagree and to dispute. Neither the Soviet Union, nor of course the British Raj in India, could meet his hopes and demands. Nor, he soon found, would Japan be able to meet them, particularly as it went on to occupy and misrule other Asian countries. Tagore's pessimism about the world found sadly eloquent expression in his last public speech, 'Crisis in Civilization', in April 1941.

5

Was Rabindranath too highly focused on the priority he gave to reasoning and freedom? Certainly, his unwillingness to give serious consideration to Gandhiji in the world of rational arguments was based on his presumption that Gandhiji was simply ignoring critical reasoning (the acknowledgement of Gandhiji's 'greatness' could not rub away that strong indictment). But if he was advocating the complete precedence of reason, it is hard to understand how and why he appeared to many discerning observers in Europe and America as being the exact opposite: an advocate of blind faith with a penchant for mystification, rather than clarity. How can we understand this odd reversal in understanding Tagore?

In the 1960s a close friend of mine, Nimai Chatterji, whom I knew from Santiniketan, wrote from his home in London (where he was then working at the Indian High Commission) a stream of letters to literary stalwarts of the time, asking their views on Tagore. To my surprise, most of them not only replied but did so at length. While a few of them (Henry Miller was one) expressed continuing admiration, others – from Lionel Trilling to T. S. Eliot – either expressed simple disdain or acknowledged a deep disappointment after an initial burst of what they later saw as misguided admiration. Tagore's alleged mysticism and rejection of reasoning were among the most common grounds of criticism, combined with a perceived lack of literary merit in his writings.

A good example of the nature of the misunderstanding of Tagore's attitude to reasoning and rationality can be found in the letters that Bertrand Russell wrote to Nimai Chatterji. In a frank letter in 1963, Russell wrote:

> I recall the meeting [with Tagore] of which Lowes Dickinson writes only vaguely. There was an earlier occasion, the first upon which I met

Tagore, when he was brought to my home by Robert Trevelyan and Lowes Dickinson. I confess that his mystic air did not attract me and I recollect wishing he would be more direct . . . His intensity was impaired by his self-asorbtion [absorption]. Naturally, his mystic views were by way of dicta and it was not possible to reason about them.

In a second letter, four years later, Russell was even sharper in his denunciation of what he took to be Tagore's aversion to reason – adding a little generalization, in passing, about what he saw as a folly of many Indians:

His talk about the infinite is vague nonsense. The sort of language admired by many Indians unfortunately does not, in fact, mean anything at all.

6

There is surely a mystery here. Why would Tagore, so focused on the priority of reason, appear to be just the opposite to some of the towering intellectuals in Europe and America? To understand what is going on here, especially in Russell's assessment of Tagore, we have to consider three factors, only one of which was specific to Bertrand Russell – his propensity to dismiss what was not immediately clear to him. Rabindranath certainly got the raw end of that in Russell's reactions to him, but in this he did not fare any worse than, for example, Nietzsche, who was peculiarly caricatured in Russell's *History of Western Philosophy*. Since my college days I have been an immense admirer of Russell's writings, but I was appalled to read the simulated conversation between Nietzsche and Buddha that Russell concocted, to bring out the stupidity – as well as the nastiness – of Nietzsche's ideas as he saw them. I liked Russell's admiration for Buddha, which was not altogether dissimilar from mine, but how could someone characterize Nietzsche in the ridiculous way that Russell did?

While Russell's impatience helps to explain his odd statements on Tagore, this still leaves open the much larger question of the widespread misunderstanding of Tagore in the West. There is some evidence, though, that Rabindranath was flattered as well as upset and confused by the type of praise he received so plentifully. He wrote, with anxiety and disappointment, to my grandfather, Kshiti Mohan, immediately after the famous literary evening at Yeats's home which would launch him as a rising literary star in the Western world. This was on the morning of 28 June 1912, and it was a sad personal letter, offering his doubts about the way he was being promoted:

> Kshiti Mohan Babu, last night I dined with one of the poets here, Yeats. He read aloud the prose translations of some of my poems. It was a very beautiful reading in the right tone ... People here have taken to my work with such excessive enthusiasm that I cannot really accept it. My impression is that when a place from which nothing is expected somehow produces something, even an ordinary thing, people are amazed – that is the state of mind here.

That launch would lead to the ecstasy with which the 'great mystic' would be received in the West, which would bring Tagore, initially, many triumphs (the Nobel Prize in Literature being one of them), followed eventually by a long-running dismissal.

The promoters of Tagore had chosen to advance a view of him in which his poetical exposition of what can be seen as extraordinary features of the world – particularly in *Gitanjali* – overshadowed his deep involvement with ordinary but very important things that make up the world (his debates with Gandhiji are good examples). His Western promoters left no room for any way of contrasting Rabindranath's deeply reflected beliefs about the world – expressed in poetry as well as prose – and the particular poetry of *Gitanjali* which had been itself over-mysticized in its English rendering with the help of Yeats. In fact, Yeats even added explanatory remarks to the translation of Tagore's poems to make sure that the reader got the 'main point' – the simple religious point – eliminating altogether the rich ambiguity of meaning in Tagore's language in the treatment of love of human beings and the love of God, which, to many of his Bengali readers, animates *Gitanjali*.

For a while Rabindranath played along with this re-creation of his work. At one point – I think a rather unguarded moment (given his nearly blind admiration of Tagore) – Kshiti Mohan told me, 'I think he loved the affection initially, despite his reasoned doubts, and by the time he was ready to make a public protest, his Western image had been well established, and he did not quite know how to get out of that idol inside which he was placed.' Tagore was aware how much misconstruing was going on in the enthusiastic reception he was receiving in the West. He wrote to his friend C. F. Andrews in 1920, 'These people ... are like drunkards who are afraid of their lucid intervals.' And yet, caught in a web of gratefulness and doubt, he went along with it, without disagreeing in public.

Another, a third, factor was the particular position of Europe when Tagore's poems became all the rage in the West. Tagore received his Nobel Prize in Literature in December 1913, very shortly before the start of the First World War, which was fought throughout Europe with unbelievable brutality. The barbarity and killing in the First World War had made many intellectuals and literary figures in Europe turn to insights from elsewhere, and Tagore's voice seemed to many at that time to fit that special need splendidly. When, for example, the pocket book of Wilfred Owen, the great anti-war poet, was recovered from the battlefield on which he had died, his mother, Susan Owen, found in it a prominent display of Tagore's poetry. It included the poem with which Wilfred had said goodbye to his family before leaving for the battlefield (beginning, 'When I go from hence, let this be my parting word'). Those lines, Susan wrote to Rabindranath, were 'written in his dear writing – with your name beneath'.

Tagore soon became thought of in Europe as a sage with a message – a message of peace and goodwill from the East – which could, quite possibly, save Europe from the dire predicament of war and disaffection in which it recurrently found itself in the early twentieth century. This was a far cry from the many-sided creative artist and careful reasoner that people at home found in Tagore. Even as Tagore urged his countrymen to wake up from blind belief and use their reasoning ability, Yeats was describing Tagore's poetry in thoroughly mystical terms: 'we have met our own image' or heard, 'perhaps for the first time in literature, our voice as in a dream'.

It must also be accepted that, led by his Western admirers, Tagore had fallen into the belief that the East really did have a message to give to the West, even though this fitted quite poorly with the rest of his reasoned commitments and convictions. Nevertheless, there was a serious mismatch between the kind of religiosity that the Western intellectuals, led by Tagore's sponsors such as Yeats and Pound, came to attribute to him (Graham Greene thought that he had seen in Tagore 'the bright pebbly eyes' of the Theosophists) and the form that Tagore's actual religious beliefs really took. These are perhaps best represented by one of his poems:

> Leave this chanting and singing and telling of beads!
> Whom do you worship in this lonely dark corner of a temple
>   with doors all shut?
> Open your eyes and see your God is not before you!
> He is there where the tiller is tilling the hard ground and
>   where the path-maker is breaking stones.
> He is with them in sun and in shower, and his garment is
>   covered with dust.

An unalienated God, who is not a source of fear but of tolerant love, and who is present in daily life, had a large role in Tagore's thinking, and he combined that with transparent reasoning. But the real Tagore received very little attention from his Western audience – neither from his sponsors who championed his alleged mysticism, nor from his detractors who shunned the beliefs attributed to him. When an otherwise sympathetic writer such as Bernard Shaw jokingly transformed Rabindranath Tagore into a fictional character called 'Stupendranath Begorr', there was not much hope that Tagore's real ideas would receive the attention they deserved.

7

These misleading impositions have for a long time clouded views of Rabindranath's thought. One important aspect of it was his willingness to accept that many questions may be unresolved even after our best efforts, and our answers may remain incomplete. I found Tagore's outlook very persuasive and it had a great influence on my own thinking. The domain of unfinished accounts would change over time, but not go away, and in this Rabindranath saw not a defeat, but a beautiful, if humble, recognition of our limited understanding of a vast world.

Another belief, in his distinctive view of education, was a particular emphasis on the need for gathering knowledge freely from everywhere in the world, but then using it only with reasoned scrutiny. As a student at the Santiniketan School, I felt very privileged that (as I mentioned in Chapter 3) the geographical boundaries of our education were not confined only to India and imperial Britain (as was typically the case in schools in British India), that we learned a great deal about Europe and Africa and Latin America, and even more extensively about other countries in Asia.

Rabindranath also worked hard to break out of the divisive communal thinking based on religious hostility that was beginning to be championed in India during his lifetime and which would peak in the years following his death in 1941 when the Hindu–Muslim riots suddenly erupted in the subcontinent and moved the country towards a partition. He was extremely shocked by the violence that drew on the singular identity of people as members of one religion or another, and he felt convinced that disaffection was being foisted on a normally tolerant people by political instigators.

Tagore did not live to see the emergence of a secular Bangladesh, which drew part of its inspiration from his firm rejection of communal separatism and the similar stance of others dear to him (including the poet Kazi Nazrul Islam). On independence, Bangladesh chose one of Tagore's songs ('Amar Sonar Bangla') as its national anthem, making him – since India had already adopted his song 'Jana Gana Mana' – perhaps the only person ever to have authored the national anthems of two major countries.

8

If Tagore's voice was strong against communalism and religious sectarianism, he was no less outspoken in his rejection of nationalism. Despite his persistent criticism of British imperialism, he was also critical of the display of excessive nationalism in India (and this contributed to the tension with Mahatma Gandhi as well). Tagore wrote many essays on the nastiness and violence that can accompany nationalism, including a collection of speeches and articles that appeared under the title of *Nationalism*, but his concerns are well reflected also in some of his fictional writings. The delusional and destructive power of nationalism is brought out sharply in Tagore's wonderful, universalist novel *The Home and the World*, which would later on be made into a beautiful film by Satyajit Ray.

Rabindranath's criticism of nationalism, including in the subtle form it took in his novel *The Home and the World*, had many detractors, not just among dedicated nationalists in India. Georg Lukács, the Marxist philosopher, found the novel to be 'a petit bourgeois yarn of the shoddiest kind', 'at the intellectual service of the British police' and 'a contemptible caricature of Gandhi'. This reading verges on absurdity. Sandip, the anti-hero, was no Gandhi and Tagore did not model him that way at all – indeed, very far from it. Sandip lacked the genuineness and the humanitarianism that characterized Gandhiji, as the novel clearly brought out. But Rabindranath was deeply worried about the passions that nationalism was arousing, and there was certainly a warning in the book about the power of nationalism to create mischief, despite its sometimes lofty aims. Bertolt Brecht, who was a Marxist in a very different mode from Lukács, noted in his diary his strong endorsement of Tagore's concerns, arguing that *The Home and the World* was a 'strong and gentle' warning against the corruptibility of nationalism.

Despite Rabindranath's great admiration for Japanese culture, history and education, he would chastise Japan later for its extreme nationalism and its mistreatment of China and East and South East Asia, despite his continued appreciation of many features of Japanese society. He also went out of his way to dissociate his criticism of the Raj from any denunciation of British people and culture. Gandhi's famous witticism, in reply to a question he was asked when in England, about what he thought of British civilization (Gandhi had said, 'it would be a good idea'), could not have come from Rabindranath's lips, even in jest.

6

The Presence of the Past

I

I studied in Santiniketan for ten years, from 1941, when I came from St Gregory's, until 1951, when I went to Presidency College in Calcutta. My great loves at Santiniketan were mathematics and Sanskrit. In the last two years at the school, I specialized in science, particularly physics and mathematics, which I was preparing to study in Presidency College. It is not rare to be fascinated by mathematics, but being a fan of Sanskrit at school was more unusual. I was very absorbed in the intricacies of that language, and for many years Sanskrit was close to being my second language after Bengali, partly because my progress in English was very slow. At St Gregory's in Dhaka I had resisted education in general, but English in particular, and when I moved to Santiniketan the medium of instruction was very firmly Bengali. The language of the Raj somehow passed me by – at least for many years.

In contrast with my neglect of English, there was no reason for me to lag behind in Sanskrit, indeed I had constant encouragement at home from my grandfather to proceed further. He did not actually have to push me very hard, as I was quite enchanted by Sanskrit literature already. My focus was mostly on classical Sanskrit literature – though I could also read, with help from my grandfather, some Vedic and epic Sanskrit, which had flourished earlier, with Vedic Sanskrit going back to around the fifteenth century BC.

I became thoroughly engrossed in Sanskrit's linguistic discipline. Reading Panini, the great grammarian from the fourth century BC, was as exciting an intellectual adventure as any I have undertaken in my life. In fact in many ways Panini taught me the basic demands of intellectual discipline, well beyond the cultivation of Sanskrit itself. His insight, that most of what we understand as knowledge is essentially a categorization of distinct understandings, has come back to me again and again throughout my life.

There is much advocacy these days for reviving the teaching of Sanskrit in Indian schools. I have been sympathetic to the basic idea – encouraging students to study one classical language or another. It could be Sanskrit, but also, alternatively, it could be ancient Greek or Latin or Arabic, or Hebrew or classical Chinese or old Tamil. However, the voices in favour of Sanskrit are often those of people who would not allow such a wide choice. It is Sanskrit they want: no other classical language will do. These Sanskrit champions typically tend to see it as the great language of Hindu scriptures. Of course, it is that, but Sanskrit is so much – so *very* much – more as well. It is also the vehicle of rationalist – indeed, materialist (including atheist) – thinking in ancient India, and that literature is remarkably large. Sanskrit, along with Pali (which derives from and remains quite close to it), is also the language of Buddhist scholarship and, through the spread of Buddhism, Sanskrit became something of a lingua franca for much of Asia through the first millennium.

2

The thought that I must put my understanding of ancient India into some kind of systematic framework became strong – in fact close to an obsession – as I was completing my education at Santiniketan. I spent many hours thinking about it, trying to put together the disparate elements necessary for an integrated understanding. I am not sure I succeeded (and the exercise books I used did not survive my moving from place to place), but I got something from the process of thinking about all this, particularly in my last academic year at Santiniketan School, which ended in the summer of 1951.

Within Sanskrit literature, I loved the great plays of Kalidasa, Shudraka, Bana and others, which were fun to read, but also extremely thought-provoking about philosophical problems for which they served as introductions. I was also immersed in the epics, *Ramayana* and *Mahabharata*. Even though these epics are often taken to be religious texts – or at least semi-religious – they are in fact storytelling epics (like the *Iliad* and the *Odyssey*), without any foundational religious standing. Even *Bhagavadgita*, which is wholly contained in *Mahabharata*, and which is much revered by many religious people as the divine Krishna's victory in argument over the dissenting warrior Arjuna (who began by expressing his reluctance to fight a major war and kill many people), is only a very small part of the grand epic. In fact, *Mahabharata* presents visions that go well beyond *Gita* itself and Krishna's advocacy that it was Arjuna's duty to fight the just war. It includes the tragic scenario that is described towards the end of the epic as the aftermath of the war – rightly won by the noble Pandavas – when the country is covered with burning funeral pyres, and women weep over their lost men. That picture is arguably closer to Arjuna's anti-war vision than to Krishna's insistence on Arjuna's duty to fight in the war no matter how grim the consequences.

3

Although Sanskrit is the language of priesthood, it also has a larger body of firmly agnostic and atheistic literature – in the works of the Lokayata and Charvaka schools among others – than can be found in any other classical language in the world. It contains, too, the deeply rationalistic and firmly agnostic reasoning of Gautama Buddha from the sixth century BC.

I have often wondered why I have been so deeply moved by Gautama Buddha, right from the time I first encountered his thoughts when my grandfather gave me a short book about him. I must have been about ten or eleven then, and I remember that I was completely bowled over by the clarity of reasoning Buddha used and his accessibility to anyone who could reason.

As I grew older, my attachment to Buddha deepened. When I thought about his approach, I decided that I was so moved by him because of at least four different aspects that distinguished him from most proponents of ethics and verged on the borders of what was – sometimes mistakenly – taken to be religion.

First, Buddha's approach focuses on reasons to accept one position and reject another, without any appeal to unargued beliefs. True, he also presented a metaphysics of the world, but his championing of particular ethical conclusions – such as the equality of all human beings irrespective of community and caste, the treatment of animals with kindness and the replacement of hatred towards others by universal love – was not conditional on accepting that metaphysics. On the contrary, each ethical conclusion demanded support from reasoning, even if it was sometimes implicit rather than explicit.

Second, Buddha seemed to me to be clearly human, with our usual anxieties, in a way that God – or the powerful gods and goddesses – were not. When young Gautama left his princely home in the foothills of the Himalayas in search of enlightenment, he was moved by the sight of mortality, morbidity and disability – concerns he shared with ordinary human beings. What distressed him then continues to worry us today. Unlike with most religious leaders, there was no real distance between him and us.

A third feature that made Buddha so attractive was what he was trying to defend. After reading whatever I could get hold of among Buddha's expositions, I became convinced that he had managed to turn our religious concerns from belief – about God and other existential suppositions – to behaviour and action, to be determined here and now. It was Buddha who changed the religious question from 'Is there a God?' to questions such as 'How should we behave?' no matter whether there is a God or not. He identifies that it is possible for people to agree on good action without necessarily agreeing on a bigger metaphysical view of the universe. This is, I believe, immensely significant.

Finally, Buddha's approach to ethics differed substantially from the morality of the 'social contract', which appeared forcefully – if intermittently – in Indian thought (for example in the *Bhagavadgita*) and that has become such a dominant feature of post-Hobbesian and post-Rousseauvian thinking in Western ethics. A social contract takes the form of each contracting party doing specified good things for others *on condition that* the others must also do what they owe to everybody else. Buddha argued instead that doing good should not be so transactional, that people have a duty to do what they recognize to be good unilaterally, even if others do not perform their corresponding duties.

In a document known as *Sutta Nipata*, Buddha illustrates this line of reasoning by pointing to a mother's duty to do for an infant what it cannot do for itself. This provides a compelling reason for the mother to help the infant – it is not because she expects the infant to do something for her in return, as in a social contract. Buddha argued that making morality transactional is to miss its central requirement – and even applied this to what human beings have reason to do for helpless animals.

Buddha was not in fact alone in arguing an unconditional case for doing the right thing. Jesus argued similarly in the story of the Good Samaritan in St Luke's Gospel. When the Samaritan goes to help the wounded man, he is not driven by any kind of social contract – either implicit or explicit. He sees that the person lying on the other side of the road needs help and, since he is able to give that help, he provides it. The much-recognized Christian duty to help one's neighbour provides no justification here, if the normal use of the word 'neighbour' is understood. Yet Jesus wins the argument with the local lawyer who is questioning him by making the concept of neighbourliness stretch to include all those who we can help. Buddha and Jesus ultimately arrive at the same conclusion, but Buddha takes a directly ethical route, whereas Jesus's reasoning is irreducibly epistemological.

During a literary evening at Santiniketan School, I tried to argue for the superiority of the ethics of 'unconditional duty' (*shartaheen kartavya*) over that of 'social contract'. I doubt that I persuaded many listeners, though some of my classmates cheered me on. For some years whilst I was in Santiniketan, I actually tried to register my religion as Buddhist. The school authorities took this to be a prank and wouldn't allow it. Was I not deterred by the fact that there was no other Buddhist within hundreds of miles? I did not make myself popular by responding that this fact made it all the more necessary for me to see that my religion was recorded. I did win one or two skirmishes in this debate, but altogether lost the war. The school authorities laughed away my claim to be registered as a lonely Buddhist.

4

As I was becoming more and more involved in the world opened up by Sanskrit, the analytical challenges of mathematics began to capture my mind as well. This was particularly so with the philosophy of mathematics. I remember my excitement when I first encountered the use of axioms, theorems and proofs – how we can begin with one type of understanding and derive many other sorts of awareness from it. I would have given anything for a ticket to ancient Greece so that I could go and invade the privacy of Euclid. The elegance and reach of analytical reasoning and the attraction of proofs have engaged me throughout my life – indeed, I have spent a lot of my academic life trying to establish results in social choice theory and decisional analysis for which my interest in the foundations of mathematical reasoning has been central.

Luckily, I soon discovered that there was a strong complementarity between my interests in Sanskrit and in mathematics. I greatly enjoyed the fact that I could easily move from Kalidasa's elegant poetry in *Meghaduta* and Shudraka's intriguing play *Mricchakatika* (among my favourite literary writings) to the mathematics and epistemology of Aryabhata, Brahmagupta or Bhaskara (indeed, both the Bhaskaras – there were two, each very distinguished). In fact, in the Sanskrit writings of these mathematicians, my two principal interests seemed to find a secure home together.

If the diverse – but compatible – temptations of Sanskrit and mathematics was one plurality that shaped my educational explorations in my schooldays, my fascination with abstract thinking and greedy curiosity about the world around us pulled me into another. As I look back on the little work I have been able to do over my life (I wish it had been more), it seems to be broadly divided into quite abstract reasoning (for example pursuing the idea of justice and exploring various avenues in social choice theory, with axioms, theorems and proofs) and the rather earthy practical problems (famines, hunger, economic deprivations, inequalities of class, gender and caste, and others). The foundations of both were quite firmly established in my schooldays.

I was made to reflect on all this when the Nobel Foundation asked me to give them, on long-term loan, two objects that have been closely associated with my work, to be displayed in the Nobel Museum. The generous citation with which the Swedish Academy had announced my prize was heavily inclined in the direction of my analytical work in social choice theory, quoting chapters and verses (in fact, theorems and proofs), but they also briefly mentioned, at the end of the statement, my work on famines, inequality and gender disparity. After some dithering, I gave the Nobel Museum a copy of *Aryabhatiya* (one of the great Sanskrit classics on mathematics from AD 499) from which I had benefited so much, and my old bicycle which had been with me since my schooldays.

I had used the bike not only to collect data on wages and prices from inaccessible places, such as old farm sheds and warehouses, when studying the Bengal famine of 1943, but also to transport the machine to weigh boys and girls up to the age of five to neighbouring villages from Santiniketan, to examine gender discrimination and the gradual emergence of the relative deprivation of girls. I was tempted to give the Nobel Museum the weighing machine as well. I was proud that I had to take over whenever my research assistant was deterred by the fear of being bitten by toothy children. I became an expert on weighing without getting teeth-marks. As the Nobel Museum travelled around the world, starting in Stockholm, I often received questions about what a bike had to do with Aryabhata's mathematics. I was happy to be able to explain why the answer had to be 'a great deal'.

The bike – a simple Atlas – was a gift from my parents and, as I received it when I was still growing, it is somewhat shorter than normal adult bikes are. But I went on using it for more than fifty years – from 1945 to 1998, when the Nobel Museum took over its custody. The bike not only gave me much faster mobility within Santiniketan, but also allowed me to get to the villages around us when we started running a night school for tribal children who had no access to primary education (as described in Chapter 3). Some of my classmates and fellow teachers at the night school did not have bicycles and so it was rare for me to ride without a passenger at the back, and sometimes also another on the horizontal bar connecting the steering handle with my seat.

5

The India that I came to know from my early studies had several distressing features – in particular the powerful hold that the caste system had over the country (about which Buddha had already protested in the sixth century BC) – and, at the same time, many extraordinarily interesting and inspiring ideas, a duality that goes back to ancient times. I had to supplement my readings in epic and classical Sanskrit through the first millennium with the reasoning and speculations of later thinkers (from Jayadeva and Madhavacharya to Kabir and Abul Faz'l, the adviser and collaborator of Emperor Akbar) whose robust heterodoxy was particularly thrilling. But if the greatness of the heritage captivated me, the attempts to confine Indian culture in narrow sectarian perspectives, which were also going on, were immensely distressing.

The perception that human identity does not demand a singular confinement came to me quite powerfully from the ancient classics. Think of Vasantasena, the heroine of Shudraka's *Mricchakatika* ('The Little Clay Cart') from around the fourth century – a radical and subversive play that offers several distinct, but important, themes. One of them was the need to see a person as having many identities – this was an idea that helped me to resist the imposition of a single, overwhelming identity based on religion or community (including focusing only on Hindu–Muslim divisions), which was becoming more and more common as my schooldays progressed.

Vasantasena is a great beauty, a rich courtesan, a dedicated lover and a loyal partner of the persecuted Charudatta, an impoverished member of the gentry who is also a social reformer, a political revolutionary and ultimately an insightful and forgiving judge. When it is Charudatta's turn to judge the miscreants after a successful revolution against the ruling clique, he chooses leniency and decides to free the hired hand who, on behalf of the corrupt rulers, had been trying to kill both him and Vasantasena. She applauds his far-sighted decision to focus not on retribution but on social – attitudinal – reform that would be in the best interests of the people. Charudatta then startles everyone (except possibly Vasantasena) with his judgment that they should free the would-be murderer because it is society's 'duty to kill the miscreant with benefaction' (the Sanskrit phrase for that innovative punishment – *upkarhatastakartavya* – is very elegant in itself), a grand idea that fits as well on Vasantasena's lips as it does on Charudatta's. Finally, Vasantasena – who earlier in the play had spoken so eloquently and movingly on the injustice of inequality of power and of the corruption of the rich, and urged the people to revolt – joins Charudatta in rejecting revenge in favour of exercising a generosity that could reform the miscreant and help society to move away from conflict and violence.

A second idea which *Mricchakatika* prompts us to think about is the theory of jurisprudence that Charudatta presents to the world. When I read the play first in my schooldays, I felt transformed by Shudraka's way of reasoning. Rejecting the tradition of retribution, Charudatta invites us to think about all the consequences of an action – in this case of a particular punishment. The approach helps us to distinguish between two different interpretations that I would try to pursue in *The Idea of Justice* more than sixty years after I first read *Mricchakatika* with awe and admiration. The distinction is between the concepts of justice represented respectively by two Sanskrit terms: *niti* and *nyaya*. Among the principal uses of *niti* are the virtues of following well-defined rules and organizational propriety. In contrast with *niti*, the term *nyaya* stands for a comprehensive concept of realized justice. In that view, the roles of institutions, rules and organizations, important as they are, have to be assessed in a broader and more inclusive perspective on the world that actually emerges from the process of justice, not just the institutions or rules we happen to have. I interpreted Charudatta's priority to be the pursuit of *nyaya*, seeking a good world in which we can live with fairness, rather than obeying the *niti* of fixed rules, including required punishments that are supposed to 'fit' the crime in question in standard theory.

To consider a particular application, early Indian legal theorists talked disparagingly of what they called *matsyanyaya*, 'justice in the world of fish', where a big fish can freely devour a small fish. We are warned that avoiding *matsyanyaya* must be an essential part of justice, and it is crucial to make sure that the awful 'justice of fish' is not allowed to invade the world of human beings. The central recognition here is that the realization of justice in the sense of *nyaya* is not just a matter of judging institutions and rules, but of judging the societies themselves. No matter how proper the established organizations might be – and the rules erected by the society (for example, about punishments) – if a big fish can still devour a small fish at will, it must be considered a patent violation of justice as *nyaya*. We needed a different – and a better – world, not just to follow old rules and hallowed conventions.

I would find out many years later that when an English translation of *Mricchakatika*, *The Little Clay Cart*, was staged in New York in 1924, the drama critic of *The Nation* (Joseph Wood Krutch) wrote in a rave review that he found the drama 'profoundly moving', and went on to declare his boundless admiration for the play. 'Nowhere in our European past do we find . . . a work more completely civilized.' This may be a little excessive, but Krutch was surely right to point to the importance of the understanding that in that remarkable play 'passions' are being 'reconciled with decisions of an intellect'. Since the reconciling of passions with intellectual reflections was one of the ideas I was most interested in in my days as a student, I found a lot to admire in Krutch's comments on Shudraka's play.

6

My attempts to take a capacious view of ancient Indian literature, which got me into arguments in my schooldays, would still perhaps encounter resistance today. Consider the *Vedas*, the four-part book which is often seen as the foundational treatise of Hinduism. Reverence for the ancient *Vedas* is championed by many political advocates of religious persuasion in India – it was common enough in my younger days, and is no less common today. I was led to an exalted view of the *Vedas* from the time I first tried to read them more than sixty years ago – but not because they have been seen as the foundations of Hinduism, nor indeed because (as is sometimes wrongly claimed) we can find sophisticated mathematics there. If there were reasons for worry about the confused claims of allegedly profound 'Vedic mathematics' in my schooldays, they are much greater now, when some universities in India offer post-graduate instruction on the allegedly academic subject of 'Vedic Mathematics' (you can even get a postgraduate degree in this largely fictitious field). India's profound contributions to the world of mathematics would come much later, from the fifth century onwards, led by Aryabhata, Brahmagupta and others, and to look for such contributions in the *Vedas* is an extraordinary folly.

What we have reason to cherish instead is that the *Vedas* are full of wonderful verses – reflective, daring, elegant and evocative. Many of them are deeply religious, but they also include a powerfully articulated argument for doubt and agnosticism: the so-called 'Song of Creation' from Mandala X of the *Rig Veda*, quoted before, is an example of its profound scepticism.

When I first read the verse as a young boy, guided by my grandfather, at a time when my own convictions as a non-believer were taking root, I felt thrilled by this support from 3,500 years ago. One way of approaching the Vedas – the *Rig Veda* in particular – is to see them as the response of precarious human beings, expressed in beautiful poetry, to the unequal power of natural forces. There is clearly a temptation to attribute some kind of supernatural status to these forces which are hugely powerful and beyond our control. If that leads to a polytheistic panorama, it also generates speculation about the possibility of one God – a creator, a preserver and a destroyer – who rules over all these disparate powerful forces. There are elegant verses which tend in that direction in the *Rig Veda*, but (in the opposite direction) it also acknowledges the critical minds of those early thinkers in considering the possibility that there is no such unifying force – no one God who created it all and still remembers what he had done. There is a strong suspicion that behind the natural forces there is, perhaps, nothing. The verse in Mandala X is an expression of that agnosticism.

7

The intellectual history of ancient India includes fun and games as much as it does religious thoughts of various kinds. In understanding India's heritage we cannot expunge any of that, and should not want to. Chess may be the most well known of games originating in India (and perhaps the most sophisticated too), but there are many others. One that seemed to me to offer some insight into the way human lives are so dependent on chance is the ancient Indian board game Gyan

Chaupar, also known as Moksha Patam, which came to Britain a century or so ago – where it became known as Snakes and Ladders.

Even the *Vedas*, I was delighted to see, had room for discussing games – real games that can influence human lives. The religious reader of the *Vedas* may easily miss an instructive passage headed the 'gambler's lament' in the *Rig Veda*:

> The trembling hazelnut eardrops of the great tree, born in a hurricane, intoxicate me as they roll on the furrowed board. The dice seem to me like a drink of Soma from Mount Mūjavant, keeping me awake and excited.
>
> . . .
>
> When I swear, 'I will not play with them', I am left behind by my friends as they depart. But when the brown dice raise their voice as they are thrown down, I run at once to the rendezvous with them, like a woman to her lover.
>
> The gambler goes to the meeting-hall, asking himself 'Will I win?', and trembling with hope. But the dice cross him and counter his desire, giving the winning throws to his opponent.
>
> . . .
>
> This is what the noble Savitṛ shows me: 'Play no longer with the dice, but till your field; enjoy what you possess, and value it highly. There are your cattle, and there is your wife, O gambler.'

The gambler recognizes that he should do something useful – such as cultivating land – rather than giving in to his addiction. But, despite his desire not to gamble, he constantly ends up in gambling joints, thereby ruining his life. As I became increasingly interested in philosophy, I thought that this might be the first discussion in the world of the well-known problem of the 'weakness of will' (what the ancient Greeks would call *akrasia* and study extensively) – a subject that remains very important in contemporary philosophy as well.

The verse has another distinguishing feature that I thought was fun when I first read it: it is almost certainly the first complaint about the 'mother-in-law' – still popular material for middle-brow humour in the contemporary world. The Rig Vedic gambler laments: 'My wife's mother hates me, and my wife pushes me away; the man in trouble finds no one with sympathy.' To read the *Vedas* without its human qualities – the deep vulnerabilities as well as the flights of imagination – would be an impoverishing approach. Anxiety about your mother-in-law's disapproval has a place there.

8

My school's refusal to register me as a Buddhist was particularly disappointing for me since, in ancient days, Bihar – then very prosperous – was the original centre of Buddhist religion, culture and enlightenment. Its capital Pataliputra (now called Patna) also served as the capital of the early all-India empires for more than a thousand years, beginning in the third century BC. Among its greatest glories was the foundation of Nalanda, the oldest university in the world, which flourished there as a Buddhist foundation from the fifth century to the end of the twelfth. For comparison, the oldest European university – in Bologna in Italy – was founded in 1088. Thus by the time the University of Bologna came to life, the university in Nalanda had already been functioning for more than 600 years – educating thousands of students each year from many countries in the world.

Since students had come to Nalanda University from all over East Asia, the so-called East Asia Summit in 2009 made a strong attempt to re-establish it. 'Ritorno a Nalanda' headlined *Corriere della Sera*, the largest circulating Italian newspaper, when classes began again in September 2014 at Nalanda. It was a notable moment in the history of higher education in the world. It was also, for me personally, as the Chancellor of the newly re-established Nalanda University, a deeply nostalgic moment. I recalled the time – nearly seventy years before – when, as an impressionable child, I had wondered whether Nalanda could ever come to life again. 'Is it really gone forever?' I had asked my grandfather, Kshiti Mohan. 'Perhaps not,' said the old man, who always generated cultural optimism, 'it could do us a lot of good today.'

When classes were held at Nalanda more than 1,500 years ago, it was the only place in the world offering instruction of a kind that we now expect from universities around the globe. Nalanda broke completely new ground, and established itself as a distinguished institution offering advanced education in a great many fields, not only in Buddhist studies, but also in languages and literature, astronomy and observational sciences, architecture and sculpture, and medicine and public health care. It drew students not only from all over India, but also from China, Japan and Korea, and other Asian countries with Buddhist connections, and by the seventh century it had 10,000 residential students. It was in fact the only institution of learning outside China to which any ancient Chinese ever went for higher education. The world – not just India – needed a university like that, and Nalanda went from strength to strength. As the excavations of the old ruins have revealed – both in Nalanda and in the neighbouring areas all over Bihar where educational institutions were springing up, inspired by Nalanda's example – it was contributing something of great value to the world.

Despite my personal proximity to Nalanda from a very early age, it was striking for me to see the recent excavations going on in Telhara (near Nalanda) and the process of unearthing lecture halls and student hostels that must have been unique in the world more than a thousand years ago. The last thing we would expect to see as we excavate historical ruins now is a set of large halls, presumably used for lectures and instructions, and clusters of small bedrooms, akin to present-day hostels for students. As an institution of higher learning, where the entry qualifications were high, Nalanda was fed by a network of ancillary educational organizations. Some Chinese students, including the famous Yi Jing (AD 635–713), who studied in Nalanda for ten years and wrote the first inter-country comparative study of medical systems, comparing Chinese and Indian medical practices, first went from Guangzhou to Sumatra (then the base of the Srivijaya empire) to learn Sanskrit. After acquiring adequate Sanskrit in the schools there, Yi Jing took another boat journey, ending up in Tamralipta, not far from modern-day Calcutta, on his way to Nalanda. There were four other Buddhism-based universities in Bihar by the seventh century, largely inspired by Nalanda, and by the tenth century one of them – Vikramshila – had emerged as a serious competitor.

After more than 700 years of successful teaching, old Nalanda was destroyed in the 1190s in a series of attacks by invading armies from West Asia, which also demolished the other universities in Bihar.

There are serious debates about whether Bakhtiar Khilji, the ruthless invader whose conquering army ploughed through north India, was himself responsible for the sacking of Nalanda (as is told in popular accounts), but the fact of the violent destruction by invading armies is well established. The library, a nine-storey building full of manuscripts, is reputed to have burned for three days. The destruction of Nalanda took place shortly after the development of the University of Oxford from 1167, and about a decade before the University of Cambridge was founded in 1209. The patronage of higher learning in India by well-settled Muslim monarchs, Mughals in particular, would come much later, by which time nothing of Nalanda remained.

9

Nalanda is part of India's and the world's heritage, and attempts to revive it in a modern setting in the contemporary world had encouragement and support from other Asian countries, particularly those participating in the East Asia Summit. The Indian government was initially very enthusiastic, but, after the political powers governing the country changed around 2014 and the priorities of Hindutva and of political Hinduism became dominant, there have been significant lapses in the plans for reviving Nalanda and its Buddhist world vision.

However, the need for the classical Nalanda remains. Part of the necessity arises from Nalanda's focus on quality education – a much-neglected requirement in Indian higher education today. The specifically Buddhist features of Nalanda, including its non-sectarian view of humanity, may not appeal to those whose interest in interpreting ancient India as Hindu India is now extremely strong. It is also important to recognize that the enormous blemish of division in India's old traditions, including caste hierarchy and untouchability, was strongly resisted by Buddha and the Buddhist tradition, and the main twentieth-century intellectual fighter against this divisiveness, Dr B. R. Ambedkar, converted to Buddhism to establish his position. Nalanda is associated with that egalitarian vision which is extremely important for education in general, and higher education in particular.

There is also something in Nalanda's method of pedagogy that remains relevant for the world today. Nalanda's method of instruction, as its Chinese students noted, was to make plentiful use of dialogues and debates (even greater, it would appear, than in ancient Greece). This dialectical method was not only unusual, but also extremely effective. The spread of the influence of Nalanda across Asia, which the Asian Civilization Museum in Singapore called the 'Nalanda Trails', came from talking to and learning from each other.

On one occasion when I was visiting the new campus of Nalanda and conducting a seminar on Asian history, a question came up on the impact and influence on Nalanda of the Silk Route, which extended for over 4,000 miles and enabled merchandise to move between Asia and Europe. Silk was one of the principal exports of China – hence the name. Originally established between the third century BC and the third century AD, during the Han Dynasty, the Silk Route was of profound importance not only for trade and commerce, but also for the intermingling of people and ideas.

The critical question that can be asked is not about the importance of the Silk Route, nor about the crucial role of trade in linking people with each other across borders – neither is in dispute. It is, rather, about whether a persistent focus on trade and commodity exchange in human contacts, and a consequently magnified reading of the role of the Silk Route, may downplay other influences through which people have interacted with each other across frontiers and borders, including the massive civilizational interactions that the 'Nalanda trails' generated and sustained.

There have even been some confusing attempts recently to see old Nalanda itself as a by-product of the Silk Route. That would be a huge mistake, not merely because Nalanda was not on – or even strongly linked with – the Silk Route, but also because it was central to a different avenue of interaction in which the trade of commodities was not the prime mover. If trade gets people together (and it certainly does), then so does the pursuit of knowledge and enlightenment. Mathematics, science, engineering, music and the arts, along with religious and ethical commitments, have prompted people to seek them across regions, by land and sea, over millennia. The motivation behind these journeys was not the pursuit of commercial gain, but the search for ideas – including, but not limited to, religious ideas. The huge modern popularity of seeing global connections through the prism of trade, of which the Silk Route is a leading example, should not be allowed to eclipse the fact that reflective engagements have motivated the movement of people across countries and regions for just as long. Globalization is a result not only of seeking business, but also of talking to – and learning from – each other.

10

Old Nalanda belonged to a globally interactive tradition, the need for which remains strong today. The campus of new Nalanda, which is a few miles away from the ruins of the old university, is at the edge of the old town of Rajgir, then called Rajagriha. This is exactly where the first 'Buddhist Council' met not long after Buddha's death 'to resolve differences by discussion'. A later Buddhist Council, the third, which met in Pataliputra (Patna) at the invitation of Emperor Ashoka in the third century BC, has become the most famous, both because of its size and also on account of the importance of the differences that were addressed there through discussion. So Nalanda sits right next to the location of the very first attempt, possibly in the world, to bring about what in the nineteenth century Walter Bagehot, following John Stuart Mill, called 'government by discussion'. In the history of democratic thought, the past has a huge presence, a history that is both inspirational and instructive in the contemporary world.

Many of us among the students at Santiniketan School went on frequent excursions to Rajgir and Nalanda late in the year. We stayed in tents and suffered a little from the cold, but the outdoor fire around which we sat and chatted until well past midnight always provided some warmth. The conversations were often far from profound (despite efforts by the teachers with us to bring in some pedagogy), and there was much irreverent humour. Sometimes mild romances developed at considerable speed – and foundered equally rapidly – among the co-educational students on these trips. But none of this interfered with the diligent exploration of Buddhist trails and ancient history during the day.

PART TWO

7

The Last Famine

By the early months of 1942 I felt well settled in Santiniketan. The tranquil nature of 'the abode of peace' was quite striking. And being able to go everywhere on foot or on a bicycle was very enjoyable. The near total absence of motor vehicles was a boon that I came to appreciate more and more as I got used to the way of life there. I particularly relished the relaxed academic atmosphere at Santiniketan School and the opportunity to learn about all kinds of extraordinarily interesting things, often much outside our curriculum. I continued to roam around in our open-access and user-friendly library, tasting this and getting into that, with an abandon that transformed my life.

Yet, even as my own life was going so well, I was becoming increasingly aware that there were great tensions in the world around me – inside India and outside it. A ferocious world war was going on, the eastern front of which was moving closer and closer to us. But India's problems were not only of external origin. There were politically cultivated tensions between Hindus and Muslims. And on top of that there were rapidly rising food prices; the intense hardship they caused was a subject of constant conversation in many – I imagine most – homes in Bengal. All these problems and concerns worried my grandparents with whom I was living, and also our relations, including of course my own parents, who would visit us frequently in Santiniketan. When I went to Dhaka in the school vacations to be with them, I found the state of anxiety there to be even more palpable.

2

I saw the first signs of famine in April 1943 – the so-called 'Great Bengal famine' which would kill between 2 and 3 million people. Food prices had started rising quite sharply during 1942, the year before the famine.

At the end of a class in the spring of 1943, we were told by some younger students that a man with evident mental derangement, who had just appeared on the Santiniketan campus, was being cruelly teased by a couple of school bullies. We went to the scene of this barbaric activity – near the cricket ground – and, while the two bullies were individually stronger than each of us on our own, there were a great many of us who together could give them pause. After the tormenters left with some angry words, we tried to talk to the victim. He was barely coherent, but we gathered that he had not eaten anything for nearly a month. One of our teachers joined us as we were conversing, and we gathered from him that prolonged starvation often does produce mental derangement.

That was my first direct contact with a famine victim. But soon there were others who came into our neighbourhood in the hope of escaping starvation. Their numbers grew as the classes stopped in May for the summer vacation. My parents joined me in Santiniketan (it was my father's holiday too, at Dhaka University) as famished victims kept arriving in larger and larger numbers. By the time the school reassembled in July, the trickle had grown into a torrent of miserable humanity. They were looking for anything whatever that they could eat. Most of them were on their way to Calcutta, nearly a hundred miles away, having heard rumours of arrangements there for the feeding of destitutes. These rumours were vastly exaggerated. The government was not, in fact, providing any relief and private charities were woefully inadequate. But because of the rumour it was to Calcutta that the starving wanted to go. From us, they wanted a little help with food – maybe even leftover or rotten food – to allow them to survive as they continued their journey, on the way to Calcutta.

The situation continued to worsen, and by September we thought that perhaps 100,000 destitute people had passed through Santiniketan on their long journey to the big city. The continuous cries for help – from children and women and men – ring in my ears even today, seventy-seven years later. My grandmother allowed me to give a cigarette tin full of rice to anyone who begged for food, but she explained, 'even if it breaks your heart, you cannot give any more than one tin-can of rice to anyone, since we have to help as many people as we can.' I knew that small cans of rice would not go very far, but I was glad that we could at least do something to help. One of those who arrived at that time, as I related earlier (in Chapter 4), was Joggeshwar, an almost fatally hungry boy of fourteen from Dumka, about forty miles from Santiniketan, whom my aunt fed immediately to save his life.

3

When the famine erupted with great ferocity between the spring and summer of 1943, I was about to have my tenth birthday and I felt very confused. I listened to the anxious discussions on the possibility of impending doom ('if things continue to go this way'). My parents and grandparents, my uncles and aunts all had views on why prices were rising and how – if it continued and intensified – there would be widespread starvation. 'I don't rule out a big famine,' my maternal uncle Kankarmama said one morning in what would have been, I think, early 1943. I was not yet absolutely sure what a famine really was, but I was full of apprehension. I did not, of course, know any economics, but I was aware that if food prices kept rising without people's incomes going up, many would end up starving – and dying. Listening to these family conversations on tragedy and doom was a sobering way of growing up fast.

The immediate question was: what was causing the sharp rise in the price of food in 1942, and of rice in particular, the staple food in Bengal? Remember that 1942 was not the year of the famine, but the year before it. Was the commonly aired understanding that food prices were already rising fast in 1942 (hence causing panic) correct? When, as an economist, I decided, thirty years later, to study famines in general and the Bengal famine in particular, I found that the popular beliefs were entirely correct. For example, rice prices in the College

Street market in Calcutta (for which I could obtain fairly reliable data) were already up by 37 per cent between the beginning of January and the middle of August 1942. By the end of the year those prices had risen by 70 per cent. For people living on miserably low incomes, a severe price hike of this kind resulted in very serious survival problems. In 1943 the problem would intensify, and by August 1943 the price of rice was five times what it had been at the beginning of 1942. By then starvation had become impossible to avoid for a substantial section of the population of Bengal.

Why was this allowed to happen? Although the Indians did not have the power to initiate anti-famine policies, what about the British? Was the famine really so difficult to stop? In fact, quite the contrary. The problem was not that the British had the wrong data about how much food Bengal had, but their theory of famine was completely wrong. The British government was claiming that there was so much food in Bengal that there couldn't be a famine. Bengal, as a whole, did indeed have a lot of food – that's true. But that was on the supply side; demand was going up very rapidly, pushing prices sky-high. Those left behind in a boom economy – a boom generated by the war – lost out in the competition for buying food.

This was at a time when the Japanese soldiers were at the border of Burma and India. In fact, part of the Japanese Army – along with the anti-British Indian National Army (recruited from Indian-origin residents and captured soldiers in East and South-east Asia, raised by the Indian leader Netaji Subhas Chandra Bose) – was actually reaching India, at Imphal. The British Indian Army, the British Army, and later the US Army, were all buying food. They – and all the people hired for the war effort, including for military construction – were consuming a lot of it. War-related construction projects generated new jobs and incomes; for example, I remember many new aerodromes were being built all over Bengal. There was a huge demand-led price rise, which was further enhanced by panic and market manipulation in the buying and selling of food.

People can't live on the knowledge – no matter how secure – that there is a lot of food around. They have to rely on their ability to buy the food they need – competing with others in the market economy. There is a huge difference between food availability (how much food there is in the market as a whole) and food entitlement (how much food each family can buy in the market). Starvation is a characteristic of people not being able to *buy* enough food in the market – not of there being not enough food in the market. In the 1970s, when I studied famines across the world, it became clear how important it was to focus on food entitlement – not food availability.

I should emphasize that this basic analysis of the causes of the famine was not complicated, nor particularly new. The food supply in Bengal had not fallen dramatically, but the rise in demand in the war economy was pushing food prices sharply higher, which made them go beyond the reach of the poor labourers dependent on fixed – and low – wages. Urban wages were – to varying extents – flexible upwards because of the increasing demand for labour in the war economy, but rural wages did not rise much or at all. So the largest group of famine victims were the rural workers. The government was not particularly worried about them, since it was afraid mostly of urban discontent because of its potentially weakening effect on the war effort.

To ensure that the urban population had enough food, particularly in Calcutta, the government arranged for the distribution of food at controlled prices through ration shops in Calcutta. The rationing system effectively covered the entire Calcutta population. The food needed for distribution in Calcutta was bought in the rural markets at whatever price had to be paid to buy it, which pushed up rural food prices further, causing more rural poverty and starvation, while urban residents had heavily subsidized inexpensive food from ration shops. The distress in rural areas was thus reinforced through government policy.

4

The Bengali cultural magazines were convinced that the starvation occurring in Bengal could have been stopped by getting more food into the economy, and they blamed the British government for not dealing with the famine. One of these magazines, *Desh*, ran a striking editorial in July 1943 which presented the analogy of Emperor Nero playing the violin while Rome burnt. The editorial was sarcastically headlined 'The Glory of the Churchill Government'. It proclaimed in powerful Bengali why the famine could have been averted if Prime Minister Winston Churchill had allowed more food to be brought into Bengal. This diagnosis may have overlooked some of the features of the government's inability to understand what had caused the famine and the different ways it could have been prevented, but the basic thrust of its criticism of government policy was not seriously mistaken.

The Bengali daily newspapers were heavily censored during the famine period, but the cultural magazines, with a relatively small readership, were rather freely sold. My grandparents used to take a couple of these periodicals regularly – among them *Desh* (a Bengali weekly) and *Prabashi* (a Bengali monthly) were particularly well regarded. My grandmother Didima read them most afternoons while resting on her favourite wooden bed after lunch, and often shared with me the accounts she read. I felt very involved – more than just interested – in the arguments presented in these articles. Some of my older cousins, who visited us from time to time, also wanted to find out what they could about the terrible developments around us. I had a great many discussions with them, particularly with Khokonda (Kalyan Dasgupta), who was two years older than me; he often intervened with his more 'grown-up' point of view. My uncle Kankarmama gave me a copy of Pearl Buck's *The Good Earth* (published in 1931), and I slowly read her long fictionalized account of a Chinese famine with morbid fascination.

One day, Didima read out to me a striking analysis of 'the food problem' from *Prabashi* in the issue for Shrabon (a monsoon month), which would have been out in August 1943. I checked later that my memory was correct about what the piece had actually said. It did link the rise of food prices with the extra expenditure and bigger food purchase in urban regions resulting from the war efforts, including the consumption of soldiers stationed in Bengal and beyond, who were facing the Japanese not far from us. *Prabashi* did not dispute the need for the war effort, but questioned the complete lack of attention by the authorities to the hardship that resulted from it, including the impact on food prices, which ruined the lives of the rural poor.

5

Did the Parliament in Westminster not discuss the calamity of the famine? Not until it was nearly over, in October 1943. Indeed, news of the famine was carefully kept away from the British public until then. This was critically important because, even though India had an autarkic imperial rule, the governance was controlled by a functioning democracy in Britain. This contradiction was a favourite subject of conversation in Santiniketan as well as in Dhaka. Those among my relations who were members of, or close to, the Communist Party, scoffed at the idea of trusting an impotent 'bourgeois democracy', and their anti-colonialism was further confused by Soviet cooperation with the British in fighting the war (following Stalin's turn-around in June 1941). Others, such as Gandhians, Congress Socialists, followers of Subhas Chandra Bose (of whom more in Chapter 9), attributed the inaction of the British Parliament to a policy choice, rather than to any innate inability to respond to a catastrophe on the scale of the Bengal famine. I found the arguments enormously engaging, but very hard to sort out. Forty years later, I would recollect how transfixed I had been, sitting at one corner of the living room, trying to decide who among my uncles and aunts had 'won' the argument.

The fact is, however, that, even as Bengal was ravaged by a famine the likes of which it had not seen since the eighteenth century (at the beginning of British rule in Bengal), neither the Parliament in Westminster nor the ever-active British newspapers had sufficiently extensive reports or discussions about it. Indeed, the British public was kept amazingly uninformed. The high-circulation Bengali newspapers were, as I have said, censored (to avoid damaging rumours while fighting the world war), and the grand English newspaper of Calcutta, *The Statesman*, which was British-owned and edited by a loyal Englishman, Ian Stephens, voluntarily chose a policy of not discussing the famine in the interest of solidarity for the war effort – though it did publish some sad photos of starving people, without commentary or explanation.

The informational blackout ended only when Ian Stephens revolted in October 1943. Until then, the censorship imposed by the Raj, combined with the *Statesman*'s silence, had prevented any large-scale journalistic discussion of hunger and famine in Bengal. All the members of my extended family, despite their political differences (they included nationalists, socialists, communists and liberal democrats) were united in fury about the suppression of news and analyses of what was going on.

6

The war efforts continued and intensified, and food prices rose faster and faster in 1943, driven not only by increased economic activity and fast-growing market demand, but also by panic and speculative manipulation of the market. The price of rice continued to rise rapidly until by August (as I mentioned earlier) it was about five times what it had been at the beginning of 1942. I did not, of course, know the numbers then, and *Prabashi*, *Desh* and other Bengali periodicals did not dwell on them either. But they did make enormous efforts to draw the attention of their readership to the general facts about the causes and consequences of price rises and their impact in spreading hunger, as well as criticizing the inaction of the Raj in dealing with the deprivation generated by the war's unaddressed consequences.

Like almost all famines, the Bengal famine of 1943 was a class-based calamity. No one who came from a relatively well-off family, including those in my extended family or the families of my classmates in school, had any difficulty in surviving a calamity that took millions of lives. Of course, everyone grumbled about the rise of food prices, but the relatively affluent were not being pushed to the edge of starvation.

7

In early October, when the famine was in its most intense phase, I went with my father to Calcutta for a few days. He had some work to do there, and I liked the idea of visiting the big city where I had had such an interesting time in the preceding December (despite the Japanese bombs on the distant Khidirpur dock). But the Calcutta I now saw was altogether different – and terrifying. There were famished, destitute people on all the streets, and for the first time in my life I saw people actually dying of starvation. There were a few feeding programmes in different parts of the city, organized by private charities, which did provide food for limited numbers. All of them opened at the same moment so that no one could go and eat at more than one. The starving fought with each other to get a place in the queue before the cut-off number was reached.

The famine generated a kind of moral degeneration in people ravaged by circumstances beyond their control. The jostling to get ahead of others was hard to watch. But even as a ten-year-old child I could understand that this was inescapable given the circumstances. My grandmother told me about an occasion at which she had observed a mother crying profusely while eating the food she had obtained from somewhere, rather than giving it to the emaciated child on her lap. 'We are no longer human beings – we have become animals,' she told Didima.

The nightmare of the Bengal famine began to generate a determination in me to do what I could to prevent famines from occurring ever again. When I told this to one of my school teachers, he smiled and applauded my ambition, but he also 'brought me down to earth' (as he put it) by saying that famines are almost impossible to eliminate. I remembered that discouraging conversation when, in the 1970s, I started analysing famines in the hope of finding a solution that would facilitate at least a partial prevention.

8

Bengal and the Idea of Bangladesh

I

One afternoon in 1944, a man came through the gates of our home, bleeding profusely and screaming in pain. I was back in Dhaka during the school holidays and alone in the garden of our house, Jagat Kutir. The man, a Muslim day-labourer called Kader Mia, had been severely knifed in his back as well as at the front. He was going home after some work in a nearby house – for a tiny reward – and had been stabbed on the street by communal thugs in our largely Hindu area. Badly wounded and in huge pain, Kader Mia asked for some water and for help. In the bewildering moments that followed, I ran to get some water, while shouting for my parents. My father rushed him to the hospital, but Kader did not, alas, survive the stabbing.

I was then approaching eleven. I knew, of course, that communal divisiveness could be very nasty. But that afternoon, as I tried to support Kader's bleeding body and help him to drink some water, even as his breathing was becoming heavier, I could suddenly see the beastly horror and terrible consequences of engineered divisions and cultivated hostility. Aside from the savagery of the incident, I found it impossible to understand – or to fathom at all – why Kader should have been killed by assassins who did not even know him. All that mattered to these dedicated murderers was the knowledge that Kader was a Muslim – that he had a particular communal identity.

When I had sufficiently recovered from the shock and sadness, I got into a long discussion with my parents about what had happened. 'For every incident of viciousness you will come to know,' said my father (who was becoming increasingly pessimistic during those odious times), 'there is probably another that would be even more abhorrent.' 'No,' said my mother, 'people cannot continue to live in a state of such barbarity.' 'This is another face of man, full of irrational violence,' said my father, 'no less real than the kindly and humane face that we like so much.'

The memory of that afternoon would come back to me again and again, as I thought about the brutality that so often lies hidden in the community-based identification of people. Surely, if we regard religious community to be our principal – perhaps even our unique – identity, we will end up seeing people as just Muslims, or just Hindus, or by some other exclusive identification. At a time of communal strife, that reduction of human beings to one dimension can serve to incite violence. If I have been a sceptic about communitarian philosophy throughout my life, despite the bonding and sympathy it can also produce within a particular group, it is because of my early experience of the inhumanity of community-based categorization. When, many decades later, I wrote a book called *Identity and Violence: The Illusion of Destiny*, published in 2006, on the dangers of seeing other people – and ourselves – in terms of a singular identity, I could not help feeling that I was merely completing a journey that I had begun many decades earlier, on that blood-soaked afternoon of Kader Mia's murder.

2

When my father was taking him to the hospital, Kader Mia told him that his wife had pleaded with him not to go into a hostile area during the communal riots. But he had to go out in search of work, to earn a little wage, because his family had nothing to eat. The penalty for that economic lack of freedom turned out to be death. Kader Mia need not have gone in search of a tiny bit of income in those troubled times if his family could have managed without it. Kader told my mother that he looked at his starving children and simply had to go out to earn something in order to buy them food.

I thought again and again about Kader's wife, pleading with him not to take such a risk. The incident dominated my thoughts for a

long time, and I came to recognize the huge reach of poverty in rob-
bing a person of all freedoms – even the freedom not to take a highly
probable risk of being murdered. Class comes into this story in a big
way. It is obviously sound advice (as we tend to hear again and again
during riots) to tell people not to leave their homes, but what can you
do if staying at home means starving children? It is not surprising that
most of the victims of communal riots come from the poorest layers
of the society – those who are always the easiest to kill. I was not very
old before I realized the pressing need to bring economic class into an
understanding of the horrors of communal violence and carnage in
India. Most of the people killed in the Hindu–Muslim riots of the
1940s shared a class identity (they came from families of workers and
the dispossessed), even though they differed in their religious or communal identity (in being a Muslim or a Hindu).

There was, of course, a lot of talk about class among my family
members, on my maternal as well as paternal sides, during my early
years. My mother's only brother, Kankarmama, belonged to the
socialist wing of the Congress Party, and one of their cousins, Satyen
Sen, or Lankarmama as we called him (who I saw as another uncle),
was in the Communist Party. After Partition, Lankarmama would
stay on in East Pakistan and become active in the development of left-
wing politics there. Another 'uncle', my father's cousin Jyotirmoy
Sengupta (Shidhukaka to me), had started as a nationalist revolutionary, but gradually came to have sympathy with the communist
movement, under the strong influence of Muzaffar Ahmad, one of the
founders of the Communist Party of India, who he had met in a British Indian jail (a good place in those days to meet intellectuals).

My mother was an ardent listener to their somewhat differing, but
all basically class-oriented, analyses of what the real problems were in
India – going well beyond the inequity of British rule. To be sure, they
were fighting the Raj too, and in my childhood these uncles were periodically in British Indian jails (as I will relate in Chapter 9). In contrast
to my father, who remained sceptical of the ability of nationalist politics to drive out the British, my mother was much more receptive, and
especially favoured the ideas of the leftist activists. She had a special
interest in Marxist thinking and liked talking with me about politics,
often adding 'your father would probably not agree'. With the

famines and riots all around us, it did seem to me that class analysis could offer at least a partial understanding of what was ailing us, including the poverty and inequality and the deprivation of basic freedoms (including the freedom not to take huge risks with one's own life). I shall return to those discussions later on in the book. But aside from the influence that these thoughts would have on my political understanding and on the questions I wanted to ask, they also indicated that human lives were gaining prominence in my curious mind, compared with the abstractions of mathematics and my fascination with historic cultures.

3

Communal rioting was not an altogether novel phenomenon in Bengal. There had been occasional Hindu–Muslim riots there at different times in the twentieth century (there were some in Calcutta in 1926), as in the rest of India, fed by sectarian incitement. But what happened in the 1940s was truly extraordinary and quite unprecedented. The politics of partition demanded by some and resisted by others made the invoking of Hindu–Muslim disunity dramatically more common than had been the case earlier. The simmering violence of the decade – which was an inescapable presence in my life in Dhaka, as it was not, for obvious reasons, in my school town of Santiniketan – reached its peak as independence and the partition of the country approached just before 1947.

It was the Muslim League, led by Muhammad Ali Jinnah, which had forcefully demanded the partition of the country, with a separate homeland for Muslims. This demand was backed up, in some of the League's statements, by the thesis of there being 'two nations' – of Hindus and Muslims – in undivided India. The thesis was much discussed in my family, and there was complete unity on its total falsity. My grandfather, Kshiti Mohan, thought it was based on comprehensive ignorance of the history of India. My family viewed the ongoing connections between Muslims and Hindus to be constructive and generally cordial, and regarded their differences to be basically unimportant, except in the actual practice of religion.

Though the demand for the partition of the country began with the Muslim League, many upper-class (and mostly upper-caste) Hindus in Bengal moved rapidly towards wanting to partition the province, as a part of the general bifurcation of India. Bengal had a substantial majority of Muslims, and if the whole of it were to go to Pakistan, the comparatively privileged Hindus, who were dominant in civil and professional life, and significantly richer on average, would lose their power and prominence. The extent to which the privileged parts of the Hindu middle and upper classes worked *for* the partition of Bengal has been well brought out recently in a highly illuminating study by Joya Chatterji.

Contemporary observation, with limited access to information, cannot obviously match the conclusions arrived at by later, more comprehensive historical studies, but, even to a young observer living in Bengal through that period, a change in the rhetoric among the Hindu elite on the unity of Bengal – moving from firmly positive to doubtful or confused – was hard to miss. This upset Kshiti Mohan greatly, though he was even more cast down by the possibility of the comprehensive partition of India as a whole.

4

There is, in fact, quite a history of partitioning, or attempted partitioning, of Bengal. In October 1905, Lord Curzon, then Viceroy of India, had tried this, making Dhaka the capital of a new, sequestered, province of 'Eastern Bengal and Assam'. Among the reasons for Curzon's decision was a concern about the part that a united Bengali nationalism was playing in generating sentiments against British rule. Even though the British decision to partition Bengal was taken in the hope that it would gain support from Bengali Muslims (who would become the dominant political group in Dhaka), it turned out that resistance to Curzon's partitioning came from all parts of Bengali society. Curzon eventually had to abandon his move, and Bengal was reunited in 1911, at the same time as the decision to move the capital of British India from Calcutta to Delhi. One of the results of the anti-partition movement was Rabindranath Tagore's composition of the evocative and moving Bengali song 'Amar Sonar Bangla' ('My Golden Bengal'), which he released and sang at an anti-partition meeting in 1906. In 1972, after the formation of Bangladesh, it was this song that would be chosen as the national anthem of the new country.

In the 1940s there was in fact a possibility that Bengal could remain undivided but made into a country on its own – old India thus being separated into three parts, namely India, Pakistan and Bengal. This was indeed one of the alternatives that some Bengali political leaders proposed. But while it had some Muslim supporters, the proposal received very little backing among the Hindu privileged classes. My own family was divided about the case for a united Bengal in a partitioned India, giving it only limited support. Basically they were all opposed to any kind of partitioning of India.

5

We had a great many Muslim friends, in Dhaka, in Calcutta and in Santiniketan. Given the class barriers within which friendship typically flourishes, most of our Muslim friends belonged to a similar social stratum as us. But that group was a relatively small minority – much smaller than the affluent Hindus. I became aware, on the basis of observation as well as discussion with my family, that there were relatively few Muslims among the university-educated elite, civil servants, the professions – doctors, lawyers and such – and more generally among the reasonably prosperous middle classes. There was a big contrast here with North India, where the Muslims were well represented within the elite. I always found the contrast striking when I visited the northern city of Lucknow, to which I went frequently, largely because my mother's sister, Mamata (Labumashi to me), lived there with her husband, Sailen Dasgupta, Professor of History at Lucknow University. I loved to visit that campus as a schoolboy – but most of all I liked Lucknow because I could spend time with Labumashi and Sailen's son Somshankar (Bacchuda to me) and their daughters, Ilina and Sumona.

I was also impressed by the richness of Lucknow culture, which was dominated by upper-class Muslims. The upper classes in Lucknow had traditionally been Muslim gentry, including a network of people – not just the erstwhile rulers, the Nawabs – who were Muslims too. The leisurely, congenial and benign lifestyle of Lucknow's Muslim elite, even as the doom faced them in the form of conquest by the British, would be beautifully portrayed in one of Satyajit Ray's great movies, *The Chess Players* (1977). Dhaka had, of course, its own share of Muslim Nawabs, but outside that small group the vast majority of Bengali Muslims were not typically very well off.

There is an oddity here, since Bengal had been ruled by Muslim kings for many centuries. But these Bengali Muslim rulers did not seem to want to displace the comfortable position of the Hindu upper and middle classes, nor to force them to embrace Islam. Hindus did not have to denounce their own religion to serve as officers for Muslim rulers in the court or in the military. There are striking descriptions of swearing-in ceremonies in the Mughal army, with Muslim officers taking their oaths in the name of Allah and Hindu officers taking theirs in the name of Vishnu.

This acceptance of religious plurality was the firmly declared policy of the Mughals in general, beginning with Emperor Akbar in the second half of the sixteenth century. (Even while Giordano Bruno was being burned at the stake for apostasy in Campo de' Fiori in Rome, Akbar was lecturing on the importance of religious tolerance in Agra.) While many Hindu historians have commented sharply on the 'communal' nature of later Mughal rule, particularly under Emperor Aurangzeb a century later, my grandfather, Kshiti Mohan, used to dispute that piece of received wisdom – much emphasized in the strife-ridden years when I was growing up – as 'imagined history'. Aurangzeb had a large number of Hindus in his court and among his close circle. Kshiti Mohan was hard to restrain on this subject. This was, I think, largely because he saw sectarian anti-Muslim history as playing a very nasty role in generating disaffection and violence, and in hardening the communal divisions in India.

Even before the Mughal conquest in the sixteenth century, the Muslim rulers of Bengal (Pathans from Afghanistan) were already content to accept Hindus at court and in the military. In addition to there being few conversions to Islam among the top layers of the Hindu society, there was relatively little influx of upper-class Muslims from the north of India into Bengal. Certainly, there were 'Ashrafs' who claimed their ancestors came from west of the Khyber Pass, from the Persian, Arabic or Turkish kingdoms, that is from lands within the core Muslim domain; but the immigrating Ashrafs were not numerous. The main conversions to Islam (which were numerically significant from the fourteenth century) took place among the less affluent, often from the outer reaches of Hindu society. Indeed, it is not actually very clear whether all those embracing Islam could be said to have converted from Hinduism to Islam, for they had often been barely integrated into Hindu society itself.

The gulf between Hindus and Muslims was enhanced under the British rule, initially under the East India Company. In 1793, a proclamation (known as the Cornwallis Code) by Lord Cornwallis, the British Governor General, settled 'permanently' the revenue to be paid by landowners to the state, giving them immunity against revenue increase, in addition to security of ownership. Many of these secure landowners were Hindus, and there grew up a class of them who lived off the rent from their land, but who actually resided far away and did not cultivate it themselves. Most of the tenants, who paid rents to the landlords and were severely exploited, were Muslims. The Permanent Settlement did extraordinary harm to the economy by removing almost all the incentives to improve the performance of agriculture and by freezing inequalities based on land ownership.

6

As I grew older and began to develop some understanding of the importance of class categories, it became clear to me how far-reaching was the impact of these economic inequalities between Hindus and Muslims in pre-Partition Bengal. My mother, strongly influenced by her activist cousins and cousins-in-law, gave me fragmentary information on the social distance created by ownership of means of production, which in this case was primarily land. She was certainly on to something important, but she never quite followed up her lines of thought, even in the magazines she edited for many years.

My family did not own any significant amount of land – to the extent they had any prosperity it was from their professional incomes – but over the years, in Calcutta, I came to know a huge number of absentee Hindu landlords who owned varying amounts of land and drew regular incomes from them. The historian Ranajit Guha (later a friend and colleague), who produced a definitive and far-reaching study of the origins of the thoroughly iniquitous system of Permanent Settlement, acknowledged that as a member of that absentee landlord class he was a beneficiary of the system himself:

> In his early youth the author, like many others of his generation in Bengal, grew up in the shadow of the Permanent Settlement: his livelihood, like that of his family, was derived from remote estates they had never visited; his education was orientated by the needs of a colonial bureaucracy recruiting its cadre from among the scions of Lord Cornwallis's beneficiaries; his world of culture was strictly circumscribed by the values of a middle class living off the fat of the land and divorced from the indigenous culture of its peasant masses.

Another important historian, Tapan Raychaudhuri, describes his own experience as a member of a landowning family, but one which owned a lot more than Guha's family, and who actually lived close to their holding in the district of Barisal. Raychaudhuri himself had strong egalitarian commitments and brought out the inequities of the land ownership system in Bengal with striking clarity:

> Being zamindar [landowner] meant being treated as royalty by the poor peasant farmers who were our tenants . . . When we encountered the *ryots* [cultivators], they did treat us as their lords and masters . . . the Bengali zamindars . . . dominated the rural, and to some extent, the urban, society in that part of the world for more than a century.

Some of the subservient *ryots* were Hindus from lower stations in life, but many – indeed most – of them were Muslim.

Given this economic inequality, Bengali Muslims were easy to recruit in the politics of discontent, and the Muslim League's temporary success in Bengal during the mid-1940s in capturing Bengali Muslim loyalty, which was hugely important for the partition of India as a whole, had close links with this issue of land ownership. However, despite the potential for the exploitation of communal divisiveness, Bengali Muslims continued to support communally integrated political parties until up to 1943. Fazlul Huq served as the Premier of Bengal – a position based on electoral politics, but of limited power under the Raj – in various coalitions, first with the Muslim League and then with the Hindu Mahasabha. His own party was the secular Krishak Praja Party ('Peasants and Tenants Party'), dedicated to land reform and the removal of Cornwallis's Permanent Settlement. It was not a communal party but, given the nature of Bengal's economics, most of the supporters of his party were in fact Bengali Muslims.

Fazlul Huq was attacked by some in the Congress as 'communalist'. They could cite his frequent statement that he was 'Muslim first, Bengali later' and that he was persuaded by Muhammad Ali Jinnah to move the Muslim separationist 'Lahore Resolution' in 1940. But Huq continued to pursue his own priorities as the leader of Bengali Muslims, with their very different economic position from Muslims elsewhere in the subcontinent, and was actually expelled by Jinnah from the Muslim League in 1941.

Certainly, the interests of Bengali Muslims were firmly associated with the essentially secular issues of land reform and the removal of inequalities and exploitation in land ownership in Bengal. Huq himself was concerned for the wider interests and glories of Bengal. To give a small example, after an excellent performance at the examinations, Tapan Raychaudhuri even received a telegram from Fazlul Huq congratulating him for having advanced 'the glory of Barisal'. There were a lot of arguments between members of my family about 'what Fazlul Huq really stands for', but since many of them, including my father, knew him well and were sympathetic to his basic commitments, Huq used to emerge from these discussions endorsed and vindicated.

7

There are many things that have changed in Bengal since my schooldays, but what has altered most radically is the removal of the dead weight and inequity of the Permanent Settlement. Tapan Raychaudhuri describes how the lifestyle of affluent landlords disappeared 'almost overnight in 1947–48'. It is fair to say that this 'overnight' change made a Bangladesh with a strong commitment to secularism feasible in a way it probably was not in the 1940s. There is, however, more to the story, in particular the development of very well-reflected secular politics under the leadership of Sheikh Mujibur Rahman (or Bangabandhu), the great statesman of Bangladesh.

Once 'the land question' – that major Muslim grievance which restrained Fazlul Huq's secularism – suddenly became obsolete, there was room for more integrative Bengali political movements in East Pakistan, of which the Bengali language movement (the *bhasha andolan*) was the pioneer from February 1952, less than five years after the partition of India and the establishment of East Pakistan. This is not to say that the emergence of such non-divisive Bengali movements was inevitable once land inequities had been transformed. Rather, the possibility of them – and it was no more than that – opened up.

The idea of a secular and democratic Bangladesh needed constructive political cultivation, which was pursued – with much difficulty – over the years. Ultimately it required a far-reaching and affirmative vision, which came from Bangabandhu, Sheikh Mujibur Rahman. Importantly, Mujibur Rahman could draw on Bengal's special history of communal relations over the centuries, and its recent past of intense sectarian violence. When I thought about Bengal's cultural history – whether I was in Dhaka, Calcutta or Santiniketan – the connections between all these elements were clearly relevant in addressing the difficult question of whether we can legitimately talk about 'the Bengali people'.

A Bengali identity has always been important for me, without being invasive enough to obliterate my other loyalties of occupation, politics, nationality and other affiliations, including that of my shared humanity with all others. A mixture of different historical sources of culture is very much a part of what has emerged as a Bengali identity. When, at his Hibbert Lectures in the early 1930s, Rabindranath Tagore told his Oxford audience, with some evident pride, that he came from 'a confluence of three cultures, Hindu, Mohammedan and British', this was both an explicit negation of any sectarian confinement, and an implicit celebration of the dignity of being broad-based rather than narrowly sequestered.

The affirmation of political and cultural secularism does not rob a Bangladeshi Muslim of his or her religious Muslim identity, and this is entirely consistent with the assertion that people's religious identification can be separated from their political self-recognition. The same can be said of a Bengali Hindu, whether in Bangladesh or in India.

8

In thinking about these debates, what should we look for in the history of Bengal? When Buddhism disappeared as a practice from much of India after a thousand years, it continued to flourish in Bengal until the late eleventh century, with the Buddhist Pala kings representing the last bastion of Buddhist regal power in the country. After a short period, Hindu rule was supplanted by the arrival of Muslim conquerors from the early thirteenth century onwards. Even though these early Muslim rulers (the Pathans), who came from Afghanistan, had a ruthless history of confrontation and destruction, Muslim rule in Bengal put down roots within a fairly short time. Indeed, several of the early Muslim kings, who learned Bengali despite their origins elsewhere, were sufficiently impressed by the multicultural history of the region to commission good Bengali translations of the Sanskrit epics, *Ramayana* and *Mahabharata*. This was in the fourteenth century, and these early translations are still among the most read versions of these ancient epics. There are moving accounts of how one of the Muslim kings wanted to hear the old Sanskrit stories again and again every evening. They were not, of course, in any way abandoning their own Islamic beliefs, but were establishing non-religious affiliations in addition to their own religiosity, showing very clearly – 700 years ago – that a person's religious identity need not annihilate every other affiliation.

The energy of new Muslims coming into the region is described and celebrated at the end of the sixteenth century (around 1590) by the leading Hindu poet, Mukundaram, in his *Chandimangal*. Mukundaram went on to note that their economic activities, apart from yielding the usual benefits, had even driven out the dreaded tigers from the region:

From the West came Zafar Mian,
    Together with twenty-two thousand men.
Sulaimani beads in their hands,
    They chanted the names of their *pīr* and the Prophet.
Having cleared the forest,
    They established markets.
Hundreds and hundreds of foreigners
    Ate and entered the forest,
Hearing the sound of the ax,
    Tigers became apprehensive and ran away, roaring.

Industrial enterprises, including the manufacture of textiles involving high levels of specialized skills, such as the famous muslin of Dhaka, grew rapidly. And, even though settled agriculture came later to east Bengal than to the west, the eastern regions were soon competing and often overtaking western Bengal in productivity. The integration of Muslims and Hindus in economic activities was well established, but already encompassed the disparity in land ownership that would dramatically develop and expand under early British rule, particularly through Cornwallis's Permanent Settlement.

9

What unites the Bengalis in Bangladesh is not only a shared economic or political history – though it does play a big role – but the common language of Bengali and pride in its richness and accomplishments. The language has had an amazingly powerful influence on the identity of Bengalis as a group on both sides of the political boundary between Bangladesh and India. As I have mentioned, the politically separatist campaign in what was East Pakistan that led to the war for independence and eventually to the formation of the new secular state of Bangladesh was pioneered by the 'language movement' in defence of the Bengali language. The pioneering meeting on 21 February 1952 at university campuses, which the Pakistani authorities tried forcibly to break up, with significant loss of life, is widely celebrated in Bangladesh as 'Language Movement Day' – and also, across the world, as 'Mother Language Day', as the United Nations designated it in 1999.

One of the strongest voices – both for the quality of his literary contributions and in championing his integrationist view – was that of Kazi Nazrul Islam, the most popular poet in Bengal after Tagore. Nazrul's approach to communal divisions was not really very different from Rabindranath's (Nazrul had a reputation, in his youth, as a great reciter of Tagore's poems), but he wrote more emphatically and combined his humanist Bengali view with a strong left-wing commitment to economic and social equality. He was a friend of – and much influenced by – Muzaffar Ahmad, whom I mentioned earlier in this chapter as the inspiration for my uncle Jyotirmoy Sengupta while he was in a British Indian jail. Ahmad also wrote a wonderful biography of Nazrul Islam, particularly about his commitments to secular humanism and social equity.

A literary magazine linked with the Communist Party was called *Langal* ('Plough') and was established in 1925. The first number carried a review of a biography of Karl Marx and another of a translation of Maxim Gorky's *Mother*, as well as some of Nazrul's poems which it promised to publish on a regular basis. *Langal*'s chosen motto, which appeared as a kind of a masthead, was from the fifteenth-century Bengali poet Chandidas:

> Shunoho manush bhai,
> Shabar upor manush satya
> Tahar upor nai.
> (Please hear me, my brother human being,
> Man is the highest truth we seek
> There is no truth above that.)

Nazrul's influence on Bengali thought was profound. His reputation as the *bidrohi kabi* ('rebellious poet') had secured for him special devotion, and in many political contexts even great fans of Tagore would look for the strong Assam tea of Nazrul rather than the delicate flavour of Tagore's Darjeeling. There were very few Bengalis in my time who could not recite by heart a poem that goes by the title 'Kandari Hushiyar', which can be freely translated as 'Careful, Captain of our Boat'. A particular admonition to the captain warned him:

'Is this drowning person a Hindu or a Muslim, asks someone. Leader, tell him that the person is a human being – the child of my mother.'

Since my grandfather, Kshiti Mohan Sen, was, as I have discussed earlier, deeply engaged in researching, lecturing and writing on the extensive interactions between Hindus and Muslims in Bengali culture, I had regular home tutorials on the subject, in addition to my reading of what Kshiti Mohan wrote. He also had a great collection of stories to tell about the narrowness of cultural separatists. One I liked a lot, because of its gentle advocacy of integration, but also because of the way it reflected a common Bengali scepticism of priests. It concerned an evening when Kshiti Mohan's elder brother, Abani-mohan, was chatting with a friend – a Muslim priest – called Mahafizuddin, at his home, sharing a smoke from a hubble-bubble with him. They saw a Hindu priest called Chakravarty going past and Mahafizuddin invited him warmly to join them. Chakravarty declined, and pointed to the difference between him, a pure Brahmin priest, and the Muslim Maulavi. They were 'very different', Chakravarty insisted, and it would be inappropriate for them to smoke together. The Maulavi replied: 'My friend, there is really no difference between us. You live by exploiting the vulnerabilities of ignorant Hindus, and I live by exploiting the vulnerabilities of ignorant Muslims. We are engaged in exactly the same business.'

10

As a student, I was particularly impressed by a striking illustration of multicultural integration in Bengal, which is largely forgotten now but has in fact a remarkable history: the Bengali calendar, called the 'San'. The San is the only extant calendar in the Indian subcontinent in which the influence of Emperor Akbar's abortive attempt at establishing an all-Indian non-denominational calendar, the Tarikh-ilahi, survives. In the late sixteenth century, as the end of the first millennium in the lunar Muslim calendar or Hijri approached, Akbar wanted a multicultural calendar for India that would be solar, like the Hindu or Jain or Parsee calendars, but which would include some important features of the Muslim Hijri in it. The zero year was fixed at AD 1556 (the year of

Akbar's ascent to the throne), which corresponded to 1478 in the Hindu Saka calendar and to 963 in the Muslim Hijri.

Despite Akbar's lofty hopes, the Tarikh-ilahi never caught on in Delhi or Agra, despite its use in Akbar's own court. But it had a good reception in Akbar's recently acquired addition to his empire, Bengal, where the reformed old Bengali calendar, strongly influenced by Akbar's Tarikh-ilahi, survives robustly today and is critically important also for many Hindu ceremonies. As I write these lines, it is the year 1427 in Bengali San, an identification that commemorates the Prophet Muhammad's move from Mecca to Medina, in a mixed lunar–solar system of counting – Muslim lunar until 963 and Hindu solar since then. A religious Hindu may not be at all aware of this connection with the Prophet of Islam when he or she invokes this date in a Hindu ceremony.

I remember being both impressed and amused by this neat combination when the history of the Bengali San was clarified, primarily by the brilliant scientist Meghnad Saha in the mid-1950s. However, forty years later there was scope for further reflection when Samuel Huntington's thesis of 'the clash of civilizations' drew much attention across the world through his book of that title published in 1996. A devotee of civilizational partition along Huntington's separatist lines has to figure out whether the Bengali San is a part of 'Hindu civilization' or of 'Muslim civilization', between which Huntington saw such a sharp dissonance. The answer of course is that it is both, and it cannot be fitted into the devastating simplicity of Huntingtonian categorization.

The history of Bengal is thus a tale of integration, rather than one of religious partition and cultural disintegration. It is that philosophy, that understanding, which makes a united and secular Bangladesh a feasible and elevating idea, and allows it to face the world on its own terms.

9

Resistance and Division

'How is Ranjit?' asked my uncle Shidhu (cousin of my father) in a letter from Burdwan jail to my aunt Bani. He complained about the complexity of the name Amartya, grumbling that in giving such a 'teeth-breaking' name to a small child, Tagore showed evidence of having 'turned completely barmy in his old age'. 'I will call him Ranjit,' declared uncle Shidhu – 'How is he?' The affectionate letter was written on 22 August 1934, before I was one year old. Shidhu, or Jyotirmoy Sengupta (which was his proper name), had been in prison since the summer of 1932, before I was born. He had been sentenced to seven years, having been convicted of the general charge that he was working for the destruction of the British Empire (which he certainly was) and of the particular crime that he had helped to channel government money to a revolutionary group dedicated to violent rebellion. Shidhu was moved around from one prison to another: Dhaka Jail, Alipore Central Jail, Burdwan Jail, Midnapore Central Jail, among others. As a little boy, I was taken to visit my uncle with some regularity in these various houses of incarceration.

When Shidhu was sentenced, he chose to embrace rigorous imprisonment, with leg chains and all, even though as a political prisoner from an educated middle-class family he could have placed himself in the much more comfortable and less degrading confinement permitted by the class-conscious British Indian prison system. He regularly wrote to his mother that he was 'excellently well', but the malnutrition that he experienced in the different jails almost certainly contributed to the serious case of tuberculosis that he developed, which made his weight drop alarmingly, as his fellow prisoner Muzaffar Ahmad reported. Since the severity of his TB threatened his life, and as he gave no one any trouble in the various prisons where he had been held, Shidhu was ultimately released in December 1937, somewhat before completing his seven-year sentence. By then, alas, he was not far from death. However, luckily for me, I did have many conversations with him after he was released and have some warm memories of listening to him on important subjects such as the unity of India and the political triviality of the Hindu–Muslim division. My mother was a huge admirer of Shidhu, and was very keen that 'Ranjit' could chat with, and learn from, his visionary and courageous uncle.

2

As I was growing up, I was struck by the fact that so many of my uncles, including my mother's only brother Kankarmama and various cousins on both sides, were in one jail or another. They were all kept in custody not because they had been convicted of doing anything, but because the colonial rulers had decided that they could harm the Raj if they remained at large. They were therefore imprisoned under the widely used colonial practice of 'preventive detention'. A few of them did have connections with organizers of violent events, but most of them, like Kankarmama, were staunchly committed to non-violence. However, non-violent writing and speeches in favour of independence, especially those aligned with Mahatma Gandhi, were enough of a qualification to be preventively detained by the Raj.

Shidhu, however, was not such a detainee, but the only one of my imprisoned relations who had actually been convicted in a court. His specific crime was to be in touch with, and provide aid to, the activists who had robbed a train in Dhaka that was carrying, in a sealed compartment, government funds for military use, which the rebels offloaded and passed on to the revolutionaries. The raid was carried out just as the train left Dhaka station. It is not absolutely clear how directly Shidhu was involved in the raid itself, but he did help carry the money to the anti-Raj activists (the driver of the car that was used for this transfer turned 'state witness' in a plea bargain and apparently identified Shidhu).

My father, Ashutosh Sen, was never involved, or inclined to be involved, in these activities. He did admire the courage, dedication and self-sacrifice of the rebels, especially those who killed or wounded no one, and was very willing to help the activists in the privations of their personal lives. But violent rebellion was not his thing and he had no time at all for what was called 'terrorism' (in the Raj's preferred terminology) which mostly took the form of trying to bomb British officers. My father thought such activities were brutal and beastly as well as completely useless in a campaign to free India from colonial rule. His admiration for the courage and dedication of these activists did not stretch to admiration for their morality or reasoning.

The captured money was passed on to the rebels the morning after the raid, and my father asked one of the cousins involved – not Shidhu, I think – where they had kept the money that night, as the police were looking vigorously for it everywhere in Dhaka. My father was astonished, and not very pleased, when the activist told him that they had kept the money in his – that is in my father's – house, in a decorated old chest he used to have on the veranda downstairs ('we knew they would never come to your house'). Much later I would learn from Tom Stoppard's wonderful play *Professional Foul* that similar strategies for escaping authoritarian detection through hiding searched-for items among the possessions of the trusted are used across the world. I understand that Ashutosh gave an irate lecture to the activists for their moral as well as political failings, but left it at that.

Shidhu underwent a political transformation during his years in jail, coming strongly under the influence of the political and social ideas of Marx and Freud. Both cast a spell on him, but it was Marx who made him gradually convinced that terrorism was a huge mistake, and what was needed instead was the nurturing of organized mass movements. His wide reading in various prisons made him thoroughly opposed to the terrorist folly of injuring or killing British officials, and he kept on planning a future life in the organization of workers and peasants through the trade union movements (which he would go on to pursue for the brief period he had left after being released from jail). As I mentioned earlier, in prison he came to know well Muzaffar Ahmad, one of the founders of the Indian Communist Party. After his own release, Muzaffar agitated for Shidhu's too, explaining that he had cut any links that he might have had with the terrorists and intended to concentrate only on union work.

3

Since I regularly visited my uncles, and loved chatting with them, I was fascinated by the fact that they differed from each other and belonged to different political parties – Kankarmama was in the Congress Socialist Party (part of the general Congress), Lankarmama in the Communist Party and so on. I was taken to visit them with adult members of the family, and remember being quite moved when, on one occasion, Kankarmama told me that he was very happy that he had just been shifted to a room outside which was a tree, something he had not seen for quite a while. 'It is a very soothing sight,' he told me, 'especially for being reminded that there is a normal world outside the high walls of the jail, where new leaves come out in the spring.'

He told me that he was also very happy to have a picture of some ducks, drawn by me, that I had sent him on a postcard – ducks from our own compound. On one occasion I had asked him about the difference between communists and socialists, and he told me that while he could not have a political discussion in the closely supervised 'visiting hour' in the jail, he would talk with me on that subject as soon as he was released. He was very critical of communists, especially for their 'slavishness' towards the Soviet Union ('it is a kind of political bankruptcy,' he told me).

My grandmother Didima, Kankarmama's mother, was always rather emotional when saying goodbye to him at the end of the weekly visiting hour. My grandfather, Kshiti Mohan, did not help by looking unaffected and sturdy. He made the short visiting hour even shorter (especially for Didima) by telling us, at regular intervals, that we had only twenty (or fifteen, or ten, or five) minutes left – 'any important thing you want to discuss must be discussed now' – warnings that made all conversations stop. I learned of his ever-present sadness about his son's imprisonment only when he and I had long walks early in the morning before dawn, with stars still shining overhead.

Other than visiting her son in jail, my grandmother also tried to appeal to some officers of the Raj whom she knew (or was related to), pleading that her son was innocent and should not be kept in preventive detention. I went with her on one occasion when she visited a well-known Indian Civil Service (ICS) officer, B. R. Sen, who was a distant relative. Binay Ranjan had been District Magistrate in Midnapore, but when Didima visited him he was helping to coordinate the food policies of the Raj. (He had the misfortune to be a senior officer with that responsibility when the Bengal famine occurred.) We waited for him in an outer reception room, being told that he would see Didima after he had shaved. We waited for about two hours, durng which we heard the sound of some light conversation going on inside his quarters, with occasional laughter. I remember asking Didima whether perhaps he had a very thick beard.

Eventually he had time for Didima – a couple of minutes – allowing her to explain to him that her son was not involved in any violent activity at all. 'I can't help him,' B. R. Sen told her, 'unless he changes his political attitude towards the Government. The charge against him is not violence, but that his writings create discontent about the empire. He will be released the moment he stops this.' I went back home with Didima, who was extremely disappointed, but later on she liked quoting my more positive view of the encounter. 'He was very well shaved,' I had told Didima.

After 1947, when the former ICS officers who had been dedicated to serving British rule (including keeping rebellious Indians in jail) were given prominent positions in the international world as representatives of a newly independent country, B. R. Sen became the Director General of the Food and Agriculture Organization (FAO), based in Rome. Efficient in everything he did, he served very creditably in that office – as he had served his British masters earlier. He apparently did take some imaginative initiatives on world food problems, but guardians of the Raj culture would be relieved to learn that in the FAO he continued the tradition of senior officers of British India in never being seen to carry his own briefcase – his orderly, walking two steps behind, always carried it for him. This amused my Italian friends in Rome, who had come to know about him. To them I had to explain the immutable 'orderly culture' of the Raj.

4

During my childhood, the movements for Indian independence were becoming stronger and more determined. There were many different kinds of actions and agitations, and as I was growing up I wanted to try and understand how they differed – and why.

Then suddenly the Second World War became the major concern of the British rulers of India. In 1939 Lord Linlithgow, the Viceroy of India, made a unilateral declaration announcing that India was a party to this war, of course on the side of the British. When that announcement was made, I was nearly six, and we were on our way back from Mandalay to Dhaka, where my father resumed his teaching duties at the University. The Linlithgow declaration, made without any kind of consultation in India, was hugely criticized, and I was dimly aware that, even though nearly all the adults in my family seemed very opposed to Nazi Germany, they thought that India should not be brought into the fight without first consulting the Indians.

It was not so much any lack of sympathy for Britain's stand against Nazism, but rather the denying to India the right to be consulted that caused much frustration and anger. There were other, bigger, issues too, beyond the right to be consulted. The Indian National Congress was ready to cooperate with the British provided the issue of the independence of India was sorted out. The war was taken seriously in India and it would soon come to Burma, from where we had just returned, but already many Indians were aware of the stories of Japanese atrocities in China, which drew much condemnation.

To deal with the rising discontent in India, a Mission was sent in March 1942 by the British government to talk to Indian political leaders about cooperating more fully in the war efforts. It was led by Sir Stafford Cripps, one of the most senior figures in the Labour Party, who – I gathered from my parents and uncles – was a 'very good man'. He was supposed to talk to the Indian leaders and urge them to cooperate in the war effort in exchange for a firm promise that Indian independence would be seriously considered after the war. There would, however, be no immediate concession to Indian independence from the British rulers.

Gandhi found this lack of any immediate change quite unacceptable, but Cripps was not allowed by the Churchill government to offer any deal that might have been more welcome to the Indian leaders. The negotiations, Cripps promised, would start after the war ended. Gandhi remained unenthusiastic. When Cripps asked him why he seemed so unmoved, Gandhi apparently said that he was trying hard to figure out what exactly he could do with 'a post-dated cheque on a crashing bank'. There was some speculation as to whether Churchill had sent Cripps to India not so much to win the cooperation of Indian political leaders (which Cripps could not possibly achieve given what he was authorized to offer), but rather to undermine this 'very good man' from the Labour Party, who at this time was being spoken of as an alternative prime minister, if Churchill fell.

On 8 August 1942, following the failure of the Cripps Mission in April, Gandhi launched the 'Quit India' movement. This had the cooperation of Congress leaders, and the day after that declaration, nearly all of them – Gandhi, Nehru and others – were arrested. By the summer of 1942 more than 30,000 people were being held as political prisoners in British Indian jails. The 'roll of honour', as it would be called by the rebellious nationalists, included several members of my extended family. Kankarmama and several of my other uncles went back to jail. The 'August rebellion' prompted by the Quit India movement was strong, not least in Bengal, and I remember being moved by accounts of the heroism of those participating in it. By the end of the year, however, the rebellion, now largely leaderless – because all the Congress leaders were in prison – was over. What was not over were the debates generated everywhere by the rapidly moving events, including at my home and at my school.

With the German attack on the Soviet Union in June 1941, the Indian Communist Party too gave priority to winning the war against the Axis powers over the cause of Indian independence. Communists came under huge fire from nationalists for this abrupt change of their attitude and would suffer quite a debacle in the provincial elections in 1946. The debates around this issue split the adult members of our extended family. Lankarmama, as an active member of the Party, did his best to offer plausible reasons for the shifting Communist position, but no other member of my extended family was at all sympathetic to the U-turn by the Party. Nevertheless, there were many sympathizers among them who thought that the defeat of Nazi Germany was more important than any 'nationalist' issue with which Congress was so totally preoccupied.

So there was criticism of Congress too: even Kankarmama, who was himself in the Congress Socialist Party, told me, 'We have to remember that there is a world outside India and Britain.' But he was much more critical of the inability of the Communists to 'resist toeing the Soviet line'. The Communists did not join – and in many ways acted against – the 'Quit India' movement, and the speed with which the Party aligned with what some called 'their Soviet masters' drew sharp criticism in family discussions, to which I was an avid listener.

5

A uniquely interesting development of that period involved Subhas Chandra Bose, a great leader of the independence movement (typically called 'Netaji' – the leader). Bose was an important figure in Congress and inspired people to fight for India's independence; by 1938 he had been elected to be Congress President. His radical political views and his uncompromisingly secular commitments had made him popular in my extended family. There were some doubts, however, concerning his ambiguity about violence as a means of gaining Indian independence, and the followers of Gandhi in the family (such as Kankarmama) had reservations about him for that reason. In 1939 he was ousted from his role in the Congress leadership. This exclusion was effectively Gandhi's doing, by means that could be seen as somewhat underhand.

Bose was imprisoned by the Raj in Calcutta not long after his ejection, and then placed under house arrest, from which he escaped in 1941 (helped daringly by his nephew Sisir Bose). He found his way to Afghanistan, and eventually, in April of that year, to Germany. He wanted to raise an army of Indians, with German help, to fight for independence. We would learn only later that Bose had a girlfriend in Germany, from an earlier visit there in 1934, called Emilie Schenkl. He was also keen to return to her. They went on to have a daughter in 1942. Despite helping to set up a Free India radio station, the German commitment to Indian independence seemed to Bose to be rather minimal. He decided to relocate again, and ultimately managed to reach Japan during the early months of 1943 after a perilous sea journey, mostly in a submarine.

Things then started to move fast. Bose – or Netaji – raised a significant number of troops from the captured Indian soldiers in South East Asia, from where the British had withdrawn under Japanese attack. This army, called the Indian National Army (INA) or the Azad Hind Fauj, also had many recruits from expatriate Indians in South East Asia, which added to its strength. The INA fought side by side with the Japanese, and reached Imphal on the easternmost edge of India. By then the war was turning: the INA, like the Japanese army, suffered a series of setbacks and was compelled to retreat. By 1945 it was all over, following the dropping of atom bombs on Hiroshima on 6 August and on Nagasaki on the 9th. A little over a week later, on 18 August, Bose, who was being flown out of Japan by the Japanese before the Allies arrived, died in a plane crash. Just three days before his death, on 15 August 1945 (as it happens, exactly two years before Indian independence), he reiterated the goal behind all his activities in a speech to the nation, saying, 'There is no power on earth that can keep India enslaved. India shall be free and before long.'

As the news of Netaji's movements and actions filtered through to us in India, there were many debates in my school and within the family about both the effectiveness and the propriety of what he was doing. Some people were deeply moved and excited; others were doubtful whether joining forces with Japan and Germany could possibly be right in the context of the global war; still others were simply puzzled about what to think on such a difficult issue. Bose had not, in fact, been an admirer of Nazi Germany, or even of militant Japan, and indeed in his Presidential Address to the Indian National Congress in Haripura in 1938 he had described the newly emerging expansionist Japan as 'militant, aggressive and imperialist'. But evidently, given the overwhelming goal of ending the British Raj in India, Bose was ready to work with Japan, which did not have an imperial past in its relations with India.

The Raj had banned the INA broadcasts, and listening to them was now seen as a serious crime, but of course many of us tuned our radios to hear the prohibited communications. We would gather in a room in the student hostels in Santiniketan, typically in Satish Kutir, and, after closing all the windows, turn on the radio – low but clear. There was excitement even when we could not fully believe what the INA spokesman was telling us. Even those who strongly doubted the political wisdom of the steps that Bose had taken could not but admire what he and his followers were trying to do for India – and taking a great personal risk, in a very difficult world.

When the British rulers of India started bringing captured INA officers to military trial, there was huge discontent across the country, for these officers were, by then, seen in India as patriots. I remember that – like most students in my school – I wore badges in support of freeing the INA officers. At this point, however, Britain's Indian empire was beginning to collapse and the officers awaiting trial were eventually freed by the British.

6

Nothing perhaps was as momentous at this time for the future of British India as the emergence of the Muslim League, under the leadership of Muhammad Ali Jinnah, a seasoned politician. The Muslim League had started as a political entity in the 1920s, claiming to represent the interests of Muslims in the subcontinent. It gradually became an important political force, advancing the view that nothing short of the partition of the country – with a Hindu India and a Muslim Pakistan – would satisfy the requirement of fair treatment for Indian Muslims. This view was not, of course, popular in my extended family, strongly secular as they were. But, more importantly, the family – especially Kshiti Mohan Sen (as discussed in Chapter 8) – was completely convinced that the Hindu–Muslim division, while important in terms of religious beliefs, was of no political importance (it could have political significance only if religious identities were artificially inserted into politics).

Jinnah was, however, becoming immensely influential. This came slowly at first. In the provincial elections of 1937, the League had failed to get anything like a majority even in the Muslim-majority states of Bengal and Punjab. But it grew in influence sharply between the late 1930s and the 1940s, and the Lahore Resolution of 1940, arranged by Jinnah, added something like a plan for partitioning India on religious lines.

To many Indian Muslims, this divisive line of thinking was completely unacceptable. As Rafiq Zakaria, a leading political analyst in India, put it in his account of *The Man Who Divided India* (2001), Jinnah propounded his 'pernicious Two-Nation theory' only to pursue his narrow objectives. He propagated extensively his theory that Hindus and Muslims formed two distinct nations and used it to justify his demand that 'India must be partitioned and Muslims given a separate homeland.' That diagnosis of perniciousness was shared by many Indian Muslims at the time, but those who were positively inclined to accept the Two Nation theory were also growing in number in the 1940s. In the provincial elections in Bengal in January 1946, just one year before Partition, the Muslim League won, for the first time, a convincing plurality – though not quite a majority – of all seats.

At the time of the Lahore Resolution in 1940, I was not yet seven. But that turning point was pivotal in the discussions that took place through my school years. As Hindu–Muslim riots became familiar events in what was previously taken to be a well-integrated Bengal, the incendiary nature of the Lahore Resolution featured strongly in conversations that were going on around me. Jinnah backed up his political programme in 1946 with a demand for 'direct action' by Muslims to accomplish the partitioning of the country. A gigantic burst of communal killing – both of Muslims and Hindus – erupted in Calcutta and elsewhere in Bengal, far greater than anything that had occurred before. The political options available for secular governance were rapidly shrinking.

However, to blame exclusively Jinnah and the Muslim League for starting the violence and riots has two significant limitations. First, although an overwhelming majority of Congress leaders – from Nehru to Abul Kalam Azad – were committed to secular politics, even in pre-Partition India there were many voices in support – explicitly or by implication – of Hindu majoritarianism. Even the Two Nation theory was first proclaimed not by Jinnah but by Vinayak Damodar Savarkar in his presidential address to the Hindu Mahasabha in 1937.

Savarkar was a strong proponent of Hindu politics: it was he who coined the term 'Hindutva' that can be translated from Sanskrit as 'the quality of being Hindu', which is so much in circulation now. His thought remains very influential in Hindu majoritarian thinking in India today, but he was not alone in arguing for a 'Hindu Rashtra' (and Hindu political dominance) rather than a secular multi-religious India. An important figure on the Hindutva side was Madhav Sadashiv Golwalkar, who provided much-needed organizational leadership for the movement as well as rather idiosyncratic theories of Hindu separateness.

Second, the Congress did far too little to retain the loyalty of its Muslim supporters. As Rafiq Zakaria pointed out, 'There was no concerted rational approach on the part of the Congress to expose Jinnah's game which threatened to put Hindus and Muslims at loggerheads and thus to undermine the composite character of the nation.' I remember how frustrated Kshiti Mohan felt that many centuries of collaborative work by Muslims and Hindus had received so little airing from the Congress leadership, whose focus did not seem to stretch beyond passive tolerance of each other. 'Much more than living peacefully together is involved in the India we have *jointly built*,' Kshiti Mohan kept on telling me.

7

Subsequent research, particularly by Ayesha Jalal, has brought out that Jinnah himself was not really very keen on a clear-cut partition. He wanted a conditionally split country, a Hindu-majority India and a Muslim-majority Pakistan, with shared foreign policy and defence – very far from what actually emerged. Jalal has provided a powerful commentary on Jinnah's ambiguity on the subject of Partition and the internal problems in the policies he pursued. She asks, 'how did a Pakistan come about which fitted the interests of most Muslims so poorly?' That question gained in relevance as time passed, and as the dominance of the military in Pakistan became increasingly clear. Jinnah was not particularly religious (his persona was that of a whisky-drinking Westernized gentleman), and indeed he made a speech shortly before the birth of Pakistan, when he became its first Governor General, arguing for religious freedom and equal rights for all. But by an irony of politics he helped to create a national polity in which appeal to Islamic fundamentalism would rapidly gain ground. Lord Mountbatten, the new Viceroy of India, with Nehru's agreement, seemed willing to deliver to Jinnah even more than he had really wanted.

The problems of religious extremism and the ascendancy of the Pakistan military in the name of religion would, of course, emerge only gradually. But in the world of the 1940s, the divisive politics of Muslims and Hindus ran amok, resulting in chaos and bloodshed, and making Hindu–Muslim riots a norm in the country, including in Bengal. Ultimately, when the partition actually occurred, around 1 million people were killed in the violence of the riots and organized communal killings, thousands of women were raped and 15 million people were displaced from their homes. Saadat Hasan Manto, the brilliant writer, captured our sense of frustration when he described how the riots showed how human beings can be 'slaves of bigotry ... slaves of religious passions, slaves of animal instincts and barbarity'.

8

When the agitations for the partition of India gathered momentum, my father was still teaching in Dhaka University. But the riots and disorder made classes hard to hold in Ramna, the area of Dhaka where the University was situated. Two years before Partition, but after many months of disrupted teaching and research, a number of the university teachers in Dhaka decided to leave. Along with my father, the group included the physicist Satyendra Nath Bose (of the Bose–Einstein statistics), the economist Amiya Kumar Dasgupta, the literary author Buddhadeb Bose and a number of others. Our beloved home in Wari in Dhaka was locked up and my parents moved to Calcutta. I was in Santiniketan already, which – like Calcutta – would be a part of West Bengal in the divided India. Dhaka would become the capital of East Pakistan.

Even after leaving Dhaka, my father continued to take serious interest in the politics of his university. He was fed up with the Congress politics of Bengal, dominated as it was by Hindu landowners, and he sought a more humane alternative. One of his close friends at the university, Fazlur Rahman, who had joined the Muslim League, kept in touch with him. Despite his membership of the League, he claimed, through 1945–6, to be trying to achieve some kind of genuine secularism. Ashutosh viewed Rahman's candidature for the provincial elections sympathetically, arguing that more weight must be given to the nature and 'quality' of a person than to the party to which he belonged. He and Amiya Dasgupta corresponded extensively on the choices involved. In the provincial election in the Dhaka University constituency, Rahman won on behalf of the Muslim League, with the support of a number of Hindu professors, including my father and Amiya Dasgupta.

Rahman was evidently a decent man, but Ashutosh and those colleagues of his who cast their vote for him must have been quite naive to think that, in the political atmosphere of 1946–7, a member of the Muslim League would have much freedom to pursue any kind of an independent political line. Ashutosh remained an eternal optimist, with great faith in a human being's ability to be an independent thinker and agent, and my uncles were probably right in deciding that my father persistently underestimated the role of parties and organizations.

9

As the partition came to look more and more inevitable, we moved full-time to Santiniketan and it was there that I continued to study as a student. However, my father needed to earn an income, so my parents set themselves up in rented premises in Calcutta.

At first Ashutosh wanted to start a business, making inexpensive porcelain cups and dishes for affordable daily use. He borrowed some money for it and set up a new factory, going at it with great energy but evidently rather little business skill. It did not prove to be a success, and within a year or so he started looking for a job with a salary. In his business he was quite horrified, he told me, by the crude and sometimes cruel treatment that Calcutta labourers received at the hands of factory managers (this would eventually be addressed – indeed, more than addressed – by the militant unions that took root in the city and provided a solid basis for a militant Communist Party from the 1970s onwards). Ashutosh could not change things in his factory, but nor could he reconcile himself to what he saw happening in his 'own' factory. He strongly wanted to leave it for something more ethically acceptable.

Eventually, Ashutosh did get a job with a salary, or – more accurately – the promise of a job from the central government in Delhi, with the proviso that, in exchange for a commitment to work for the government for at least five years, he would be trained in America for project management involving agriculture. (His own speciality within chemistry was soil chemistry.) So, along with five others, he went off to be trained in the USA for about six months, visiting institutions such as the famous Tennessee Valley Authority. But while my father and the others were receiving American training, the government changed its mind about the programme. The trainees were told on their return that their five-year undertaking was cancelled and the programme would not now hire anyone – indeed, would cease to exist. The uncertainties of Indian economic planning were beginning to become plain.

Meanwhile Ashutosh had returned from the USA with a large but inexpensive Chevrolet, a home movie camera, a projector (which had a tendency to give mild electric shocks to the user) and some newly available ballpoint pens. All this was quite jolly, especially for the rest of the family, but my father still had to look for a job. Happily, he was soon hired by the local Delhi administration for an interesting position with the grand title of Land Development Commissioner. The outdoor life suited him very well, and the new Commissioner went enthusiastically around the environs of Delhi with an army of tractors and land movement equipment, together with the aim of achieving good habitations, efficient cultivation and careful environmental preservation.

When I visited Delhi, I liked going around the countryside with him, but particularly enjoyed being in the lovely house he was given by the Delhi Administration on the graceful Alipore Road – north of

New Delhi, on the other side of Daryaganj. I loved spending my vacations there, on one side of the historical 'Ridge' where some of the last battles of the Mutiny of 1857 had been fought, with Delhi University on the other side. I ventured across the hill into the campus quite regularly, where more than a decade later I would actually teach. On those early occasions, my ambition was limited to walking around in the campus, exploring the library on a day pass, and drinking cups of cold coffee in the coffee house there. Typically during the summer vacation, the outside temperature was 115 degrees Fahrenheit (around 46 degrees Celsius), which made my journey up and down the steaming Ridge a challenging experience.

10

The British eventually left India in a great hurry, and its partition was perhaps the most rapidly decided bifurcation that any country has experienced before or after. Sir Cyril Radcliffe was given less than two months to draw the famous Radcliffe Line, splitting the country into two, beginning his work in late June and finishing in mid-August 1947. He was mainly guided, of course, by the proportions of Muslims and non-Muslims in different districts in British India, but many exceptions had to be found, some of which were understandable (such as geographic viability), while others looked unfathomable and arbitrary. I was sympathetic to the rumour that Radcliffe might have fallen asleep while working late at night, drawing his line. He returned to Britain as rapidly as he had come, with no visible attachment to the land that he had just divided.

There is, however, a postscript to the story. Many years later, in 1973, when I was teaching at the London School of Economics, I was invited to give a rather hyped-up set of lectures on economic problems at Warwick University called 'the Radcliffe Lectures', named after Sir Cyril. I spoke on the subject of economic inequality. Lord Radcliffe (as he had by then become) was, of course, an important person in Indian history and I asked the university whether I could go and see him, since he lived quite close to the campus. I was told at first that he did not particularly like talking to visiting Indians, but when he was told that I was not visiting but lived in London, he informed my hosts that he would be willing to have a cup of tea with me if I did not linger long. I was happy enough with that response (since I wanted to see him), and agreed to come for tea. But, just as I was preparing to leave the Vice Chancellor's room at Warwick University, I was told that Sir Cyril had just changed his mind and did not want to have tea that afternoon after all.

That gave me a bit more time to talk with my host, John Blackstock Butterworth, the first Vice Chancellor of Warwick University – an engaging academic often known as 'Jolly Jack', with whom I had a very pleasant conversation. He commented on the disappearance of my tea with Lord Radcliffe. He confessed he was very amused by the unpredictability of the 'old India hands'. 'I always wonder,' he told me, 'how this lot actually managed to run an empire.'

10

Britain and India

I

The British Empire in India was in effect established at the Battle of Plassey on 23 June 1757. The battle was swift, beginning at dawn and ending close to sunset. It was a normal monsoon day, with occasional rain in the mango groves at the town of Plassey, which is between Calcutta, where the British were based, and Murshidabad, the capital of the kingdom of Bengal. It was in those mango groves that the British forces faced the Nawab Siraj-ud-Doula's army and convincingly defeated it.

Among the questions that engaged us, as our schooldays were coming to an end nearly 200 years later, was the reason for the ease of the British victory. Why was it such a cake-walk for the British to defeat the Nawab of Bengal, a rich kingdom in a region that was well known in Europe? The British, although they had a significantly smaller army, had much greater firepower and stricter military discipline. Such standard military reasons were undoubtedly important, and yet there were also questions about the role played by the divided nature of Siraj's forces.

During the British rule of the subcontinent that followed the battle, much would be made of the supposedly irreconcilable hostility in India of Hindus and Muslims (the British were allegedly there to keep these communities apart) and a theory was advanced that it was the disunity between them that helped to ruin Siraj. This was, however, not the case at all. There was no significant hostility between Hindus and Muslims in Bengal, and Siraj's government in Murshidabad had not departed from the even-handed treatment of Hindus and Muslims that had characterized Muslim rule in Bengal after the initial asymmetries of Muslim conquest. Siraj had placed a Hindu, Mir Madan, in one of the highest positions in his court and Madan remained Siraj's only loyal general to the very end: he died fighting against the British at Plassey. Siraj's Chief Minister, Mohan Lal, was also a Hindu, who remained totally loyal to the king. Siraj's army had three divisions, led by three conspirators against him – two Muslims, Mir Jafar (Siraj's uncle) and Yar Latif Khan, and one Hindu, Rai Durlabh.

When Robert Clive was marching towards Plassey and still pretending to be seeking peace (this deception was, of course, a part of his strategy), he wrote to Siraj proposing that their disputes could be placed for arbitration before people whom the young Nawab trusted, namely, as Clive put it, 'Jagat Seth, Raja Mohan Lal, Mir Jafar, Rai Durlabh, Mir Madan and the rest of your great men'. This is a list of one Muslim and four Hindus in what Clive saw as the inner circle of the Muslim king of Bengal.

The divisions and intrigues in Murshidabad which Clive managed to foster were on entirely different lines from those of religion. They were mainly driven by the search for power and profit. With the decline of previous imperial powers in Bengal, double-dealings were a regular part of the activities both of the local moneyed gentry and of the European traders in Bengal. This included not only the British and the Indian merchants and financiers, but also the French. Indeed, the French remained in alliance with Siraj until Plassey, and gave him periodical reassurances of support – but provided no help when Siraj needed it most. The person at the centre of the treason turned out to be Siraj's uncle, Mir Jafar, whose desire to seize the throne was both strong and much encouraged by Clive. Mir Jafar's role was quite crucial in the military combat. Right in the middle of the battle, the division that he commanded on the Nawab's side suddenly left the fight. It simply quit, which seemed to have been his arrangement with Clive.

On the evening of his victory, Clive received a felicitating letter from Mir Jafar, the key conspirator: 'I congratulate you on executing your design.' Clive went on to execute Siraj, who remained courageous and defiant to the end. He put Mir Jafar on the throne, with nominal power, at the mercy of his British masters. The empire thus began with an event that turned not on any religious division, but on an elaborately worked out conspiracy that rewarded betrayal. Had Plassey been a cricket match, Skipper Clive would have been barred from participating in further games for many years to come.

British rule ended nearly 200 years later with Jawaharlal Nehru's famous speech on India's 'tryst with destiny' at midnight on 14 August 1947. As the Union Jack was being lowered across the subcontinent, there was no lack of discontent about erstwhile colonial dominance, and one did not have to stay up late listening to Nehru to understand the joyful significance of its ending. It is no secret that many Indians found it agreeable that the favourite tune of the British Army was 'Beating Retreat'. However, in 1944, when I first heard that haunting piece of music, there was little sign that the British were ready to retreat from India. When independence came rather suddenly three years later, ending 'the biggest Empire ever, bar none', as the distinguished historian Niall Ferguson describes it in his engaging book *Empire* – a guarded but enthusiastic history of British imperialism – there was some surprise and much celebration in India.

2

Two hundred years is a long time. What did the British achieve in India, and what did they fail to accomplish? In the chatty life of Santiniketan these questions came into our discussion constantly. They remain important even today, not least because the British Empire is often invoked in discussions about successful global governance. It has also been invoked (again by Niall Ferguson) to try to persuade the United States to acknowledge its role as the pre-eminent imperial power in the world today: 'Should the United States seek to shed – or to shoulder – the imperial load it has inherited?' It is certainly an interesting question, and Ferguson is right to argue that it cannot be answered without an understanding of how the British Empire rose and fell – and what it managed to do.

Arguing about all this at Santiniketan, we were bothered by a difficult methodological question. How could we think about what India would have been like in the 1940s had British rule not occurred? The frequent temptation to compare India in 1757 (when British rule was beginning) with India in 1947 (when the British were leaving) would tell us very little, because in the absence of British rule India would of course not have remained the same as it was at the time of Plassey. The country would not have stood still had the British conquest not occurred. But how do we answer the question about what difference was made by British rule?

To illustrate the relevance of such an 'alternative history', we may consider another case – one with a potential imperial conquest which did not in fact occur. Let's think about Commodore Matthew Perry of the US Navy, who steamed into the bay of Edo in Japan in 1853 with four warships. Now consider the possibility that Perry was not merely making a show of American strength (as was in fact the case), but was instead the advance guard of an American conquest of Japan, establishing a new American empire in the land of the rising sun, rather as Clive did in India. If we were to assess the achievements of the supposed American rule of Japan through the simple device of comparing Japan before that imperial conquest in 1853 with Japan after the American domination ended, whenever that might be, and attribute all the differences to the effects of the empire, we would miss all the contributions of the Meiji Restoration from 1868 onwards, and of other globalizing changes that were going on. Japan did not stand still; nor would India have done so.

While we can see what actually happened in Japan under Meiji rule, it is extremely hard to guess with any confidence what course the history of the Indian subcontinent would have taken had the British conquest not occurred. Would India have moved, like Japan, towards modernization in an increasingly globalizing world, or would it have remained resistant to change, like Afghanistan, or would it have hastened slowly, like Thailand? These are impossibly difficult questions to answer. And yet, even without real alternative historical scenarios, there are some limited questions that *can* be answered which may contribute to an intelligent understanding of the role that British rule played in India. We can ask: what were the challenges that India faced at the time of the British conquest, and what happened in those critical areas during the British rule? There was surely a need for major changes in a rather chaotic and institutionally backward India.

3

To recognize the need for change in India in the mid-eighteenth century does not require us to ignore – as many Indian super-nationalists fear – the great achievements in India's past, with its extraordinary history of accomplishments in philosophy, mathematics, literature, arts, architecture, music, medicine, linguistics and astronomy. India had also achieved considerable success in building a thriving economy with flourishing trade and commerce well before the colonial period – the economic wealth of India was amply acknowledged by British observers such as Adam Smith (as we discussed in Chapter 2). The fact is, nevertheless, that even with those achievements, in the mid-eighteenth century India had in many ways fallen well behind what was being achieved in Europe. The exact nature and significance of this backwardness were frequent subjects of lively debates in the evenings at Santiniketan School.

In thinking about this, an insightful essay on India that Karl Marx published in the *New York Daily Tribune* in 1853 particularly engaged the attention of some of us. Marx pointed to the constructive role of British rule in India, on the grounds that India needed some radical re-examination and self-scrutiny. And Britain did indeed serve as India's primary Western contact, particularly in the course of the nineteenth century. The importance of this influence would be hard to neglect. The indigenous globalized culture that was slowly emerging in India was deeply indebted not only to British writing, but also to books and articles in other – that is non-English – European languages that became known in India through the British. Consider, for instance, Christopher Bayly's important example (in his all-encompassing book *The Birth of the Modern World, 1780–1914*) that the Calcutta philosopher Ram Mohan Roy, born in 1772, 'made in two decades an astonishing leap from the intellectual status of a late-Mughal state intellectual to that of the first Indian liberal ... [He] independently broached themes that were being simultaneously developed in Europe by Garibaldi and Saint-Simon.' To understand Roy's creativity, it is necessary to appreciate that his far-reaching deliberations were influenced not only by his traditional knowledge of Sanskrit, Arabic and

Persian texts, but also very strongly by the growing familiarity of Indian intellectuals with English writings circulating in Calcutta under the East India Company's patronage.

Ram Mohan Roy was only one of many such radical intellectuals. After him, in Bengal itself there were also Ishwar Chandra Vidyasagar, Michael Madhusudan Dutta and several generations of Tagores and their followers who were re-examining the India they had inherited in the light of what they saw happening in Europe in the eighteenth and nineteenth centuries. Their main – often their only – source of information were the books (usually in English) circulating in India, thanks to British rule. That intellectual influence, covering a wide range of European cultures, survives strongly today, even as the military, political and economic power of the British has declined dramatically. I was persuaded that Marx was basically right in his diagnosis of the need for some radical change in India, as its old order was crumbling as a result of not having been a part of the intellectual and economic globalization that the Renaissance and the Industrial Revolution had initiated across the world (along with, alas, colonialism).

There was arguably, however, a serious flaw in Marx's thesis, in particular in his implicit presumption that the British conquest was the only window on the modern world that could have opened for India. What India needed at the time was more constructive globalization, but that is not the same thing as imperialism. The distinction is important. Throughout India's long history, it persistently enjoyed exchanges of ideas as well as of commodities with the outside world. Traders, settlers and scholars moved between India and further east – China, Indonesia, Malaysia, Cambodia, Vietnam, Thailand and elsewhere – for a great many centuries beginning more than two thousand years ago. The far-reaching influence of this movement – especially on language, literature and architecture – can be seen plentifully even today. There were also huge global influences by means of India's open-frontier attitude in welcoming fugitives – and other settlers from abroad – from its very early days.

Jewish immigration into India began right after the fall of Jerusalem in the first century and continued over many hundreds of years. Baghdadi Jews, such as the highly successful Sassoons, came in large numbers even as late as the eighteenth century. Christians started coming at least from the fourth century – possibly much earlier. There are colourful legends about this, including one which tells us that the first person that St Thomas the Apostle met after coming to India in the first century was a Jewish girl playing the flute on the Malabar coast. We loved that evocative – and undoubtedly apocryphal – anecdote in our discussions in Santiniketan, because it illustrated the multicultural roots of Indian traditions.

The Parsees started arriving from the early eighth century – as soon as persecution began in their Iranian homeland. Later in that century, the Armenians began to leave their footprints on India, from Kerala to Bengal. Muslim Arab traders had a substantial presence on the west coast of India from around that time – well before the arrival of Muslim conquerors many centuries later, through the arid terrain in the north-west of the subcontinent. Persecuted Baha'is from Iran came only in the nineteenth century.

I have already described the long-established trading connections, stretching back nearly two thousand years near the mouth of the Ganges – close to the location from where the East India Company launched its first conquest of India in the eighteenth century. At the time of Plassey, there were businessmen, traders and other professionals from a number of different European nations well settled there already. Being subjected to imperial rule is thus not the only way of making connections with, or learning things from, foreign countries. When the Meiji Restoration established a new reformist government in Japan in 1868 (which was not unrelated to the internal political impact of Commodore Perry's show of force a decade earlier), the Japanese went straight to learning from the West without being subjected to imperialism. They sent people for training in America and Europe, and made institutional changes that were clearly inspired by Western experience. They did not wait to be coercively globalized via imperialism.

4

In reflecting on all this in our debates on British rule in India at the time of independence, we tried to make extensive use of the global history on which Santiniketan School was so very keen, going up and down our open-shelf library at all hours of the day. We concluded that

the British probably did give India a much-needed jolt, but the awakening could have come in other ways as well.

However, we had no firm account to champion as an alternative to
British rule. The reforms that came from British administrators were,
by contrast, admirably concrete. Britain did become India's pre-
eminent Western contact, and this was certainly intimately bound up
with the Empire. To recognize this is not in any way to ignore the
alternative courses that India could have taken if it had not fallen
under British subjugation – that is an important but completely separate question. However, what did actually happen – the process of
change that in fact occurred – certainly deserves special attention.

What do we find on that line of enquiry? One of the achievements
to which British imperial theorists tended to give a good deal of
emphasis was the role of the British in producing a *united* India. In
this analysis, India was a collection of fragmented kingdoms until
British rule made a country out of these diverse regimes. It was argued
that India was previously not one country at all, but a thoroughly
divided land mass. It was the British Empire, so the claim goes, that
welded India into a nation. Winston Churchill even remarked that,
before the British came, there was no Indian nation. 'India is a geographical term. It is no more a united nation than the Equator.'

If this is true, the Empire clearly made an indirect contribution to
the modernization of India through its unifying role. Reforms of the
kind that Japan undertook in the Meiji period would have been hard
to achieve in a country without some unity. However, is the grand
claim about the big role of the Raj in bringing about a united India
correct? Certainly, when Clive's East India Company defeated the
Nawab of Bengal in 1757, there was no single power ruling over all
of India. Yet it is a great leap from the proximate story of Britain
imposing a single united regime on India (as did actually occur) to the
huge claim that only the British could have created a united India out
of a set of disparate states.

That way of looking at Indian history would go firmly against the
reality of the large domestic empires that had characterized India over
the millennia. The ambitious and energetic emperors from the third
century BC (beginning with Chandragupta Maurya) did not accept
that their regimes were complete until the bulk of what they took to

be one country was united under their rule. There were major roles here for Ashoka Maurya, the Gupta emperors, Alauddin Khalji, the Mughals and others. Indian history shows a sequential alternation of large domestic empires with clusters of fragmented kingdoms. We should therefore not make the mistake of assuming that the fragmented governance of mid-eighteenth-century India at the time of Clive was the state in which the country typically found itself throughout history, until the British helpfully came along to unite it.

Even though in history textbooks the British were often assumed to be the successors of the Mughals in India, it is important to note that the British did not in fact take on the Mughals when they were a force to be reckoned with. British rule began when the Mughals' power had declined, though formally even the Nawab of Bengal, whom the British defeated, was still their subject. The Nawab still swore allegiance to the Mughal emperor, without paying very much attention to his dictates. The imperial status of the Mughal authority over India continued to be widely acknowledged even though the powerful empire itself was missing.

When the so-called 'sepoy mutiny' threatened the foundations of British India in 1857, the diverse anti-British forces participating in the joint rebellion could be aligned through their shared acceptance of the formal legitimacy of the Mughal emperor as the ruler of India. The emperor was, in fact, reluctant to lead the rebels, but this did not stop the rebels from declaring him the Emperor of all India. The eighty-two-year-old Mughal monarch, Bahadur Shah II, known as Zafar, was far more interested in reading and writing poetry than in fighting wars or ruling India. He could do little to help the 1,400 unarmed civilians of Delhi whom the British killed as the mutiny was brutally crushed and the city largely destroyed. The poet-emperor was banished to Burma, where he died some five years later.

As a child growing up in Burma in the 1930s, I was taken by my parents to see Zafar's grave in Rangoon, which was close to the famous Shwedagon Pagoda. The grave was not allowed to be anything more than an undistinguished stone slab covered with corrugated iron. I remember discussing with my father that the British rulers of India and Burma must evidently have been afraid of the evocative power of the remains of the last Mughal emperor. The inscription on the grave noted only that 'Bahadur Shah was ex-King of Delhi' – no mention of 'empire' in the commemoration! It was only much later, in the 1990s, that Zafar would be honoured with something closer to what could decently serve as the grave of the last Mughal emperor.

5

In the absence of the British Raj, the most likely successors to the Mughals would probably have been the newly emerging Hindu Maratha powers near Bombay, who periodically sacked the Mughal capital of Delhi and exercised their power to intervene across India. Already by 1742, the East India Company had built a huge 'Maratha ditch' at the edge of Calcutta to slow down the lightning raids of the Maratha cavalry, which rode rapidly across a thousand miles or more. But the Marathas were still quite far from putting together anything like the plan of an all-India empire.

The British, by contrast, were not satisfied until they were the dominant power across the bulk of the subcontinent, and in this they were not so much bringing a new vision of a united India from abroad as acting as the successor of previous domestic empires. British rule spread to the rest of the country from its imperial foundations in Calcutta, beginning almost immediately after Plassey. As the Company's power expanded across India, Calcutta became the capital of the newly emerging empire, a position it occupied from the mid-eighteenth century until 1911 (when the capital was moved to Delhi) and it was from Calcutta that the conquest of other parts of India was planned and directed. The profits made by the East India Company from its economic operations in Bengal financed, to a great extent, the wars that the British waged across India in the period of their colonial expansion.

What has been widely called 'the financial bleeding of Bengal' began very soon after Plassey. With the Nawabs under their control, the Company made big money not only from territorial revenues, but also from the unique privilege of duty-free trade in the rich Bengal economy – even without counting the so-called 'gifts' that the Company regularly extracted from local merchants. Those who wish to be inspired by the glory of the British Empire would do well to avoid reading Adam Smith's *The Wealth of Nations*, including his discussion of the abuse of state power by a 'mercantile company which oppresses and domineers in the East Indies'. As the historian William Dalrymple has observed:

> The economic figures speak for themselves. In 1600, when the East India Company was founded, Britain was generating 1.8% of the world's GDP, while India was producing 22.5%. By the peak of the Raj, those figures had more or less been reversed: India was reduced from the world's leading manufacturing nation to a symbol of famine and deprivation.

While most of the loot from the financial bleeding accrued to British company officials in Bengal, there was widespread participation by the political and business leadership in Britain: nearly a quarter of the Members of Parliament in London owned stocks in the East India Company after Plassey. The commercial benefits from Britain's Indian empire thus reached far into the British establishment. The robber-ruler synthesis did eventually give way to what would become classical colonialism, with the recognition of the need for law and order and a modicum of reasonable governance. But the early misuse of state power by the East India Company put the economy of Bengal under huge stress. What the cartographer John Thornton, in his famous chart of the region in 1703, had described as 'the Rich Kingdom of Bengal' experienced a gigantic famine during 1769–70. Contemporary estimates suggested that about a third of the Bengal population died. This is almost certainly an overestimate and we spent quite a bit of time in Santiniketan trying to figure out how high the numbers might actually have been. There was no doubt, however, that it was a huge catastrophe, with massive starvation and mortality – in a region that had seen no famine for a very long time.

This disaster had at least two significant effects. First, the inequity of early British rule in India became the subject of considerable political criticism in Britain itself. By the time Adam Smith roundly declared in *The Wealth of Nations* that the East India Company was 'altogether unfit to govern its territorial possessions', there were many British voices making similar critiques. The strongest indictment came famously from Edmund Burke, in his parliamentary speech at the impeachment of Warren Hastings in 1789. Burke's denunciation of Hastings was both powerful and eloquent, but his notions of Hastings's personal perfidy were seriously misplaced. Hastings tried, and to a great extent succeeded, in stopping the comprehensive British pillage of India, in contrast with his predecessors in charge of the Company, including Clive, whom – oddly enough – Burke greatly admired. However, Burke's general diagnosis of the extent of nastiness of the Company rule of India was not mistaken. Second, the economic decline of Bengal did eventually ruin the Company's business as well, hurting British investors themselves, and giving the powers in London reason to change their business in India into more of a regular state-run operation. By the time Burke denounced Hastings, the period of so-called 'post-Plassey plunder', with which British rule in India began, was giving way to the sort of colonial subjugation that would soon become the imperial standard, and with which the subcontinent would become more and more familiar over the following century and a half.

6

How successful was this long phase of classical imperialism in British India from the late eighteenth century to independence in 1947? The British claimed a huge set of achievements, including democracy, the rule of law, railways, the joint stock company and cricket, but the gap between theory and practice – with the exception of cricket – remained wide throughout the history of imperial relations between the two countries. Putting the tally together in the years of pre-independence assessment, it was easy to see how far short the achievements were compared with the rhetoric of accomplishment.

Indeed, Rudyard Kipling caught the self-congratulatory note of the British imperial administrator admirably well in his famous poem on imperialism:

> Take up the White Man's burden –
> The savage wars of peace –
> Fill full the mouth of Famine –
> And bid the sickness cease.

Alas, neither the stopping of famines nor the remedying of ill health was part of the high-performance achievements of British rule in India. Nothing could lead us away from the fact that life expectancy at birth in India as the empire ended was abysmally low – at most thirty-two years.

The abstemiousness of colonial rule in neglecting basic education reflects the view taken by the dominant administrators of the needs of the subject nation. There was a huge asymmetry between the ruler and the ruled. The British government became increasingly determined in the nineteenth century to achieve universal literacy for the native British population. In contrast, the literacy rates in India under the Raj were very low. When the Empire ended, the adult literacy rate in India was below 15 per cent. The only regions in India with comparatively high literacy were the 'native kingdoms' of Travancore and Cochin (formally outside the British Empire) which, since independence, have constituted the bulk of the state of Kerala. These kingdoms, though dependent on the British administration for foreign policy and defence, had remained technically outside the Empire and had considerable freedom in domestic policy, which they exercised in favour of more school education and public health care.

The 200 years of colonial rule were also a period of massive economic stagnation with hardly any advance at all in real GNP per capita. These grim facts were much aired after independence in the newly liberated media, whose rich culture was in part – it must be acknowledged – an inheritance from British civil society. Even though the Indian media was very often muzzled during the Raj – mostly to prohibit criticism of imperial rule, for example at the time of the Bengal famine of 1943 – the tradition of a free press, carefully cultivated in Britain, provided a good model for India to follow as the country achieved independence.

Indeed, India received many wonderful things from Britain that did not – could not – come into their own until after independence. Literature in the Indian languages took some inspiration and borrowed genres from English literature, including the flourishing tradition of writing in English in India. Under the Raj, there were restrictions on what could be published and propagated (even some of Rabindranath Tagore's books were banned). These days the government of India has no such need, but alas – for altogether different reasons of authoritarian domestic politics – the restrictions are sometimes no less intrusive than during the colonial rule.

Nothing is perhaps as important in this respect as the functioning of a multi-party democracy and a free press. But often enough these were not gifts that could be exercised under the British administration during imperial days. They became realizable only when the British left – that is, they were the fruits of learning from Britain's own experience which India could use freely only after the period of Empire had ended. Imperial rule tends to require some degree of tyranny: asymmetrical power is not usually associated with a free press or with a vote-counting democracy, since neither of them is compatible with the need to keep colonial subjects in check.

7

A similar scepticism is appropriate about the British claim that they had eliminated famine in dependent territories such as India. British governance of India began with the gigantic famine in 1769–70 and there were regular famines in India throughout the duration of British rule. The Raj also ended with the terrible famine of 1943, which I discussed in Chapter 7. In contrast, there has been no famine in India since independence in 1947.

The irony again is that the institutions that helped to end famines in independent India – democracy and a relatively free media – came directly from Britain. The connection between these institutions and famine prevention is simple to understand. Famines are easy to prevent, since the distribution of a comparatively small amount of free food, or the offering of some public employment at comparatively modest wages (which gives the beneficiaries of public employment the ability to buy food), allows those threatened by famine the ability to escape extreme hunger. So any government should be able to stop a threatening famine – large or small – and it is very much in the interest of a government in a functioning democracy, facing a free press, to do so. A free press makes the facts of a developing famine known to all, and a democratic vote makes it hard to win elections during – or after – a famine, hence giving a government the additional incentive to tackle the issue without delay.

India did not have this freedom from famine for as long as its people were without their democratic rights, even though it was being ruled by the foremost democracy in the world, with a famously free press in the metropolis – but not in the colonies. These freedom-oriented institutions were for the rulers but not for the imperial subjects.

In the powerful indictment of British rule in India that Rabindranath Tagore presented in 1941 (in a lecture given on the occasion of what proved to be his last birthday), he argued that India had gained a great deal from its association with Britain, for example from 'discussions centred upon Shakespeare's drama and Byron's poetry and above all . . . the large-hearted liberalism of nineteenth-century English politics'. The tragedy, he said in this last lecture ('Crisis in Civilization'), came from the fact that what 'was truly best in their own civilization, the upholding of dignity of human relationship, has no place in the British administration of this country'. The distinction between the role of Britain and that of British imperialism could not have been clearer. As the Union Jack was being lowered across India, it was a distinction of which we were profoundly aware.

PART THREE

The author, *c.* 1953.

11

The Urbanity of Calcutta

1

Rudyard Kipling called it 'the city of dreadful night'. Calcutta (or 'Kolkata' as the name is now spelt in English in an attempt at congruence with Bengali pronunciation), notorious for its poverty, wretchedness and squalor, would later move the saintly Mother Teresa to come and work there with the suffering and deprived. It continues to be seen across the world today as the embodiment of urban misery. It was, as discerned earlier, the 'big city' on the horizon of my childhood, the city through which we passed when moving between Dhaka and Santiniketan, where I was so struck by the variety of lifestyles that coexisted. It was in Calcutta as a child of nine that I stayed up late to see the Japanese bombs falling on the docks and where, the following year, I saw people dying from hunger on the streets. It was mostly to Calcutta that I went to see the members of my family held in 'preventive detention' by the Raj and where I began to reflect on the inequity of imperial tyranny.

While studying at Santiniketan School what was then called 'Intermediate Science', with the intention of doing my bachelor's degree in physics and mathematics, the idea of going to Calcutta came largely from wanting to study at Presidency College. I often talked with fellow students (Dipankar Chatterjee, Mrinal Datta Chaudhuri, Tan Lee, Amit Mitra, Shiv Krishna Kar and others) about the excellent education Presidency College apparently provided and its outstanding academic atmosphere. But I was also attracted by the big city itself, by the *Mahanagar* (literally, 'the great city') as Satyajit Ray called it in his wonderful film, lovingly describing Calcutta as a 'monstrous, teeming, bewildering' place.

Rudyard Kipling's condemnation of Calcutta had many distinct elements. One of them was his amazement that Job Charnock, an English trader, chose to found what was to become a modern city on such a terrible spot on the banks of the Ganges (or Hooghly):

> Where the cholera, the cyclone, and the crow
>> Come and go;
>
> . . .
>
> Stands a City – Charnock chose it – packed away
>> Near a Bay –
> By the sewage rendered fetid, by the sewer
>> Made impure,
> By the Sunderbunds unwholesome, by the swamp
>> Moist and damp;
> And the City and the Viceroy, as we see,
>> Don't agree.

Kipling's bewilderment at Charnock's decision to develop a city in what was seen as a most unfavourable spot has been shared by many others down to our times. Geoffrey Moorhouse, author of a well-researched and well-written history of the city, described it as 'an idiotic decision'. Idiotic or not, Charnock's decision was momentous. In August 1690, a little over 300 years ago, Charnock sailed up to a village called Sutanati (often spelt as 'Chuttanutti' by the uncertain English) and effectively established the local headquarters of the East India Company there. Sutanati was one of the three small towns that formed a cluster around which modern Calcutta grew, the other two being Gobindapur and Kalikata.

Over the next hundred years the city was transformed from the headquarters of a trading company into the capital of British India. Before the Battle of Plassey, the seat of the government of Bengal had been Dhaka, followed by Murshidabad, where the Nawab of Bengal was based. After Clive defeated and executed Siraj-ud-Doula, Calcutta became the natural place from which to govern the Company's territory in India, since this was where the British were already established.

2

Calcutta soon became 'the second city of the empire'. It was certainly larger than any other contender for that title until the middle of the twentieth century. That was, I suppose, reason enough, but Calcutta's attraction for me had nothing directly to do with that imperial history. For anyone interested in education, especially in science, Calcutta was hard to beat. In addition to Presidency College, there were many other good colleges for undergraduate education, such as St Xavier's College, Scottish Church College, City College and Asutosh College, and many other research institutions and centres of higher learning. Calcutta University, founded in 1857, was already famous. There were the Royal Asiatic Society of Bengal (later renamed the Asiatic Society), the Indian Statistical Institute, the Indian Association for the Cultivation of Science, the Saha Institute of Nuclear Physics, Bengal Technical College (which would serve as the base for the new Jadavpur University where I would work from 1956 to 1958, beginning my teaching life), the Bengal Engineering College, the Medical College, and many others. All this created a sense of exciting intellectual life in the city.

It was also the place where the so-called 'Bengal renaissance' had ushered in aspects of a modern culture into an ancient land, primarily through interactions of Indian culture (or cultures) with contributions from Europe. As Sushobhan Sarkar, the great historian who taught at Presidency College in Calcutta (and inspired a great many students there, including me) has powerfully argued, there was a basic intellectual awakening produced by the dialectical influence of the British on local traditions, whose profound impact on the lives and attitudes in Bengal makes the term 'renaissance' quite plausible. The traditional intellectual resources of Bengal were drawn into this radical process, allowing good use of Bengali, Sanskrit and Persian scholarship that was present among many of the educated Bengalis and residents of Calcutta.

Change was already under way in the late eighteenth century, especially after Warren Hastings – who may have been responsible for some colonial atrocities, like every other leader of the East India Company, but was also a great patron of culture and Indian traditions – took

charge of British administration in Calcutta. The founding of the Royal
Asiatic Society of Bengal in Calcutta in 1784 not only vastly expanded
interest in, and scholarly studies of, ancient India among the British,
but also dramatically increased the interactions between European
and Indian scholars. From the beginning of the nineteenth century new
colleges were founded, libraries were set up, systematic legal practice
received attention and support, theatres were developed for a growing
urban public, and there was a general spirit of excitement about the
need for change and the possibility of progress.

Through the influences of Ram Mohan Roy, Ishwar Chandra Vidyasagar, Bankim Chandra Chattopadhyay, Michael Madhusudan Dutt
to Rabindranath Tagore, Kazi Nazrul Islam and on to more recent
generations of Bengali writers (including Buddhadeb Bose, Bishnu
Dey, Jasimuddin, Shamsur Rahman, among others), Bengal has been a
great location of cultural transformation. Many of these writers challenged old ideas and modes of expression, and developed new ones,
struggled with old preconceptions and new criticisms, and helped to
establish urban and rural cultures in which debate and dispute, as well
as literary and cultural creation, became defining characteristics. By
the middle of the twentieth century, this intellectual ferment in Calcutta had given the city a reputation that was hard to match.

As I moved to Calcutta in July 1951, carrying my earthly possessions in a rusty old steel trunk, the city was water-logged after a
couple of days of heavy monsoon rain. Avoiding the puddles and
looking for a sensible path through the water, I could see that there
was a challenging life ahead.

3

While the British may have established modern Calcutta, many of
them, perhaps even most of them, did not like it much. They were
proud of what they had done there – and in the rest of India *from*
Calcutta – but not very happy with the way the city itself had
developed. Calcutta did, however, earn the reputation of being the
'city of palaces'. These were mostly new palaces constructed by the
British themselves, with Indian participation, since there was little to

inherit from India's past in the villages around which Calcutta was built. The city was quite unlike Dhaka and Murshidabad in this respect. The phrase emerged at the end of the eighteenth century, but it was James Atkinson who gave it its most famous literary outing in 1824, in a poem entitled 'The City of Palaces':

> I stood a wondering stranger at the *Ghaut*,
> And, gazing round, beheld the pomp of spires
> And palaces, to view like magic brought;
> All glittering in the sun-beam.

That poem, which was once much celebrated, does not capture the image of Calcutta in the popular imagination today, and perhaps never did. The palaces didn't interest me much, even though I liked the large marble building called the Victoria Memorial Hall, in the middle of the maidan (the large old open space separating the business districts of Calcutta from the Ganges). The reality of the city was better captured for me by Kipling's unease than by Atkinson's admiration. Kipling's 'A Tale of Two Cities' (1922) contrasts Calcutta very unfavourably with Simla:

> As the fungus sprouts chaotic from its bed,
>   So it spread –
> Chance-directed, chance-erected, laid and built
>   On the silt –
> Palace, byre, hovel – poverty and pride –
>   Side by side;
> And, above the packed and pestilential town,
>   Death looked down.

Ved Mehta points out that Kipling's outlook, 'when not that of an imperialist, was that of a pragmatic Lahori with perhaps a trace of the spirituality of Allahabad'. Despite this and other speculations that Kipling poured into his denunciation of Calcutta, his views are still well remembered, largely because, as Mehta argues, 'the passing of years has only preserved and multiplied the horrors of the city.'

Did Kipling really see it right? If he did, why is Calcutta so loved not only by those who end up living there, but also those who have had the chance to reflect and the opportunity to choose, and yet firmly decide to stay on? The cultural and intellectual richness of the city is certainly part of it. This does nothing to wipe out the poverty and chaos of Calcutta, of course, but those who love to live in Calcutta come for the many positive things the city offers.

Even though the Bengal renaissance was a direct result of the response of local traditions to the arrival of European thought, through British rule, the British were barely aware of what was going on. This was partly because of a lack of genuine interest on the part of the colonial masters, but also because much of what happened was in a language – Bengali – that the British rulers and merchants did not typically understand or try to learn.

Amit Chaudhuri (now a Professor at Oxford) notes the strangeness of the phenomenon:

> For the Englishman, both Indian modernity and the Indian modern were invisible. In a sense, then, Calcutta, to him, was invisible. Kipling, writing in the midst of the Renaissance, populates his magical stories of India with talking wolves, tigers, cheetahs, and orphan Indian children who have no trouble communicating with animals. No one would know, reading Kipling, that Bagheera, Sher Khan, and Mowgli are neighbours and contemporaries of the novelist Bankim Chandra Chatterjee and the poet Michael Madhusudan Dutt. In Kipling's universe – and to a considerable extent, in Britain's – the Renaissance, and Bengali and Indian modernity, might as well have never happened in India's uninterrupted, fabulous time.

4

Was Kipling's accusation about the stupidity of the choice of Calcutta as the location for the capital of the East India Company well reasoned? The question 'why there?' interested me long before I moved to Calcutta and was one of the subjects of my informal research in Santiniketan's open-shelved library – 'my favourite location' as I had told my grandfather. Kshiti Mohan was a great help in pursuing my interest in the long history of the Calcutta region. The question can be divided into two parts: first, why *generally* there – near the southernmost end of Gangetic Bengal, broadly around the Hooghly river? And, second, why *specifically* on that spot, on the east bank of Hooghly, in the terrain holding the three minor towns of Sutanati, Gobindapur and Kalikata? The second question can be answered easily enough. The British had the southernmost site among the factories then in existence, closer to the sea than those of the Portuguese and the Dutch manufacturers and traders, and better placed for exporting goods. Another advantage of the downriver location was that any hostile attack from the north – for example from the Mughals if they decided to challenge what was happening in Bengal – would have faced the Dutch and the Portuguese first. Furthermore, by choosing a site on the eastern side of the river, Job Charnock was also better placed to challenge land-based armies coming from the west – whether from Murshidabad or Delhi, or from the rising power of the Marathas near Bombay.

The bigger question, however, is the choice of the general Calcutta region. When the East India Company – founded by a group of merchants in London in 1600 – came to India shortly afterwards, it was to trade. Conquest and the establishment of an Indian empire was far from English intentions at this time, even though it is too much to say, as was once famously claimed, that the British Empire was created in 'a fit of absence of mind'. For about fourteen years before he was sent to Bengal, Charnock was elsewhere in India – mostly in Patna, developing the British trade there in saltpetre. As his role in the Company's business expanded, he had to make secure and expand the far more lucrative trade of the Company in various locally made products of Indian industry, including cotton, muslin and silk goods, famously made in Bengal, but also commodities produced in north India that came downriver from the Ganges, the Jamuna and their tributaries, to be shipped overseas.

Charnock was anxious to secure the authorization of the Company's activities from the Mughals in Delhi (which he sought and obtained), but he also took note of the weak hold, by then, of Mughal officials in charge of Bengal. There was no question of relying on Mughal protection to make his base there secure. Charnock knew how important the downriver trade was to the Company, and how significant Bengal itself was as the richest province of India at that time. Thornton's famous chart of the Hooghly River, drawn in 1703, with a map of the plentiful towns and trading settlements along the lower Ganges, described the province in large emphatic letters as 'the Rich Kingdom of Bengal'.

And, of course, the English were by no means the only foreigners to understand the economic importance of the region. The Portuguese had arrived there nearly a century earlier in 1518 and built three different settlements in the same Hooghly district. The Dutch came in 1632 and established a factory in neighbouring Chinsurah. As J. J. A. Campos explained in his *History of the Portuguese in Bengal*, published a hundred years ago, 'In Indo-European history there is not, undoubtedly, a more interesting Indian town than Hooghly because there, within a range of a few miles, seven European nations fought for supremacy: the Portuguese, the Dutch, the English, the Danes, the French, the Flemish, and the Prussians.'

Charnock's choice of the general Calcutta area could hardly be seen as eccentric.

5

The history of the Calcutta region and its economic role go much further back than the period in which the Europeans became active there. The Bengali *Mangal Kavyas* (narratives in poetry), which were written from the thirteenth century onwards, dwell on it in great detail. As a boy I had read the most famous of them, *Manasamangal* by Bipradas, who apparently lived near today's Calcutta in the fifteenth century. Bipradas refers to both Kalikata and to nearby Kalighat (the location of an old temple of Kali) as towns that his rebellious hero Chand, a naval merchant and oceanic trader, described as he went down the river towards the sea.

Perhaps more significantly, the region has had urban settlements since at least the second century BC. There are ancient sites within a short distance of Calcutta, and the archaeological excavation at one of those sites, called Chandraketugarh (only about twenty miles from the city), was in progress when I was moving to the city; it was gradually revealing extensive remnants of an ancient town, including fortifications and public buildings. Almost any serious digging in the region seemed to yield commodities for use in an urban setting – ornaments, statuettes, exhibits and of course utensils – going back to the Sunga period, more than 2,000 years ago (flourishing between 185 BC and 73 BC), and the Kushana period that followed it.

I kept reading about the excavations, but could not find the time and opportunity to go and see them for myself. Road transport in Bengal has always tended to be poor, and even the twenty miles to Chandraketugarh – as the crow flies – would have taken a long time on the shockingly bad roads. I eventually managed to get there in 2005, after a friend, Gopal Gandhi (the grandson of both Mahatma Gandhi and another leading statesman, C. Rajagopalachari), became Governor of Bengal. We went there together in his car: it took a couple of hours on still rickety roads. I was very interested to listen to Gopal describe his own research into the history of the region – an unusual activity for a governor to undertake.

Ancient remains from this part of Bengal's past are scattered around the general Calcutta region, but their presence within the city of Calcutta itself – the present location of the ancient urban complex – has come to light only recently, driven in the first instance not by archaeological interest but rather by demands of modern town planning. When the underground metro system was built in the city between 1972 and 1995 by Indian Railways (it was the first underground railway in India), the digging unearthed pottery and other materials for ornament and use from more than 2,000 years ago. Then, in 2001, when the city decided to restore the house in which Robert Clive had lived, the excavations there produced remnants of an urban civilization from the same Sunga–Kushana period, including ancient pottery, fine fabric, bricks for buildings, a floor made of lime and brick, a hearth, and coins and seals that were evidence of vigorous trading activities from at least the second century BC. The findings were not entirely a surprise, given what was already known about the Calcutta region, but they left no doubt that Charnock had decided to base his business in a region that had been an important centre of transport and commerce for a very long time.

I was tempted at one time to consider the possibility of writing a 'real history of Calcutta' – and perhaps someday I will. On the basis of my reading in the Santiniketan library, I was quite sure already that the city I was moving to was not just 300 years old, as Calcutta is so often described. It was also clear that the founding was not so much a case of the East India Company bringing global trade to Calcutta, but of the region bringing global trade to the Company – which decided to settle in an area of established urban living and a long history of being economically active.

6

By early 1951, I was becoming more and more excited about joining Presidency College and living in Calcutta. An immediate question was where should I stay? Presidency College had two student hostels, but the hostel system continued the British policy of maintaining communal divisions between Muslims and Hindus, which looked like a perpetuation of the old 'divide and rule'. I was offered accommodation in what was called the 'Hindu Hostel'. I did not warm to the idea. Indeed, I thought that communal divisiveness did not fit at all with post-independence secular India, nor with the completely nondenominational nature of Presidency College itself. Even though the College had been named as a 'Hindu College' in the early nineteenth century, it was never only for Hindus and never discriminated on the basis of the religion of the student. In fact, by 1855 – nearly a hundred years before I arrived – it had abandoned its sectarian name as well. Having seen so much communal bloodshed during my schooldays, I was resistant even to the symbolic aspect of settling myself somewhere – the Hindu Hostel – with a clear communal identification.

So I found a place – a shared room (and later a modest single room) – at the YMCA hostel at Mechua Bazar, which involved a walk of about twenty minutes from the College. I moved there in early July 1951. The YMCA was not, of course, meant specifically for Christians – students from all religions could be found there. And the residents, all of whom were students, studied different subjects at a number of colleges in Calcutta. I greatly enjoyed this diversity, and enjoyed talking frequently with my co-residents. We often stayed up late into the night, conversing on the spacious verandas of the old YMCA.

Calcutta is a great city for idle chatting – what Bengalis call *adda* – an agenda-less free discussion on any topic that might come up. I soon discovered that I loved *adda* more than almost any other way of passing time. I had a nice *adda* with the Warden of the YMCA on the day I arrived. Mr Mukherjee, who was a devoted Christian, was toying with the idea, he told me, of voting for the Communist Party in the up-coming election. 'Do you agree with the Party's policies?' I asked him. 'No,' he said, 'they are not very nice to those they do not like, and they are against all religions, and I am against them really. But they can probably do a lot of good for the state of West Bengal, where the ruling Congress Party does not seem to want to do anything at all.' As I sat down for my first evening meal and chatted with Mr Mukherjee, I decided I liked his point-counterpoint approach. It somehow fitted in with my image of Calcutta and my expectations of the city. My initial scepticism that Mr Mukherjee might be a babbler soon gave way to real admiration for someone who was clearly willing to think in unusual ways about politics and society and the political demands of religion, despite what I assumed was his strict religious upbringing.

The most convenient walking route from Mechua Bazar to College Street, where Presidency College is located, went through some rather impoverished areas, as well as others with well-stocked shops and offices, particularly on Harrison Road (now called Mahatma Gandhi Road). Then, as I came closer to Presidency College and turned the corner from Harrison Road into College Street, there was suddenly a massive constellation of bookshops of every kind. From books protected by glass-fronted wooden bookshelves inside the solidly built shops to heaps and heaps of books precariously balanced on ad hoc pedestals on the pavements – a million books calling for attention. I had the wonderful sense that I had come to the right place on earth.

7

I was amazed how quickly I got used to living in Calcutta. As a child who grew up in Dhaka, I did of course have a little sense of rivalry with long-term Calcutta residents – 'Calcuttans' as they used to be called then, or 'Kolkata-*basi*' (residents of Kolkata) in proper Bengali. India had been partitioned four years earlier and Bengalis had been relocated into two different countries. The Hindu–Muslim hostility, much of which, as I have discussed earlier, had been politically engineered, was by then giving way (on both sides of the border) to a reaffirmed sense of Bengali unity, even though occasionally political sectarians would do their best to stir up trouble.

Calcutta was, and is, a wonderfully multicultural city. Of course, Bengalis form the majority of the population, but there are large communities of Biharis, Tamils, Malayalis, Oriyas, Marwaris, Anglo-Indians (Eurasians), Chinese, Nepalese, Tibetans, Armenians and others. Among the languages that are widely spoken are Bengali, Hindi, English, Bhojpuri, Maithili, Urdu, Chinese and many more. If there is something of which Calcutta can be proud, it is that, unlike other metropolitan cities, it has not had to contend with significant anti-immigrant movements. By contrast, in the politics of Bombay (or Mumbai, as it has been renamed), activists favouring, say, Maharashtrians, have sometimes been forcefully anti-Tamil. There have been very few attempts at such anti-immigration politics in Calcutta.

It is also particularly striking to see how Calcutta's British colonial heritage, once deeply resented, has been absorbed into the tolerant memory of a warm multicultural history. Nationalist movements against British rule had strong support in Calcutta from the latter part of the nineteenth century. The powerfully nationalist Indian Association, led by the famous Surendranath Banerjee, was established in Calcutta in 1883, two years before the first meeting of the Indian National Congress in Bombay. Subhas Chandra Bose also came from a solidly Calcutta family. Unquiet nationalists who were willing to consider the use of violent rebellion in the battle for Indian independence were significantly more plentiful in Bengal than anywhere else in India.

And yet, today, the relics of British rule are among the city's most treasured landmarks. The beautiful Town Hall, built in 1813 for social gatherings of Europeans in the days of the East India Company, has been carefully renovated by the Calcutta Municipality, who have meticulously reconstructed a replica of the old building. Similarly, the Victoria Memorial Hall, built between 1905 and 1921, is sparklingly well preserved, and full of materials and illustrations from the time when the British were very much in command. Its museum receives more visitors each day than any other museum in the city – indeed, I am told, more than any other museum of any kind anywhere in India.

8

Calcutta was the first city in which I lived alone and experienced the life of a college student. The sense of freedom I had there might have reflected an element of liberation from my family, but I also adored the opportunities for *adda* in the coffee house next to my college, in the public spaces in the YMCA hostel, and of course in the homes of my friends. But I also soon discovered that Calcutta is a great city for walking, especially in the evening after the traffic dies down. And, since I was moving from being an early riser in Santiniketan to the 'late to bed' life in the big city, I could chat with friends in their homes and walk back to the YMCA well after midnight. Unlike in Trinity College, Cambridge, to which I would go later, where the college doors shut at 10 p.m., the YMCA had no strict curfew and no exact time by which one had to return, though you were required to tell the Warden if you were going to be late. I loved those long walks through the nocturnally quiet city. One of the results of Partition was that many of our friends and relations moved from the new East Pakistan to India, a huge proportion of them to Calcutta. This new proximity allowed these old relationships to become much closer and more accessible. Before I moved to Calcutta, I had not imagined how strikingly enjoyable my friendships with cousins such as Mejda, Miradi, Khokonda, Ratnamala, Babua, Rabida, Piyali, Dula and others would become. I sometimes reached up a generation for conversations with cousins of my parents too, such as Chinikaka, Chotokaka, Kankarmama and others, all involved in different walks of life. Since my immediate friends at Presidency College or at the YMCA were almost invariably young, the generational variation added nicely to the reach of our conversations.

Walking around in Calcutta was itself always pleasant. Though I sometimes passed through areas known for crime, I never – absolutely never – encountered anyone who tried to rob me, or even stop me. I did not know then, as my later probing into urban statistics would reveal, that Calcutta had not only the lowest rate of serious crime in India, but one of the lowest homicide rates of all major cities in the world. That is an odd feature for one of the poorest cities in any country, and it raises a serious question about poverty being a major cause of crime.

If this rare characteristic of Calcutta is largely hidden – and largely unsung – its unusual distinction in terms of books and theatre and other forms of culture was more easily identified. Calcutta has hosted annually for many years the largest book fair (or *boi mela*) in the world where hundreds of thousands of people gather day after day over a fortnight or more. (The *boi mela*'s claim to be the largest book fair in the world is, of course, based on the number of people coming to the *mela* – not the volume of financial transactions, an accolade that must go to Frankfurt or London.) The huge crowd of visitors come to view new books and even to read bits of them, typically without being able to afford to buy them. The *boi mela* is a gigantic cultural event which brings a fresh burst of life to the city in early spring.

When I moved to Calcutta in 1951, the annual *boi mela* had finished, but theatre was certainly a source of much excitement and engagement. The city's reputation as a place with regular theatre was by then well established – it was the only one in India where you had the choice of several plays in different theatres on any night. Calcuttans understandably took pride in this and, as a new resident, so did I. Tickets were inexpensive and affordable, so I went often. It was a joy to have a choice of Bengali plays every evening, many of them with strong social and political themes.

The first theatre in Calcutta was the so-called Calcutta Theatre, founded in 1779, on the initiative of the British, although traditional plays known as *jatra* had been attracting a huge following in Bengal over the centuries. In 1795 a Russian dramatist, Herasim Lebedef, came to Calcutta and staged a couple of Bengali plays in collaboration with Bengali artists. His theatre house, the Hindu Theatre, was so successful that, when it caught fire, a rumour circulated rapidly in the city that the envious British had burnt it down (there was, in fact, little truth in that). But by the nineteenth century, many other regular theatres were being established.

One feature of the Bengali theatre in Calcutta was that women were able to play female parts decades before they were allowed to do so in any other city in India. Despite this unusual modernist tendency that distinguished Bengal at the time from much of the rest of India, there was still a disapproving gentry in Calcutta who were convinced that it was unseemly for women from 'good families' to be on the stage. Since my mother, coming from a family of academics, played the leading part in several of Tagore's dance dramas in the 1920s, I was aware of the debates surrounding this when I was very young (I discussed this cultural heterodoxy earlier on in the book). My mother's appearances had been seen as a scandal in some – happily rather limited – circles and a point of celebration and admiration in others.

The conservative circles in Calcutta not only disliked seeing 'respectable' women on the stage, they were sometimes opposed even to *jatra*s in Bengal. I enjoyed participating in the debates on this, and was particularly amused to learn about a famous Bengali educationist, Heramba Maitra, Principal of City College in Calcutta, who found himself with a moral dilemma when he was asked on the street by a young man whether he knew where the Minerva Theatre was. Disgusted by the young man's deplorable taste (Minerva was one of the theatres with regular women actors), Maitra replied with scorn that he did not know. Then, realizing that he had just lied, he ran back, huffing, to catch the baffled enquirer, grasped him by the shoulders, and said, 'I do know, but I will not tell you.'

9

Mahatma Gandhi, who was in many ways a traditional moralist, took a liberal – and supportive – attitude to the theatre, and indeed while he was passing through Calcutta went to see Bengali plays, despite the barrier of language. Gandhi's first visit to the city was on 4 July 1896, when he arrived by ship from Durban, but he left the same day. When he returned on 31 October that year, he decided to go and see a play on his very first evening, despite, I imagine, being tired from the long journey. Not discouraged by the language difficulty, he went again, to another Bengali play, on 7 November.

I did not know then the exact dates of those events, but I did know that Gandhi had seen Bengali plays on his way through the city, and I was curious about what he saw. That curiosity remained unsatisfied until his notes from that time were studied by his grandson, Gopal Gandhi. Thanks to Gopal's research on Calcutta's cultural history, we know that his grandfather had the choice between four Bengali plays, running on those nights in the Royal Bengal Theatre, the Emerald Theatre, the Star Theatre and the Minerva Theatre (though alas we do not know which of these Gandhi actually chose). Nevertheless it is clear that the pioneering Bengali theatre could take pride in the patronage it received from the person we like to see – with good reason – as 'the father of the nation'.

10

By the time I came to live in Calcutta, the voice of the left had become particularly strong in cultural matters, a development in which the Indian People's Theatre Association (the IPTA) played a leading role. This was in response to a number of influential events. The Bengal Famine of 1943 led directly to a very successful Bengali play entitled *Nabanna* ('New Crop' – the name of a traditional harvest festival), which presented a strong critique both of the colonial government and of the heartlessness of the market manipulators. It was written by Bijon Bhattacharya and directed by Sombhu Mitra – both very active in the IPTA – and was immensely successful. This inspired several other plays and a wonderful Hindi film of 1946, called *Dharti Ke Lal* ('Children of the Earth'), directed by Khwaja Ahmad Abbas. The new theatre movements recognized the powerful social causes which needed literary articulation, and this had an inspirational effect on the theatre-going Calcutta population – which definitely included me.

The film industry was still rather bound by convention all over India, but that too was beginning to change. A robust film of left-wing social critique, *Udayer Pathe*, appeared in 1944, and was often revived in the early 1950s. Quite the rage by my time was Italian neorealist cinema, which included *Bicycle Thieves* (1948) and *Miracle in Milan* (1951), both directed by Vittorio de Sica. The Italian neorealist tradition, which began with Luchino Visconti and Roberto Rossellini, was immensely popular and much discussed in our student circles. The impact of these films on the young in Calcutta is hard to over-estimate. Those influenced included Satyajit Ray, also a student at Presidency College ten years before me, who was deeply moved by *Bicycle Thieves*. Ray saw it in London – earlier than we could in Calcutta – and he wrote, 'I knew immediately that if I ever made *Pather Panchali* – and the idea had been at the back of my mind for some time – I would make it in the same way, using natural locations and unknown actors.' Soon enough that is exactly what he did.

I I

Despite all that Kipling listed in his charge sheet, I was rapidly falling in love with the city, much as I think Satyajit Ray had done. Discussing the choice of material for his films, Ray asks what his films should be about:

> What should you put in your films? What can you leave out? Would you leave the city behind and go to the village where cows graze in the endless fields and the shepherd plays his flute? You could make a film here that would be pure and fresh and have the flowing rhythm of a boatman's song.
>
> Or would you rather go back in time – way back to the Epics, where the gods and the demons took sides in the great battle where brother killed brother and Lord Krishna revivified a disconsolate prince with the words of the *Gita*? One could do exciting things here, using the great mimetic tradition of the *Kathakali*, as the Japanese use their Noh and Kabuki.
>
> Or would you rather stay where you are, right in the present, in the heart of this monstrous, teeming, bewildering city, and try to orchestrate its dizzying contrasts of sight and sound and milieu?

Those 'dizzying contrasts' engaged me profoundly. I recognized how quickly these variations and contrasts had become part of my life when I moved to Calcutta. I could see that I had been captivated, and even knew how it had happened.

12

College Street

I

Presidency College's long record of training some of the best scientists in the country gave it an academic dazzle that made it unique in my day – as indeed it still is. There was a galaxy of exceptional figures who had studied at the College and gone on to produce original work of major significance. Among the ones I knew well, Satyendra Nath Bose is well remembered for a number of major breakthroughs in physics, including the development of the 'Bose–Einstein statistics', and for categorizing, in effect, half the particles of the universe. Paul Dirac, the great physicist, whom I met later in Cambridge, had insisted on calling these particles 'bosons' in recognition of the critical importance of Bose's work. I had the opportunity of a brief conversation with Dirac about this when Piero Sraffa introduced me to him, in (I think) 1958, when we happened to be walking in the playing fields of St Johns, Dirac's college. Dirac was much better known than Bose, and I was struck by his concern to ensure that young Bose received the recognition he deserved.

Satyen Bose was an outstanding mathematical physicist who had a major impact on theoretical physics. He was a family friend and a colleague of my father at Dhaka University, which they had left together in 1945. What emerged as the Bose–Einstein statistics were first formulated by Bose while giving a lecture in Dhaka. At first he thought he had made a mistake, but then recognized that he had made a huge discovery. Whenever I visited Satyen Bose at his home and had the opportunity of chatting with him, I found myself quite mesmerized by his intellect. I was also very pleased that he seemed to have plenty of time to talk – in a relaxed way – in fact his abundant willingness to do so made me wonder when he found time for research.

A scientist of a very different kind, but who had also taught at Presidency College (before my time there), was Prasanta Chandra Mahalanobis. Not content with the excellent work he was doing in physics, he went on to become one of the founding fathers of the newly emerging subject of statistics. Mahalanobis was not only a close family friend, he was also a great Santiniketan personality. He had worked for some years as Rabindranath Tagore's academic secretary (a rather extraordinary choice of employment for a leading scientist at the peak of his creativity) and I knew him from the time I started walking. (My mother's album had a number of pictures of me as a child on Mahalanobis's shoulders, looking rather pleased, presumably because of the great height I had achieved.) By the time I was talking about going to college, Mahalanobis was busy running his new academic institution, the Indian Statistical Institute, which he made into one of the leading centres of statistical research and teaching in the world. But it was at Presidency College that his ideas of stretching the boundaries of statistics, especially in sampling theory, had emerged.

The fact that amazing things can be done with clusters of numbers through foundational reasoning in statistics came to me from one of my closest friends, Mrinal Datta Chaudhuri, who liked keeping track of developments in foundational statistics. He was interested in the work that Mahalanobis was doing on sampling, both at the theoretical level and with specific applications to randomly collected Indian data on such subjects as crops, food and people. Mrinal started his own investigation of the underlying analytical structure of statistical reasoning while still at our school in Santiniketan, and I remember having some captivating discussions with him about whether there was something in need of explanation in the fact that roads are empty most of the time even though there are such a lot of cars around. I understood something about random distributions of different kinds, but wondered whether we could really get *empirical* information about the world (such as relatively empty roads) on the basis of expectations formed through *analytical* reasoning (including ideas of randomness). Mrinal and I spent some time debating whether what looks like analytical reasoning may be no more than just a glorified description of what we are observing. Like me, Mrinal moved from Santiniketan School to Presidency College in July 1951, but, predictably, he chose to study statistics there.

2

It was on a monsoon-drenched day in July 1951 that I registered to do economics, with mathematics, at Presidency College. I had originally planned to study physics and mathematics, but changed my field of study, partly influenced by my friend Sukhamoy Chakravarty, who had already begun his study of economics at Presidency. Sukhamoy had visited Santiniketan a number of times during my last academic year. He came initially as a guest of a brilliant student (Bheltu, whose proper name was Subrata) with whom – and with his brother Chaltu – I used to spend a lot of time at Santiniketan. I met Sukhamoy then, and had really engaging conversations with him. He continued to visit quite regularly, to see more of the place – he was particularly keen on seeing the paintings of Mukul Dey, who lived in Santiniketan. I had never met anyone who knew so much and who could reason about any subject whatever with such ease and command. It was also apparent that Sukhamoy shared my concern about social inequality in India.

Sukhamoy asked me, 'Why don't you join me and do economics?' He pointed out that economics related more closely to my – and his – political interests, and that it gave just as much scope for analytical – and mathematical – reasoning (which he knew I liked) as the natural sciences. On top of that, economics was human and fun. And, not to be ignored (he added), the afternoons were free from laboratory work (unlike for the science students), so we could go to the coffee house just opposite the College. To Sukhamoy's arguments I could add the attraction of being in the same class as him and the chance of chatting with him regularly. I was gradually being persuaded to study economics (along with mathematics) rather than physics.

Unlike most universities in India at that time, in Presidency College learning mathematics was already seen as a necessity for doing serious economics and made the study of the subject more interesting. It also integrated more easily with interests from my schooldays, which included maths, along with Sanskrit. In addition I had a growing recognition that economics would be much more useful to me given my social interests and political involvements. I was already harbouring the idea of working for a different kind of India – one not as poor, nor as iniquitous and not at all as unjust as the country around me. Knowing some economics would be vital in the work of reshaping India.

I had wonderful discussions on these issues with Professor Amiya Dasgupta, who was another close family friend and a remarkable economist. Amiyakaka, as I called him, was Professor of Economics at Dhaka University, which he had left in 1945 (along with Satyen Bose, my father and others). Amiyakaka was very pleased to hear that I was considering the possibility of studying economics rather than physics. He gave me a couple of books by John Hicks, which I read with huge interest: *Value and Capital* and *The Social Framework*. The first was a model of clear-headed analysis in economic theory, dealing with some fundamental problems in price theory, and the second was a very broad attempt to see how the economic relations in a society actually work through their interdependence. I loved reading Hicks – the clarity and lucidity of his analyses were disarming – and I would come to recognize him as one of the leading economic thinkers of the twentieth century. Much later, when I came to know Hicks well at All Souls College at Oxford (we were colleagues there) and I told him about my early reading, he remarked with a broad smile, 'Now I know, Amartya, how deep-rooted your delusions about economics are!'

3

Even though Presidency College had become a government college a century before I arrived there to study, it began as an educational institution set up by an initiative of civil society in Calcutta nearly 200 years ago. The Hindu College (as it was called until 1855, though, as I have said, it was never only for Hindus) welcomed students from all communities in Calcutta, and had a good mixture from different backgrounds within a few decades. Its foundation committee was chaired by Raja Ram Mohan Roy – a great scholar (in Sanskrit, Persian, Arabic, Latin and several other European languages) and a tireless social reformer. The initiative to establish the College was a joint effort by leading intellectual figures in the city and, even though the governors and directors of the College were all Indians, its establishment was much inspired by the efforts of a remarkable Scottish watchmaker living in Calcutta at that time, David Hare, who worked in close collaboration with a local intellectual, Radhakanta Deb. The process was also greatly helped by the work of one of the activists in the city, Buddinnath Mukherjee, who secured the support of Sir Edward Hyde East, the Chief Justice of the Supreme Court in Calcutta. East called a meeting of 'European and Hindu gentlemen' at his house in May 1816 to plan the College, which opened the following year on 10 January 1817 with twenty scholars. By 1828 the enrolment had risen to 400.

This social initiative was an early component of a radical intellectual movement in Calcutta, rather self-consciously called 'Young Bengal' (the example of near-contemporary 'Young England' must have been something of an inspiration). It was championed by a seriously radical group of thinkers, quite firmly anti-conservative, who were sceptical of traditional thinking both in India and in Europe. Since it was non-denominational in outlook, it was only natural that when the Hindu College was transformed into Presidency College in June 1855, it reaffirmed very clearly that it offered educational opportunities to non-Hindus as well as Hindus. Two years later, when Calcutta University was established, Presidency became one of its constituent colleges. Nearly a century later, in 1953, it was from Calcutta University that I received my BA degree in Economics with Mathematics.

4

The role of Presidency College in the emergence of Young Bengal is important to recognize. The most prominent member of Young Bengal was a Eurasian of mixed Indian and Portuguese ancestry called

Henry Derozio, who was formally a Christian but in reality a non-believer and self-described atheist. Born in April 1809, Derozio was appointed a lecturer at the College in May 1826, when he had just turned seventeen. His precociousness was extraordinary and he became a powerful intellectual influence in Calcutta as a legendary teacher of history and literature. All of Derozio's achievements – he accomplished an amazing variety of things – came in a very short life: he died suddenly of cholera in 1831, at the age of twenty-two. As well as being a great teacher and rebellious reformer, Derozio was a considerable poet. Most importantly, he was an active advocate of free and fearless thinking, and a huge inspiration to his students as well as to many of his colleagues in the College and the elite of Calcutta. Young as he was, Derozio had a profound influence on the development of the free-thinking tradition of Presidency. Almost a century and a half later he figured a great deal in our college debates as we continued to celebrate his intellectual distinction and social leadership.

Derozio wanted the conservative societies around him in India to reform radically. He championed the ideas behind the French Revolution (which had occurred only a few decades earlier), going firmly against the general weight of opinion around him, particularly in British circles in Calcutta. But he was also an Indian nationalist, keen on making his country fearless in thought and liberal in practice – free from all unreasoned restraints. In a poem entitled 'To India – My Native Land', written in deliberately arcane language, Derozio contrasted India's historical achievements with its badly diminished present:

> My country! In thy day of glory past
> A beauteous halo circled round thy brow,
> And worshipped as a deity thou wast –
> Where is that glory, where that reverence now?
> Thy eagle pinion is chained down at last,
> And grovelling in the lowly dust art thou:
> Thy minstrel hath no wreath to weave for thee
> Save the sad story of thy misery!

Derozio's students were fired by his critical outlook as well as his capacious imagination. The so-called 'Derozians' helped to establish the College's spirit of critical, rational enquiry and were influenced by their reading of David Hume, Jeremy Bentham, Thomas Paine and other rationalist thinkers; Derozio himself clearly liked Voltaire much more than religious thinkers in either continent. He also ruffled feathers by recommending that students should study Homer rather than Christian texts. Opposed by the Hindu orthodoxy as well as the Christian establishment, his open advocacy of non-religious, rationalist thought eventually cost Derozio his job.

The new intellectual movements springing up in Calcutta at this time were not invariably hostile to religion. A rapidly expanding new society, the Brahmo Samaj, led by the scholarly reformer Raja Ram Mohan Roy, became a powerful religious movement of a staunchly reformist kind, making relatively free interpretations of ancient Hindu texts; some of these interpretations have a striking resemblance to Unitarian writings. Derozio was central to the emergence of a robust tradition of free thinking in Presidency College – a tradition from which many later generations of students would greatly benefit.

5

My new interests in economics were amply rewarded by the outstanding teaching we received from our college. I was particularly influenced by Bhabatosh Datta and Tapas Majumdar, who were both economic theorists, but there were other fine teachers as well, such as Dhiresh Bhattacharya, who gave brilliant lectures on applied economics, particularly related to the Indian economy. Instruction on politics came from Upendranath Ghosal and Ramesh Ghosh, who were also very engaging and had excellent pedagogic skills. I found it wonderful to be able to talk with teachers of such distinction – in economics, politics and mathematics, but also in history. In particular, Sushobhan Sarkar, a visionary historian, with a leaning towards Marxian analysis, was inspirational.

Bhabatosh Datta was probably the most lucid lecturer in economics I have ever heard. Extraordinarily complicated problems in theories of value and distribution were analysed with remarkable clarity and easy accessibility. I adored his classes, but I was surprised that he seemed disinclined to try to make a research contribution of his own. He was a very modest man, and I imagine he felt happy enough to be a superb intellectual intermediary, bringing complicated economic theory within our easy reach. Nothing could take away the gratefulness with which we listened to – and learned from – Bhabatoshbabu (as we called him), but I remember thinking that if I had the creative talent that he clearly had I would have liked to have done some research of my own.

Tapas Majumdar's approach to teaching was different from Bhabatosh Datta's. Tapasda (as I called him) was a very young teacher who had just completed his own studies. Both because of the quality of his own mind, and I imagine because of the influence of Bhabatoshbabu (who he always treated as something of a guru), Tapasda was also a superbly clear and lucid lecturer. He was very engaged in nurturing the intellectual self-confidence of his students, and furthermore did really interesting research of his own. Later on, Tapasda made quite remarkable contributions in the economics of education as well as in social choice theory. He brought out in a very imaginative way how social choice theory can contribute to educational planning and development.

Since I preferred to challenge rather than accept at face value the ideas and knowledge we were being offered, and sometimes questioned what we were getting from the books and well-respected articles, I was very attracted by Tapasda's bolder approach, which was less respectful of prevailing traditions. One day, after about an hour of argument with him on why I thought the contents of an article on which he had just lectured was wrong, he told me, 'If some analytical theory you read appears to you to be wrong, it could be that you have not followed the reasoning (and you must check that), but it could also be – don't dismiss the possibility – that the received argument, despite common belief, is simply incorrect.' That was a huge piece of ammunition for me in strengthening my argumentative resolve. I remember then thinking that if I learned from Bhabatoshbabu how to lecture, I must also learn from Tapasda how to question.

I came to know Tapasda well soon after his first lecture, as we went on to discuss what he had just taught us. I often visited him – involving a long bus ride from College Street – at his home in Dover Lane in south Calcutta where he lived with his mother, whom we called Mashima. She was a wonderful person, and great fun to talk with. Tapasda's father, Nani Gopal Majumdar – a very talented archaeologist who was a leading explorer of sites of the Indus Valley Civilization – had died young. Since archaeology interested me greatly, it was a pleasure for me to slip away from economics for a while and discuss with them the archaeological exploration of India's, and the world's, past. Mashima and Tapasda were both extremely tolerant of a young undergraduate who arrived unannounced (telephones were quite a rarity in Calcutta in those days) to chat for a long time over cups of hot tea and Mashima's savoury delights.

6

I have excellent memories of my lecturers at Presidency, but also of my fellow students. I had the great fortune of having wonderful classmates, including of course Sukhamoy, but also several others, such as Suniti Bhose, Tushar Ghosh and Samir Ray (we called him Samirda, because he was a little older and joined us after having been out of college for a while), and Jati Sengupta, who would later make a much-deserved name for himself in the new subject of 'stochastic programming'. And there were other brilliant students who were pursuing subjects other than economics, such as Partha Gupta, Barun De and Binay Chaudhuri in history. Indeed, there was an astonishing cluster of superb scholars in a remarkable variety of subjects at Presidency at that time, including Nikhilesh Bhattacharya, a real star in maths and stats. There was also Jyotirmoy Datta in English literature and Minakshi Bose in philosophy, who would later marry each other. Students often met in social gatherings, and there was a very active poetry circle which met regularly and in which I was quite active, along with Jyotirmoy, Minakshi, Mrinal and a number of others. The poetry circle met not to write poetry or to critique each other's work, but to appreciate it; this sometimes involved discussions of neglected poets – for example, I often imposed Andrew Marvell, one of my favourites, on the others.

Presidency was also firmly co-educational, having admitted women since 1897 – as was Santiniketan right from its inception. (Indeed, until I moved to England and to Trinity College, Cambridge, I had not studied in any single-sex college.) We had a cluster of highly talented women students in our class in Presidency College, and I did not fail to notice that some of them were very charming and good-looking as well. But one-to-one meetings were both rare and rather difficult to arrange, given the College's – and society's – conventions at that time. Our meetings were mostly in restaurants, including in the College Street coffee house, and occasionally in cinemas or in the maidan.

The hostels prohibited visitors of the opposite sex from coming to the residential rooms. This applied to my YMCA hostel as well, and I was pleasantly surprised – indeed amazed – when a female friend whom I knew very well managed to visit me in my room when I was slightly unwell. I asked her, 'How did you manage to get in?' She told me, 'by informing the Warden that you are sick, possibly quite seriously ill, and need immediate attention'. The Warden told her, 'You must go and find out what he needs. Please look after him and tell me whether I should do something.' She did give a 'report' on my medical condition to the Warden when she left. An account of this event was soon being widely circulated in the College.

7

The intellectual challenges that Presidency presented were really exciting, but I would not be describing my life there accurately if I gave the impression that it was focused mainly around classes and formal studies. For one thing, the conversations in the coffee house absorbed nearly as much of my time as class hours.

The coffee house had originally been a workers' cooperative, was taken over by the Indian Coffee Board, and then became a cooperative again. It was an amazing place for *adda* as well as for serious learning. I remember hundreds of arguments there about politics and society, often not at all related to themes in our studies. I cannot describe adequately how much I learned from others, mostly fellow students, telling me what they had read or had found out in some other way, including from lectures they had attended (in various subjects – from history and economics to anthropology and biology – in one college or another). But more than direct transmission of snippets of knowledge, there was the remarkable impact of closely knit arguments, disputing each other's understanding and convictions. The splendid historian Tapan Raychaudhuri, who was a student at Presidency in the 1940s, exaggerated only a little when he wrote: 'Some of us got all our education from our fellow students in that seat of learning [the coffee house], without ever bothering to cross the street to attend classes in the other institution.'

The clientele of the coffee house was not just from Presidency College, but also from the rest of Calcutta University, a large part of which was also located on College Street and nearby, including the Medical College, the Scottish Church College, the Sanskrit College, Central Calcutta College (previously called Islamia College, and later on renamed again as Maulana Azad College), among others. One remarkable student often present at the coffee house came regularly from a relatively more distant college, St Xavier's, and later from the University College of Science. He was a budding anthropological star – André Béteille – who was a little younger than me. I came to know him well only later, when I returned to Calcutta in 1956, but I was already struck by his intellectual creativity.

I soon plunged into the multitude of bookshops that dotted the coffee-house corner of College Street, providing another source of enjoyment as well as education. My favourite was Das Gupta, established in 1886, which I used as a kind of library. The proprietor-manager was remarkably tolerant and allowed me and Sukhamoy to linger in his shop, reading newly arrived books. This was a fantastic opportunity since we did not have the money to buy much. Sometimes he even allowed us to take books home for a night, on condition that we returned them as we found them (he would often wrap the covers in newspaper). When a friend of mine who was keeping me company in the bookshop asked him, 'Do you not mind that Amartya does not have money to buy books?' he replied, 'Why do you think I sell books rather than make much more money selling jewellery?'

8

The memory of the Bengal famine of 1943, in which between 2 and 3 million people had died, and which I had observed as a child, was still fresh in my mind when I arrived at Presidency College in 1951. I had been particularly struck by the thoroughly class-dependent character of the famine. Calcutta, despite its immensely rich intellectual and cultural life, provided constant reminders of the proximity of unbearable economic misery. Unsurprisingly, the student community of Presidency was very politically active. Though I was not enthusiastic enough to join any specific political party, the quality of sympathy and egalitarian commitment of the political left appealed to me greatly, as it did to most of my friends and fellow students. The kind of rudimentary thinking that had inspired me at Santiniketan to run evening schools for illiterate rural children in the neighbouring villages now seemed to be badly in need of systematic rolling out across the country. Like many of my contemporaries, I spent time in the Student Federation, a broad alliance of leftist students, with close links with the Communist Party. For a while I had an active role as leader of the Student Federation, even though I had many reservations about the austere narrowness of the Communist Party.

Despite the high moral and ethical standpoints of its social commiseration, political dedication and a deep commitment to equity, there was something disturbing about standard left-wing politics at that time, in particular its scepticism about democratic procedures that permitted liberty-respecting pluralism. The major institutions of democracy received no more credit from the standard left-wing organizations than a kind of measly acknowledgement, as result of seeing such frameworks as typical of a 'bourgeois democracy'. The nefarious power of money in democratic practices around the world was rightly identified, but the alternative – including the terrible abuses of authoritarian non-oppositional politics – did not receive strong enough critical scrutiny. There was also a tendency to see political tolerance as a kind of 'weakness of will' which might deflect political leaders from promoting social good, without let or hindrance.

While I was at Presidency, and indeed before I started there, I developed strong convictions about the constructive role of opposition and dissent, and a commitment to general tolerance and pluralism. I had some serious difficulty in integrating those beliefs with the form of left-wing activism that characterized mainstream student politics around College Street. It seemed to me that in creating a constructive civil society and attempting to understand each other, not only should we recognize the liberal political arguments that had so clearly emerged in post-Enlightenment Europe and America, but we must also pay attention to the traditional values of tolerance of plurality which had been championed over the centuries in many different cultures – not least in India. To see political tolerance merely as a Western liberal inclination seemed to me a gigantic error.

Even though these issues were unsettling, I was happy that, then and there, they forced me to face some fundamental political questions which I might otherwise have neglected. Along with resenting authoritarianism in any form, I was becoming more and more suspicious of political piety – of which I saw too much around me.

When piety surfaced in unexpected quarters, there could be a shocking quality to it. For example, we all tremendously admired the writings of J. B. S. Haldane, and I was much taken by his left-wing, egalitarian sentiments which complemented nicely the strictly scientific principles in his academic work. I learned a lot from reading him, especially his series of articles on 'A Mathematical Theory of Natural and Artificial Selection'. So it came as a blow to me when I found him saying, 'I had gastritis for about fifteen years until I read Lenin and other writers, who showed me what was wrong with our society. Since then I have needed no magnesia.' This was a remark made in 1940 to a journalist, and many of my fellow left-wingers in Calcutta liked quoting it with approval – in and out of context. Perhaps Haldane intended it as a frivolous remark, but if he had really meant it as a serious political or scientific observation, then I had to part company – very definitely – with his thinking. I would, I thought, vastly prefer magnesia to political piety.

I left Presidency College for Cambridge in 1953, the year of Stalin's death and well before the misdeeds of his regime in the Soviet Union were brought under the spotlight by Khrushchev at the Twentieth Congress of the Communist Party of the Soviet Union of 1956. But even in the early 1950s it was hard for discerning readers of world affairs to think of 'purges' and 'trials' in the USSR as anything other than forced confessions of alleged guilt which were dealt with by the heaviest and most unjust punishments. These issues often came up in discussions in the coffee house, and I sometimes found myself feeling rather deserted by most of my friends. Between the rightists who thought Marx was all wrong (a hugely mistaken diagnosis) and 'true leftists' who thought there was no tyranny in Russia, only the operation of 'the democratic will of the people' (a belief of unfathomable naivety, it appeared to me), some of us had a difficult passage. I began thinking about the need to be less dependent on securing the agreement of others, pleasing as it always is.

While remaining deeply sympathetic to the removal of inequality and injustice in the world, and continuing to be suspicious of authoritarianism and political piety, I soon decided that I could never be a member of any political party that demanded conformity. My political activism would have to take a different form.

9

While my studies and my new life in Calcutta were proceeding well, an intellectual discovery came my way which would influence the direction of my work through much of my later life. Kenneth Arrow's path-breaking study of social choice theory, *Social Choice and Individual Values*, was published in New York in 1951, when Sukhamoy and I were in the first year of our undergraduate studies at Presidency College. Sukhamoy promptly borrowed a copy – I believe the only one to arrive at Das Gupta's – and read it quickly and formed a view. This was quite soon after the publication of the book and, while chatting in the coffee house soon after that, Sukhamoy drew my attention to the book and expressed his admiration for Arrow's work on social choice theory. Both Sukhamoy and I knew just a little about the field of social choice theory, which eighteenth-century French mathematicians such as the Marquis de Condorcet had initiated. Sukhamoy knew more about it than I did, and I clarified my understanding by talking with him.

So what is social choice theory? We can introduce many mathematical links and formal connections, but to obtain a rough understanding of this rather technical discipline, we can think about it this way. A society consists of a group of people each of whom has some priorities and preferences. To obtain fitting social decisions on behalf of the group as a whole, those decisions must take serious note of people's – possibly diverse – views and interests. Social choice theory links what can be reasonably seen as social priorities and preferences to the preferences of the individuals that make up the society.

These links can take many different forms, which we can express in terms of axiomatic requirements. For example, one axiom may demand that if every member of the society prefers x to y, then x must be socially preferred to y. Another can demand that if everyone ranks x and y in exactly the same way in situation A as they each respectively do in situation B, then the social preference over x and y must be exactly the same in the two situations (A and B), no matter how different their ranking of other alternatives (that is, other than x and y) may be in the two situations. And so on.

Arrow established a stunning 'impossibility theorem' which showed, basically, that no non-dictatorial social choice mechanism can yield consistent social decisions when certain elementary requirements of apparently reasonable procedures (like the two outlined in the last paragraph above – and others like them) have to be satisfied. This is an extraordinary mathematical theorem: powerful, unexpected and elegant.

In some ways Arrow's impossibility theorem can be seen as an extension of a result established earlier by the Marquis de Condorcet, the French mathematician and social thinker referred to above. Condorcet had already shown in the eighteenth century that majority decisions can be inconsistent, and in some voting situations there may be no majority winner at all. For example, in a three-person community, if person 1 prefers x to y and that to z, and person 2 prefers y to z and that to x, and person 3 prefers z to x and that to y, then in terms of majority comparison, y will be defeated by x, while x is defeated by z, and lastly z is defeated by y. So there is no majority winner in this case.

Majority rule, which is otherwise an attractive way of making a social choice, may be severely inconsistent or inconclusive. Arrow vastly generalized Condorcet's pessimistic result and showed – in his 'impossibility theorem' – that *all* social choice rules that satisfy some minimal conditions of apparent reasonableness will turn out to be inconsistent or unusable. So it seems to be impossible to get a convincingly attractive social choice rule that will work. Arrow pointed to the dire prospect that only a very unattractive social choice rule, namely dictatorial choice, may survive and work consistently. That is a gloomy result – gloomier than Condorcet's.

Sukhamoy gave me the copy of Arrow's book he had borrowed from Das Gupta's bookshop. He lent it to me for a few hours – and I was completely absorbed. The proof of Arrow's formidable 'impossibility theorem' was quite complicated, and it would have to be simplified later (as it indeed was). We had to pursue quite a sustained argument in mathematical logic to understand the theorem fully and how exactly the unexpected result emerges. This was a very different kind of mathematics from what we were doing in our college courses, which had been fashioned to serve the needs of physics and which insisted on a higher degree of precision of the variables involved than could be expected in social phenomena (the subject matter of Arrow's theorem).

Moving away from the maths and the proof, there was also the question: how significant is the result? Did it really offer an excuse for authoritarianism, as many commentators had claimed? I particularly remember one long afternoon sitting next to a window in the coffee house, as Sukhamoy talked about alternative interpretations of Arrow's result, with his deeply intelligent face glowing in the mild winter sun of Calcutta. He felt that it was not immediately clear what the implications of Arrow's theorem were for political democracy and for integrated social judgements, and there was a lot to be done to work out how to proceed from Arrow's stunning mathematical result to the practical world of social choice and of political and economic decisions. Later on, when I was engaged in doing just that, I often thought about Sukhamoy's early pessimism.

Those were formative years in the development of my own understanding of systematic mathematical reasoning about social choice. Those – and related – exercises established an interest in me that has lasted for the whole of my life. In the newly independent India, which was trying to be a successful democracy, the feasibility of consistent democratic politics was a crucially important issue. Could we have democratic consistency at all, or was that a chimera? In many academic discussions in Calcutta at the time, Arrow's ideas got a good deal of airing. A common interpretation was that you simply couldn't have democratic consistency. In particular we needed to scrutinize the apparent conditions of reasonableness of the conditions – or axioms – that Arrow tended to impose. I was not at all convinced that we could not choose other axioms that were also reasonable and which permitted non-dictatorial social choice. There was, I persuaded myself, a need for (to borrow a phrase from Hegel) some 'negation of negation'.

Social choice problems, as investigated by Arrow, became critically important parts of my long-term intellectual engagement. When I look back, I am happy to remember that this began in my first year in Calcutta as an undergraduate, with a book borrowed by a friend from a local bookshop for overnight reading.

13
What to Make of Marx

I

In the academic circles around College Street in Calcutta in my student days, no one could compete with Karl Marx for intellectual standing and stature. A great many who were politically active saw themselves as 'Marxists', while some insisted that they were emphatically 'non-Marxist' or even 'anti-Marxist'. Although some brave souls declared their rejection of any Marx-based classification, there were very few who did not have a view on the soundness – or penury – of Marx's claims.

I too had taken a great interest in Marx's ideas from my teenage years. This was not only because some of my relatives saw themselves as Marxists (and were often quoting him) but mainly because in the corpus of Marx's writings I found concepts that seemed to me to be important and nicely discussable. Apart from the significance of the issues he was presenting to the world, arguing about Marx was fun.

Marx was not, however, much discussed in economics classes at Presidency College – or, for that matter, in any other college in Calcutta. He was mostly seen as the hero of some kind of alternative economics. I remember trying to understand this near-complete exclusion of Marx from the teaching of standard economics – with his towering presence looming on the periphery. There were some simple theses about his absence from the economics we were taught in college, one of which was that modern economists just disliked Marx's loyalty to the 'labour theory of value', which appeared to many to be naive and simplistic. In one of the versions of this theory, the claim seemed to be made that the relative prices of commodities reflected the amount of labour involved in producing those goods or services, which would point towards the existence of 'exploitation'. Capitalists get things produced through the use of labour, but the labourers themselves are paid far less than the value of the labour they put into producing the commodities. Profit (or surplus) comes from the difference between the labour value of what the workers produce and the smaller sum (even sometimes a pittance) they are paid for it by their employers, in the form of wages.

Those opposed to Marxian economics tended to believe that the 'labour theory' was based on an elementary mistake – so elementary that it is almost embarrassing to have to point it out. There are, surely, factors other than labour that contribute to production, and the use of these non-labour resources must be included in the price of what is produced. Relative prices of commodities do not reflect only the amounts of labour used in making them. True, labour theory might conceivably be useful in giving us a rough first approximation to prices, ignoring non-labour resources, but this is hardly a captivating picture. So, no matter how attractive the labour theory might have appeared to earlier 'classical' economists (such as Adam Smith – who had preceded Marx and strongly influenced him), Marx should have dropped the defective labour theory of value, rather than embracing it. A fuller understanding, with non-labour factors of production included in the picture along with labour, would make it hard to diagnose exploitation, since the prices of commodities must also include the rewards of non-labour resources, such as capital, which the capitalists contribute to the process of production. With these additional factors acknowledged, we cannot have a theory of prices in terms of labour alone, and the theory of the exploitation of helpless workers also disappears. So much for Marx, said the self-satisfied teachers of mainstream economics as they passed tea and biscuits to each other in the teachers' common room.

2

Is this a convincing dismissal of the Marxian understanding of value and exploitation? Does it explain why Marx was so neglected in the standard economics curriculum in colleges and universities, including ours? Aside from the kindergarten nature of these dismissive arguments, there are at least two problems with this summary explanation for Marx's absence from the economics curriculum. First, many of Marx's ideas were not about the labour theory of value at all (we will look at some of them presently), so that the usefulness of Marxian economics did not depend solely on whether or not the labour theory of value was an interesting theory of prices. Second, to the extent that Marx used the labour theory of value, did he really see it as a good theory of prices? This then raises the question: why was Marx using the labour theory of value?

Paul Samuelson, a great economist I liked reading on my own during my years at Presidency College and the YMCA (he taught at MIT in America), provided some clarification in terms of good and bad approximations. He accepted that the labour theory could certainly be treated as an approximation for a theory of prices, but that it was not a good approximation – so why use it? Dobb quotes Samuelson's remark making this apparently convincing point: 'Modern science and economics abound with simplifying first approximations, but one readily admits their inferiority to second approximations, and drops them when challenged.' So why use the labour theory when we can easily develop theories that can go much further? Why stick to a theory that at best gives us crude approximations? Why not drop the labour theory altogether (as Samuelson would prefer)?

This simple dismissal of labour theory of value – as a bad first approximation – was placed under scrutiny by Maurice Dobb, a Marxian economist in Cambridge, in an essay entitled 'The Requirements of a Theory of Value' which appeared in his book *Political Economy and Capitalism*. He argued that a first approximation need not be sensibly rejected if 'there is something in the first approximation that is lacking in later approximations'. But what is this 'something'?

Dobb argued that the labour theory of value can come into its own when the role of labour in production is emphasized. The labour theory can be viewed from different perspectives. As a theory of prices, it is no more than a first approximation, and not typically a close one. As a normative theory with a moral content, it tells us something about inequalities in the world and how the poor labourers get a raw deal under capitalism. Each of these perspectives may have some relevance, but – going further – the labour theory of value can also be seen as, primarily, a descriptive theory, delineating the role of human work in the making of goods and services. Marx was keen to pay special attention to human involvement in almost everything he studied. Taking his cue from this, Dobb argued that the labour theory is 'a factual description of a socio-economic relationship'. The fact that this description focuses on human labour in particular does not make it false: it reflects a particular – and important – perspective in which to see the relation between different social agents – workers, capitalists and so on.

We can compare this with other labour-based descriptions we may find in historical generalizations, such as the historian Marc Bloch's apt characterization of feudalism as a system in which feudal lords 'lived on the labour of other men'. Did they? There is an aptness in the description – focusing specifically on labour (in particular hard labour) – which does not deny that the land owned by the feudal lords is productive too. But Bloch's statement focuses on the asymmetry of different roles for different people in production and that there may be no comparison between, on the one hand, the hard labour of the serfs in the production process and, on the other, the contribution that the feudal lords make by allowing the land they own to be used for productive purposes. 'Working hard' and 'allowing one's land to be used' may both be productive, but they are very different types of productive activities. We can go well beyond the mechanical symmetry on which what economists call 'marginal productivity' concentrates – without discriminating between different kinds of resource use.

To examine another type of distinction within the production process, consider the famous statue of David in Florence. We can sensibly say, 'Michelangelo made this statue of David.' The truth of the statement does not depend on denying the need for marble, or for chisels and hammers, in making the statue (Michelangelo surely did need them). In a multi-factor description, these different 'factors of production' are all involved in the making of the statue. And yet we bring out another, crucial, aspect of the production process when we focus particularly on the artist, Michelangelo, and do not equate his role with what is provided by the assembled marble and the hammers and chisels.

Production can thus be described in many different ways. Concentrating on the labour involved is certainly one legitimate way, and it can be seen as appropriate depending on the purpose and context of the description. In presenting his characterization of feudalism, Marc Bloch did not have to apologize, or confess to some error, when he chose a particular aspect on which to focus – to wit, hard labour – the fact that feudal lords 'lived on labour of other men'. Marx did not have to confess to any blunder – nor did Dobb. The relevance of the labour theory of value depends on which perspective we are trying to highlight.

I remember vividly the long evening when I digested Dobb's immensely readable essay 'The Requirements of a Theory of Value'. I finished it late at night, thinking that I could now consider a different perspective on Marx's use of the labour theory of value. I also had a personal thought: if I was ever to go to England, I must try to meet Maurice Dobb.

3

I shall come presently to other aspects of Marx's writings that I found particularly interesting. But, before doing so, I want to discuss briefly some of his idiosyncrasies which became increasingly clearer to me as I continued reading his work. Compared with the extensive economic analyses in which Marx was clearly interested – involving the labour theory of value, unequal ownership of the means of production, widespread exploitation of labour, the falling rate of profit and so on – Marx's scrutiny of political organization seemed oddly rudimentary. It is hard to think of a more breathless bit of theorizing than the idea of 'the dictatorship of the proletariat', with underspecified characterization of what the proletariat's demands are (or should be), and very little by way of how the actual political arrangements under such a dictatorship might work. In fact there seemed to me a striking lack of interest in Marx's writings in the problem of how to move on from people's preferences and priorities to actual social decisions and governmental actions – important aspects of 'social choice'. Since I was becoming more and more interested in understanding social choice, Marx's evident reluctance to get into much of that was rather disappointing.

Also, there is an important lacuna in Marx's treatment of democracy. As John Kenneth Galbraith would make us understand, democracy may be well served if one powerful group exercises 'countervailing power' over another, so that no potentially irresistible group becomes too powerful. Galbraith's ideas began to emerge in my mind as a good supplement to Marx in understanding how democracy might actually work.

It is not, of course, fair to blame Marx (as he sometimes is) for the authoritarian practices of the communist regimes that claim that his thinking was their inspiration, since he neither devised nor recommended them. But surely he would have had reason to appreciate that his reluctance to talk about how power is to be distributed, or exercised, in a post-capitalist society would leave gaps that could be filled with dangerously authoritarian additions. The constructive role of oppositional politics seemed to escape Marx's attention significantly.

Also, Marx could not be accused of being indifferent to liberty, or to freedom of choice. In fact he was very interested in the freedom to choose. However, his neglect of political organization and of safeguards against authoritarianism may well have contributed to a distortion of the demands of liberty through the unaddressed role of pressure groups and the unchecked use of political power. The lack of liberty and freedom that has been a persistent problem of regimes with Marxist credentials may not have been in any way advocated by Marx, but nevertheless it had a favourable atmosphere in which to flourish as a result of his reticence to comment on power and pressure groups.

And it is true that in Marx's famous defence of individual freedom of choice (in his book, *The German Ideology* (1846), jointly written with Friedrich Engels), he captured important ideas that many authors – indeed, most authors – often tended to miss. He powerfully illustrated his praise for bringing 'the conditions for the free development and activity of individuals under their [own] control', by noting that it 'makes it possible for me to do one thing to-day and another tomorrow, to hunt in the morning, fish in the afternoon, rear cattle in the evening, criticize after dinner, just as I have in mind, without ever becoming hunter, fisherman, shepherd or critic'. There is a marvellous airing here of the nature and importance of individual freedom, even if one's confidence in Marx's empirical understanding of the rural world is placed in some doubt by his evident belief that evening is a splendid time to rear cattle. He was on more familiar ground with the freedom to 'criticize after dinner' (which he must have practised quite regularly). There can be little doubt that Marx did have a powerful understanding of the importance of liberty of choice – and its necessity for the richness of the lives that people lead.

4

Marx had a fair share of my evening hours after dinner at the YMCA, though he had to compete with others, including Aristotle, Adam Smith, Mary Wollstonecraft and John Stuart Mill. In my second year, as I was settling down into a kind of equilibrium in my political philosophy (with some ideas influenced by Marx and others far away from him), I decided that I must be clearer in taking note of those ideas I liked to which Marx had made a big contribution. His illuminating distinction between the principle of 'non-exploitation' (through payment according to work, in line with the accounting established by his version of the labour theory of value) and the 'needs principle' (arranging for payments according to people's needs, rather than their work and productivity) was a powerful lesson in radical thought.

In his last book, *The Critique of the Gotha Programme*, published in 1875, Marx took the Social Democratic Workers' Party of Germany to task for seeing 'equal rights of all members of society' as the workers' right to get 'the undiminished products of labour'. The congress of the Workers' Party was due to take place in the town of Gotha: the 'Gotha Programme' was the party's proposed manifesto to be presented there. While equal rights is entirely in line with the avoidance of exploitation, Marx sharply pointed out that this was not the only way of seeing people's claims and entitlements (he even described this kind of right as a 'bourgeois right'). He then considered a rival principle by which each person received what he or she needed. Marx went on to discuss alternative arguments that could be presented in favour, respectively, of each of the two competing principles. He was very critical of the Workers' Party's evident inability to see that these two principles were thoroughly distinct and in competition with each other and explained that they led to two quite different approaches to organizing society; a workers' movement has to choose in a clear-headed way which of the two principles should be given priority – and why.

Marx ultimately preferred the needs principle – since people do have important needs that can vary, it would be unfair to ignore the differences – but he also noted that it may be very difficult to combine this principle with an adequate system of incentives for work. If what one earns is not linked to one's work, a person may lose the incentive to be diligent. So, after making a strong case for the needs principle, Marx saw it as only a long-term objective – at some distant point in the future when people would be less driven by incentives than they were at present. Although Marx considered the needs principle to be fundamentally superior, he accepted that in the near future it would not be possible to have a system based on it. So he was ready to support, for the time being, the Social Democratic Party's demand for payment according to work, but it remained important to acknowledge that work-based distribution is ultimately not adequate for social justice.

Marx's championing of the needs principle has not been forgotten in public dialogue since that time. Its moral force ensured that it featured in debate across the world again and again. A bold but ultimately disastrous attempt to break the barrier of feasibility came with Mao Tse-tung's efforts to achieve the so-called 'Great Leap Forward', when a version of the needs principle was imposed without waiting for the emergence of a more cooperative and selfless culture. When this did not work (the Great Leap Forward was a failure, as Marx might have predicted), Mao followed up with an attempt to force through a major 'Cultural Revolution' – seeking a radical change in the immediate future, again without waiting, as Marx had suggested, for long-term cultural transition. Mao's attempt to out-Marx Marx came to an end eventually, without evident success.

The impracticability of the needs principle as a comprehensive policy goal meant it had to be abandoned in the short term. Nevertheless, recognition of the importance of needs in a less comprehensive form – to which Marxian ethics gave such a prominent place – did receive, if only slowly, an accepted place among political ambitions and aspirations across the modern world. For example, the National Health Service (NHS), which Britain introduced in 1948 and which became fully operational in Britain shortly before I arrived there, was a heroic and path-breaking attempt to implement a crucial component of the needs principle, as far as health care in particular was concerned. As the originator and staunch defender of the NHS, Aneurin Bevan, who had studied Marx's writings as a student in the Central Labour College in London, put it, 'no society can legitimately call itself civilised if a sick person is denied medical aid because of lack of means'. Further, the whole concept of the European welfare state is based on loyalty – to the extent that that is feasible – to the needs principle.

If it is correct to claim that the often-repeated slogan attributed to Marx – 'from each according to his ability, to each according to his needs' – is at odds with what Marx thought would actually be feasible in the near future, it is also true that some version of a Marxian ethics of needs and freedom has been among the major progressive and enlightening principles that had a deep influence on Europe following the devastation of the Second World War.

In the other direction, recent attempts – especially after the financial crisis of 2007–2008 – to force 'austerity' on many European countries, with disastrous results, have been closely linked with the perceived imperative (often wrongly theorized, particularly through the neglect of Keynesian insights) to reject the needs principle in favour of the immediate demands of economic management, specifically to deal with high levels of public debt. The tussle between the demands of need and those of incentives (and work-related entitlements) remains as alive today as it was when Marx was writing his far-reaching *Critique of the Gotha Programme*.

I should add that in the context of distinguishing between different principles of payment, Marx comments on a few general facts for which the plural identity of human beings is important. He argued that we have to see human beings from many different perspectives.

His criticism of the Social Democratic Party included that in interpreting 'equal rights of all members of society' only in terms of what a person produces as a worker, there is neglect of the other aspects and identities of that person. Being a worker cannot be the sole identity of any person. As Marx put it, through its exclusive concentration on workers' rights and non-exploitation, the Gotha Programme ends up seeing human beings '*only as workers*, and nothing more is seen in them, everything else being ignored'. In his famous invitation in the 1848 Communist Manifesto – 'Workers of the world unite!' – there is no obliteration of the fact that every worker is also a human being with many different aspects.

Given the prominence of attributing single identities to people in today's tumultuous world, with 'everything else being ignored' (as Marx put it), we can find a vitally important message in his determination to avoid seeing individuals as one-dimensional. What was merely a passing remark by Marx in 1875, in the context of an ongoing debate, clearly has a much greater relevance for the identity-based conflicts that so dominate the battles in our own time.

5

There were other departures in Marx's thinking that attracted me. One idea that I found both exciting and deeply intriguing was his highly original concept of 'objective illusion', and, related to that, his discussion of 'false consciousness'. An objective illusion is an apparent reality that may seem objectively true from a particular vantage point, but which in fact needs to be supplemented by other observations in order to undertake a critical examination and to decide after suitable scrutiny whether what appears to be true from the initial position is in fact so. For example, the sun and the moon may appear to be of about the same size when we observe them from the earth. But to conclude from such observations that the sun and the moon are in fact of the same size in terms of physical mass or volume would of course be a total mistake. And yet to deny that they do seem to be the same size as observed from the earth would be a mistake too. Marx's investigation of objective illusion (what he called 'the outer form of things') is a pioneering contribution to the understanding of the epistemic implications of positional dependence of observations and observation-based reflections.

The idea of objective illusion was important for Marx's social and economic analysis. There are truths we can establish by combining observations with critical scrutiny that may not be immediately reflected in an assessment based on a particular position. Marx considered as an example of objective illusion the apparently fair and equitable relationship between workers and capitalists thanks to free exchange. But in reality, he argued, there was economic exploitation because of the workers' lack of bargaining strength. Workers do not receive the value of what they produce because of the way markets work, with huge inequalities in the ownership of the means of production. He argued for better ways of thinking about the demands of fair exchange.

What emerges from Marx's work-based accounting is far from what we actually observe in a market, which gives the impression of 'equal values' being exchanged equally. To consider an example proposed by Maurice Dobb, if it turns out (perhaps after some litigation) that you happen to own a gate that allows – or prohibits – movement from one side of a factory to the other, you may be able to charge a huge amount for the use of the gate because of the 'productivity' of opening it. It is possible to subject this 'productivity' to extensive – and possibly devastating – scrutiny. The critically located gate, which produces nothing except the potential ability to disrupt production, is not really a productive asset, despite the apparent 'marginal product' from *refraining to use it*. It may generate the illusion of productivity, but that illusion can be rejected by reasoned arguments.

This idea of objective illusion, which had many applications well beyond Marx's own use of it, had a deep impact on my youthful thinking, not least in my understanding of class and gender inequalities. These inequalities may not be immediately obvious, since it might often seem that different people – workers and capitalists, or women and men – are being similarly treated when in fact there are serious discriminations that are subtle but strong and (in the absence of serious political discussion) overlooked. As my college days proceeded, I became more and more interested in equity-enhancing politics, and spent some time examining cases of objective illusion – particularly the deceptive failure of the workers in an unequal society to see clearly the nature of their exploitation.

6

There was a lot to get from Marx's work, and he could certainly be seen as a strong source of alternative economics. There is, however, a danger in viewing Marx in narrowly formulaic terms, for example in seeing him as a 'materialist' who allegedly interpreted the world in terms of the importance of material conditions, while denying the significance of ideas and beliefs. This materialist reading is frequently adopted, but it is a serious misreading of Marx, who emphasized two-way relations between ideas and material conditions. It would also be sad to miss out on the far-reaching role of ideas in social understanding on which Marx threw so much light.

Let me illustrate the point with a debate about historical explanation that came to prominence around the time I was moving to Cambridge. In one of his brilliant, but lesser known essays, 'Where Are British Historians Going?', published in the *Marxist Quarterly* in 1955, Eric Hobsbawm discussed how Marx's appreciation of the two-way relationship between ideas and material conditions offered very different lessons in the twentieth century compared with those in the world Marx saw around himself in the nineteenth century, when the prevailing intellectual concentration – chosen for example by Hegel and the Hegelians – was on highlighting the one-directional influence of ideas on material conditions. In responding to that misunderstanding – and in resisting that misuse – Marx's characterization of the relationship tended to focus much more on the opposite direction of influence – that of material conditions on ideas – in the empirical debates in which he was actually engaged. This corrective focus of Marx, to rectify the prevailing bias in his own days (which emphasized the influence of ideas on material conditions – ignoring the opposite), is neither suitable for our own times, nor fair to Marx's interest in influences going in both directions.

The dominant focus has tended to change in our own time. The tendency of most prominent schools of history in the mid-twentieth century, Hobsbawm noted (citing the hugely influential historical works of Lewis Namier), had come to embrace a type of materialism that saw human action as being almost entirely motivated by a simple kind of material interest, in particular narrowly defined self-interest. Given this completely different kind of bias, in many ways the opposite of the idealist traditions of Hegel and other influential thinkers in Marx's own time, Hobsbawm argued that a balanced two-way view must now emphasize in particular the importance of ideas and their influence on material conditions, since it had come to be so neglected. Marxian analysis in the twentieth century would thus need to take a different direction from the one Marx had provided in his own time, without departing from his diagnosis of a two-way relationship between ideas and material conditions.

For example, it is crucial to recognize that Edmund Burke's strongly influential criticism (in the famous impeachment hearings) of Warren Hastings's misbehaviour in India was directly related to Burke's firmly held ideas of justice and fairness, whereas the self-interest-focused materialist historians, such as Namier, saw no more in Burke's discontent at Hastings's policies than the influence of his financial concerns in the management of the East India Company. The over-emphasis on materialism – and materialism of a particularly narrow kind – needed serious correction from the broader Marxian perspective. As Hobsbawm argued:

> In the pre-Namier days Marxists regarded it as one of their chief historical duties to draw attention to the material basis of politics . . . But since bourgeois historians have adopted what is a particular form of vulgar materialism, Marxists had to remind them that history is the struggle of men for ideas, as well as a reflection of their material environment. Mr Trevor-Roper [a famous conservative historian] is not merely mistaken in believing that the English Revolution was the reflection of the declining fortunes of country gentlemen, but also in his belief that Puritanism was simply a reflection of their impending bankruptcies.

While studying in Calcutta I took a serious interest in the ideas presented by Burke at the impeachment hearings of Warren Hastings, and I was concerned that Burke's ethics seemed to play such a small role in what were seen as 'smart' historical readings – by Namier and others – of that impeachment. I thought that Burke was muddled to attack Hastings while praising Robert Clive (who was, in my judgement, a much nastier man and much more of an imperialist than Hastings was). But I was moved by Burke's broad-minded sympathy for the Indian subjects in the early days of British rule, finding it difficult to see his eloquent anti-imperial critique simply as a reflection of his financial self-interest. When I read Hobsbawm on Namier and Burke in Cambridge, I had the sense of a penny dropping.

7

While studying mainstream economics – both in Calcutta and later in Cambridge – we were strongly encouraged to assume that everyone puts self-interest first, without any other values influencing our concerns and decisions. This seemed to me both crude and erroneous. Was it something that Marx assumed too, thereby absorbing a distorted version of mainstream economic theory rather than questioning such a highly limiting assumption about human behaviour?

The general lesson that was slowly taking root in my mind was the importance of paying adequate attention to Marx's capacious pedagogy about human behaviour. What had to be avoided was the narrowing of his ideas through simple formulas – particularly in connection with the priority of materialism (and especially in the form of a universal assumption of self-interest). Such a narrowing should have been difficult to sustain since Marx talked extensively about many different types of motivation (for example in *The German Ideology*) and wrote movingly about the emergence of cooperative values over time (for example in *The Critique of the Gotha Programme*). Hobsbawm's commentary on Marx clarified this issue as well.

Hobsbawm's paper came out just around the time I was graduating in Cambridge. I was aware of a few of his early works before I went to Cambridge, and when I arrived there I wanted to meet him. Happily this proved not to be so difficult, since as a young Fellow of King's College, Eric was easily approachable, and I got my friend Prahlad Basu, who was at King's, to invite us to tea (along with

Morgan Forster, which greatly added to the occasion). I remember the excitement of those early Cambridge meetings, at a time when I was much impressed by the intellectual reach of Marxism, but without being tempted to become a Marxist. For me there were too many other sources of ideas, not all in harmony with the tenets of Marxism. I was, however, also generally bothered by what seemed to me to be the decadence of a great – and once very creative – Marxist tradition that was, by the 1950s, much too engaged in producing formulaic and conformist analyses of literature, economics and history. Eric, quite strongly Marxist as he was, stood apart from this intellectual dereliction – just as Maurice Dobb and Piero Sraffa did, among other inspiring figures in Cambridge. Later, Eric became a close friend. I was happy to try to learn from the richness of the Marxian tradition reflected in his thought and work, while rejecting the formulaic learning championed by its more mechanical practitioners.

8

Recently, Gareth Stedman Jones, a fine historian, has written a splendid re-examination of Marx, *Karl Marx: Greatness and Illusion*. He highlights some of the reasons for the distortion of an understanding of Marx, from the end of the nineteenth century through the twentieth, which led to a view of Marx as an infallible leader of thought and an unquestioned guru of politics. Stedman Jones puts it thus:

> The figure that had emerged was a forbidding bearded patriarch and lawgiver, a thinker of merciless consistency with a commanding vision of the future. This was Marx as the twentieth century was – quite wrongly – to see him.

The aim of Stedman Jones's book, by contrast, is to 'put Marx back in his nineteenth-century surroundings, before all these posthumous elaborations of his character and achievements were constructed'.

To understand and interpret Marx's writings we do indeed have to see him in his surroundings, as Stedman Jones does very illuminatingly. He discusses all the contingencies that circumscribed Marx's choice of deliberations, debates and political engagements – and (I could add) anger and jubilation. To that, however, we must also add a Hobsbawm-inspired point, which gives an alternative emphasis and motivation in understanding Marx, running parallel to Stedman Jones's perspective. We also have to recognize that those of Marx's ideas that are relevant at other times – specifically in our twentieth- and twenty-first-century world – cannot be fully understood in terms of Marx's own application of his general theses in his nineteenth century. If we need contextualization for some purposes, we also need decontextualization, or a context change, when circumstances shift. To understand the reach and force of Marxian analyses in quite different contexts from Marx's own, we need to employ a suitable versatility.

The enormous power of ideas in changing material conditions is a theme that is thoroughly Marxian, as Hobsbawm demonstrates, but it is not a theme to which Marx himself gave the attention he could have done, had he detached himself from engaging in battles against the contrary ideas in his own time. Indeed, I would argue that some of the most fruitful uses of Marx's ideas in our world today – the reach of coherent description, the relevance of objective illusion, the plurality of distributive goals, the dual role of ideas and of material conditions – have to draw on his general reflections, sometimes even passing observations, that he aired and very briefly illustrated, often without pursuing them further.

To get the most from Marx, I was becoming increasingly convinced, we have to go well beyond the priorities reflected in his own writings. Many of our arguments in the College Street coffee house attempted to examine this broader philosophy. We were not always successful in our reinterpretations, but we did try to see how far we could go – in the Marx-obsessed world that came with our daily coffee.

14

An Early Battle

I

Hypochondria and I had been friends for a long time, but I did not know that the friendship would save my life one day. Just as I reached my eighteenth birthday, I noticed that I had a smooth lump in my mouth – on the hard palate, about the size of a split pea. It was painless and gave me no trouble, but it was quite different from anything I had ever seen before. I was worried.

This was in November 1951. By then I was well settled in my YMCA hostel in Calcutta and so I went to see the doctor who was meant to look after all of us at the hostel. The doctor thought nothing of the lump and said that it would go away on its own. I shouldn't worry. His lack of concern worried me, since he offered no explanation of what the lump might be and what could have caused it. This anxiety deepened when, in reply to my demand for a plausible explanation, he said, 'We doctors often do not understand minute features of the world that God has created for us, but we do not panic about them!' Recollecting my long-term intellectual companion, the old materialist philosophy of Lokayata, I thought about one of its central propositions that 'material events have material causes – don't look for any world beyond them'. I did not see any reason to ignore that advice from the sixth century BC.

The lump was still there when I returned to the hostel in January after the Christmas vacation – in fact, it seemed to have grown a little larger. I was determined to pursue the matter more fully. The word 'growth' kept circling in my mind, and I used the University Library to look up a few popular books on cancer to quieten my mind. This actually had the opposite effect and, led by my readings, I started to think about an odd thing called a 'carcinoma'. I wanted to get to the bottom of it and, since I could not afford expensive medical care (my parents were still in Delhi and knew nothing about all this), I went to the Outpatients Department of the Carmichael Hospital, one of the large public hospitals in Calcutta. (It would be later absorbed into the large complex of R. G. Kar Medical College and Hospital.) The hospital had a reputation for having excellent doctors and surgeons and also of treating indigent patients with dignity.

I stood in a queue for a couple of hours. When I reached the doctor, who looked impressive, he smiled nicely. I told him that I had a lump on my hard palate and I thought it might be a carcinoma. He smiled broadly, in a very friendly way, and immediately started humouring me, evidently inclined to dismiss a medical diagnosis by an economics undergraduate. 'Yes, yes, I see,' he said, 'you think you have a carcinoma! Well, I had better examine it very carefully, but before that, tell me, are there any other suspicions of serious disease you are harbouring in your mind?'

'No,' I replied firmly, 'just carcinoma.' So he examined me with a bright lamp that focused on the roof of my mouth. He said little until I asked him, 'Are you going to biopsy it?' 'No,' he said, 'it would be pointless. There is nothing of any consequence there. It is just a little swelling, which will certainly go away. If you want to speed the process, you can bathe it in some antiseptic – perhaps you could do some gargling with Dettol.'

'But,' he said after a little pause, 'here is a better idea. If you can hang around until late afternoon, when I have some minor surgeries scheduled, I can remove the lump under local anaesthesia.' The lump would then be gone and 'so would your fears and panic'. The little reading I had done on cancer had taught me enough to think that this would be an extraordinarily bad idea – to have the lump roughly cut off by someone who did not even think that he was dealing with a case of possible cancer. So I thanked him and left, and went back to my hostel dejected rather than reassured. The idea that I might have cancer and yet could not get a firm diagnosis began distracting me from my studies, and even from relaxed conversations in the coffee house.

I did wonder whether I was being foolish. I had already had two fully qualified doctors look at the source of my concern and neither had found anything suspicious at all. I knew of course that my tendency to suspect some serious disease or other was incorrigible, and a source of amusement to my friends. I remembered an episode that had marked me out as 'impossibly worry-minded', as our school doctor at Santiniketan had put it (it sounds better in Bengali, but it is not a term of approval). That remark was justifiably prompted by an event which had shown me at my worst. I had decided one day that I might have an early case of cholera, because of some stomach-related symptoms, which I will not describe but which the beleaguered British imperialists used to call 'Delhi belly'. My school doctor assured me that I did not have cholera, and he then went on to make a very interesting observation. He said that he had noticed in his medical practice that cholera patients tend to be typically very optimistic, and the fact that I had panicked so much was further proof that I did *not* have cholera.

I found that remark tremendously consoling. I stopped panicking and became optimistic. And then, of course, I was seized with a new panic, because my optimism was surely an indicator, by the doctor's criterion, of my having rather than not having cholera. When I shared that thought with him, my doctor was exasperated and said, 'Amartya, we obviously can't reassure you, but you must restrain your propensity to worry!' When I recollected his advice years later in Calcutta, hypochondria strengthened my resolve. I told myself that I did have some reason – no matter how low the probability – to think that I might have a serious disease in my mouth. I had to pursue it, if for no other reason than to get this concern out of my mind.

2

There was a rather smart and friendly co-resident at the YMCA who was training to be a doctor at the Calcutta Medical College. (I am sad that I cannot now recollect his name but this was sixty-eight years ago.) I began a long conversation with him, and after explaining my predicament, asked him whether he would have a look at my oral lump. 'I have not completed my studies,' he said, peering at my palate, 'but it does seem to me what a carcinoma tumour might look like.' He was the first person I had met who responded to my worry. Next morning he went to the library of the Medical College and brought me a couple of books on carcinomas.

I retired to bed in the evening with the two large books. It was nearly midnight when, after some intense reading, I found myself absolutely convinced – on purely morphological grounds – that I did have squamous cell carcinoma in the form of the lump. I told myself I had to see a cancer specialist now without delay. But who? There was a cousin of my mother, Dr Amiya Sen, Amiyamama (as I called him), who was an excellent doctor and a famous surgeon in Calcutta. He lived at the southern end of the city, in Ballygunge, and, after calling him and saying that I was coming to seek his advice, I got into a double-decker bus which plied from the northern end of the town close to his home. I remember thinking, looking out at sunny Calcutta from the top deck, that on a wonderfully sparkling day I might get the terrible confirmation of my fear of a very dark world waiting for me.

Amiyamama took the lump seriously and said that a biopsy might be needed, but that there could also be explanations other than cancer, so he wanted me to try some local antiseptic first. I think the one he gave me was called mercurochrome, a red coloured liquid, which tended to leak a little from the recess of my mouth, and colour a spot or two on my lips. This gave me the reputation among my classmates that I must be constantly kissing girls who wore heavy lipstick. 'I would say, kissing at least one,' said a friend, who explained that he was opposed to extremism in politics as well.

The red liquid did nothing for me, so on Amiyamama's advice I registered at the newly opened cancer hospital in Calcutta, the Chittaranjan Cancer Hospital, for a day surgery and biopsy with local anaesthesia. By now it was early May and Calcutta was beginning to heat up for the summer. Amiyamama himself did the excision of the lump, cauterizing its base with diathermy, and sent it for a lab test. This was two days before he left for London for a conference, followed by a few months' work engagement in England. By the time the diagnosis came, he was hard to contact, and after a few tries I gave up.

While all this was going on and I was waiting for my biopsy results, my parents moved to Calcutta from Delhi. I had not told them anything and their move was just a coincidence – my father had a new job as a member of the West Bengal Public Service Commission, whose duty was to interview applicants for government employment and make selections for public appointments. He liked the job, and both my parents liked Calcutta, as did my sister Manju who joined them, and I was happy to move from my hostel to our new home. Everything was rather cheerful, except that I was worried about the delay in receiving my results. I then shared with my parents what had happened so far, marshalling as much gung-ho as I could muster. They wanted to get in touch with Amiyamama immediately, but he was still in England and unreachable.

I had been told by the hospital that the biopsy result would come to me by post, but if there was any need for urgency, they would telephone. Nothing came. I would clearly have to go and get the result. But the Chittaranjan hospital was not easy to penetrate, and I knew they didn't like giving results directly to the patients, especially to young ones. After some family discussion about this, my father's cousin, Ashoke Sen (whom I called Chinikaka), went and picked up the report for me.

My parents saw the report before I did. When I arrived home from my classes, there was a funereal atmosphere. My mother was obviously crying (even though she tried to conceal it); my father had turned into a melancholy statue; my sister Manju looked awfully glum; and Chinikaka was sitting there with a very heavy face. 'The biopsy results have come,' my father told me, 'I am very sorry to have to say that it is squamous cell carcinoma.' I was, of course, terribly dejected, but also triumphant. 'I knew it,' I told them. 'I diagnosed it first,' I said with some feeling of scientific pride.

I felt devastated. We had a very quiet dinner, and my father said that he had an appointment at the Cancer Hospital next morning, but he would go there directly from his office, and I need not – indeed, should not – accompany him so that the doctors could be free to tell him things that they might not want to tell me.

As I lay in my bed that night – my bedroom looked more like a study because of the bookshelves all around my bed – both my predicament and the fact that I had diagnosed it first went through my mind many times. I remember thinking that I was really two persons. One was a patient, who had just got some absolutely terrible news;

but I was also the agent in charge of the patient, who had carefully diagnosed the patient's ailment by reading books, insisting on a biopsy being done, and had obtained a result that would, with any luck, make the survival of the patient possible. I must not let the agent in me go away, and could not – absolutely could not – let the patient take over completely. That was not, of course, a consolation – nothing could be – but it was an energizing thought. I would need that energy, I told myself, for my battle through the coming months. It turned out – as I did not then know – to last decades. The first task, the agent told the patient, was to find out what the best treatment would be, and what kind of chances this patient had.

When I finally fell asleep, dawn was breaking. A poor door-to-door peddler was already hawking quite loudly, trying to sell something – vegetables grown in his own garden, I think. He was full of determination, despite the adversities of his life. His vocal presence and his fight to survive encouraged me, giving me a sense of resolve too. There was also something comforting about another day starting – with brilliant sunshine. I needed sleep, but I really did not want it to be long – or everlasting.

3

The biopsy report dated 14 May 1952 said, 'Squamous Cell Carcinoma Grade II'. I knew enough by then to know that Grade II was not a nice number. Grade I carcinoma have cancer cells that resemble non-cancerous cells quite closely: they are, as the labs put it, 'well differentiated', rather like our normal cells. Grades III and IV are very poorly differentiated and meant to be vigorous and terrible. What I had was 'moderately differentiated' – an intermediate case. It was not automatically doom, but there were certainly grounds for worry and for haste. And that is what the Chittaranjan Cancer Hospital told my father. They thought that I should receive radiation treatment as soon as possible.

I went to the hospital with my father and met the Director of the Hospital, Dr Subodh Mitra. Dr Mitra knew about cancer in general, but had no particular expertise in oral cancer. In fact, he was a leading

gynaecologist, who had done some innovative work on vaginal surgery (not quite my need). He was becoming well known at that time
with what came to be called 'the Mitra Operation' (more prosaically,
extended radical vaginal hysterectomy), about which several essays
had appeared in medical journals. He received some kind of an award
in Vienna for this, even as I was being treated in his hospital.

I asked who were the oral cancer specialists in the hospital, but
could not quite get a satisfactory answer, though a cluster of names
were mentioned, without pointing to any specific expertise. I was told
that the radiologist would take care of me – not to worry. My father
was a little uncertain about how to assess all this, but he was very
disturbed by the diagnosis of my disease and wanted to act with maximum speed. I was also surprised to see that my father, normally a
very reserved man, was talking a little too much, cutting into medical
conversations between the assembled doctors (in what must have
been a 'tumour clinic'), thereby losing the hearing that his intelligent
questions might otherwise have received.

My readings on oral carcinoma had convinced me that I would
expect to have surgery, followed by radiation. But what was being
prescribed was just heavy-dose radiation. I worried about this a little,
and also more generally that Chittaranjan Cancer hospital was very
new – it had been established only in January 1950, two years before
I went there. One of the doctors told me that the hospital had been
inaugurated by Marie Curie, the winner of two Nobel Prizes (in Physics and Chemistry). That did not, however, reassure me much – partly
because pedigree does not translate into expert medical treatment, but
also because I knew that Marie Curie had died in 1934 (from aplastic
pernicious anaemia, a kind of leukaemia caused by her work with
nuclear material) and could not have opened a hospital, or indeed
done anything else in Calcutta in 1950.

A little further research revealed that it was the daughter of Marie,
Irène Joliot-Curie, herself a Nobel Prize winner in Chemistry, who
had opened Chittaranjan Hospital. I was grateful for that knowledge,
but my question still remained: who was going to provide expert
guidance for my treatment? The answer was obviously, if only by
elimination, the resident radiologist himself. Through repeated insistence, I arranged a couple of meetings with him. He looked very smart

and somewhat unusual in having slightly reddish hair, which is very rare among Bengalis. I am ashamed that I have forgotten his name, though he was important enough in my life for his name to be indelibly imprinted in my memory.

The radiologist was quite convincing. Oral carcinomas are hard to eliminate, and mine being Grade II did not help. When I pressed for the statistics of cure he was reluctant to give an answer, but it eventually emerged that the kind of number they tend to expect, given what I had, was around a 15 per cent chance of survival for five years. That was certainly very discouraging, even though the radiologist reassured me that each case of cancer was different, and he was sure (for reasons that he did not specify) that I would do much better than these numbers. The aggressive treatment that they were planning to give me would certainly work, he said reassuringly.

Why no surgery? The radiologist said something about the possibility of spread being greater with surgery – and there would also be a resulting delay in giving me radiation (when speed was important, he emphasized). Most types of oral carcinoma respond very well to heavy radiation, he assured me. To my question – what if my type is not of the kind that responds well? – I did not receive an answer that I would call reasoned, but he somehow believed mine was of the kind that would respond. The hospital had just acquired a radium mould which they would use, in a lead case so that the other tissues in the mouth were not affected. I spent a lot of time then getting a lead mould constructed, with a recessed chamber for the radioactive material to be placed in it.

I was told that I had to have a lot of radiation – 8,000 rad. This, I knew, was exceptionally high. I asked him why I needed such a heavy dose, to which he replied, 'You know, I can't repeat this treatment, and I have to hit it as hard as I can, as much as you can bear. I am looking for what is minimally needed to kill the cancer, but which is also within the maximum you can tolerate.' I babbled to him something about being familiar with other 'minimax' problems in mathematics, and went back home with much anxiety, though also some resolve. I knew later that the kind of radiation I received from radium, an element that Marie Curie herself had discovered (along with another element called polonium – named for her Polish origins), could not penetrate very far and would soon become obsolete, as deeper X-rays were developed. I did not know then that work on medical linear accelerators, which generate more penetrating radiation – with better targeting – was beginning in the early 1950s, even as I was being treated with good old radium.

Over seven days, in an old-fashioned radiological way, I was going to get just enough to kill the disease, but not me. My treatment was a part of a new adventure for the hospital: I was one of the earliest cases to receive a hefty dose of radiotherapy with their newly acquired radium mould. I was told that they were all very excited about this. So, of course, was I.

4

On 26 June, as the monsoon broke on Calcutta, I checked in to the Chittaranjan Cancer Hospital. It was located on a very busy street, S. P. Mukherjee Road, near a corner with another street with heavy traffic, Hazra Road. There was a little open space across the street from the hospital where children played football in a field too small for the game and with a ball too soft for real soccer. My parents came to settle me in, and I also had visits from a couple of friends and a huge number of family members. My father's elder sister – my *pishima* – sent me a silver object with a vermilion mark that had been somehow blessed (I was not quite sure how) and which would bring me, I was told, good luck.

To add to the gloom, a frail cancer patient from Dhaka also arrived that evening for some 'last try' treatment, and in fact died the next day before my treatment began. On the first morning, I moved around the ward and saw lots of young people – some of them small children – suffering from cancers of various kinds. At eighteen, I thought I was comparatively grown up.

The radiation was a gruelling experience – not because it was painful (it was not) – but because it involved extremely boring confinement to a rickety metal chair, with the radium mould inside the cavity of the lead case lodged in my mouth, every day for seven days. I had to hold it tightly against my palate and then sit stationary for five hours each day. There was a window some distance away, through which I could see a dreary compound with many dustbins and a solitary tree with very few leaves. I was grateful for that tree and remembered that my uncle Kankarmama had told me how wildly happy he felt when the British rulers transferred him, as a 'preventive detainee', from one prison with no window to another where there was a window with a tree outside.

Fearing the boredom that would be generated by being radiated, sitting rigidly on a chair for five hours at a stretch each day, I had brought some books. They were not economics books, but mainly stories and plays by George Bernard Shaw – those I had not yet read – and also some unread plays by Shakespeare. I read *Coriolanus* again: I thought I needed that resolve – that defiance – and wondered whether it could be achieved without his dismissive attitude towards other people and his sense of unexamined superiority. As with all Shakespeare's plays, the underlying tension repeatedly circulated in my mind. I also read a few of Eric Hobsbawm's early writings and got some material from local leftists on the plans for a new history journal, *Past & Present*, which was just then being launched in England.

On the first day of radiation, my kindly *pishima* sought divine grace in the ways known to her, and I remember wishing that she knew how to bring good luck, which I certainly needed. I also remember reading Shaw's short story about the predicament of a news reporter from London sent to investigate a case in which the religious people in an obscure village claimed that after they had buried a sinful drunkard in a churchyard on the bank of a river, the church had moved overnight to the other side of the river, parting company with the sinner. The newspaper reporter – it might have been from *The Times* in Shaw's story – had been sent there to write a piece on the hold of superstition in the minds of the ignorant villagers. The reporter encountered a problem, however, when he found that the villagers were right, that the church had indeed crossed the river to the other side.

So he wrote just that to his editorial office, which promptly told him that he was there to report how irrational the villagers were, rather than to confirm their inane beliefs: he could not expect to return to his old job if he came back under a spell of superstition himself. Faced with the certain prospect of losing his job, the reporter did the only intelligent thing he could. In the middle of the night he dug up the coffin of the drunkard in the old location of the church (from where the church had crossed the river) and carried it over to the new location of the church across the river. As soon as the alcoholic was reburied in the newly positioned graveyard, the church promptly moved back across the river to where it had been earlier. The reporter then wrote eloquently to his editorial office confirming that the church was still where it had always been and denounced the superstition of villagers in no uncertain terms. I allowed myself to think that some such small, science-defying miracle would be very welcome in my situation.

I emerged from the ordeal at the end of seven days in early July and returned home. There was no reaction immediately to the radiation and peering at the roof of my mouth with a mirror revealed that the base of the excised tumour looked exactly the same. But then a couple of days later a veritable inferno began in my mouth. The entire region swelled and turned into something like mush, and I could not eat anything, nor touch my face, nor recognize myself in the mirror, nor – and this made my mother cry all the time – speak or smile without blood coming out of my traumatized mouth. There was pain (of which I had been warned, though perhaps not adequately), but most of all a peculiar sense of discomfort, too unusual to be anticipated by any warning.

I had read a lot about Hiroshima and Nagasaki, which had been bombed only seven years earlier, and I could suddenly see myself as part of a population that had been similarly attacked. There was suddenly even more fellow feeling for the Japanese victims than I already had. I could not help thinking that this must surely be my end – the radiologist must have calculated the maximum tolerance of radiation wrongly. He told me later that there was indeed a problem in predicting the response. He had expected something pretty bad, as part of the process of the cure, but had not anticipated quite that degree of reaction. Radiation kills cancer cells by being more destructive of young tissues – cancer cells are new in the body. However, since I was quite young myself, all my cells were relatively young – hence the unexpected over-reaction. I could see that the horrendous events in my mouth might be contributing to some broadening of medical understanding in the new Chittaranjan Cancer Hospital about radiation treatment for young patients. I cannot, however, claim that this worthy thought was uppermost in my mind, as I painfully sipped the liquid food my mother made for me – which was all I could put into my mouth.

In two weeks' time the doctors were jubilant to see that the remnant of the biopsied tumour had disappeared altogether. I was happy too, except that I could not be sure what else might also have been flushed so devastatingly out of my body. My parents and sister were wonderfully sympathetic and did their best to help me retain optimism – about things sorting out 'soon – very soon'. My mouth did begin to gradually re-emerge, and two months later – they were a terrible couple of months – I looked more like I did before I checked into Chittaranjan Hospital. The first day I dared to go out of our house and perch on the lawn I had a visit from Satyen Bose, the physicist. He joined me on a neighbouring chair on the lawn and talked with me on a great number of subjects, including how he got into physics research ('you should not have left it,' he said encouragingly). He added that adversity sometimes makes one more determined to continue one's work.

The forced exclusion from college life had given me time to think a lot about my own work commitments, and about what I should do in the future if I were to survive. I had time enough to think also about my plans and hopes – and efforts – to do something about illiteracy and poverty in India. I was becoming more and more anxious to get back to Presidency College and to my friends. I had missed a lot of classes, but throughout the period my friends had brought me reports on what was going on, and even gave me their notes on the lectures I was missing. Samirda in particular had visited me almost every day with accounts of what had been happening. There was a rumour in the College that I was on my deathbed, and it was particularly nice for me and for my close friends when I could re-emerge and quash the speculation.

5

I returned to College Street in September – and what a joyful return it was. My world was restored. The pleasures of chatting with classmates and arguing vigorously about politics were re-established. The girls seemed as intelligent and attractive as they had been when I left, and the coffee house as energizing as ever. I had a warm welcome from the Poetry Circle and Jyotirmoy gave me some rare books of poetry with exhilarating poems.

Shortly afterwards, along with my friend Partha Gupta, a brilliant scholar training to be a historian and a wonderful man, I went off to Baharampur, about 120 miles from Calcutta, for an all-Bengal debating competition. We had some success there, and I was particularly happy that on the train Partha and I could resume our former political discussions. Among other grim subjects we talked about the Soviet treatment of Eastern Europe and news of the purges and trials in the Soviet Union – a controversial topic for those on the left, as Partha and I both were. Partha said that John Gunther, the American journalist, had reported in his book *Inside Europe* that Bukharin and others, who had been on public trial, looked quite healthy and not as if they had been tortured. I told Partha that if he believed Gunther's account, then he would believe anything.

Partha did not need much persuasion. Like me, he was very concerned about the possibility that Stalinism (though we were not yet using that term) was now obliterating the promise of freedom that communism had initially proclaimed. My days at the College after my return from radiotherapy were particularly full of political discussions, including some catching up.

There was another, more personal, debate in which I could not but get involved as I made progress in my recovery from the radiation. I was reasonably well known in academic circles in Calcutta and my treatment became a subject of much discussion among these groups. The story went round that I had been wrongly diagnosed and thus wrongly treated. There was even a rumour that the authorities of the Chittaranjan Cancer Hospital had rushed my father into settling for radiation treatment for me for a price (though it was a public hospital), thereby getting a little money for the institution as well as finding some use for their newly acquired radium mould, which had been waiting to be used on a gullible target. The rumour went further: that I was nearly killed by the hospital when I had nothing for which I needed to be treated, especially by something as lethal as heavy radiation.

There was no truth in all this, except of course that the decision to go for radiotherapy was certainly rushed. Our own family doctor in

Calcutta (Dr Kamakhya Mukherjee), who was away during the decision period, felt very unhappy about what had been decided and
wrote in his report: 'The parents of Shri Sen became very anxious
[with the biopsy report] and without taking a second opinion and
without having a second specimen examined for confirmation, hur-
riedly had a radium treatment done in June, 1952.' There could indeed
have been a case for a second opinion and a second biopsy. But there
was also a need for urgency, and good reasons for promptness given
the diagnosis, which made for a difficult decision. I found no reason
at all to question what we had done. I thought my parents had acted
wisely and that the hospital had done its best, with the help of their
energetic radiologist, who made up for his lack of experience by
extensive reading. Also, post-radiation, I could not see the point of
revisiting what had already happened. Indeed, if it were to turn out
that I had gone through the radiation ordeal unnecessarily – because
of a medical mistake – that would have greatly added to my sense of
anguish, rather than reinforcing the sense that I actually had undergone all that suffering for a very good reason.

6

About a dozen years after my radiation, the great scientist J. B. S. Haldane died of rectal cancer after being treated in another hospital in
Calcutta. Haldane had become an Indian citizen in the early 1960s and
lived, with his wife Helen Spurway, in Bhubaneshwar. We met in the
period between my cancer and his, and I was thrilled that I came to
know him a little: his writings, which I knew from my schooldays, had
a big influence on me. I regret that when he became ill I did not manage to come to see him from Delhi, where I was by then teaching.

Haldane wrote a poem on cancer as he lay in his hospital bed in
Calcutta. I imagine that this remarkable poem, which was published
in the *New Statesman* on 21 February 1964, was written to keep his
spirits up, not with blind affirmative faith but with critical reasoning,
as we would expect from him. He began by noting the high incidence
of cancer:

Cancer's a funny thing:
I wish I had the voice of Homer
To sing of rectal carcinoma,
This kills a lot more chaps, in fact,
Than were bumped off when Troy was sacked.
. . .
I know that cancer often kills,
But so do cars and sleeping pills;
And it can hurt one till one sweats,
So can bad teeth and unpaid debts.
A spot of laughter, I am sure,
Often accelerates one's cure;
So let us patients do our bit
To help the surgeon make us fit.

Haldane may have overestimated the medical value of a positive attitude – the statistical evidence is very divided on how much it helps. But, although in 1952 I had not read his poem (it had not yet been written), I followed the advice that Haldane would give on trying to remain cheerful. It may not have made any difference to the outcome, but I don't think I could have easily gone through the rigours of a nearly lethal dose of radiation without cultivating some deliberate cheer. The thought of having to 'do my bit' certainly made a difference to the life I was trying to lead, despite the adversities.

Whether or not Haldane was right to expect that an actual cure is helped by having an affirmative attitude, it certainly makes the experience of treatment and its aftermath bearable in a way that pessimism cannot. This is perhaps not as minor a point as some people might think. Our life consists of a sequence of experiences, and a period of medical treatment is a part of that sequence. So we have to look not merely for the 'end result' – whether or not we die from the disease that afflicts us – but also for the life that we lead even as we are battling with our affliction. Or, to put it in another way, we have reason to be concerned not merely with the life after our battle – if there is one – but also with life *during* the battle, which in the case of cancer can be quite a prolonged period.

Palliatives are of course important for our lives, but the judgement that the doctors sometimes like presenting – with great emphasis – that a treatment is 'only palliative' (for which read 'it makes no difference to the outcome'), is perhaps less conducive to a good life than attention to the overall experience, including our knowledge and concerns, and our fears and hopes (even perhaps wild hopes). Haldane was, I believe, right to see mirth as a part of the battle with cancer.

7

Back at Presidency College and the coffee house, I resumed my old College Street life – reading, arguing and debating. I felt completely happy. The cancer threat would not, of course, go away, and the radiation damage to bones and tissues would have its own consequences and need attention and management for decades to come. But, for the moment, hypochondria could be given a rest. I now felt the compelling need to lead my life – and to lead it vigorously. I was back arguing about subjects that mattered not just to me (as my carcinoma clearly did), but to the world. I wanted to celebrate victory over the inescapable self-centredness that cancer imposes.

As I sat on the edge of a veranda in Presidency College one evening in early October 1952, I thought of Henry Derozio, separated from me by more than a century, who had given the academic community in Calcutta such a tremendous start by being critical and fearless in his ideas about education. I felt that he would have understood my present state of mind, which allowed my sense of celebration to overwhelm my concerns. There was now nothing between me and the joys of intellectual deliberation, drinking coffee with our friends in the coffee house across the street – nothing, except rows and rows of bookshops and over-packed book stalls on College Street. It was an exhilarating moment.

15
To England

I

The idea of my going to England to study had first germinated in my father's mind. He had greatly enjoyed his three years doing a Ph.D. in agricultural chemistry at the University of London, working mostly at Rothamsted Research in Harpenden, Hertfordshire. When I was undergoing radiotherapy for my cancer, he and my mother wanted me to have something to look forward to when the medical turmoil was over. My father asked me whether I would like to go to the London School of Economics, about which he had heard good things. 'That would be great,' I replied, 'but can we afford it?' It was a natural question to ask, since the family was not rich, and as a long-term university teacher my father's salary had been quite modest.

My father said that he had been doing some calculations and he had come to the conclusion that he could – just – afford to pay for me to be in London for three years, including the university fees. There were hardly any scholarships to go to England in those days, and certainly nothing for which I could be considered at that time, but happily the university fees were also extraordinarily low – less than a small fraction of what they are today, even after adjusting for inflation.

This led me to do some research on what I should consider doing after the debilitating effects of high-dose radiation receded. I also had a chat with Amiya Dasgupta, whom I mentioned earlier. Amiyakaka thought I should indeed go to England – not to the LSE (where he himself had done his Ph.D. in the early 1930s), but to Cambridge, which he thought was then the leading school of economics in the world.

So I went to the British Council library to obtain information about colleges and universities in England. That library was one of my favourite haunts – it was charming and very easy to use. As I looked through the material on the different colleges in Cambridge, Trinity jumped out at me. I knew something about the College for several different reasons. My cousin Buddha had spent six months there as a trainee in the Indian Administrative Service just after independence. I liked Buddha a lot, from the days when as a child I heard the stories behind the plays of Shakespeare from him (he was the living embodiment of the Lambs' *Tales from Shakespeare* for me) – before I could even read English. Later, as a grown-up boy of sixteen, I took serious note of Buddha's joyful admiration for Trinity, soon after he returned. I even enjoyed his account of the college clock in the Great Court telling the time alternately in male and female voices (that is, in low and high pitch).

I also knew a fair amount about Newton and Bacon, about Russell, Whitehead, Moore and Wittgenstein, not to mention the Trinity poets (Dryden was my favourite, followed by Marvell, Byron, Tennyson and Housman), the Trinity mathematicians (Hardy and Littlewood, and the redoubtable Ramanujan) and the Trinity physicists and physiologists.

The deciding moment came when I found that Maurice Dobb, perhaps the most creative Marxist economist of the twentieth century (some of whose writings I had read), was there, as was Piero Sraffa – a major thinker in both economics and philosophy, who had been a close friend and associate of the great Marxist thinker Antonio Gramsci. And to them had to be added the name of Dennis Robertson, the leading utilitarian economist and a brilliant conservative thinker who had also done outstandingly original work on aggregative economics, in some ways anticipating the ideas associated with John Maynard Keynes. The possibility of being able to work with Dobb, Sraffa and Robertson was altogether thrilling. I was so certain of my choice that not only did I apply for admission to Trinity, but I applied to no other college. In effect I decided, 'Trinity or bust'.

2

And, promptly, it was bust. Trinity rejected my application with remarkable rapidity, with a formulaic explanation that there were 'this year' too many good applicants from India. That was sad. So I planned to continue my studies at Calcutta University. I was finishing my second year at Presidency College, which would lead to a BA degree of some kind at the end of the year (I was nineteen when I eventually got it), but in another two years I could get a serious university degree, which – though called a Master's degree – was meant to be of roughly the same standard as a BA at Cambridge. I told myself that I could perhaps still go to Trinity later on for postdoctoral work, but now I could have two more enjoyable years in Calcutta with my friends – Sukhamoy Chakravarty, Mrinal Datta Chaudhuri, Jyotirmoy Datta, Minakshi Bose, Barun De, Jati Sengupta, Suniti Bhose and others – who were studying a variety of subjects (I knew that, alas, another close friend, Partha Gupta, wouldn't be there since he had already secured a place at Oxford and was preparing to go). In the cooling monsoon rain of 1953, Trinity bust did not seem so bad after all.

Suddenly one morning in August a cable came from Trinity saying that some of the accepted Indian applicants had dropped out and that I could study there after all, if I could make sure to get to Cambridge by the beginning of October. Arrangements had to be made quickly. I went with my father to BOAC, the precursor of British Airways. They were very polite, but it turned out that we could not afford the air fare, which was very expensive in those days. However, we discovered that going by boat from Bombay to London was much cheaper than the cheapest flight, despite nineteen days of comfortable accommodation, free meals and free wine (which I hadn't started drinking yet, although I was certainly curious), free frivolities on deck and even free bingo every evening (if one were willing to play the most boring game in the world). So my father purchased for me a ticket on P&O's SS *Strathnaver*, which would arrive in England in good time.

There followed some shopping for jackets, ties, an overcoat and some other things I had never needed in Calcutta. My father was excited, almost as if he was himself going back to university in England again. He would get up in the middle of the night and make lists of things I needed. Eventually we left together on a train for Bombay to catch my boat – my parents, my sister Manju and me. At the Calcutta railway station (the Howrah station, as it is officially called), I saw some others going to Bombay to catch the same ship. Tapanda, the historian, greeted me warmly, and there was a kind of festival of students as we settled down to the two-day rail journey to Bombay. The festivity reminded me, rather ominously, of an early scene from the Italian neorealist film *Bitter Rice* (*Riso Amaro* – made in 1949, which was popular among the students in College Street, not just because of the stunning Silvana Mangano), when the newly employed harvesters going to the Po Valley were gathering joyously at the railway station before tragedy hit them at their destination.

3

In Bombay we stayed for three days with a cousin of my mother, Ajay Gupta – Ajaymama to me – the son of Tuludi, my grandmother's sister, who in my early schooldays used to keep me energized with a constant flow of puzzles and brainteasers. I was also very fond of Ajaymama, and particularly admired his far-sighted decision to join the dedicated effort of an early Indian pharmaceutical firm, CIPLA. Established in 1935 by an Indian nationalist with great scientific skill, Khwaja Abdul Hamied, CIPLA tried to rival Western firms, an ambition which is now largely fulfilled and with which in its early days Ajaymama was closely involved.

Some of that great success came only very recently, after Ajaymama's death. I thought of him when CIPLA managed the great feat of busting the world cartel in the retroviral medicine essential for the treatment of AIDS, slashing dramatically the international price of the drug. The new generic product caused a huge stir, in being sold in the developing world from Africa to Latin America at a tiny fraction of the previously prevailing price, making retroviral treatment of AIDS suddenly a lot more affordable across the world. CIPLA has continued to work determinedly to bring medicine to people who are deprived of it for reasons of unaffordability. Now, if a patient with a drug-resistant urinary infection (even in the USA) wants to use a special antibiotic called Zemdri – originally developed by Achaogen, which is now bankrupt and gone – the source of supply has to be CIPLA, which has continued to produce this effective drug.

As I prepared to sail, I had several chats with Ajaymama, who talked about wanting to do what he could to make India an economic success. The thought was in some respect nationalistic, but what he said did not have a touch of exclusivity. He expressed his admiration not only for Hamied's talents and gifts, but also for his broad mind. The fact that Hamied, a Muslim, had married a Jewish woman was just one illustration of that broader vision (and I would later come to know well their son Yusuf, who had by then very ably taken over the leadership of CIPLA). Ajaymama also admired Hamied for responding to the colonial dominance of pharmaceuticals by Western countries by trying to beat them in manufacture and commerce, rather than manoeuvring to shut down competition through government control. As a committed leftist, he expressed surprise that people on the left in India thought international trade to be such a bad thing; I agreed with him that there was a big intellectual deficit there.

Some of our conversations were also on practical matters, in which Ajaymama did his avuncular duty. One piece of advice which stuck in my mind was about not getting into a mess by promising more than one could reasonably deliver, which he thought was a chronic problem with Indian students in Britain. This included, he said, relations with a girlfriend. He was keen that I should understand the huge distinction between a genuine relationship with a partner and the frivolity of thoughtless fun. I accepted the epistemic soundness of this distinction, but could not get Ajaymama to discuss whether thoughtless fun and spontaneity might have some merit in normal life too.

I felt I did not know enough about Ajaymama – other than his political and economic views. His life in Bombay seemed solitary and I was unaware of any personal involvement he might have had when he had been studying abroad. The mystery was handsomely resolved when his charming Scottish girlfriend Jean arrived in Bombay to join him. They promptly married and produced three wonderful children. But contact with them became harder, because after some years in Bombay they decided to move to live in Australia. All that was many years after our conversations on the eve of my departure for Cambridge.

4

It was a sunny evening when I boarded SS *Strathnaver*, ready to sail for London. We all went together to the docks, where I said goodbye to my family. I had a strange mixture of excitement and undefined anxiety. I knew that transcontinental travel was too expensive to allow me to come back to India until after I had finished my degree in Cambridge. And of course I knew that I was leaving behind people who were very important to me – through joyful days as well as difficult ones.

As I stood on the deck looking at what I could see of India receding in the setting sun, I remembered something from the memoir of Maxim Gorky about the time when he arrived to join Moscow University, accompanied by his father. He clutched his father's hand as he went up the famous front steps of the University. As he stood alone after saying goodbye, he felt a sense of isolation of a kind he had not known before. I understood Gorky better, I thought. Outside India, I had only known Burma, and that was at a very early age. The thrill of going to a new place – to Britain and to Cambridge – was mixed with the sorrow of leaving the country to which I had such a strong sense of belonging.

No less importantly I was anxious about going to the metropolis of the empire which I had learned to battle from my earliest days. This was only six years after independence, and relations between the erstwhile empire and its former colonial subjects had not yet been normalized. My memories of sitting in the waiting rooms of British Indian prisons to see my uncles and cousins, who were in 'preventive detention', were still fresh and vivid. As I watched a team of white men running the ship and ordering us around, I recollected a small, and not especially momentous, experience of my father, when he was working for his Ph.D. in London in the 1920s. He told me that he greatly enjoyed being in Britain, and yet thought often about the abnormality of the ruler–ruled relationship. There was an occasion when he was about to send a letter home and was trying to find out whether the stamp he had put on it was adequate. As he whispered the question to a neighbour who did not hear him clearly enough – this was at a busy railway station – a young boy (my father thought he could not have been ten yet) rushed over and told him, 'Yes, that is exactly right – it is the same postage anywhere in our empire.' The idea that this child had an empire was amusing to my father, though of course the boy was just trying to be helpful.

On *Strathnaver*, I was not short of fellow passengers I knew well – there were about two dozen Indian students going to England to study. They included Tapan Raychaudhuri and Partha Gupta, both on their way to Oxford. The summer before we left for England, Partha and I had vacationed together at the hill station of Darjeeling. We took long walks in lovely mountainous terrain, discussing an amazing variety of subjects, including the troubled politics of the left in India. Both of us identified mostly with the left, but had considerable doubts about the democratic credentials of communist parties across the world. We had a long discussion, among other subjects, of the treatment of Bukharin, the foremost Leninist philosopher in the Soviet Union, who ended up having to confess that he was a traitor and was subsequently executed. Even though Calcutta was full of admirers of Joseph Stalin, Partha and I both wondered what he really stood for.

Tapan was several years older than me (I called him Tapanda, following the Bengali custom of addressing one's elders), and I had only seen him once in Calcutta before we left for Britain. His later writing on land ownership, which I quoted in Chapter 8, was only one of many reasons why he became a legendary professor of history at Delhi and Oxford.

There was another extremely talented historian on board called Romila Thapar, who belonged to the upper class and a smarter part of society in Delhi. She combined her rapidly growing intellectual reputation with other talents: her elegant lifestyle, including her skilful ballroom dancing. I had not known her before, and I am sad to report that I did not manage to talk with her on the boat either, even though I saw her often enough moving around gracefully in her well-chosen saris. Ours were different worlds – I did not even know how to dance, without stepping on my partner's toes (generating a howl from her). But Romila and I would become friends many years later, in Delhi.

As we crossed stretches of water from the Arabian Sea to the Mediterranean, I had hugely enjoyable conversations with Tapanda and

Partha Gupta, mostly about contemporary affairs. As the journey went on, Tapanda became a little aggrieved about what he thought was the high-handed treatment the Indian students were receiving from the British and Australian staff of the ship, particularly the waiters in the dining rooms. He complained about this to an officer of the ship who gave his concern a very patient hearing, but we noticed no remedial action.

Also on the boat was the Indian women's hockey team, who were going to Britain for some kind of international competition. A number of them seemed to me to be quite approachable and rather marvellous. I spent many hours in their company, and had to answer to my friend Partha's highbrow puzzlement, 'Isn't it a strain for you, Amartya, to spend hours chatting with these hockey women?'

One particularly charming member of the hockey team, who seemed quite keen to have coffee and conversation with me, asked, 'Are you going to England for education?' I was slightly embarrassed to confess to such a mundane purpose, but said that this was indeed what I was intending to do. 'Really?' she answered, 'I always hated school. What's the use of education?' I wasn't certain how to respond to such fundamental scepticism, but managed some kind of a reply. 'I don't know how to play hockey,' I said, 'so I had to choose education.' 'Oh, playing hockey is easy,' she said, 'I will teach you.' I quibbled, 'But if you did that, that would be education too – you would be educating me.' 'Yes,' she agreed, 'but it would be great fun – much more than the boring maths you were doing all afternoon on deck.' I had to concede defeat.

5

There were a number of people from India and Pakistan on the boat with whom I chatted a great deal. Perhaps the most rewarding new friendship I made on board was with a young East Pakistani from Bengal called Kaiser Murshed. The Murhseds were well known in the intellectual subset of the rather anglicized part of Calcutta. Kaiser's father K. G. Murshed was a senior civil servant, one of the celebrated members of the cadre of Indian Civil Servants (ICS officers) who managed much of the running of the country on behalf of London. I had heard that K. G. was the smartest of them all and showed much humanity in his exercise of the power that the Raj delegated to these officers.

Kaiser came to me one morning when I was standing on deck watching the Arabian Sea turning a little more turbulent. He said hello and, with a well-wrapped bar in his hand, asked me, 'Would you care for some chocolate?' I had not heard that way of making an offer before – 'care for?' (English was still my third language, after Bengali and Sanskrit). I remember wondering whether I was being asked a question about my taste (did I think well of chocolate as an object of consumption?) or being offered a gift (did I want a piece?). Since I wanted to chat with this evidently agreeable person, I simply said 'yes, thanks', even though I did not actually like chocolate much. I was promptly given a piece of what turned out to be delicious Swiss chocolate. I relished the opportunity to talk often with this remarkably clever person and our friendship lasted much beyond our journey.

Kaiser had studied at St Xavier's in Calcutta, where the English-speaking residents of the city preferred to be educated. He was on his way to Oxford to study law, and he loved this prospect in a general kind of way, but I could not get a very clear understanding of what motivated him. I would learn later that he did not go on to pursue a legal career, despite doing very well at Oxford, and also qualifying at Lincoln's Inn and getting a brilliant Master's degree in law from Harvard. Instead, he joined the Pakistan Civil Service and excelled in it, both in East Pakistan and later in Bangladesh, and retired as the head of the foreign service of Bangladesh. While he undoubtedly made a great public contributions in his life and work, I could not later help feeling some parochial sadness that the academic world did not manage to recruit a thinker of such extraordinary promise.

There was also a lively young woman from Odisha called Lily, who was travelling with her mother, who was no less lively than her daughter. I learned a little about Lily's thoughts on how she would pursue a legal education in England, in ways that – she explained – were not entirely clear to her yet. Since I knew with some certainty what I was going to do in England – study economics at Trinity College with Maurice Dobb and Piero Sraffa – I found Lily's open-mindedness agreeably baffling.

Lily's charming ruminations and Kaiser's well-reflected uncertainties made me wonder whether my own certainty about what I wanted to do was really as normal as I had previously thought. As we crossed the blue waters of the Arabian Sea, I asked myself whether I really knew more about where I was going than Columbus did.

6

Our first stop after crossing the Arabian Sea was Aden in Yemen, which was then a little-known country, but is now alas well recognized as a place where people are going through terrible hardship and difficulties, including devastating bombardments from abroad. In 1953 it was still peaceful, and we were taken in a bus to see this exceptionally arid, starkly beautiful part of the world. Then, after crossing the Gulf and the Red Sea, SS *Strathnaver* reached the port of Suez. We were told that we were going to have a day's halt and that we could go ashore if the Egyptian authorities permitted it. As we were waiting to hear whether that might be possible, I heard some strong words of criticism of the alleged chaos of Egyptian administration, from a group talking on the deck in powerfully upper-class English. The previous year King Farouk, loyal to the West, had been overthrown and a new revolutionary government of Egypt led by President Naguib had taken over. Within the temporary government, Gamal Abdel Nasser was already a strong force – and he would take over the presidency a year later. There were disputes simmering about the control and use of the Suez Canal. The bitterness in Anglo-Egyptian relations was already quite strong, though it would not burst into open warfare until three years later.

So there was some tension as we waited on board, hoping that the Egyptian officers would soon come, as they eventually did, all neatly dressed in well-starched white uniforms. We passengers had formed a long queue from the deck that gave access to the shore, right to the top of the ship. I was sandwiched between two groups of rather loud men talking about the lethargy and other failings of Egyptians, and the gullibility of Egypt-loving Englishmen such as T. E. Lawrence and the archaeologist Leonard Woolley.

An Egyptian officer came up the steps, stopped and looked at me, and asked where I was from. When I told him that I was from India, he took me straight down off the ship to the line of waiting buses, to join a cluster of people of colour (to use a modern term not then in use) who were getting into them. This was the only occasion in my whole life when my Indian citizenship resulted in favourable treatment at a border control. Since I still have only Indian citizenship, I am very used to standing in long queues at passport checkpoints, answering questions about whether I might be tempted to stay on in whatever country it is I am passing through. I did not understand at the time how unusual this episode of favoured treatment would be.

Our buses went off one by one, and when I returned to the ship after a day of wonderful sightseeing, I could not help hearing loud conversations about the apparently neglectful and demeaning treatment of British and Australian passengers who had been delayed by Egyptian border control and had had time only for a very short tour. 'We must take the canal off their hands,' said one penetrating voice. Some years later, when I recounted this incident to an Egyptian friend in Cambridge – a Christian Egyptian in fact – he asked me whether 'the Brits were really angry'. I told him, 'I am afraid they were.' 'Good,' said my Egyptian friend, 'very, very good.'

7

We slowly went through Port Said, with a brief stop, and then continued on through the Mediterranean. We glimpsed Europe from time to time, and one night we even saw Stromboli, the volcano, spitting fire – justifying its reputation as 'the Lighthouse of the Mediterranean'. We went through the Strait of Gibraltar and crossed the Bay of Biscay, and then, going around the head of Brittany, we had an unofficial stop at Cherbourg on the French coast. I was excited to be there and went downstairs to look out. Some exchange of commodities was taking place between men on the ship and some shadowy people on the ground, through a little side door. I was watching this with fascination, when an officer asked me 'What the hell are you doing here?' My reply that I wanted to see Europe was rejected as completely inadequate and I was quickly sent back up.

And then, after a little more voyaging, we finally reached Tilbury Docks. It was a wet day there, with occasional rain. An insufferable officer from the Indian High Commission came on board and lectured us – the Indian students – on how the natives behaved (such as not speaking loudly), which we should emulate. It was the kind of advice which – had it been given to Captain Cook in time – might well have saved his life, but it seemed hugely inappropriate, and extraordinarily long, when we were itching to get off the boat and land in England.

We eventually set off on a slow train for London. By the time we got to St Pancras station, a mild afternoon sun was shining. The elegant structure of St Pancras, with the sun breaking into the station here and there, generated a bewitching sight.

A cousin of my father – known in the family as 'Khyapa Jyatha' which literally means 'the mad uncle' (not a flattering name, but Bengali nicknames often have that mock-derogatory quality) – was standing on the platform, with a young Indian who worked with him in his firm. As we drove through London to Khyapa Jyatha's house in Hampstead for dinner, the twilight gave a rather dreamy appearance to the buildings and parks. The quietness was in contrast to the jolt I had expected when seeing – at last – the metropolis from which my country and so much of the world had been run.

After dinner with Khyapa Jyatha's family, I went to stay at a lodging house in Kilburn that had been arranged by Narayan Chakravarty, an ex-student from Santiniketan. As I drifted off to sleep I wondered whether I should be more exuberant at having arrived in London. It was not so much that I was disappointed, but I did think that a bit more urban boisterousness would have suited me better. 'That's for tomorrow,' I told myself, and felt quite cheerful next morning as I was awakened by children talking loudly to each other on the street.

8

I had a pleasant conversation with my landlady in the morning, while experiencing a huge English breakfast. I realized for the first time that one must treat a cooked tomato with due respect, since it is much like a hot-water bottle and spurts boiling liquid all over you if you decide to attack it with a knife. During the day I learned to use the Underground and made some essential purchases from department stores in Oxford Street, carefully keeping track of my meagre budget. And of course I did some sightseeing. I spent hours in Bloomsbury and Regent's Park, absorbing the beauty of the city. Much later, I would live very happily in London for more than two decades and realize that my first impressions had already told me something.

In the evening I had a visit from a woman called Winifred Hunt, who – I had been told by my parents before I left for Britain – had been my father's girlfriend in his student days, decades earlier. Winifred was extremely nice and gave me all kinds of helpful advice, staying to eat dinner with me at my lodgings. Winifred said a few things about my father's younger days which were enlightening for me. 'I sat behind him on his motorcycle across the country,' she said, 'but it was hard for me to convince Ashu that he tended to go far too fast.' A few years later, when I talked with a family friend, Anil Chanda, who also knew my father in England, he confirmed this passion for speed – 'I would say 70 to 80 miles an hour is rather fast on English roads.'

Later on, there was an occasion when I was advising my own daughter Nandana, who is an actor (and a writer of children's books), that she really must conform to family traditions in her behaviour. Nandana was shooting a film – an 'action film' as it was rightly described – in which she had to jump from the twenty-second floor of one building to the twenty-second floor of another – closely adjacent – building. When we go from the twenty-second floor of a building to the twenty-second floor of a neighbouring building, I said, the family tradition is to take a lift down to the ground floor of the first building, walk to the next, and then take a lift up to the twenty-second floor of the other building. No other route is permissible. But, even as I was lecturing my daughter, Winifred's remarks came back to me and I could not be quite sure what my energetic father would have done in his youth.

Winifred had been born a Quaker (and still was one), and her family, especially the male members, had been sharply denounced during the First World War for refusing to fight. Their critics were constantly writing 'conshy' on the outside walls of their house. Being described as 'conscientious objector' was, I suppose, bad enough when it was presented as an insult. Winifred said she was less sure about the moral demands at the time of the next – Second – World War, given what she had come to know about the terrors and exterminations under Nazi rule. 'But,' she added, 'I guess I still remained a conshy.'

Winifred's visit was a slightly unexpected way of spending my first free evening in London. But it was important, both because it gave me the sense that London – and in fact England – was far from an alien place, and because we discussed the unacceptability of violence, even in a good cause, which had been so divisive an issue in India in the battle against the Raj. Here I was, at the hub of the empire (even though it was only Kilburn), discussing the universal need for non-violence, just as those fighting for independence under Gandhi's leadership shared the same conviction. I did not know Kilburn, I told myself, but I did know why someone might be a conshy.

PART FOUR

In the Great Court of Trinity College, c. 1958.

16

The Gates of Trinity

I

Two mornings after my arrival in London in September 1953, I took a slow train from King's Cross to Cambridge. In those days, the faster trains went from Liverpool Street, but King's Cross was easier for me to get to with my heavy luggage. This included a large cabin trunk which had been my father's when he had come to London as a student, and now, in addition to some clothing and my personal effects, it contained lots of books on economics and mathematics that I thought I might need. The slow train to Cambridge took about two hours, and I kept looking out anxiously to see the names of stations we went through. Eventually the sign for Cambridge appeared. A very helpful porter assisted me with getting the trunk into a taxi, and I went off to a bed and breakfast that had been booked for me in Park Parade.

Trinity had put me in digs – a room in a house with a landlady – not in a college room. That was the convention then – first-year students went into digs, and as you gained seniority you were allowed to move into the College. I thought this was a terrible system, as it is so much harder for a newly arrived student to live in an unfamiliar place in an unknown city. The house was on Priory Road, off Huntingdon Road – quite a distance from Trinity. But the room was not ready until the beginning of October and it was still only 29 September. This is why I went temporarily to Park Parade, close to the centre of Cambridge, overlooking a wonderful park – green and inviting, as so many English parks and meadows are in the summer.

The Park Parade room had been fixed for me by a Pakistani friend of the family from Dhaka, called Shahabuddin. He was studying law in Cambridge and had readily agreed to help; he himself was moving to new digs, but he would get me a room at his current place for two nights. Unlike my pleasant host in London, the landlady here was full of grumbles. Shahabuddin went off early in the morning to the Law School to use the library, and the landlady wanted me to convey a complaint to 'your friend'. 'You know, don't you, that a bath costs one shilling, since hot water is expensive?' I said, 'I know now, and I will of course pay you a shilling for my bath last night.' 'That is not my point,' the landlady said. 'Your friend is a cheat. He has a bath four times a day, and lies about not having them. He says he has just one bath a day, and only washes his feet the other times. What a liar!' I had to explain to her the demands of cleanliness before Muslim prayer.

The landlady was adamant. 'What is the point of washing your feet so often?' I talked a bit more about the need for purification before praying. 'Do you do that?' she asked quite aggressively. I tried to re-assure her, 'No, I am not a Muslim and I don't pray – I don't believe in God.' That threw me from the frying pan into fire. 'You don't believe in God?' she exclaimed in horror, and I started wondering whether I should start packing my trunk immediately. But then the crisis passed: business interests prevailed and she asked me whether I would talk with my friend and remind him that each bath costs a shilling. I prom-ised that I would. When I saw Shahabuddin that evening, I advised him to have a fuller conversation with the landlady. 'She is crazy,' Shahabuddin said. 'I am moving out of this house tomorrow.' Indeed, both of us left Park Parade next morning, and I reflected that the landlady probably thought herself lucky not to have to host lodgers who were either liars or godless – or perhaps both.

2

My long-term landlady at Priory Road proved altogether different. Mrs Hanger, as she was called, was enormously kind and interested in the world. However, she confessed, she was very worried about having me in the house since she had never met a non-white person before (though, she added, she had seen them in trains and buses). She had in fact told Trinity that she would prefer not to have a coloured person, to which the College had responded by offering to take her off the list of land-ladies altogether. At this she panicked and said she had no objection to anyone at all. The accommodation officer probably then had a bit of fun in promptly sending an undeniably coloured person to her home.

It turned out that Mrs Hanger's fear of coloured people had some rational basis in her understanding of science. On my first day, after welcoming me warmly, she popped the question. 'Will your colour come off in the bath – I mean in a really hot bath?' I had to reassure her that my colour was agreeably hardy and durable. She then explained to me how electricity works, and how I could be seen from outside in a well-lit room if I did not draw the curtains, even when what I see outside is dark. Once these matters were settled, all her efforts were concentrated on making my life happier and better. After a couple of days, she decided that I was much too thin (what a nostal-gic thought that is to me today) and badly undernourished, so she ordered full-fat milk for me to drink. 'You must drink this, Sen, every morning, for me – at least one glass please: we have to build you up.'

3

On my first day in Cambridge, when I was still in Park Parade, I went to find my college and arrived in front of the Great Gate of Trinity, standing majestic and tall, just as I had seen it in pictures. I knew vaguely that Trinity's Great Gate pre-dated the College itself, since it was originally built during the period of King's Hall, founded in 1317. In 1546 Trinity College was established by Henry VIII by merging two pre-existing colleges: King's Hall and Michaelhouse. King's Hall is, in fact, the second oldest college in Cambridge, after Peterhouse. With that merger, the gates of King's Hall became the Great Gate of Trinity. It was not only the special history of that grand gate (the name King's Hall is inscribed in Latin on Trinity's Great Gate), but also its elegant beauty that I found so impressive from my very first sight of it.

I slipped through the smaller of the two doors that the Great Gate accommodates – the larger door was shut, as it usually is. I went first to the Porter's Lodge, just beyond the Gate. The porters were extremely welcoming and expressed delight in seeing me, together with some surprise that I was not Chinese. The Deputy Head Porter said, 'We have had a few Sens from China, but they all wanted to be called by their first name.' 'You can call me by my first name too,' I said, 'and without the Mr.' The Porter shook his head and said with a laugh, 'That just won't do. Also, I have seen your first name, and it will be far easier for us to manage Mr Sen.' He went on to give me a little map of the College and point out what was where.

I went then to the chapel, and found the history of the College there in three dimensions before me – a statue of a reflective Isaac Newton next to others of Francis Bacon and Thomas Macaulay, together with memorials to many other Trinity luminaries. But, perhaps most importantly, I saw for the first time the names of all the members of the College who had lost their lives in the First World War carved on the walls of the chapel. I was struck by the extraordinary number of casualties. I could scarcely believe how many Trinity men had fallen, and tried to take in the fact that they all came 'from just one college, from one particular age group, in a war lasting just four years'. There were so many names from 1914–18 that space had to be found in the ante-chapel for those who fell in the Second World War. Though I knew the raw numbers, I had never fully appreciated the scale of the carnage. I had to sit down on one of the wooden benches in the chapel, trying to understand the brutality involved. By the time the Second World War came, the leaders of most of the combatant countries had found ways of transferring the bulk of the casualties to the civilian population – from Coventry and Dresden to Hiroshima and Nagasaki.

It was in this somewhat shaken state that I returned to the beauty of the Great Court, and then, past the screens, saw for the first time the breathtaking elegance of Nevile's Court, designed by Sir Christopher Wren. The Wren Library, which is on one side of Nevile's Court, was one of the finest buildings I had ever seen. When I went inside the Wren Library and saw the shelves of old books, and looked up at the sunlight coming through the high windows, I wondered whether it really would be possible to treat a place of such outstanding beauty as one's day-to-day workplace.

'Are you one of the new students?' asked a lively young woman, who was obviously part of the library staff. 'I hadn't fully realized that summer is over and the term is about to begin. Let me show you round,' which she did with efficiency. I asked myself whether anything could be more attractive than the possibility of working in such a place – with one's own choice of timing. I predicted that I would be there very frequently. While I get many things wrong, I got that one absolutely right.

4

Next morning I went to see my tutor, Mr John Morrison, who was full of cheer and warm welcome. A tutor in a Cambridge college does not teach you, but is in charge of your college life and tells you who to see for your college teaching. Morrison was not an economist but a distinguished classicist and a renowned scholar in ancient Greek. He asked me about my journey and about settling down in Cambridge, and also told me that I should go and see Mr Sraffa, who was going to be my Director of Studies – the person who would be in charge of my teaching arrangements and would send me to those who would be supervising my studies.

As a part of his welcome, Mr Morrison also offered me some sherry, which I declined. He said, 'That's quite right – get on with your work, but you must come to my sherry party in a few days – I will send you a card.' I did show up in the party and met quite a number of my fellow tutees. But if one liquid avoidance problem was deflecting the full-fat milk arranged by Mrs Hanger in Priory Road, I now faced another. Mr Morrison handed me a large glass of sweet sherry. Sherry is a drink I hate with a passion, and sweet sherry with a feeling stronger than passion. But I was too shy to tell him, so had to find a flowerpot in the passage between his two rooms. When he saw me with an empty glass, Mr Morrison immediately filled it up again. So after a bit of dithering I walked through the passage once again. After that I gathered the courage to tell him, 'Thanks so much, but no more please.' In my future visits to his rooms I checked rather nervously whether the flowering plant was still there and unharmed. Happily, it was flourishing.

When I went to see my Director of Studies, Piero Sraffa, at 10 a.m. in Nevile's Court on my second morning in the College, he had finished his breakfast but was still getting ready, he told me, to wake up properly. He asked me to come back in an hour's time, which I did. He informed me that my immediate supervisor was going to be Mr Kenneth Berrill, a young Fellow at St Catherine's College. It turned out that I thoroughly enjoyed working with Berrill, and formed an excellent friendship with him, but at that moment I was disappointed. I had come to Trinity to work under the guidance of Maurice Dobb and Sraffa himself. My disappointment could not be disguised. Sraffa was very sympathetic, but assured me, 'You will like Ken Berrill – a very smart economist and a wonderful economic historian. But do go and have a chat with Maurice Dobb too, and remember you can come and see me any time.'

The weekly supervisions with Ken Berrill proceeded very well (as anticipated), but I did drop a line to Maurice Dobb and went to visit him. I am not sure how much he liked the fact that I had views on a number of his writings, and he expressed surprise that I could have been reading them while in distant Calcutta. In my many years at Trinity College, when Maurice Dobb became a close friend, he would often tell me that he was astonished by what he would describe as 'your odd taste in reading'. In my second year Maurice became my main supervisor, though the College also arranged for me to see Aubrey Silberston for lessons on the British economy (my ignorance on that subject was, I suppose, immediately clear to all). Aubrey too became a close friend – a friendship that lasted until his death in 2015. I sometimes wondered about the speed with which I was acquiring mentors.

5

When Piero Sraffa told me to come and see him at any time, I am not sure he really expected to see me quite as often as he did. In effect I treated him as an extra supervisor. Aside from the lessons in economics I had from him, he introduced me to some very agreeable things, including the merits of ristretto (the first flow of espresso coffee that appears in the initial few seconds, after which you have to stop the flow). This was a taste changer for me. It was nearly as illuminating as his first advice to me about why I should be sceptical of at least some of Cambridge economics.

Sraffa told me: 'You have now come to a place where economists love proposing new theories all the time, which may or may not be a bad thing, but you have to understand that no Cambridge economist thinks the job is completed until his or her theory has been boiled down into a one-line *slogan*. That you have to try to avoid – hard as it is in Cambridge.' This proved to be very useful advice, especially when navigating through a minefield of slogans in Cambridge economics.

Later, when I became a Prize Fellow of Trinity, I had a lot of opportunities to chat with Sraffa and came to understand his role in drawing Wittgenstein away from his thinking in the *Tractatus* towards a trailblazing concentration on the rules of language – a change that had also engaged Sraffa's friend Antonio Gramsci. I will come to that debate later on.

I also learned something from Sraffa about self-scrutiny and self-criticism. I was quite excited when, as an undergraduate, I found a clear mistake in an essay by a well-known economist published in *The Economic Journal* – a leading periodical in our discipline. I wrote a rebuttal, took it to Sraffa and asked him whether he thought *The Economic Journal* would publish it. Piero looked at the erroneous article in the journal and then at my rebuttal, and said, 'I am afraid they will definitely publish it.' He went on to add, 'You must not go that way. Do you want to begin your academic publications with a correction – fine as it may be – on such a trivial issue?' My first attempt at being published in a respectable professional journal was thus thwarted, but I was very grateful to Sraffa that he prevented me from making a serious error of judgement about what I could sensibly publish.

6

My teachers at Trinity were very fine economists and each original – and inspiring – in their distinct ways. But they did not agree with each other. Dennis Robertson had Tory sympathies, but told me that he voted Liberal. Sraffa and Dobb were very much on the left – Dobb was, in fact, a member of the British Communist Party. All three got on very well with each other despite these significant differences.

When Robertson had initially conveyed to Dobb the offer of a job at Trinity, Dobb promptly accepted, but – I was told by Sraffa – felt compelled to write to Robertson the next day: 'When you offered me the job, I failed to tell you, for which I apologize, that I am a member of the British Communist Party, and if in view of that you want to withdraw your kind offer to me, I would like you to know that I would not hold that against you.' Dobb got a one-sentence reply from Robertson: 'Dear Dobb, as long as you give us a fortnight's notice before blowing up the chapel, it will be all right.'

What was intended to be a two-year stay at Trinity for a rapidly earned BA degree (following on from what I had done in Calcutta) ended up being my first period of ten years there, from 1953 to 1963 – first as an undergraduate, then a research student, then a Prize Fellow and eventually as a Lecturer and Staff Fellow. Even after I left Trinity in 1963, it remained my base whenever I came to Cambridge.

Much later – forty-five years after I had first passed through it – I would stand formally attired outside the firmly closed Great Gate. I had to knock three times on the small pedestrian gate at one side of the Great Gate. The Head Porter opened the small door and asked, 'Who are you, sir?' To which I had to reply – as confidently as I could muster – 'I am the new Master of the College.' The Head Porter then asked, 'Have you got the letters patent?'(the letter from the Queen appointing me as Master of Trinity). I had to reply, 'Yes, I have,' and hand it to him. The Head Porter then banged the small door shut after telling me that all the Fellows had assembled in the Great Court to check the authenticity of the document. The letters patent were then, I understand, passed around for inspection by the Fellows, while I loitered outside the Great Gate. After the genuineness of the royal document had been established, the big door of the Great Gate was opened and the Vice Master came forward, took off his hat and said to me, 'Welcome, Master.' After being introduced to the Fellows (many of whom I knew already, of course), I had to walk slowly to the chapel to be installed in a rather charming ceremony.

As I waited outside the Great Gate for the Fellows to check the authenticity of my appointment, I could not help recollecting my first entry in October 1953 through the small door of the Trinity Gate. Later, as the chapel ceremony proceeded, I looked again at the names on the memorials, names I had seen on my first day in the College. There was now a bond linking me to the fallen Trinity men, killed in a completely unnecessary European war, long before I was born in a far-away land.

The complexities of our multiple identities were only just becoming clearer to me as my ties with Trinity – and England – expanded. They had started at the British Council in Theatre Road in Calcutta and continued as I anxiously boarded the SS *Strathnaver* in Bombay. As I stepped through the gates of Trinity, I could feel them advance further, along with a powerful attachment and an extraordinary sense of belonging.

17
Friends and Circles

The first – and for a while the only – investment I made in Cambridge was to buy a bicycle. Walking to Trinity and to the centre of the University from Priory Road took a long time. I also needed to get around to different parts of the town – to visit other colleges, to attend lectures, to reach libraries, to meet my friends and to go to political, social and cultural gatherings. Unfortunately my budget did not allow me to buy a bicycle with gears. I bought a simple, gearless bike second hand – and consoled myself that going up Castle Hill on my way back to my digs in Priory Road on this antiquated machine would give me just the exercise I needed.

I met Mahbub ul Haq from Pakistan even before I had managed to get a bicycle – he was at King's, a short walk from Trinity, and we met while I was on my way to the first Cambridge lecture I ever attended. The term had just started and I was hurrying along King's Parade to hear Joan Robinson, the famous economist whose book *The Economics of Imperfect Competition* (1933) I had read with much admiration in Calcutta, and whose lecture I was anxious to hear. It was a fine autumn morning, and Mahbub, elegantly (indeed nattily) attired, was walking rapidly down King's Parade on his way to Joan Robinson's lecture, like me.

We were both a little late (Joan Robinson was, in fact, even later) and we began to talk while keeping our pace. It is my good fortune that the conversation which began somewhat breathlessly during that encounter in October 1953 continued through our lives, right up to Mahbub's sudden and tragic death in 1998. Outside the classrooms, when we walked together on the Backs next to the river Cam, or chatted in his room or mine, we grumbled about mainstream economics. Why did it take so little interest in the lives of human beings? Mahbub and I were not only fond of each other (and, later on, I would come to know well his spirited wife Bani, or Khadija – a Bengali from East Pakistan) but shared many intellectual interests. Mahbub's pioneering work in launching the Human Development Reports in 1990 reflected his passion – a thoroughly well-reasoned passion – to broaden the coverage of economics.

Lal Jayawardena from Sri Lanka was at King's too. Lal and I would also form a lifelong friendship, combining affection with a shared commitment to try to extend the reach of economic thinking. Many years later Lal would give shape to that commitment as the founding director of the research institute of the United Nations University in Helsinki, established in 1985. For a while, I worked with him there, but even before that I helped him to choose an appropriate name for his institution. We settled on the World Institute for Development Economics Research, which gets nicely recognized by its acronym, WIDER – a good description of what Lal wanted from economics and the social sciences. When I look back at some of the global initiatives in which I have been involved, I realize how fortunate I was to meet as fellow undergraduates the people who would eventually establish and lead them – Mahbub and Lal in particular.

Yet another reason to frequent King's in my first few weeks was to talk with Michael Bruno from Israel, then doing mathematics, but who would move to economics soon afterwards. His Jewish family had left Germany in 1933, when he was one year old, just in time to avoid the massive butchery that would follow. Bruno was an excellent economist, and among other roles served as a remarkably successful Governor of the Central Bank of Israel. As President of the International Economic Association, when he had to arrange the Association's World Congress, he courageously – and successfully – located it in the Arab state of Tunisia, rejecting a number of alternative proposals from Europe and America. Given his democratic and left-leaning politics, we agreed on many issues in the world, but disagreed on what was likely to happen to the Arab residents of Palestine.

Michael was very committed to peace and tolerance but he was, alas, much too optimistic about the Israel–Palestine situation. With my experience of the terrible Hindu–Muslim bloodshed of the 1940s, I was very aware how easy it is to generate hostility and violence by fanning the flames of division in artificially generated identity confrontations. When Michael and I argued about Palestine in the 1950s, I hoped that his optimism would be vindicated. It gives me no pleasure to find that my pessimism has been proved right.

2

Despite acquainting myself with many students outside Trinity, my main circle in my first year was inside the College. My college friends included some very engaging mathematicians, particularly David Epstein from South Africa and Allan Hayes. There were also historians – one of whom, Simon Digby, became a major scholar of Islamic studies, much admired in India and Pakistan. (His grandfather William Digby had famously denounced British rule for creating poverty in India.) And I was very lucky to meet, more or less immediately, Ian Hacking, who later had a major influence on philosophy. I have been able to draw on our friendship throughout my life.

I found that I often hung around with a group of recently arrived foreign students who arranged regular get-togethers, none of them particularly quiet. There was Salve Salvesen from Norway, Jose Romero from the Philippines, Hisahiko Okazaki from Japan (known to us as Chako) and a number of others in that very lively group. They were not, to say the least, tremendously involved in their studies (with the possible exception of Chako), which suited me fine, and we spent many hours chatting away in large and small groups. We were occasionally joined by Anand Panyarachun from Thailand, an extremely talented thinker, who had been in Trinity for a year already when we neophytes arrived.

In their later lives, members of the Trinity foreigners' gang had successful careers. Anand became Prime Minister of Thailand twice. Chako was a leading diplomat, and for a while headed the foreign relations office of Japan. After retirement, he became the Director of the Okazaki Institute in Tokyo, named in his honour. Joe Romero became an ambassador. Much later, visiting me at the Master's Lodge, he told me that he had some difficulty adjusting to my new role in the College. ('What happened to your scepticism of rules and regulations?') Joe continued to be active in many institutions of learning, communication and social action in the Philippines after his formal retirement.

The Second World War was still fresh in everyone's memory in 1953. Perspectives on it were quite different among my Asian friends – for example between the Japanese and those from the Philippines. That was not, of course, surprising. Chako was described by our friends as 'conservative', though I was not sure what that would mean in post-war America-dominated Japan. In our first long conversation, in the Junior Parlour of Trinity, he asked me whether I knew about the dissenting opinion that the Indian jurist Radhabinod Pal had delivered in the judgment of the international military tribunal regarding Japanese war crimes.

I knew the judgment well, since it had been much discussed in India. Justice Pal – alone among the team of judges (though the French and the Dutch members of the tribunal expressed some sympathy with parts of his judgment) – found the accused to be not guilty of the most serious (called 'class A') war crimes. Pal had questioned the legitimacy of the tribunal set up by the victors of the war for the trial of the defeated military leaders in accordance with newly specified 'class A' war crimes, which had been promulgated 'ex post facto'. He did not deny that some of the Japanese actions were terrible, including the Nanjing massacre – he even described some acts of the Japanese military as 'devilish and fiendish' – but he wanted these terrible acts to be described as 'war crimes' of a more standard kind, common in most wars. He also argued that the use of atom bombs on Hiroshima and Nagasaki were serious war crimes too.

Justice Pal's dissenting statement to the tribunal judgment, delivered in 1946 (just before India's independence), was of course immediately banned in the twilight days of British India, and was published fully only after the Raj ended. I have never read the full text of Pal's dissent (I stuck to the summary after I found out that the actual dissent was 1,235 pages long), but in my student days in Calcutta we had discussed the main arguments, as reported in the press, on several occasions in the College Street coffee house. Chako said he was surprised – and pleased – that I knew Pal's arguments. I had to tell him that I agreed only partially with Pal, particularly on the issue of the criminality of the Allied acts in Hiroshima and Nagasaki.

If my memory of Justice Pal's dissent had remained vivid, it was because the subject was such a divisive one. Indians had been pleased to see Japan, an Asian power, emerge to take on the European colonialists. Also, the Indian National Army, raised by Netaji Subhas Chandra Bose, from soldiers of the British Indian Army who had surrendered to the Japanese and then fought on the side of the Japanese, had a positive place in some parts of Indian political imagination. Finally, the use of atom bombs on Japan by the Allies caused nothing short of horror in the minds of most Indians.

The Japanese themselves also took Justice Pal seriously, even though in 1953 that support was not much articulated. Later on, in 1966, the Emperor of Japan would award him the Order of the Sacred Treasure, and there are now monuments dedicated to him in two Japanese shrines (the Yasukuni shrine and the Kyoto Ryozen Gokoku shrine). In 2007, Prime Minister Shinzo Abe called on the son of Justice Pal, Prasanta (a distinguished lawyer himself), in Calcutta during a one-day visit to the city.

Chako and I also talked about many other things, serious topics such as the route that Buddhism took to get to Japan (via Korea, not through China, as is sometimes supposed) and less momentous ones, inevitably including what we thought of the people we met. Chako was then at the beginning of his diplomatic career and there was no doubt in my mind that he would bring to it his sharp intellect, if a somewhat nationalistic perspective.

3

Salve Salvesen was a Norwegian with a good sense of humour, with whom conversations were invariably fun and sometimes instructive too. He devoted an amazingly small part of his time to his studies (which he thought was 'bookish' folly), and struggled to enjoy economics, his chosen subject. Salve's mother, Sylvia, came to see her son and took us out to a great dinner in a fancy restaurant (what a change that was from the standard fare in the College), where she engaged us in energizing conversations. The Salvesens came from the top layer of Norwegian society and were close to the royal family, but Sylvia's political activism also involved radicalism and courage, which found fearless expression in her resistance to Nazi domination of Norway during the Second World War. She talked about her days fighting the German occupation and being repeatedly arrested. On the last occasion, she was sent to the Ravensbrück concentration camp in Germany, via Hamburg. Happily, she survived that ordeal and was able to serve as a witness in the Hamburg Ravensbrück trials for war crimes at the end of the war.

I found Sylvia's book, *Forgive – But Do Not Forget*, which we discussed in some detail, very moving. It contained an extremely wise discussion of how to deal with past offenders who had terrorized the lives of ordinary people. Though not directly comparable, Sylvia's thoughts were also relevant to post-imperial relations after the end of the Raj. At that time – the early 1950s – we were in the middle of rebuilding Indo-British relations. Later I realized her thoughts had even greater relevance to strategies for post-apartheid South Africa, under the leadership of Nelson Mandela and Desmond Tutu.

While Sylvia Salvesen was anti-Nazi, she was absolutely no socialist and she greatly feared the influence of socialist thinking in post-war Norway. She was full of laughter when she told me, 'I sent my son to the safety of aristocratic Trinity College to be away from Norwegian socialists, and promptly the College sent him to be taught by someone from the British Communist Party!' When I told that story to Maurice Dobb, he was very amused and said, 'I shall have to make sure that Sylvia understands that what Salve and I talk about is standard neo-classical economics!'

4

Perhaps the closest friendship I developed within Trinity in my student days was with Michael Nicholson, whom I met in my first year, but came to know much better in the second. Aside from his likeable

personality and brilliant mind, I was impressed by Michael's humanity and universalism. We talked a lot about our shared concerns when
we were undergraduates together and happily our contact continued
over the subsequent decades. In later life he became deeply involved
in finding ways to solve disputes and clashes between nations and
groups by probing analyses of the nature and sources of conflicts. I
was very happy when he came to see me at the Master's Lodge after I
moved there in early 1998. To my great sorrow, Michael died suddenly of cancer in 2001, not long after one of his visits.

Michael, like me, was not religious, but came from a strongly Christian family in Beverley, Yorkshire, near the famous Minster. When I
visited his home and stayed with his parents, who were exceptionally
kind, I saw how moving and insightful Christian humanity could be.
But one result of Michael's parents being so religious was that Michael
had to take me to the next village for a couple of pints in a pub, rather
than being seen in one in Beverley. That was not a heavy price to pay,
I thought, for having such wonderful parents, who had spontaneous
warmth and strong sympathy for all those they met – and indeed for
people across the world. Michael's mother made the best Yorkshire
pudding I have ever tasted – to be eaten on its own, of course, as a first
course.

Another very close friend at Trinity was an Italian Marxist, Pierangelo Garegnani, who had come to Trinity to study with Piero Sraffa,
arriving at about the same time as I did. He was, however, a research
student, not an undergraduate like me. The world of Italian Marxism
interested me greatly, and we had frequent conversations. Pierangelo
was a great devotee of Gramsci and displayed this devotion in a slightly
Catholic way, with a picture of Gramsci over his desk, apparently
keeping a close eye on his disciple's work. While I was a wholehearted
admirer of Sraffa, Pierangelo was more than that. He would barely
countenance criticism of Sraffa's economics, even when the critique
came, as it did in my case, from an enormous admirer.

I must also mention here my friendship with Luigi Pasinetti, who
arrived in Cambridge a little later, having first studied in Oxford. He
and I have had a lifelong closeness which still flourishes. Aside from
making major contributions to capital theory and the theory of economic growth, Pasinetti made great advances in the understanding of

neo-Keynesian economics, which started with Keynes but went much further than Keynes's own ideas. Pasinetti was interested in Marx (as most Italian economists in those days were), but he was not a Marxist in any sense. He too was clearly influenced by Sraffa and did a great deal to make the Sraffian economic perspective understood – on which more shortly.

5

Another Italian economist, Nino (Beniamino) Andreatta, was not a Sraffian, nor a Marxist, not even a Keynesian, but pursued more traditional, mainstream economics as a visiting scholar to the Economics Faculty in Cambridge. He was also politically active – he would become a senior Cabinet minister in a right-of-centre Italian government, and later on would inspire a centrist Prime Minister of Italy, Enrico Letta. He was one of the prime movers of the Ulivo (centre-left) coalition in 1996, along with Romano Prodi, and would try to resist Berlusconi's rise to political power.

I warmly remember the conversations I used to have with Nino. He was sympathetic to leftist causes, but found them, taken on their own, to be too rigid and, as a man of good humour, he could express his scepticism in amusing anecdotes. He had a great interest in India, which he later visited on behalf of MIT to give advice to the Planning Commission, then headed by Jawaharlal Nehru.

We continued our conversations when he came to Delhi, and as a seasoned iconoclast he applied his usual scepticism to my thesis that he might find his Indian servants to be far too submissive. 'As usual, you are wrong, Amartya,' Nino told me a few days later, 'as I have just confirmed while installing a calling bell in the servants' quarters. The installation was done when Giana [his wife] and I were out of the house, and when we came home and wanted to check whether the electrical work had been completed, the electrician said that it had been all done, and more.' At the request of their servant, Pradeep, another bell had been installed in the Andreatta living room, with a push button in the servants' quarters. Pradeep explained to Nino's wife, 'Madam, this is very convenient: when Madam wants Pradeep,

Madam pushes the white bell in your living room, and when Pradeep wants the Madam, he pushes the white bell installed in his room.' Aside from feeling reassured that my friend Nino had not lost his sense of humour despite the successes in his life, I also found his story of the two bells rather encouraging for the future of a changing India.

6

South Asians formed quite a distinct group in the Cambridge of my undergraduate days. I knew two Indians already before I came, having met them during their visits to Calcutta: Prahlad Basu and Dipak (Hapan) Mazumdar, who had come to Cambridge a year before me. I sought them out shortly after arriving and both became close friends. Prahlad later went into administration and became one of the leading civil servants in India, whereas Dipak became an academic like me – indeed, we were fellow teachers at the London School of Economics in the 1970s. Dipak and I often got together with his sparkling wife Pauline, a medical researcher with a gentle sense of humour.

I came to know many other Indians and Pakistanis and gathered with them on the campus, mostly in the evenings. Aparna Mehta, who would later marry Prahlad, became a very close and supportive friend and much like a family member. She had spent some of her childhood in Calcutta and spoke Bengali fluently. We often consulted each other about our respective problems. Our friends decided that we had formed a 'two-person mutual admiration society', though it would probably have been more accurate to describe it as 'mutual advice society'.

Another Indian I came to know well was Dipankar Ghosh, a very smart law student whose father, Dwarkanath Ghosh, had been one of the leading economists in India. I knew the family, but did not meet Dipankar until I got to Cambridge. He had studied at La Martinère College in Calcutta, which drew more fluently English-speaking students than my own educational background permitted. I called on Dipankar the day the term started, and we met in an Indo-Pakistani restaurant (inevitably called the 'Taj Mahal'), more or less opposite the Great Gate of Trinity. Dipankar did dazzlingly well as a law student at Cambridge (though it was hard to determine when he actually did his studying). We shared a group of common friends who gathered together quite regularly.

Dilip Adarkar, the son of another leading economist in India, belonged to the group, and, though I did not meet him until my second year, we rapidly became close friends. During our second and third years we did many things together, including a trip to Norway, Sweden, Denmark, Germany and the Netherlands. We drew on that closeness when my wife Nabaneeta and I later visited Stanford University in the summer of 1961, where he and his wife Chitra were finishing their graduate studies.

Some of the Indians I knew well were also at Trinity. I think particularly of Kumar Shankardass, who was a leading advocate at the Supreme Court of India in Delhi – he also served as the President of the International Bar Association during the 1980s, and remained a close friend. There was also Samir Mukherjee, who spent a lot of time then listening to jazz in various dives around town. When I talked with him last in Calcutta – it must be more than a couple of decades ago – I gathered that after recovering from a bout of polio, he was mainly devoting himself to writing left-wing plays for the Calcutta theatre (which was striking, given the upper-class, anglicized business background of his family). His brother Prabir, also at Trinity (and another hugely agreeable person), was sceptical of every political idea we ever discussed.

7

Indians and Pakistanis mingled with each other a great deal in those days in Cambridge, and while there was no India Society or Pakistan Society, there was a flourishing 'Majlis' (the term means an assembly in Persian) which welcomed all South Asians. It included, among my close circle, Rehman Sobhan from East Pakistan (later Bangladesh) and Mahbub ul Haq and Arif Iftekhar (perhaps the best debater I have ever heard) from West Pakistan. From my second year the Majlis became a central part of my life and I followed Rehman Sobhan as President, having been its Treasurer (guarding its non-existent treasures) during Rehman's presidential term. Rehman is probably the closest lifelong friend I have ever had, and the Majlis had a role in bringing us constantly together in the mid-1950s.

We held some joint meetings with the Oxford Majlis, and on one occasion Rehman and I went over there to debate the Cold War with them. Oxford was well represented by Kamal Hossain, who was studying law and later would be very active in the formation of Bangladesh; he became the first Foreign Minister of independent Bangladesh in 1971. Kamal told us that he had been warned that two very fiery left-wing speakers were coming from the Cambridge Majlis and was duly prepared for us. He confessed to some disappointment when Rehman and I proved to be not so scorching after all.

8

The Cambridge Majlis was quite vigorous in recruiting new students as they arrived each October. Rehman had a persuasive pitch ready to be unleashed for this purpose on any South Asian freshman. In October 1955, when the impressive Salma Ikramullah arrived at Newnham College from Pakistan, Rehman showed exceptional interest in wanting to recruit her. He urged me to accompany him when he gathered the courage to visit Salma to persuade her to join the Majlis. She smiled as Rehman brought out his well-rehearsed arguments as to why a newly arrived South Asian at Cambridge must join the Majlis immediately, or face a culturally and politically impoverished life. Salma listened with amusement as Rehman laboured, clearly unpersuaded by his hard sell. There was bemused scepticism in her eyes, but she decided to join us anyway.

I was not aware then, of course, how momentous a meeting that would prove to be in Rehman's own life, and for the lives of a great many others in the subcontinent and the world. Salma later married Rehman, and went on to join him in enterprises far larger, and far more important, than our little Majlis. She became a pioneering human rights activist and made a big difference to progressive causes in Bangladesh, passionately determined to fight social inequality in general and gender inequality in particular. As an inspiring and immensely admired teacher in Dhaka University's Law Department, Salma had fresh and far-reaching ideas on the importance of human rights, including the rights of women, and much to say on the practical ways and means of fighting against and overcoming social injustice. She also brought about a remarkable enrichment of the gender perspective and feminist understanding of social inequalities in Bangladesh and elsewhere. Among other important institutions, she founded the Ain O Salish Kendra (Centre for Law and Legal Redress), dedicated to working for the rights of those who receive little legal support from standard sources, to fight gender-related disadvantages.

Behind this work there was a deep intellectual analysis of the roots of deprivation. While legislation is often needed in defence of those who have very few recognized rights, even existing legal provisions may in effect not be useful for seriously deprived people because of other handicaps, such as illiteracy and penury. These disadvantages can prevent the downtrodden from invoking and utilizing the protective force of the law – if you cannot read what the law says, you are inescapably handicapped in using it. Along with her friends and colleagues (Sultana Kamal, Hameeda Hossain and others) who were – and are – hugely dedicated to these causes, Salma laid the foundations for a comprehensive approach to resisting human rights violations and defending the claims of the most disadvantaged members of society. Salma died suddenly in December 2003, but the Ain O Salish Kendra, with its intellectual reach and practical commitment, remains a lasting legacy of her vision and initiative.

9

I came to know Claire Royce, a student of economics, at the beginning of my second year. Her good looks and intelligence were very noticeable in the Marshall Library – the economics library – then located in Downing Street. I had many good conversations with her outside the library, chatting over coffee, and I knew that my friend Michael Nicholson adored her. Not long after our first meeting, Claire asked me whether I had any festive plans, and whether I would like to join her and her family in Coventry for Christmas. I was very happy to accept her invitation: Claire's boyfriend, Bev Pooley, was also coming, and she had asked Ken Pollak from South Africa and my friend Lal Jayawardena. We made quite a cosmopolitan group. Diana, Claire's captivating younger sister – lively and immensely charming – was there too.

I was familiar with the lights and sounds of an English Christmas, but I did not know much about the fun-and-frolic aspect of it. That deficit was certainly rectified by the festivities in Coventry. Claire's parents, Henry and Eleanor, were enormously welcoming and fascinating to talk with. They were interested in India, and also curious and caring about what I was experiencing so far away from home. I felt very much at ease in the Royce family home and had an extraordinarily merry time over the holiday.

I knew Lal Jayawardena already of course, but at the Royces' we could talk in a more relaxed way about his life and concerns. Lal was interested in being a leftist – that is the best way of putting it, I think, since neither in his inherited instincts, nor in his lifestyle, was he cut out to be one. He came from a wealthy and very successful banking family from Colombo, with a big house in a select location in Colombo-7, but his humanity and egalitarian reflections were constantly pulling him in a different direction. He was at this time writing an interesting essay on Marx (the title was, I think, 'Marx – a Much Maligned Man'). He would later marry a politically active left-wing intellectual, Kumari, who combined political fire with striking beauty.

During our Christmas in Coventry, Lal told me he was worried that he was dreaming in English, which made him feel distant from the people of Sri Lanka. 'What language do you dream in?' he asked me. When I said, 'Bengali, mostly,' he told me, 'I would like to do just that.' I told him, 'You wouldn't be able to follow it, since you don't know Bengali.' 'In Singhalese, I meant of course,' Lal said, 'but it is not easy, as I cannot control my dreams.' In the 1980s when Lal became the first Director of the World Institute for Development Economics Research (UNU-WIDER) in Helsinki, he initiated a number of major departures in the global agenda for development research, and I was proud to be able to work with him on them. His concerns and desires sprang from his egalitarian commitments, and we remained close friends until his death in 2004.

Diana Royce became a very close friend, from our time together in Coventry, and then through her subsequent visits to Cambridge. We enjoyed each other's company and that closeness enriched my life in many different ways. Diana herself later became involved in the local Conservative Party, but devoted most of her time to pro bono work for good social causes. My friend John Bradfield of Trinity explained to me how committed and effective Diana had been in improving Addenbrooke's Hospital in Cambridge. If her becoming a Conservative politician had surprised me (it had), there was no surprise in her dedication to social welfare in general and medical care in particular. Diana married a most likeable Cambridge man called George Abbott who, after studying in Cambridge, ran a small but very friendly travel agency in the centre of the town.

Claire also remained a close friend, and at different stages I have played various roles in her colourful life, including being a 'Dutch uncle' when her life got complicated. But my biggest contribution to Claire's life was surely my introducing her to Luigi Spaventa. Luigi, a stunningly brilliant economist, was my first research student (of which I am very proud). He came to Cambridge after studying at the University of Rome (La Sapienza) in 1957, the year I was elected to a Prize Fellowship at Trinity. When I returned from Calcutta to Trinity the following year, and began doing some teaching in addition to research, Luigi asked me to be his supervisor – he was primarily interested in the nature of deprivation in Italy's poorer southern region (the so-called Mezzogiorno). He was only a little younger than me, and I learned at least as much from my conversations with him – on economics, politics, Italian wines and on the social problems of Europe – as anything he could have possibly learned from me. Luigi did not go on to submit his thesis for a Cambridge Ph.D., even though he could have done it with very little extra effort ('not much use to me in Italy,' he explained), and he became professor at various Italian universities – a process the Italian system makes you go through – ending up with a professorship at his old university in Rome. He became active in politics as well, and was a member of the Italian parliament from 1976 to 1983, for the Communist Party which was then transforming itself into the Democratic Party of the Left. He served for a period as a Cabinet Minister and went on to hold various official leadership positions in economics, including being the head of CONSOB, the government commission that oversees the operation of business companies and regulates the Italian securities market and stock exchange.

One morning – it was in 1960 I think – Claire dropped into my rooms in New Court in Trinity, which overlooked the avenue over the river Cam. I was supervising – at least pretending to supervise – Luigi. It was clear that they made an immediate impression on each other, but they would not initially admit it. When Claire left, Luigi commented on the 'strait-laced English girl'. Claire similarly told me, not long afterwards, that my friend was 'much too well-behaved and much too well-informed, and must have been born with the *Manchester Guardian* tucked underneath his elbow'. I was agreeably surprised when a year or so later they told me they were about to get married, which they did. There followed a wonderful life together, with an enormous closeness, mutual support and complementarity.

10

Among my new circles, there was one which originated in medical necessity. I had come to Cambridge just one year after the heavy-dose radiation for the treatment of my oral cancer. The chances of recurrence were known to be high, and the dangers of radiation damage were very considerable too. My Calcutta hospital – Chittaranjan – had been so disorganized that I could not get from them a case history to take with me to Cambridge. Many years later, when I visited the hospital to check what records they had of my illness and of the treatment I had received, I was told that they couldn't find anything at all.

Luckily, my father, being the systematic man he was, had pages and pages of notes covering the diagnosis and medical consultations, the alternative treatments that were discussed, the precise amount of radiation that was being given to me and what my post-radiotherapy reactions had been. When I seemed to have recovered, my father placed the records neatly into a file, tied it – I remember this vividly – with a red string and told me, 'I hope – in fact I am sure – we shall not have to open this file again.' In fact I did open the file again, as it proved to be an invaluable resource, given the delinquency of

Chittaranjan Cancer Hospital's record-keeping. My mother's cousin Amiyamama, the surgeon who had done the original biopsy, also gave me a page and a half of capsule history, even though he was away from Calcutta when the decisions about radiation were taken.

I had kept those papers, but was not quite sure who to go to see in Cambridge. There were no physical changes for a while in my radiated mouth. My General Practitioner, Dr Simpson, read the notes, and after examining my well-healed palate decided not to do anything. But a few months after my arrival in Cambridge, the palate seemed to be shrinking at the edges and my upper teeth became quite loose (a common result of radiation treatment), with a fair amount of pain. So I went to see a dentist, who wanted to pull the teeth out immediately under local anaesthesia. But Amiyamama had told me to be extremely careful not to do anything in the mouth without expert advice, and in particular not to use any local anaesthesia, given the after-effects of radiation. The dentist was not particularly impressed by those words of caution but, noting my worry, said that he would arrange for my teeth to be pulled out in a little surgery he had in Addenbrooke's Hospital. If I was really concerned about some unknown danger, I could talk with one of the doctors in the Radio Therapy Centre (RTC) in the hospital.

I arrived at Addenbrooke's a little early for my surgery, and insisted that I must see an RTC expert *before* the tooth extraction occurred (which clearly irritated my dentist). But my insistence worked, and someone from the RTC did come to see me. This prompted a strong response. I was asked to wait and do nothing, and soon enough a senior oncologist from the RTC arrived at the dentist's surgery. He rapidly took charge of me and insisted I go with him at once. He admonished the dentist for not having been in touch with them earlier, and told me that in future I must not go to any dentist without talking with the RTC first. 'You can bring a huge problem on yourself if you mess around with your heavily radiated mouth,' he said. 'We know very little about what is going on in the region of your mouth which has received so much radiation. Anything you want to do in the mouth, you must check with us first.'

From that moment onwards I became a ward of the RTC, with regular check-ups, close examinations and some small but carefully planned minor procedures. I cannot describe adequately how impressed I was with the National Health Service – with their quality of care, medical cautiousness, as well as their humanity.

My relationship with the RTC became one of the most important connections in my life. Between 1953 and 1963 (my years in Cambridge), I sometimes had to go there several times a month, to follow up what looked like a potentially suspicious development. The first oncologist who looked after me, with exceptional care and skill, was a young doctor called Dr Levison. When he moved to a London hospital, Professor J. S. Mitchell, the Regius Professor of Physic, took over his responsibility. He was a superb scientist and a very kind medical practitioner. As well as dealing with whatever was happening in my mouth, he would give me, once every six months, an examination of my entire physical body – in line (I thought) with the title of his chair. He explained that it was best to be sure nothing untoward was happening in any other part of my body. I don't think I have ever been examined with such concentrated care. Aside from the need for general care he had talked about, he wanted to be sure that no secondaries were developing anywhere else (though oral squamous cell carcinoma rarely causes general metastasis – it tends to kill by local proliferation and eventual suffocation).

Professor Mitchell also had strong views about my normal eating and drinking. I must not have any fried food, he told me, and should drink my tea weak and with a lot of milk. 'Is this to prevent the cancer from coming back?' I asked him. 'No,' he said, 'this is to avoid other health problems that you might develop if you have bad eating habits.' Not to drink strong tea is a difficult thing for an Indian (Mitchell was even more suspicious of strong coffee), and his attempt to put me off alcohol – totally off it – also encountered some inner resistance in me.

I was intrigued by Professor Mitchell's directives about good living and asked Dr David Bratherton, who took charge of me at the RTC after him, about them. Dr Bratherton smiled a bit about the rigour of the Regius Professor's advice, saying, 'You must remember that Professor Mitchell is a teetotaller.' When I replied, 'That surely has nothing to do with his scientific advice?' Bratherton simply continued to smile, which I realized was a rather profound observation in epistemology.

It is hard for me to describe the extent of the personal attention I received from everyone at the RTC. I was longest with Dr Bratherton, who became like a member of my own family. I visited his home a number of times, and he came and dined with me at Trinity after I was elected to a Prize Fellowship in 1957. He spent a long time after dinner asking me about my life in India and my experiences in Britain. Much later, after his wife died and he was living alone in his large house on Grantchester Meadows, I spent an enchanting evening with him, when he played the piano beautifully for me. The music was superb, but there were too many pensive notes, reflecting his mood then, which also saddened me.

Bratherton not only kept track of my medical problems even after I left Cambridge in 1963, but he also followed my professional – and academic – life with great personal interest. Sadly he died in 1997, the year before I returned to Cambridge from Harvard – so my plan of entertaining him at the Master's Lodge never materialized. I think he would have liked to have seen that the endangered boy of whom he took so much care was leading a full life after all.

When I walk past Grantchester Meadows these days, I look at David's house with a strong sense of loss, but also with an overwhelming feeling of gratitude. When I landed at Tilbury Docks I had no idea who my new friends were going to be. Some closeness came from physical proximity, some from proximity of origin, some from political affinity, others still from personal fondness, and some – as with my doctors at the Radio Therapy Centre – from my deep vulnerability. As I reflected on my new life in Cambridge, I decided it was wonderful that weakness – not just strength – can bring people closer together.

18

What Economics?

In the summer of 1954 I was given rooms in Trinity in Whewell's Court, on the other side of Trinity Street, opposite the Great Gate. The rooms were spacious, with a nice bedroom and a sizeable living room. But of course – as in most of the College at that time – I had to cross the court to get to a lavatory, and cross Trinity Street – towel in hand – into the Great Court to have a shower. Since there was no hot water (or indeed any running water) in my rooms, the bed-maker brought two jugs of hot and cold water each morning with a large white bowl to pour them into so that I could wash and shave.

I was happy to be able to live in College at last, though I was sad to leave Mrs Hanger's house in Priory Road. I had come to like her a lot. She had always been friendly, but during the year of my stay she had also transformed herself into a crusader for racial equality. From being worried in October 1953 – when I first arrived – that my colour might come off in her bath, by the time I left she was lecturing everyone in the neighbourhood on the need to understand that 'all people are equal'.

When I came to say goodbye to her in June 1954, she gave me a cup of tea with some home-made cakes, saying that she would miss me. She then went on to say some very progressive things on race relations, and described how she had ticked off an Englishwoman at a dance club she went to regularly for not wanting to dance with an African man who was waiting to find a partner ('I was very upset – so I grabbed the man and danced with him for more than an hour, until he said he wanted to go home').

In my student room in Trinity College, Cambridge, 1955. Photograph by my cousin Baren Sen.

Years later, in January 1998, when I returned to Cambridge, I wanted to see her again and thought that she might enjoy a cup of tea at the Master's Lodge, but I could not find their name in the phone directory. So I went to Priory Road, but no one seemed to know where the Hangers had gone. It had, of course, been forty-four years since my last visit to her and it was silly of me to expect her to be still there. But I was sad not to be able to have even a glimpse of my warm and kindly landlady.

2

When I moved into Whewell's Court, I was welcomed by another undergraduate, Simon Digby, whose rooms were close to mine. He had joined Trinity two years before me, in 1951, and we had friends in common, though we did not really know each other before we became neighbours. I was very touched that Simon had cooked some

Indian food to welcome me to Whewell's Court. I was, alas, delayed on the day of my move and only got there, with my luggage, close to midnight. Of course, I had no idea that Simon was waiting for me with a prawn curry. We had a delicious meal – though it was my second dinner that evening and I suspected his too.

Simon's involvement and growing expertise in Indian history, particularly in pre-Mughal Islamic history, was already impressive – our conversations were effectively free tutorials for me. We did not, however, agree on contemporary politics, since Simon wanted to see India as a Hindu country in the same way that Pakistan can be described as a Muslim country. One of his main dislikes was Jawaharlal Nehru, especially for what he saw as Nehru's pretensions as a historian ('you can hardly do worse than his *Glimpses of World History*, you know,' he explained). Simon was also strongly out of tune with Nehru's politics. My claim that being a secular democracy has some serious merits was a difficult proposition for him to accept, at least at that time. I believe his views somewhat changed later on when he found a welcoming home for his Islamic studies in India, after being (for some reason) rebuffed in Pakistan. Simon, alas, is gone, but many of his followers are continuing his work, based in India.

3

What I knew from my studies at Presidency College seemed adequate for me to get by for my first year of economics at Cambridge, except for new departures such as the book Joan Robinson was completing called *The Accumulation of Capital*. The first lecture I attended in Cambridge had been one of hers. But, despite our friendly – and warm – personal relations, which included spending a lot of time with her and her family, an academic bond did not form between us. This bothered me, since I was very fond of her, and she was always affectionate, welcoming and supportive.

Joan had strong ties with India, which she had visited as a young woman. She married Austin Robinson, who had in the late 1920s served as a private tutor to an Indian prince, the son of the Maharaja of Gwalior. This was well before Austin came to Cambridge and became a well-known and universally liked professor there. Joan loved her time in India, visiting many historical sites (with and without Austin), and making a great many friends. If Joan's fondness for nearly everything Indian – she was often attired in Indian clothing – was a very prominent feature of her personality, her attitude to economic theory was much more discriminating. She was very strongly convinced of rights and wrongs in economics, and was determined that it was her duty to help the right side win. Her rejection of standard economics – often called 'mainstream economics' or 'neoclassical economics' – was as total as it was firm, but, on the other side, she found Marxian economic thinking – though promising – to be hopelessly wrong. She was particularly keen on criticizing – even ridiculing – her Cambridge colleague Maurice Dobb, who – as I have said earlier – was the leading Marxian economist at that time in Britain.

I must confess I was not particularly persuaded by Joan's understanding of Marx, nor by the new work on growth economics and capital theory she was engaged in when I arrived. I was, however, sufficiently curious about her ideas – and about her – to want her as an extra supervisor during my undergraduate studies, along with Dobb. This was during 1954–5, the second of my two years as an undergraduate at Cambridge.

Joan was then completing *The Accumulation of Capital*, which came out in 1956. She saw her work as a definitive disposal of mainstream capital theory as well as of 'their' theory of economic growth, which she wanted to replace with what she hoped would be a new way of seeing capital and growth. My curiosity made me accept her unusual suggestion that, instead of writing weekly essays for her to comment on (as is the custom in the tutorial system in Cambridge), I could read a chapter of her new manuscript each week and present her with my critique of it. I greatly enjoyed those readings and the meetings that followed. Her ideas were certainly original and interesting, even though I did not find them persuasive.

One result of my engaging with Robinson's new book in this way was that I became increasingly convinced that, despite my admiration for her, I was not going to be a 'follower', which I think she had rather hoped I would be. I was honoured by her faith in me and I did respect her greatly, but I could not persuade myself that she was on the right track. I argued with her a few times, but really got nowhere – she was much better at speaking than listening. Indeed, Joan was not only dogmatic: there was almost a determination not to consider contrary arguments, as if such a refusal could somehow make them go away. I could not help thinking that the argumentative tradition that had been so persistently championed in Indian philosophical debates, and which included careful listening, could have made something of a contribution to Joan's convictions about what makes a thesis powerful. Her neglect of mainstream theories seemed to me to lack a reasoned defence, as did her rapid dismissal of the Marxian perspectives carefully developed by Dobb, Sraffa and Hobsbawm.

4

Though the connections were not always clear, Joan's writing was noticeably influenced by John Maynard Keynes's rejection (particularly in his work on slumps and depressions) of the adequacy of the market economy. Many of the major debates in political economy in Cambridge were firmly geared to the pros and cons of Keynesian economics and the developments that emerged from Keynes's approach. There were sharp differences, loudly proclaimed, between Keynes's followers (among them Richard Kahn and Nicholas Kaldor, as well as Joan) and on the opposite side the so-called 'neoclassical' economists (including, in different ways, Dennis Robertson, Harry Johnson, Peter Bauer, Michael Farrell and others).

If Richard Kahn was in general the most bellicose of these neo-Keynesians, and Joan Robinson the most articulate and vocal, Nicky Kaldor, whose cogent presentation of capital theory brought it more in line with Keynesian thinking, was the most original and creative among them. He regarded the battle between the distinct schools with transparent irony and humour, and seemed to see them as little skirmishes that would not leave indelible marks on our understanding of economics. My own college, Trinity, was an oasis from this constant feuding, with three remarkable economists of very different political views who seemed happy to coexist with each other and interacted often. The Marxist Maurice Dobb and the conservative neoclassicist Dennis Robertson conducted joint seminars, and often joined hands with Piero Sraffa, whose scepticism seemed to apply to all the schools of economic thought.

The main debates in Cambridge economics at the time dealt substantially with economic aggregates – including the aggregate value of capital. Those described as 'neo-Keynesians' (sometimes, to confound us more, they were also called 'neo-Ricardians') were dead set against any use of 'aggregate capital' in economic modelling; the usefulness of the concept of capital in the form of a productive aggregate is a representational device, the success of which must depend on its circumstantial merits. There were, to be sure, difficulties – even internal contradictions – with the idea of aggregate capital as a factor of production, which Sraffa had brought out with crystal clarity. Attempts to go around them had already proved abortive. Several of my fellow students and close friends were working on these issues, and two in particular – Luigi Pasinetti and Pierangelo Garegnani – made definitive analytical contributions.

But while Cambridge economics was very engaged in subjects like this, it was much less concerned with other critically important issues, such as inequality, poverty and exploitation. Cambridge economics was meant to be politically left-wing – a cause to which it was, in some ways, dedicated. However, I found it difficult to believe that the downfall of capitalism, if that were to occur, would be caused by some sophisticated mistake in capital theory rather than because of the nasty way capitalism treats human beings. A. C. Pigou (who was still alive and living in Cambridge and who tended to be dismissed by neo-Keynesians as an old-fashioned neoclassical economist because he had challenged Keynes on many of his claims in macroeconomics) expressed a much better understanding of the real problem when he said: 'It is not wonder, but rather the social enthusiasm which revolts from the sordidness of mean streets and the joylessness of withered lives, that is the beginning of economic science.'

On these issues, Joan Robinson took a position – which has actually become quite popular in India now – that in terms of priorities, what you have to concentrate on first is simply maximizing economic growth. Once you have grown and become rich, you can then turn to health care, education and all that other stuff. This approach is, I think, one of the more profound errors in developmental thinking, since the need for good health and good education is at its peak when a country is poor.

Furthermore, even though economic growth is important, the single-minded pursuit of it – while neglecting education, health care and nutrition – is not only terrible for people's quality of life, but it is also a self-defeating strategy, since these crucial components of a decent human life are also important ingredients for human productivity, as Adam Smith noted a long time ago. Somehow Joan had little sympathy for the Smithian integrated understanding of economic development. For example, she strongly criticized Sri Lanka for offering subsidized food to everyone on nutritional grounds and for the sake of good health, even though it contributed to economic expansion at the same time. She dismissed such a mixed strategy with a hugely misleading analogy: 'Sri Lanka is trying to taste the fruit of the tree without growing it.'

The divisions between schools of economic thought seemed to play a mesmerizing role in Cambridge rhetoric, particularly in classifying economists into two distinct categories: friends or foes. The contrast between neoclassical and neo-Keynesian economics often figured in these disputes. 'Neoclassical' in the context of economics was not a term I knew before I came to Cambridge, but it was an example of a neologism that had caught on and was widely used in these debates. Any hope that I could guess what it really meant to be 'neoclassical' in economics, by analogy with the more common use of the term in art, sculpture and architecture, proved to be completely hopeless. Recollecting examples of neoclassical art I had seen, such as Jacques-Louis David's masterly painting of the *Oath of Horatii*, or Antonio Canova's sculpture *Psyche Revived by Cupid's Kiss*, offered me no clue.

A little research revealed that the original use of 'neoclassical' in economics, which was apparently by Thorstein Veblen in 1900, seems to have been intended as a prelude to a criticism of what was thus described and it is still hard to dissociate the term from its original derogatory use. I decided that it was much easier to think of neoclassical simply as mainstream economics, with a cluster of maximizing agents – capitalists, labourers, consumers and so on – who follow mechanical rules of maximization by equating marginal this with marginal that.

Veblen was a productive thinker, with much greater clarity on subjects other than his rather messy delineation of neoclassical economics: we owe to him such important ideas as 'conspicuous consumption' and 'the leisure class'. I remember being struck by the similarity between Veblen's approach to 'the leisure class' and Marc Bloch's characterization of people who 'lived on the labour of other people' (discussed in Chapter 13, in relation to an important interpretation of the labour theory of value). It was, in fact, important to get away from the over-used avenues of popular criticism (which is implicit, for example, in the idea of neoclassicism) to look for clearer characterization in the critiques of standard economics.

5

Even though there were a number of fine teachers in Cambridge who did not get very involved in these intense fights between different schools of thought (such as Richard Stone, Brian Reddaway, Robin Matthews, Kenneth Berrill, Harry Johnson, Aubrey Silberston, Robin Marris and Richard Goodwin), the political lines were, in general, very firmly – and rather bizarrely – drawn. The Keynesians were perceived to be to the left of the followers of neoclassical economics, but this was very much in the spirit of 'thus far but no further', since neo-Keynesians were firmly opposed to Marxists and other clearly left-wing schools of thought.

It was soon clear to me that there was no way in which different economists could be neatly ordered in just one dimension from left to right. Dobb, who was an astute Marxist economist, was often thought by Keynesians and neo-Keynesians to be 'quite soft' on neoclassical economics. Soft or not, my observations indicated that there was often more room for friendly relations between Marxists and neoclassical economists, than between neo-Keynesians and neoclassical economists. The Marxist Dobb, for example, one of the few economics lecturers in Cambridge at that time who was interested in welfare economics, was a close friend of Peter Bauer, the conservative neoclassical economist who would later be a nominated Tory member of the House of Lords – and economic adviser to Margaret Thatcher.

Despite my own left-wing inclinations, I realized soon after I arrived in Cambridge that the right-wing Bauer was not only the best teacher of development economics but also the most accomplished thinker on the subject in the university, by a wide margin. Indeed, he was one of the most original development economists in the world, and a lot of what I came to understand about 'how development happens' was the result of our regular conversations. I felt very privileged that Peter befriended me from the time I was a young student and joined me for coffee nearly every week – 'to meet and argue' as he used to put it, which was a source of great gain for me. My friendship with Bauer lasted for the rest of his life. The fact that the neo-Keynesians saw little in his work is not, I believe, to their credit.

6

While I was impressed by the work of many different schools of economics, my interest in welfare economics – including the assessment of how well a society was doing – continued to be strong. This field within economics directly assesses the well-being of individual members of a society and makes an aggregative evaluation of the welfare of society as a whole. It was becoming clear to me that this was a subject in which I was particularly interested.

How do we determine how well a society is doing? Or, to put it in the language of welfare, how can we assess social welfare? How can we talk sensibly about advancing the welfare of a society? Since a society contains many people, the welfare of a whole society must be related, in one way or another, to the welfare of the individuals that make up that society. Any attempt at making comparative judgements about social welfare must, therefore, involve aggregation over many individuals, and that must involve social choice theory in some form.

Assessing the *collective* welfare of individuals who make up a society is one kind of social choice problem. Utilitarian social aggregation, as championed by Jeremy Bentham, gives priority to the sum-total of utilities without worrying about distribution. In contrast, the theory of justice advocated by the famous philosopher John Rawls pays more attention to inequalities and at the same time puts an end to the exclusive concentration on utilities (taking into account other concerns such as liberty). There are many possible ways of characterizing social welfare and many different ways of doing the aggregation exercise and judging them comparatively.

Another approach is that of a voting mechanism. Different individuals may demand our support and we may have some rule or other about how to choose between competing social alternatives, including the choice between different leaders of a society. The majority vote is a well-known example of a social choice rule. There are also many other examples of social choice problems.

Each social choice exercise may involve problems of a particular kind. For example, even the highly regarded majority vote may lead to inconsistencies (what is often called 'majority cycles') and to the absence of a majority winner. In line with what we briefly discussed in Chapter 12, we can use majority rule to understand the demands of inconsistency. For example, if three voters 1, 2 and 3 respectively rank in descending order three alternatives as [x, y z], [y, z, x] and [z, x, y], then in a majority vote x will defeat y, while y defeats z, and z defeats x, so that there would not be a majority winner at all. So it would be impossible to find a cogent resolution to the problem through majority rule. This problem, identified by the Marquis de Condorcet in the eighteenth century, was shown by Kenneth Arrow in 1950 to be pervasively present in social choice exercises, thus apparently making a democratic choice impossible, if we insist on certain firm rules of consistency. Social choice theorists have therefore had to look for sensible ways of tackling the general challenge of inconsistency – and the related impossibility problems. This applies as much to social welfare judgements as to voting decisions.

7

After arriving in England from India I tried to see whether I could make an intellectual connection between my principal academic concerns in economics while I was still in Calcutta and what I was hoping to concentrate on while studying in Cambridge. This proved to be hard. After reading Arrow's *Social Choice and Individual Values* in Calcutta and looking at the newly emerging literature related to it (as well as thinking a fair amount about the new subject of social choice theory for myself), I could see that my interest in the field was becoming very strong. But I could not persuade any Cambridge faculty member to take an interest in social choice, or to encourage me to work on anything that related to it.

There could have been a way of using welfare economics to connect social choice theory and the more standard economic subjects recognized in Cambridge, but welfare economics was seen as a non-subject there. Not long before I arrived, the brilliant South African economist Johannes de Villiers Graaff (known as 'Jan') had shown in a captivating thesis that without assessing value judgements about social welfare there is not a lot that can be said in welfare economics. That could, of course, have been the beginning of a critical scrutiny of how social judgements can be linked to individual welfare assessments (or individual value judgements), just as Arrow had tried to do through the use of sensible axioms in social choice theory. Instead, Graaff's analysis was seen as the end of the subject, particularly since the nature of Arrow's impossibility theorem was not adequately understood by most economists in Cambridge. In fact Arrow's conclusion was perceived as comprehensive devastation, rather than as an invitation to scrutinize the proposed axioms and their combinations. So, after Graaff, welfare economics was typically seen as a hopeless ditch rather than as a field which could be fruitfully tilled.

When I told Joan Robinson that I wanted to work on welfare economics, she said, 'Don't you know that this is a busted subject?' She told me the story that clever economists were all trying to do welfare economics, but 'the cleverest of them all, Jan Graaff, showed that all this is nonsense'. I told Joan she might be mistaken in her interpretation of Graaff's work: first, Graaff didn't in fact show that welfare economics was nonsense; second, he himself never claimed that he had. Joan was not only unpersuaded, she had no interest in listening to my thoughts on the subject. She told me that I had better work on something more useful.

I did try to recruit one or two of the other teachers in Cambridge to join me in taking an interest in social choice theory, but had no success. No one could find a reason to encourage me. Richard Kahn, like Joan, was hostile. Nicholas Kaldor did what he normally tended to do, namely encourage you on the grounds that a certain amount of folly in one's life is necessary for character-building. The only member of the Cambridge economics faculty who lectured on welfare economics was Maurice Dobb. A number of his fellow left-wingers regarded this as a great mistake on Maurice's part ('a sell-out to the right' was often their confused summary of what he did). Dobb was rather allergic to mathematical reasoning, like many other members of the economics faculty at that time, but he wanted me to explain to him the substance of Arrow's theorem and why it was interesting. He listened to me quite attentively, but then told me that the subject was too mathematical for us to work together on it. However, he was willing – indeed, eager – to chat with me about the parts of social choice theory he understood. 'This will be a nice excursion for me,' he said.

The other teacher who took some interest in my involvement with social choice theory was a Marxist too, though of a rather different kind, namely Piero Sraffa. Sraffa had (as I have said) been very close to Antonio Gramsci, the great leftist intellectual who established the Italian Communist Party. Sraffa said he wanted to discuss with me the nature of social communication that social choice theory must yield, and this – though rather neglected by Arrow – turned out to be a very interesting challenge.

8

The financial stringency I endured as an undergraduate largely disappeared when I became a research student after graduation. I was now fully covered by two scholarships. One of them was something called the Wrenbury Scholarship, which was awarded on the basis of performance in the BA examination, but it had some odd formalities attached to it. I learned that it was the duty of Dennis Robertson as the Professor of Political Economy in Cambridge to write a few lines each term on what I was doing. 'Why don't you,' he told me, 'write something in the third person about your own work so that I can send it on? But don't try humour, they don't like that in the Registry!'

Humour would not have been easy anyway, since I found it difficult to decide where to begin my research and what to choose as the subject for my doctoral thesis. Joan Robinson wanted me to join her in doing capital theory. She told me, 'This is where really original work can be done,' adding, 'let us together put the last nail in the coffin of neoclassical economics.' When I told Maurice Dobb about Joan's advice, he responded, 'Leave the nailing to her, and do whatever interests you most.'

I told Dobb that I would really like to focus on some problem in social choice theory, following up and expanding on what Kenneth Arrow had done in *Social Choice and Individual Values*. He replied, 'Do that when there are others around who are also interested in the subject. Come and talk with me on your ideas on social choice whenever you like, but take something else as your doctoral topic – some subject on which you will find others who are also interested and have some knowledge and expertise.'

So I did. I settled on working on 'choice of techniques' – specifically how to choose appropriate techniques of production, assessed from the social point of view, in an economy with a lot of unemployment and low wages. Partly to placate Joan, who became my thesis supervisor, I stuck the word 'capital' into the thesis title. This was easy to accommodate, since I was very concerned with the question of how capital-intensive production techniques should ideally be in a cheap-labour economy. There were some complications – connected with the impact of technical choice on consumption and savings – in what might otherwise seem like a question with an obvious answer. I called the thesis 'Choice of Capital-Intensity in Development Planning'. Piero Sraffa laughed at the title when I mentioned it to him, saying, 'No one will have a clue what your thesis is on.' He said he would strongly suggest changing the title before I published the dissertation. However, for the doctoral work itself, he said, 'The title is suitably mysterious – perfect for a Ph.D. dissertation.'

19

Where is Europe?

I

If there was one thing that hit me hard in my first autumn in Cambridge, it was the fact that the sun began setting so early. After lunch there would be little clear daylight. As I enjoyed the company of people around me more and more, I saw less and less clearly the town in which I was now living. Sunset at 3.30 p.m. is a beastly experience for anyone, especially for someone from the Indo-Gangetic plain. No wonder the British have had such an obsession with possessing an empire where the sun never sets.

The idea of visiting Italy was in my mind well before I left India. My fascination had begun when I became gripped by Renaissance painting during my student days, both in Santiniketan and in Calcutta. I had bought, over the years, affordable books of reproductions of Italian Renaissance pictures from the early period of Giotto, Fra Angelico and Botticelli to the later masterpieces of Leonardo, Michelangelo and Titian, and had told myself that someday I would see the real things. I was reminded of that desire as we saw the Italian coast from SS *Strathnaver* on my way to Britain in September 1953. Even angry Stromboli at night, seen from our boat, added to my strong wish to visit Italy.

This determination to visit Italy received a huge boost in my days at Presidency College from seeing Italian neorealist movies, which transformed my understanding of how films communicate. Discussions on European politics in the coffee house added to my interest, making me read a lot about how the Italian Resistance movement fought the fascist regime and ultimately triumphed over it. I did not know then that I was soon to come to know well many people who had been involved in the Italian Resistance.

There was, however, a significant obstacle in making a trip to Italy, even from the proximity of England. My father had given me a budget of £600 for my first year in Cambridge. This was adequate for normal expenses for a year, including College fees, but not much more than that. I told myself that for any indulgence I would have to cut some of my standard expenses. I could justify an overseas visit as an educational interest, but I was mainly moved by the simple, intense hedonistic urge to see my favourite pictures, statues, films and the beautiful buildings – about half the listed buildings in the world are in Italy. By the time the winter chill began to ease in March, I started calculating whether I could manage it. It was at that time that Robert, a student of 'Modern Literature', whom I knew rather distantly but liked a lot, told me that he was buying a cheap ticket for a 'Fine Arts Tour' in Italy arranged by the National Union of Students. This would take him to Italy and back on chartered flights, and it would also cover local travel and hotels and food in six cities (Milan, Venice, Verona, Florence, Perugia and Rome). I popped the critical question, 'How much will it cost?' 'Fifty pounds, everything included,' he replied.

I went home, tallied my financial records again, and then went to the NUS office and bought a ticket for the tour. I told myself that I would have to make economies in other areas. Happily, shortly before we were to leave, Trinity told me that they had just elected me to be a Senior Scholar. The emoluments were not huge (except for UK citizens whose counties were committed to supporting the academic expenses of those elected to be College Scholars), but even the basic rewards of the scholarship were considerably greater than the expenses I had incurred at the NUS travel office. And there were additional benefits of being a Senior Scholar, such as exemption from College fees and entitlement to stay without charge in College rooms throughout the year – vacations included. As I boarded our chartered flight to Milan at the old London airport, I almost felt rich.

2

The Italian trip was a great success. My companions were very agreeable – it did not hurt that the group included eighteen young women and three men (including Robert and me, and a nice school teacher in his late forties). The modest hotels we stayed in were quite comfortable and the food was excellent. What a contrast between a proper al dente pasta and Trinity's over-boiled cabbage and Brussels sprouts, stripped of both colour and flavour. The museums were welcoming and totally divine. I spent whole days in different museums (the Uffizi, Pitti Palace, the Vatican and others) and walked endlessly back and forth in the beautiful cities around them.

I also felt very happy amid the noise and conviviality of Italian life, which I found quite energizing – life in Cambridge in comparison was so restrained. One night – I think in Perugia – I was woken by very loud conversations on the street underneath my window. I lost some sleep, but enjoyed the evidence of life. At breakfast the next morning I was the only one who was not complaining about the noisiness of Italians. I liked how unrepressed they were.

I had a copy of the complete Shakespeare with me (he had contributed to my fascination with Italy as a student in Calcutta) and spent some time trying to establish correspondences between what I was seeing and what I had read. Where in Venice did Othello land after his victory? Where did Proteus talk about 'the uncertain glory of an April day' with the other gentleman of Verona? I would have loved to have read Shakespeare's diary, if he had kept one, recording his impressions of his visits to Italy, and I was hugely disappointed when I later learned that he had probably never been to Italy at all.

3

The magical tour eventually came to an end. But by then I had decided that I was not going to fly straight back to London with the others, since the Cambridge summer vacation had just begun. Robert had taken the same decision, and had left the party to go to Switzerland before we reached Rome. I said goodbye there to my very pleasant companions as they took their chartered flight back, and we all promised to write to each other – which nobody did.

I moved slowly north on my own from Rome, heading for the Dolomites. I stayed in youth hostels, moving between them mostly by hitch-hiking and occasionally, when the going proved difficult, by short train journeys at student fares. I had twenty pounds in my pocket, which seemed more than enough to cover travel, accommodation and food from Rome to Cambridge.

In Trento, at the foot of the Dolomites, when I asked someone where the youth hostel was (I knew there was one from the guidebook to youth hostels I had with me), he pointed to the top of a mountain and told me I could get there in about two hours, with some rapid uphill walking. So, with my rucksack on my back, I set off on this stamina-building walk, to arrive at a youth hostel that was still under construction. There were bathrooms and toilets, but as yet, rather awkwardly, no doors.

I was very reluctant to leave Italy and dithered by hiking for a few days with a group of English students who were staying in the hostel who had offered to show me some particularly beautiful views on the mountainous paths. But ultimately I crossed the Alps and arrived at Innsbruck. After Austria, I joined Robert for a couple of days in Switzerland and then proceeded on my own to Paris and Calais and back to England. I still had a bit of change left, and felt quite pleased with my determined survival on bread, cheese, coffee, hitch-hiking and youth hostels. On the ferry across the Channel, I felt sad that my continental visit was over, but also very happy – which was unexpected – to be returning to the familiar surroundings of my college and to what had become my home town.

4

My experience in Italy of the ease of seeing places by hitch-hiking and youth-hostelling had gripped me, and so I wanted to do this again and again – in other parts of Europe – including France, Belgium, the Netherlands and Germany. These travels happened one by one. I went sometimes with friends and sometimes without. In 1955, the summer after my Italian trip, I attempted a tour through Norway and Sweden with a few South Asians, both Indians and Pakistanis, from Cambridge. We landed in Bergen in Norway on a ferry from Harwich, and saw a lot of the country hitch-hiking – and enjoying the mountains on the way. But after Oslo, as we crossed into Sweden with the intention of going to Stockholm, hitch-hiking became rapidly less pleasant. It turned rainy, the summer was ending (this was early September), and the passing cars seemed most reluctant to stop. My hitch-hiking partner was Rehman Sobhan from East Pakistan, and I told him that his long beard was discouraging car drivers from considering us as possible passengers. Rehman resisted my strong recommendation that he should make use of a razor and he felt completely vindicated when a car went past us and then came back, with the driver telling us that his child in the back seat wanted to have a better look at Rehman's beard.

The car owner drove us a long way and even offered us a fine dinner at his home. We had engaging conversations on many subjects related to South Asia, including the variety of eating rules and prohibitions in the subcontinent. He wanted to know whether it was true that one of us did not eat beef, while the other avoided pork. Rehman explained that I was rule-blind and did not obey any food restrictions at all, but that our host was in general absolutely right – Hindus do not typically eat beef, and Muslims shun pork. But Rehman wanted him to know more, particularly with regard to the anthropology of behaviour. So he went on, 'The restrictions are, however, not at all comparable, since Hindus avoid beef because they regard cows to be holy, whereas we Muslims refuse pork because we believe pigs are dirty.'

We spent some time on that sophisticated distinction, while Rehman unleashed his pedagogic skills with the gusto of a great teacher. As we were leaving, after thanking our host, he said that he was grateful to us for expanding his knowledge. Then he added that someday he would like to continue the conversation since he very much wanted to know why Muslims regarded pigs as holy. Rehman seemed saddened by the poor results of his anthropology teaching, and I had to console him by pointing out that if he learned economics very, very well, he could be employed teaching that and then he would not have to look for a job as an anthropology teacher.

Rehman and I eventually decided that our hitch-hiking was proceeding much too slowly, so we took a bus to a railway station and then a train to Copenhagen. It was not raining there and there was more daylight. Our hitch-hiking picked up again, taking us through Denmark, Germany (we lingered in Hamburg, with its old sites and new scars from the heavy Allied bombing less than a decade before) and the Netherlands (enjoying the charm and elegance of Amsterdam), and finally to the Hook of Holland and the ferry back to Harwich.

5

There was another experience during my European travels which gave me reason to reflect. When I was invited in 1958 to go to Warsaw University to give lectures in economics for two weeks, despite being totally under-qualified (I had not even submitted my doctoral thesis at Cambridge), I was rather elated. The opportunity of seeing Poland and meeting interesting people was hard to resist. My hosts in Warsaw explained that they did not have the ability to pay me in foreign currency, but once I was in Poland they could pay me well in Polish money. They would put me up in Warsaw at an excellent hotel and look after me very well.

The proposal seemed to me attractive enough to take the risk of travelling even with my fairly empty pocket. After some hesitation, I bought myself a ticket for the long train journey from London to Warsaw, changing in Berlin. The first part of the journey was unproblematic, but my train arrived late in Berlin – late enough for me to miss the connection to Warsaw – a daily West Europe to East Europe transfer. So I was stuck in the large East Berlin station, with the prospect of spending twenty-four hours with barely enough money for a cup of coffee, let alone a room and a bed.

As I was loitering on the platform trying to figure out how I should face this little crisis, an Indian figure emerged out of nowhere. He came forward and introduced himself as Shyam Sundar De. He explained that he was from Calcutta and studying electrical engineering in Berlin. He had come to the railway station only because his girlfriend wanted to use the facilities there. He asked me why I was visiting Berlin. I told him my not particularly credible story. I must have seemed quite desperate.

Then peculiar things started to happen. Shyam arranged for me to have a pass to roam around East Germany, then another one allowing me to move about freely in West Berlin. They took me for dinner in the dining hall of one of the engineering colleges (Shyam's German girlfriend, who was also very friendly, explained to me what the 'delicacies' were that evening), and I was finally lodged in a fine guest room of the engineering college where Shyam was studying. The next day, while Shyam and his girlfriend were at their classes, I had a good look around one part of East Berlin and a larger part of West Berlin.

In the evening they saw me off at the station for the train to Warsaw. Since he thought I might run into another difficulty somewhere between Berlin and Warsaw, he insisted on tucking some money in the breast pocket of my shirt. 'But how do I return this to you?' I asked. In reply Shyam took down in his diary the train times of my connection in Berlin on the way back, fourteen days later. 'I will be here,' he said.

My Warsaw trip went well. I particularly enjoyed meeting the students and visiting Chopin's beautiful home nearby. At one point a fellow left-winger who wanted to talk took me into the bathroom and turned on all the taps so that his criticism of the regime would not be overheard. On the way back, at Berlin station, there was Shyam waiting for me on a bench on the platform. I noticed him first by his loud English greeting, 'How did you like Warsaw?' It is hard to express adequately how grateful I was.

On reflecting on this episode, I knew of course how very lucky I had been, but I also recognized how widespread such qualities of human kindness and helpfulness could be. If Shyam's inclination to help someone in difficulty was one aspect of his values, his willingness to trust – even with his money (as a subsidized student he could not have been rich) – someone utterly unknown to him must be another. Immanuel Kant – and following him Isaiah Berlin – may well have been right to warn us that 'out of the crooked timber of humanity, no straight thing was ever made'. But humanity does also have 'straight timber' that can surprise us with its admirable goodness. There are betrayals, violence, massacres and famines, but also astonishing acts of generosity and kindness.

6

Among the places I visited, the one I wanted to return to again and again was Paris, with its prodigious cultural offerings (the Louvre being at the top of the list) and neighbouring delights, such as the extraordinary Gothic cathedral of Chartres. Since I am, in general, not a fan of Gothic architecture, I was surprised how much I liked Chartres. My visits to Paris soon became frequent. It was not, however, easy to get there by hitch-hiking from England and soon I discovered that many cut-price routes existed. Once I had restrained my urge to travel on the classic route of London–Dover–Calais–Paris, there were a great many plebeian possibilities. One of them took me by bus to the edge of the English Channel, then placed me for a very short hop on a rickety plane, landing almost immediately afterwards on the other side of the water, after which we were taken by bus to Paris. It seemed like a journey calculated to defy the seriousness of the Channel. By the time the Channel Tunnel opened many years later, I had developed quite an expertise on the various inexpensive ways of travelling to the city.

One method I did not consider was trying to emulate the daring British and French souls who competed with each other to swim across the Channel. There were, in fact, also a few Indians attempting the feat. I was very impressed to see the announcement that there was a determined Bengali from Calcutta who was preparing to do it. I followed his progress in the papers with great interest, including his preparations, on which he made periodic statements. Then came the day when he was going to embark on the cross-Channel swim. Next morning I grabbed a newspaper to see how well he had done: it turned out that he had given up halfway. When asked by his rescuers whether he was too tired, or feeling ill, he said that his reason for abandoning the challenge was 'none of those'. Instead, he explained that while swimming he kept thinking about why he was doing this, and finally asked himself, 'What exactly is the point of it?' I found the resilient wisdom of our Bengali hero, halfway across the Channel, very reassuring.

In Paris I discovered the Hotel Select, at the distinguished location of Place de la Sorbonne, which ran for no more than 30 metres from the Boulevard Saint-Michel to the locked iron gates at the back of the Sorbonne campus. The services offered by Hotel Select were minimal (and there was no breakfast), but so was the price of a room, and I became a regular visitor. My usual room in the run-down hotel overlooked the very short road that began in the boisterous Boulevard Saint-Michel and ended quietly at the closed iron gates of the Sorbonne. Many years later, when the Sorbonne generously awarded me an honorary doctorate in a very colourful ceremony, I could not resist referring to my long-term connection with Place de la Sorbonne. To my embarrassment, my casual remark about longing to see those closed gates open for just a few minutes led to precisely that. It was a different perspective on an old view, but I also noticed that my old, familiar lodging had been handsomely converted into a very smart modern hotel.

One of the best things about staying at the Hotel Select in those days was the café just below it where I could drink large cups of *café au lait* with unbelievably delicious croissants. Sometimes I came to Paris with friends from Cambridge and was treated as the knowledgeable man who knew his way around in that captivating city. I would guide my friends – mostly other students – to affordable rooms in the Hotel Select and then to the breathtaking beauty of Chartres and back. If my economics failed, I thought perhaps I could run a tour company.

7

Most places I visited in Europe were for short stays – a taster of a town and its museums and galleries – and then I moved on. But in 1962 I found myself for three weeks in a charming hill town called Alpbach in Austria. The occasion was a pan-European summer school there, where I had a teaching job. This was a long time later; by then I was married and my wife Nabaneeta and I both liked the austere beauty of Alpbach. Eric Hobsbawm was also teaching at the summer school, and we drove him there from Cambridge. After Alpbach we went on to Aix-en-Provence, where Eric and I were both presenting papers at the Second International Economic History Conference – he with the entitlement of the vastly accomplished, and I with an invitation possibly indicating the conference organizer's willingness to experiment.

Our journey together was quite wonderful. Eric knew all the places en route, and told us their history wherever we stopped – in Belgium, Germany, Austria, Italy and France. Eric had a great influence on my own thinking, but I was surprised that the most brilliant Marxist historian of our time was also spectacularly well informed about ecclesiastical history, on which we could draw as we moved from one beautiful cathedral to another.

Eric and his girlfriend Marlene Schwartz were planning to wed shortly after our European voyage. During the journey Eric stopped and bought various household items from a list that Marlene had given him; later she too would become a very close friend. One of the subjects of our conversation was how the attempts which were being made then at integration might change Europe. I did not know then how increasingly important this would become in the development of European politics.

8

Some of my classmates from Santiniketan and Calcutta were studying – or being trained – in Germany, in Cologne, Duisburg, Aachen and elsewhere. I tried to visit them all. Shib Krishna Kar from Santiniketan took me and my cousin Bacchuda in a car he had borrowed from a garage whose owner he knew. We managed to get involved in an accident, with no harm to any of us but quite a dent on the car. Shib panicked, and we were all very relieved when the amiable garage owner said that, since he ran a repair workshop, he could easily fix it – 'it would have been more of a problem if you had dropped the engine'.

My visits to Germany had started much earlier – in 1955. Since the memories of the last war were still fresh in people's minds in the 1950s, I wondered what the Germans, who all seemed very pleasant and friendly, thought of the barbarities committed under Nazi rule, especially in the concentration camps, and also, from the other perspective, what they made of the atrocious fire bombings of German cities by the Allied forces. Bacchuda and Shib were both alarmed that

I might decide to talk politics in public. 'Please, please, stay off politics altogether,' Bacchuda said firmly. He added, 'In fact there are still some admirers of Hitler around – when we are on public transport we try to avoid any Nazi word or name that may be easily recognized even in an unfamiliar language.' 'What do you do,' I asked, 'if Hitler comes up in your Bengali conversation? Hitler is Hitler, surely, in every language?' 'We call him Hitu Babu,' Bacchuda said. I liked that tactful Bengali renaming, though it sounded rather too friendly for the kind of man Hitler was.

I went to sleep that night wondering what Hitu Babu would have made of it. But I also questioned how Europe would overcome the political divisions that had made such terrible use of national pride and identity through the first half of the century. Seeing so many names of Trinity men killed in the world wars engraved on the walls of the College Chapel had given me a shock that remained with me as I travelled around Europe, whose nations had been mortal enemies of each other so very recently.

The carnage in Europe in the two world wars really was appalling. It was hard to understand how countries neighbouring each other, with long histories of cultural, artistic, scientific and literary interactions, could become so remorselessly committed to killing each other. As I write in 2021, identity conflicts are largely focused on religious divisions – involving, for example, al-Qaeda, Boko Haram, the Islamic State, powerful antisemitism and organized Islamophobia, including a cultivated hostility to refugees from the Middle East and Africa. It is difficult to appreciate that, less than a century ago, Europeans were hugely occupied in fighting each other along the lines not of religious division but of national identity. Differences of citizenship – British, German or French – easily overcame the commonality of religion in the form of Christianity.

This – after my childhood experiences of sudden outbursts of Hindu-Muslim riots – was another stage in my attempt to understand the disruptive role of identity. How could the Germans and the English slaughter each other in peculiarly bloody wars and become the best of friends just a few years later? How could the Indians of the 1930s – at peace with each other – suddenly turn into belligerent Hindus and Muslims, generating huge communal riots in the 1940s? And how did it suddenly stop as quickly as it started? Can clear-headed reflection help us overcome these outbursts of violence?

9

Along with visits to my friends in Cologne, Duisburg and Aachen, I wanted to see more of other parts of Germany. The idea of a river cruise down the Rhine appealed to me, and I found that I could start off from Cologne, where I had gone to see friends. The first time I took a boat from there all the way to Mainz, stopping at various charming river ports including Linz and Koblenz, I was enchanted by the natural beauty around me. The rules of travel were very user-friendly and affordable: you could get off anywhere en route from the boat, take your break and resume your journey on another boat from there, using the same through ticket to Mainz. I loved the experience so much that I did the same journey twice more. I became very attached to the territory of the Rhine.

On one occasion, some English students I was sitting next to on the boat told me that they wanted to see what was going on at the wine festival in Rüdesheim, which had just begun, and persuaded me to join them. At one stage, a rather highbrow group of German college students arrived and wanted to know where I was from. Since both India and Bengal figured in my reply, one particularly curious member of the group wanted to know what the oldest name of Bengal was. 'Historically, that is, what was it called?' Since a united Bengal had not emerged until only a few centuries ago, I tried 'Bongo' – referring to an important region that existed before a united Bengal but was a big part of it.

One of my new German friends wanted to know whether he was right in thinking that Bongo was next to Congo. I had to disappoint him, and drew a world map on a paper napkin, locating Africa (including Congo) and India (including Bongo), with as many countries in between as I could fit in. Shocked by the distance between the two, one of the German girls became quite excited and announced, 'We have to get them together – we must!' 'Not easy,' I said, 'since geography is not readily alterable. Countries are where they are.' 'You are missing my point,' she said emphatically, 'we have to get the whole world together.' She repeated, 'We want all to be together. Do you understand?' While I was figuring out what she was trying to tell me, she made another grand statement, I think to help me: 'We are all neighbours.'

It struck me that this simple observation had some similarity with what Jesus told the disputant lawyer in Luke's Gospel in the story of the Good Samaritan. So I asked her, 'Anyone can be anyone else's neighbour? Is that what you are saying?' 'Yes,' she agreed, 'but we must work for it.' She said this with such force that it looked as if she was going to rush out of the bar and start her global work immediately.

As I went to sleep in my little bedroom thinking about that unexpected conversation, I decided that it was perhaps bringing me to recognize how the young minds of post-war Germany were shifting, through deliberate reflection, away from the nationalist frame of mind that had so dominated the country over several decades. The German girl's words from the 1950s came back to me when I recently heard Angela Merkel arguing, in response to the Syrian crisis, that Germany must take a large number of refugees, as a part of its reasoned commitment to 'our global neighbours'.

Was I right in my interpretation of what the young German student was trying to tell me? I could not be sure, but I believed I might have been. There were certainly many signs of a change in the country only a decade after a terrible war in which Germany had been the prime mover. As I tried to sleep in my little bed-and-breakfast place in Rüdesheim, I marvelled at having encountered such commitment to global amity – if that is what it was – in a local wine festival on the Rhine.

It was too late for a good night's sleep. Dawn was breaking in Rüdesheim. I was exhausted and intrigued, but also oddly happy.

20

Conversation and Politics

I

Given the international connections of left-leaning intellectuals in Calcutta, I should not have been surprised to receive a welcome from the Cambridge left when I first arrived there. Indeed, there was a warm letter waiting for me at the Porter's Lodge from Aldrich (Ricky) Brown – a talented mathematician – of the Cambridge University Socialist Club, saying that he had received 'warnings' from Calcutta about my impending arrival and inviting me to a party that the Club was holding for new students in Cambridge. I went to the party and decided to join the Club. There were a number of self-declared Marxists among its activists, but as a self-conscious intellectual snob from College Street, I was slightly shocked by their rather limited reading of Marxist classics, including Marx's own work.

I was also surprised to see how untroubled the leaders of the Club were by the severe authoritarianism in the Soviet Union and in the East European countries under Soviet dominance. True, this was only 1953, well before the Twentieth Congress of the Communist Party of the Soviet Union in February 1956 at which Khrushchev would present his devastating exposure of the Stalinist regime; it was also before the Hungarian uprising that same year, which moved many minds. However, evidence of Soviet political tyranny had been mounting for years before that, and I thought it would be impossible for anyone concerned with freedom not to think seriously about the purges and what were already being accurately called the 'show trials'. Partha Gupta and I had spent a lot of time talking about precisely this when we were holidaying together in Darjeeling, just before we both left for England.

During the war, British soldiers wrote on their tanks, 'Hold them, Joe, we won't be long.' By 1953 that solidarity had long been forgotten, as was the extraordinary moment of the liberation of Auschwitz by the Red Army in January 1945. Stories about Soviet authoritarianism were now rampant, no doubt helped by US propaganda, but not just because of that. Yet the tyranny was strongly denied not only within the British Communist Party, but also in the broader left-wing associations, including the Cambridge Socialist Club.

However, the Club did play a more constructive role in drawing attention to egalitarian concerns within Britain and across the world, and also in questioning the belligerence of the Cold War while pressing for nuclear disarmament. These concerns were closely linked with the practice of politics, but the Club's role in making use of Marxist analysis was rather less effective.

The inner circle of the Cambridge University Socialist Club had activists who seemed a bit like the extreme left of the Labour Party, but there were theorists too. These included Pierangelo (often called Piero) Garegnani, though he confessed he found the Club to be distressingly low-brow, as I suppose a Gramsci scholar might well have done. Charles Feinstein, who came from a communist background in South Africa to study history in Cambridge, was irritated by such remarks. Charles remained very much an intellectual activist of the left and I remember on one occasion I was chastised by him for being dismissive of Stalin's writings (I was also criticized for keeping Stalin's books upside down on my shelves). Later on, however, Charles would change his views rather radically and become quite apolitical – without any left-wing inclinations – as one of Britain's leading historians. The Chichele Professor of Economic History at Oxford (as he became) retained his sharp intellect as well as the human sympathies that were evident in 1953, but he was clearly becoming more apolitical – unrecognizably different from the radical newly arrived from Witwatersrand University in Johannesburg.

Despite Piero's strictures, there was no lack of intellectual quality in the Socialist Club. Eric Hobsbawm was often there, as was Stephen Sedley (an outstanding legal scholar – later a leading British judge), who joined around the time I was leaving for Delhi in 1963. Ian Brownlie, later one of the most prominent international lawyers in the world, was a student at Oxford and belonged to the sister Socialist

Club there (he was also a member of the Communist Party which he would quit only after the Soviet invasion of Czechoslovakia in 1968). I encountered Ian regularly both as a frequent visitor to Cambridge in my student days and later as a colleague at All Souls College, when he became the Chichele Professor of Public International Law.

2

One of the most remarkable people I met through my political associations was Dorothy Cole, later Dorothy Wedderburn. At the first meeting of the Cambridge University Socialist Club, Ricky Brown conveyed an invitation to me from Dorothy to drinks at her home. She had been born Dorothy Barnard, the daughter of a successful carpenter and joiner with radical views, and lived with her historian husband Max (W. A.) Cole in a house in Parker's Piece. I was hugely charmed and impressed by the glow of bright intelligence that shone through Dorothy's elegant and kindly face. She was also wonderful fun to chat with. This was the beginning of a lifelong friendship which lasted until her death at the age of eighty-seven in 2012.

Dorothy's modesty, despite her achievements, was striking. When Eric Hobsbawm wrote in her obituary in *The Guardian* that she was an 'enemy of all self-advertisement', he pointed to a quality that struck me even at our first meeting in Cambridge in 1953. All her critiques were without assertiveness, and sometimes with a measure of self-doubt too. This applied also to her scepticism about mainstream economics, which, she said, she was 'too dumb to follow', but then proceeded to present some very enlightening criticisms of what had gone wrong with major parts of it.

When Dorothy's marriage with Max Cole broke up a few years after we met, she married Bill (later Lord) Wedderburn, a distinguished lawyer and legal thinker, who was also on the left of British politics. After some happy years, that marriage too ended in divorce. Then she had several decades mostly on her own – always cheerful, always caring about others, but undoubtedly lonely. Dorothy's life, it seemed to me, was one of alternating joys and pains. She had close friends, however, on whose company she often relied in her older days, including the

Hobsbawms and Marion Miliband, a remarkably clear-headed thinker and the widow of my friend Ralph Miliband, the great Marxist sociologist (also mother of David and Ed).

When I first met Dorothy, sociology was not yet accepted in Cambridge as a proper academic field of study and she was typically described as an applied economist, which of course she was as well. After sociology came out of the academic closet, Dorothy made her mark as a leading sociologist in Britain. Among her works was an illuminating – and disturbing – analysis of the lives of the elderly in Britain and an investigation into nursing and paramedic work. She became the Principal of Bedford College, London, and, after Bedford's merger with Royal Holloway College, the Principal of the combined institution. She also chaired a major inquiry into the conditions of women in prison, and wrote a powerful book called *Justice for Women: The Need for Reform*, a book that offers some far-reaching feminist insights. I learned a lot from Dorothy's work, particularly the importance of exploring the social aspects of economic relations, and also greatly admired the contributions she made on important aspects of social neglect.

It is sad that one feature of women's deprivation – as I see it – is firmly reflected in Dorothy's own life. Following social convention, she changed her name on both occasions when she married and the bulk of her famous publications were under her second married name (Wedderburn), even after her marriage with Bill Wedderburn had ended. Thus the radically inclined Dorothy Barnard published all her books and papers under names acquired through marriage. Oddly enough, we had touched on this subject in our first conversations at Parker's Piece, when I was already forming a view that it was a big social mistake for women to change their last name when they got married. Dorothy listened patiently to the newly arrived Indian undergraduate and smiled, but did not seem particularly impressed. She said, 'I understand what you are saying, but there are surely more serious problems to deal with first.'

3

My interest in politics far exceeded my involvement with the Socialist Club, important as that was. I liked to go to political debates and discussions, and the most affordable way to do this was to become a member of the club holding the meetings and attend for free. I thus became a member of both the Liberal Club and the Conservative Club, and enjoyed discussions taking place in what sometimes felt like alien gatherings. It would have been natural for me also to join the Cambridge Labour Club, but at that time it had the odd regulation that you could not join it if you were a member of the Cambridge University Socialist Club. This reflected a fear that communists and fellow travellers in the Socialist Club would undermine the Labour Club. The illiberality of the rule was exceeded only by its stupidity. When people heard me saying that I belonged to all the main political clubs in Cambridge 'except the Labour Club', they tended to assume that my political views were quite different from what they actually were. In fact I often attended promising Labour Club meetings too by paying the sixpence entry fee.

An odd result of being in the Conservative Club was that I came to know Tam Dalyell, who was then its President. Tam, who came from an upper-class Scottish family (he was educated at Eton and later inherited a baronetcy), was beginning to have his doubts about Tory politics. When he stood for the Presidency of the Cambridge Union Society – the main university debating forum – he asked me to support him (I might have actually been the seconder of his nomination) and I helped to gather votes for him from the left. This worked well, but the Conservatives, who were in a majority among Cambridge students at that time, deserted him and Tam lost the election.

Tam moved further and further away from the Conservatives, and later became a well-known Labour Member of Parliament (representing the Scottish constituency of West Lothian) – often on the left of his Party. He was a fiery parliamentary debater and a very effective harasser of Margaret Thatcher's Tory government – most famously for what Tam saw as the UK government's deviousness (through false declarations) about the sinking of the Argentine ship the *General Belgrano*, during the Falklands War. Tam also chastised Tony Blair's Labour government for joining the United States in attacking Iraq supported by weak information and weaker reasoning. He became famous, too, after Scottish devolution, for questioning the asymmetry of Scottish MPs continuing to have a say on some regional English issues by their presence in the Westminster Parliament when the English did not have a similar voice in Scottish matters (the issue became known as 'the West Lothian Question'). Before Tam retired from Parliament, he had become 'the Father of the House', its most senior member.

Tam's qualities – his warmth, his courage, his political wisdom, including a willingness to think differently from others and to ask difficult questions – were already evident in our student days. He discusses his priorities beautifully in his very readable autobiography, *The Importance of Being Awkward*.

When I spent some wonderful days at his ancestral home, The Binns – not far from Edinburgh – I also came to know his mother, with whom I had very warm and enlightening conversations. She was a lovely person with a prodigious memory and a detailed knowledge of Scottish traditions and history. This included, of course, historical accounts of the family, beginning with the famous 'Bloody Tam Dalyell' – our Tam's ancestor who is still revered as the person who, in the seventeenth century, raised the Royal Scots Greys cavalry regiment. Tam's kindness was mainly a natural gift, but it was clearly reinforced by his mother's Christian and humanitarian convictions.

Just as Michael Nicholson had insisted, when I went to stay with his family, that we should do any drinking away from his family's village, Tam instructed me not to say anything about being an atheist when talking with his mother. That was easy enough, except that Tam had also described me as a devout Hindu, and on my second day at The Binns Tam's mother told me she had invited the Bishop of Edinburgh who very much wanted to discuss some intricate issues of Hinduism with me. Luckily, since the bishop's questions were mostly about the foundations of Hindu philosophy, rather than anything on beliefs and practice, I could come close to answering his questions.

4

Among the economists in my class, I came to know very well, as I mentioned earlier, Mahbub ul Haq from Pakistan. I also became close to Samuel Brittan at Jesus College. After Cambridge, Sam went on to become a professional journalist, beginning first with *The Observer* (of which he became the economics editor) and then for many decades as a leading commentator and editorial writer in the *Financial Times*. Just after our graduation, when Sam's columns in *The Observer* started appearing, they were accompanied by a picture of him which made him look not only extremely wise and serious (he was, of course, both) but also much older than he actually was. Dennis Robertson, who knew Sam as a student, asked me one day whether I agreed with him that this picture reflected an attempt by Sam to look more mature ('like fifty', Dennis said). We discussed that hypothesis, but I stuck to my view that Sam was just trying to look knowledgeable and sound, for which age is only one factor among many. I am not sure I won that argument.

Sam Brittan was always much more than a journalist. Later in his career, he published a number of powerfully reasoned books on social, economic and political subjects. In his collection *Essays: Moral, Political and Economic* (1998), he puts together a number of strikingly original articles, which contain a reasoned celebration of particular arguments without making a comprehensive departure. His general approach to economics and politics is well articulated in his books *A Restatement of Economic Liberalism* (1988) and *Capitalism with a Human Face* (1995); the latter title caught Sam's basic motivation very well.

When, as an undergraduate, I first met Sam in the autumn of 1954, he had just come back from a visit to Russia, which had confirmed all his worst suspicions about the Soviet Union. He explained to me that he had been a member of the Labour Club before he went, but decided after the trip to leave it and join the Liberals. I enjoyed our conversations and learned something from his general economic thinking – a well-thought-out pro-market position, but with a liberal rather than a conservative passion for letting people lead their own lives. I did not find any areas of strong disagreement with him on the need for using the market economy, or the place it must have in our economic and political thinking, nor in his liberal rather than conservative approach to institutions.

However, I was more bothered than Sam about the deficiencies of the market and what it could do, in particular its inability to deal with influences on individuals and societies coming from outside the market – what economists call 'externalities' (of which pollution, crime, urban squalor and the prevalence of infectious diseases are good examples). A. C. Pigou had already written very illuminatingly, in 1920, on externalities of different types in his outstanding book, *The Economics of Welfare*.

In 1954, even as I was doing undergraduate economics with Sam, Mahbub and others, the great economist Paul Samuelson published a powerful paper entitled 'The Pure Theory of Public Expenditure', which discussed how markets tend to go very badly wrong in the production and placement of shared 'public goods' such as security, defence, general arrangements for health care and so on. A toothbrush is a quintessential private good (if it is mine, it is not yours to use) and the market tends to deal with private goods pretty well. However, the absence of crime in the streets is a public good in the sense that one person's use of it (benefiting from a low crime rate through its favourable impact on his or her life) does not remove the usefulness of the same 'good' (the low crime rate) for another person. Samuelson's thinking, which showed the very serious limitations of the allocation of resources for public services – if made only through the market – had a big impact on my foundational concerns, and I tried to persuade Sam to share that conviction. We agreed on the soundness of Samuelson's distinction, but, I suspect, continued to differ on the importance we placed on public goods in economic decision-making. If that was one difference, another was the importance of avoiding serious economic inequalities, with which I was much concerned. Our strong agreements as well as some residual differences always made my relations with Sam intellectually stimulating and productive.

There were other students in my class who became close friends. Walter Eltis I knew well: he went on to teach at Oxford (as a Fellow of Exeter College), and also served as a senior economic adviser to various UK governments. I came to know several others, such as Ranji Salgado, who came from Sri Lanka and was a highly qualified economist but unbelievably quiet and unassertive. Later on he worked for the International Monetary Fund, where he was a great success. From his student days, he was keen on meditation and other Buddhist practices – and later on chaired the Washington Buddhist Vihara. He was a very centrist and kindly political thinker who was difficult to push into any argument (although I tried). Ranji and I had a trip together during our second Easter vacation, spending a week in Welwyn Garden City, misled by the announcement included in its name that made us think there were going to be fabulous gardens there. We were really only trying to make an inexpensive getaway at a time when Cambridge was quite deserted. When we got off the train at Welwyn and looked around at the artificially put-together town – without a garden in sight – Ranji asked, 'Are we sure?'

5

The discussion group that was most well known in Cambridge, even though it was not formally supposed to be discussed in public, was the Apostles – the so-called Cambridge Conversazione Society. It had rather ancient origins, having been established in 1820 by George Tomlinson, who was then a student in Cambridge and somewhat implausibly (given the heretical reputation of the Society) went on to become the Bishop of Gibraltar. Tomlinson joined with eleven other Cambridge students, all from St John's College, and started the Conversazione Society – often called just 'the Society'. Its membership subsequently tended to come overwhelmingly from John's, Trinity and King's. Faithful to the name, there have not been more than twelve Apostles at any one time, but on retirement an Apostle becomes an Angel ('growing wings', as the transformation is described) and remains a member of the Society forever. There is meant to be an annual dinner arranged by the president of the Society – elected from the Angels – although I think that may now have become a somewhat erratic occurrence.

The members of the Society have included many great scientists, philosophers, mathematicians, literary scholars, writers, historians and people with other unusual achievements in intellectual and creative fields. For example, in philosophy they included Henry Sidgwick, Bertrand Russell, G. E. Moore, Ludwig Wittgenstein, Frank Ramsey and Richard Braithwaite. In many ways the Apostles lived up to William Cory's description of it as 'the small intellectual aristocracy of Cambridge'.

The process of election to the Society – consisting of an evening or two of chatting with likely candidates, followed by a vote – sometimes generated controversy when the candidates had strong followers as well as detractors, and being elected was often seen as a big deal. After being elected, even Lytton Strachey, who had many other accomplishments, wrote excitedly to his mother on 2 February 1902, 'I am now a Brother of the Society of Apostles,' adding, 'I was apparently elected yesterday.'

The Society has also had some misfits who sometimes chose to resign rather than participate. Of the deserters, Alfred Tennyson's departure is perhaps most remembered – his resignation in 1830 came when the Society was only ten years old. His fellow Apostles tended to think that this was really an ejection rather than a resignation: James Fitzjames Stephen wrote, with some scorn, that Tennyson 'was turned out because he was so incurably lazy that he could not be got to write essays in his turn'. Years later the Apostles tried to make amends by electing the poet to be an 'honorary member', but Tennyson was not to be wooed. He responded to the invitation to the annual dinner from the President of the Society, William Frederick Pollock, 'Dear P. Can't come. A.T.' A later misfit was Ludwig Wittgenstein, whose election was championed by Bertrand Russell and John Maynard Keynes, among others. Wittgenstein found the Apostolic meetings to be a waste of time and was never an enthusiastic participant, but his threat to resign was averted by the pleading of G. E. Moore and Lytton Strachey.

6

The affairs of the Society were meant to be secret, and that secretiveness was widely recognized in academic circles. Some of the less admirable features of the Society were, in fact, better known than more agreeable aspects. The Society received some high-profile negative publicity at the time of the exposure of the Cambridge spies, Guy Burgess and Anthony Blunt in particular – they were both Apostles. But the frequently repeated story that the Apostles had been extensively involved in spying for the Soviet Union had never been true. It is fair to say that the political leanings of the membership have tended to be, by and large, on the left, at least in the last century, but being politically left-wing has little to do with wanting to be a Soviet spy.

For most of its long history, the traditions of secrecy have kept detailed knowledge about the Society out of the public eye. However, there have recently been publications and public speculations on the nature and proceedings of the Society, and it is difficult to resist the temptation to correct mistaken pronouncements that have tended to circulate. One famous correction about what the Society is – and does – came from Quentin Skinner, later Regius Professor of History in Cambridge, during the time he was the President of the Society (we were Apostles mostly at the same time). Quentin got a phone call from *The Guardian* before an annual dinner of the Society, requesting him to tell them all about the 'secret group'. It was clear that the public image of a sleek and cunning Society, consisting of a bunch of spies, appealed to their journalistic curiosity. While recollecting at the annual dinner his conversation with *The Guardian*, Quentin mentioned that he had to tell the journalist that not only did the Society lack spies, but if it hadn't, it would not have made the Society much smarter, since 'some of them didn't even seem capable of keeping the news of a private dinner to themselves'.

The active Apostles in my time, over the years, included (this was before the time when the Society could elect women Apostles) Jonathan Miller, Noel Annan, Myles Burnyeat, John Dunn, Quentin Skinner, Francis Haskell, Michael Jaffé, Geoffrey Lloyd, Frank Hahn, Garry Runciman, James Mirrlees, Lal Jayawardena and many others who became well known for their academic and other achievements. I must confess that I did enjoy the weekly discussions. A typical evening would involve a very interesting paper read by one of the Apostles, followed by discussion, and then there was generally a vote on some thesis linked to what had been read. No one much cared about the outcome of the vote, but the quality of the discussion was a serious concern.

7

There was usually little connection between one's academic work and Apostolic participation. Some papers prepared for discussion in the Society were discussed in wider academic circles and occasionally had quite an impact. Frank Ramsey's presentation one evening in 1925 of his paper 'Is There Anything to Discuss?' made points of such importance (for example, about unarguable differences) that it came to have a serious place in the philosophical literature.

Sometimes the link came through references to general literature in the Apostolic discussions, in which public journals were interested. I can recall one personal case of overlap. There was an interesting sequence of events following my reading of a paper – it would have been around 1959 – on Rousseau's idea of the 'general will' and the insights we can derive from game theory, particularly as it was then being developed by John von Neumann and John Nash.

I was just becoming interested in game theory at this time (I would later teach it at the Delhi School of Economics), and it seemed easy to use a small part of it to explain the contrast between Rousseau's 'general will' (what would be collectively favoured by all) and what would be chosen by each person in isolation (sometimes called the 'will of all' in contrast with the 'general will'). Garry Runciman, a very talented classicist who was turning into a sociologist, was active in the meeting and pointed out to me how the reasoning I was presenting might also throw light on the theory of justice that was being developed by the newly emerging philosopher John Rawls.

We decided to write a joint paper that explored and extended the ideas discussed at the meeting, and sent it to Gilbert Ryle, the editor of *Mind*, a leading philosophy journal. Part of the paper supported the theory of justice being then developed by Rawls, who would soon be seen as the leading moral and political philosopher of our time. But we also argued against Rawls's assumption that in a state of impartial choice only one particular choice would emerge as being favoured by all. If there are pluralities of impartial solutions, as we argued there must be, then the Rawlsian framework faced serious difficulties.

The paper, thus broadened from the secluded environment of an Apostolic discussion, was to our delight promptly accepted by Ryle. But then for several years we did not hear anything more. We eventually decided to write to Ryle again, sending him another copy of the same paper and enquiring what might have happened to it. We knew of course that Ryle wrote in longhand and perhaps did not keep copies of his own letters, but our concerns became more complex when we received another letter from him, in which he mistakenly treated the paper as a fresh submission and again accepted it for publication. Garry and I were impressed by Ryle's consistency, but had to remind him that he had already accepted the paper three years earlier and we were hoping that it might be published soon. The story had a happy ending – the paper did come out in *Mind* in 1965, under the title 'Games, Justice and the General Will', and generated some interest.

Some years later, when I was at Harvard for a year as a visiting professor, John Rawls, Kenneth Arrow and I taught a course together on political philosophy, and Rawls discussed the arguments that Garry and I had presented and gave his illuminating comments on them. I was of course a great admirer of Rawls, and he and I argued on that subject from time to time over the decades (and I addressed it further in my book *The Idea of Justice*, published in 2009). If that was an unusual development from an Apostolic discussion, it certainly lived up to the Society's tradition of encouraging argument and counter-argument.

Listening to Rawls, with his elegant face lit up with the force of his reasoning in the Emerson Hall, where our joint seminar used to take place, I considered what a wonderful Apostle Rawls would have been if Tomlinson's ghost could somehow have spirited the great Harvard philosopher to Cambridge as a student and persuaded him to join the Conversazione Society. But an essay that Tennyson had refused to write for the Society (choosing to resign instead) was on ghosts and I thought he might not have approved of my dream.

8

The discussion meetings of the Society were held once a week in termtime, on a fixed day at a fixed place. Apparently, earlier on, the meetings used to be held on Saturdays, but in my day we met in E. M. Forster's rooms in King's on Sunday evenings. As a great admirer of Forster's work, it was reward enough for me that he was often present himself and joined in the discussion as an Angel, though some evenings he preferred to go to King's Chapel, mainly (he explained) to listen to the music.

I had met Morgan Forster earlier – well before my election as an Apostle – and saw him fairly regularly at other gatherings as well. His Indian connections were still strong, and I was thrilled when one evening in 1960 he invited me to join him to see the opening performance of *A Passage to India*, made into a play by Santha Rama Rau, at the Arts Theatre in Cambridge. We were accompanied by Joan Robinson and Richard Kahn, who took us all to dinner beforehand.

Forster said he liked the play a good deal, and it was certainly absorbing enough as an event on its own, but for those familiar with the original novel, its weaknesses were hard to overlook. Perhaps this was a harsh judgement, since famous books are very difficult to turn into satisfying plays. But I sensed Forster's determination to be kind to a little known translator, and when I met Rama Rau later, she told me how elated she was by Forster's approval.

I was persistently impressed by Forster's deep interest in India. When I first met him in 1953 – in Prahlad Basu's room at King's for tea – he questioned me, in a very amiable way, about my background. Hearing that I came from Santiniketan, he said he found Rabindranath Tagore's ideas about the world – and the themes chosen by him – very likeable, but was less captured by his style of writing. Forster also said that he thought Tagore was always experimenting with his English prose and that many of the experiments did not come off. He admired Tagore for never giving up.

I did not realize until I came to know Forster much better through the Society that he was a huge admirer of Kalidasa, the classical Sanskrit playwright from the fourth century. 'Have you written anything on that?' I asked him, rather ignorantly. Forster said, 'Nothing substantial, but I have mildly complained about the lack of popular interest in India on Kalidasa's writings – very unlike the fuss we make about Shakespeare.' This took me to his collection of essays and reviews *Abinger Harvest* (1936), where there is a splendid piece of literary appreciation, as well as an elegant grumble about the lack of public interest, in the essay 'Adrift in India: The Nine Gems of Ujjain'.

Here Forster alluringly describes the charm of historical Ujjain, Kalidasa's home town (and the capital of the kingdom), with 'people singing songs of mirth in the streets', while in the evening 'women steal to their lovers "through darkness that a needle might divide"'. Excited by reaching Kalidasa's favourite river – the Sipra – Forster had waded ankle-deep into it straightaway, without pausing to take off his shoes and socks. Remembering what Kalidasa had written about Sipra and the people in it, he saw this as a great moment – a moment he had hoped would come to him one day. When his reverie ended, Forster wondered whether his socks and shoes would dry by the time he had to take his train – and, rather more importantly, about the lack of interest in Kalidasa amongst the modern Ujjain population in the historical buildings around them. He concluded, rather sadly, 'Old buildings are buildings, ruins are ruins.' It was a frustrating end to an exciting visit, but he told me that being 'adrift in India' had taught him much about what to expect, and what not, in the country he loved so much.

9

My undergraduate days ended with a bang in June 1955. This came about through attempts by one of Trinity's kindly porters to wake me up the morning after I had decided I had finished my final exams. In those days, in addition to papers that every economics student had to take for their BA degree, we had to choose two other papers on related subjects. We could, however, take three of these additional papers, on the understanding that the two with the best grades would count in the final result. I had chosen papers on statistics, political philosophy and British economic history. I cannot now recollect in which order these three exams were held, but, whatever was the case, I decided after taking the first two that they had gone well enough for me not to need the third paper to be taken into account. So I joined in the general celebration of the end of exams and went to sleep around 4 o'clock in the morning.

However, my name remained among those taking the third optional paper (whichever it was) next morning, and soon after 9 a.m. the Exam School called the Porter's Lodge in Trinity to say that I was missing in the exam hall and should come at once. By 9.20 a very nice porter called Michael took on the challenging task of getting me up. He managed to wake me, but receiving little response, he said. 'I am going to make a fine cup of tea for you, and bring some sweet biscuits, but please do start getting out of bed.' When he returned with the tea and biscuits, I had managed to transfer myself to a sofa in the living room, from which I told him, 'My exams are over.' 'No, they are not,' Michael replied. 'They have been calling from the Exam Hall in Downing Street. Please do me a favour: drink this tea, put on your trousers and a shirt, and run down there.'

I tried to explain to him that I really did not have to take the remaining exam, since the two papers already completed would count and make the third unnecessary. 'My exams really are over,' I insisted. 'Mr

Sen,' said the kindly Michael, 'everyone feels like that during the exams, and convinces themselves of unlikely stories, but you have to persevere and finish.' It took me quite some time to persuade him that I really was not going to run to the exam hall. Later on, when I saw Michael in college, he would tell me with a broad smile, 'You know, of course, they are still waiting for you in Downing Street.'

10

My parents, along with my sister Manju, came to see me get my degree in the Senate Hall – an enjoyable event since I had to do very little. Years later, as Master of Trinity, when making a recitation in Latin for each graduating student from the College, clutching their hands in mine, telling them (in Latin) whichever degree it was that they were receiving, I thought that the heads of colleges had a much harder time during the ceremony than the graduating students. By the time I was Master of the College, the students had moved on in style as well. I enjoyed the response of one of the graduands in my first year as Master, who smiled broadly and said, 'Thanks so much, mate,' which seemed like an appropriate end of a Latin conversation.

My father had an invitation to lecture in London at the time of my graduation, and the honorarium was useful for him in arranging the family's travel. We rented a small apartment in Notting Hill where we all stayed happily for almost a month. It was particularly pleasing for Manju, who wanted to see the museums and galleries in London, and I often went with her. Some of my friends came to see us in the Notting Hill apartment. I remember the visit of Dilip Adarkar in particular, who hugely impressed my parents as well as my sister, which helped to persuade them that I was keeping good company.

I was sad that many of my old Cambridge friends were leaving, although new students were coming in. Also, some old friends had stayed on, including Rehman Sobhan and Dilip, since they were doing three-year degrees. Lal Jayawardena, in the middle of his doctoral work, also stayed, though Mahbub moved on to do a Ph.D. at Yale. Among new students in 1955, Ramesh Gangolli, a mathematician, also became a lifelong friend. It was soon clear to me that he had an extraordinary intellect. With his very broad interests (ranging from high-powered research on Lie groups in mathematics to the theory and practice of Indian classical music), Ramesh enlivened our conversations in many different ways. He did his doctorate at MIT after his graduation in Cambridge, and I had the opportunity to catch up with him – and his wonderful wife Shanta – in the autumn of 1960 when I arrived at MIT myself for a year as a visiting assistant professor.

Manmohan Singh, later to be Prime Minister of India, arrived as an undergraduate at St John's in 1955, and I went to visit him soon afterwards. Manmohan has always been warm, friendly and easily approachable – qualities that I discovered as soon as I got to know him. He remained just the same even when he was leading the country as India's Prime Minister from 2004 to 2014. When I had dinner with him at his official residence, which tended to happen whenever I visited Delhi, I was amused to note that even as Prime Minister he would always wait for others to have their say before speaking himself.

Manmohan's modesty could actually have been a problem for him as Prime Minister. While being a great social virtue, modesty can be a disadvantage in active politics, especially in a world dominated by flame-throwers like many of India's present political leaders. This could make Manmohan unwilling to have his case heard by the public – he was sometimes extraordinarily quiet. But, despite this reticence, and contrary to some public criticism that he faced relatively silently (rather than loudly rebuffing it as he could have), he was in fact an excellent political leader. He achieved many things, including contributing to the fastest rate of economic growth that India has ever known – before or since. The growth rate slowed a little in his second period (2009–14), which coincided with a global economic slump, but nevertheless remained among the highest in the world. There were also other major accomplishments, including the enactment of the Right to Information Act and the establishment of the Rural Employment Guarantee Scheme.

11

Along with new students arriving in 1955, there was also the return of Dharma Kumar, a major economic historian who was researching

India's agrarian history. She had started a Ph.D. thesis some years earlier – but had then gone back to India to work in the Reserve Bank of India, where she had made quite a name for herself. She was a woman of striking beauty and charm, and I greatly admired her sharp intellect and ready wit. We soon became close friends and met to chat most days. We also took many walks together through the neighbouring villages – Coton, Grantchester and beyond – and went to a number of plays in London.

Dharma's ability to make quick judgements combined well with her lack of patience, and this contrasted sharply with my own tendency to dither. I was initially surprised by her propensity to walk out of a play after twenty minutes if she had decided that it was no good and not going to get any better. (I am the kind who tries to extract every ounce of value by watching the proceedings to the last minute – including clappings and bows.) Dharma may not be the person with whom I have seen most plays – though we did see a great many during the excellent 1955–6 season in the West End – but she is certainly the one with whom I have watched more first twenty minutes of plays than anyone else.

Dharma's path-breaking research on Indian agrarian history went back to pre-British days to help us understand what had happened during the Raj. As Sanjay Subrahmanyam, another leading historian, has said, no one quite matched her in exploding the comfortable consensus around some well-established orthodoxies. Her pioneering book *Land and Caste in South India* remains a classic of careful and original economic history, not only offering insights on the agrarian consequences of British rule, but also transforming our understanding of the nature of pre-British land arrangements in southern India, which were far less fair than was once imagined.

I saw Dharma last in 2001, when she was stricken with a brain tumour, which made her unable – and perhaps unwilling – to speak. I went to visit her shortly before she died, in the company of her daughter Radha Kumar, whose plea to her mother to say a few words to an old friend produced no response. Dharma's eyes were wide open and she looked at me with what seemed like a warm familiarity, but she would not utter a sound. What a contrast it was with the time when she was the embodiment of wit and humour.

21

Between Cambridge and Calcutta

I

By June 1956, at the end of my first year as a research student, I had a set of chapters that looked as if they could form a dissertation. A substantial number of economists at various universities were working then on different ways of choosing between techniques of production. Some were particularly focused on maximizing the total value of the output produced, whereas others wanted to maximize the surplus that was generated, and there were also some profit maximizers. Analysing these – and other – approaches, and taking note of the fact that a higher surplus, when reinvested, could lead to a higher rate of growth and through that to a higher output in the future, the different criteria could be compared through assessing alternative time series of outputs and consumption.

I was sure that the unruly literature on all this could be sorted out and nicely disciplined through comparative evaluation of alternative time series, which turned out to be fun to do. I called it the 'time series approach'. I was glad to be able to outline an easily discussable general methodology for the various alternative proposals that were being offered. I presented the general picture in an article that I sent to the *Quarterly Journal of Economics* (a leading journal in economics – then and now), which was kind enough to take the paper for immediate publication. They also accepted a second paper to come out not long after.

There were a few related concerns that were dealt with in separate papers, which also found their way to publication. By then, at the end of my first year of research, I started wondering whether I had – in the papers taken together – something like a doctoral dissertation. But I also worried whether this was a delusion of grandeur. So I asked my teacher Maurice Dobb to have a quick look and give me his assessment. I had forgotten that for Dobb there was no such thing as having a quick look. At the end of two weeks I received from him an enormous set of helpful comments on how to improve my presentation. But there was also his comforting general conclusion that there was certainly more in my chapters than would be needed for a doctorate.

Maurice warned me that the regulations of Cambridge University would, however, prevent me from submitting a doctoral dissertation at the end of my first year. The university regulations did indeed say that a student could not submit a Ph.D. thesis until three years of research had been undertaken. So I asked myself the question: should I get away to do something more interesting than the topic of the doctoral thesis which I had, for one reason or another, come to choose? And, thanks to the already completed chapters, couldn't I go back to Calcutta and forget the doctoral research for two years? I wanted a break and, on top of that, I was missing India.

So I went to Piero Sraffa who, in addition to his role at Trinity, was a Director of Research in the Economics Faculty, advising doctoral students. I sent him a copy of my putative thesis which he looked through and seemed to approve. So I asked him whether I could go to Calcutta and come back after two years. 'You are right,' said Piero, 'the University will not allow you to submit your thesis for two more years, but nor will it allow you to go away during that time, since you have to be in residence in Cambridge, at least pretending to work on your thesis here for the three-year research requirement.'

This was very disappointing for me, but the dilemma had a happy resolution, smartly worked out by Sraffa himself. On his advice, I asked the Faculty to give me permission to be in Calcutta for the remaining two years of my research period so that I could apply my theory to empirical data from India. I had to get another supervisor in India for this plan as I would not be allowed to go without one. But that was the easiest part, since in Professor Amiya Dasgupta in India there was a brilliant economist ready to help me. Additionally, I knew that any conversation with Amiyakaka on any subject would be entertaining as well as highly educational. So I wrote to him and received his welcoming consent in reply.

Having resolved the regulation problems, with Sraffa's help, I began to prepare to travel to India. I felt that at least one phase of my association with Cambridge was coming to an end – I would come back only to submit my thesis and then be off again. I also fell into the trap of a kind of premature nostalgia about missing Cambridge since I was planning to cut my presence at the ancient university so short.

2

I could afford to go to Calcutta by air this time, since between 1953 (when I came to England by sea on the SS *Strathnaver*) and 1956 the cost of air travel had greatly fallen, while the expense of travelling by ship had risen even more rapidly, because of rising labour costs. Just before I flew to India, I suddenly got a letter from the Vice Chancellor of a new university (Jadavpur University) in Calcutta, which was then being established, saying that they would be happy if I could lead the founding of an economics department there, and serve as the head of department. I was unsuitably young for that job – I was just short of twenty-three – and had little desire to be suddenly catapulted into a restrictive administrative position. But, along with the anxiety, the unlikely proposal tempted me to try my hand at setting up a department and its curriculum in the way I believed economics should be taught.

It was not an easy decision, but after some hesitation I agreed to take up the challenge. So I found myself in Calcutta, working hard in rainy August to create syllabuses for the courses to be taught as well as trying to recruit people to join me in teaching at Jadavpur. Given the shortage of staff at the beginning, I remember having to give a great many lectures each week in different areas of economics. In one particular week I think I gave twenty-eight full-length lectures of an hour each. This was really exhausting, but I also learned many new things from having to apply myself to so many different areas of economics. I hoped it might also have been of some use to my students. In fact, I was learning so much from teaching that I felt convinced I could not really be sure of knowing a subject well until I had tried to teach it to others. In economics, this applies particularly to the classificatory devices to be used in economic epistemology, and that particular thought reminded me of my old friend, the grammarian and phonetician Panini from the third century BC whose classificatory analysis had been very influential on my thinking.

Given my youth and the widespread rumour that I had got the job at Jadavpur University through nepotism rather than merit, there was a predictable – and entirely understandable – storm of protest at my appointment. On top of that there were grounds for political suspicion because of my left-wing convictions – my days of active student politics in Presidency College had been only three years earlier. Among the sharpest attacks was a series of denunciations published in the right-wing magazine *Jugabani*. Amongst other things, I learned from them that, thanks to my appointment, the end of the world had become more imminent. One of the attacks, which I have to confess I did enjoy, was illustrated by a skilfully drawn cartoon showing me being snatched from a cradle to be immediately made into a professor, standing in front of a blackboard, chalk in hand.

I was sustained by the enthusiasm of my students, for which I was tremendously grateful. Some of them were truly brilliant, such as Sourin Bhattacharya, who would go on to become a distinguished academic and a writer. In fact, most of the students who had dared to join this totally new university to study economics were very talented. Other than Sourin, there was Reba (who subsequently married Sourin), Dhirendra Chakraborti, P. K. Sen and others, making up an excellent group. I kept in touch with them for many years after I left Jadavpur University.

I enjoyed the opportunity and the challenge at Jadavpur, which was an exciting place intellectually. It had in fact been a distinguished engineering college for many decades – well before it was turned into a university by adding departments (in literature, history, the social sciences and the 'arts' in general) to their pre-existing engineering and natural science base. My colleagues in the department – including Paramesh Ray, Rishikesh Banerjee, Anita Banerji, Ajit Dasgupta and Mrinal Datta Chaudhuri, among others – were unfailingly lively.

Apart from me, all the professorial appointees, who headed different departments at Jadavpur, were well established scholars and much older than me. The chair of the department of history was Professor Sushobhan Sarkar, who had been Professor of History at Presidency

College when I was studying economics there. A superb teacher and researcher, Professor Sarkar had had a big influence on my thinking when I was a student at Presidency. It was a fantastic privilege for me to be Sushobhanbabu's colleague and, thanks to his affection for me, I also received regular advice on what I should (and, even more importantly, should not) do as a new and unacceptably young professor.

The chair of the department of comparative literature was Buddhadeb Bose – one of the leading Bengali writers, with a formidable reputation in poetry as well as in innovative Bengali prose. I was a great admirer of his work, but also knew him personally as he was the father of my college friend Minakshi who, with her boyfriend (and later husband) Jyoti, appeared earlier in this memoir. The head of the Bengali department was the well-respected scholar Sushil Dey. Both Sushil Dey and Buddhadeb Bose had taught earlier in Dhaka University, where they were colleagues of my father. More alarmingly, Sushil Dey also knew well Sharada Prasad Sen, my paternal grandfather. He would sometimes remind me that he was senior to me by more than forty years. He used this reminder particularly when we had any disagreement – Dey was quite conservative on university matters. He would supplement his reasoned arguments disputing my proposals by invoking my family tree, which left me rather helpless. 'Your grandfather, who was such a wise man, and whom I knew so well, would see the point you are having difficulty seeing without any problem at all.' Professor Dey won all the arguments I had with him.

3

In the faculty we also had a remarkably innovative historian, Ranajit Guha – I called him Ranajitda since he was a few years older than me, though still relatively young. When I ran into him for the first time on the campus shortly after classes began, I was delighted, since I knew about him and his uncanny originality of thought.

'You are very famous,' Ranajitda told me when we first met. 'I have been constantly hearing about your severe shortcomings and about the mistake made by the University in appointing you. So let's get together straightaway – in fact let's have dinner tonight.' I went to his apartment in Panditiya Road that evening, which soon became one of my regular haunts. Ranajitda was previously an active communist, but by the time I met him he had decided that this had been a mistake. He still remained a revolutionary – in a quiet and non-violent way – working for the neglected underdogs of society, but he had completely lost his faith in communist organization, particularly Stalinism, which was very much in vogue in Calcutta at that time. Ranajitda was then married to Marta, who was of Polish origin with Jewish ancestry, and together they regularly hosted gatherings of friends.

Ranajitda was in the process, at that time, of writing his first book, *A Rule of Property for Bengal*, which would establish him as a historian of unusual imagination and vision. The book investigates the intellectual background of Lord Cornwallis's deadly Permanent Settlement of land tenure, imposed on Bengal in 1793, which (as discussed in Chapter 8) did incredible harm to the economy. It was a work of quite profound originality, differing from standard works on British colonial policy in India by focusing on the role of ideas as opposed to greed and self-interest (which had become the mainstay of critical history at the time). The British officers who had a voice in the choice of land rules in Bengal were motivated by their well-considered views on how to improve Bengal agriculture. The ethics behind the rationale of permanent settlement, and on the reasoned and humane ideas that led to it, were actually different readings of good governance. What is striking is that, despite their sincere attempts at doing good, the Permanent Settlement agreement produced quite disastrous results. Guha's focus, unusually in colonial history, was not on imperial exploitation and the dominance of British interests over the concerns of the subjects, but the various well-meaning thoughts that led to a jumble of proposed arrangements for land settlement in Bengal – and their botched application.

A Rule of Property for Bengal is not, however, the work for which Ranajit Guha is now most famous. That distinction goes to a series of publications under the generic title of Subaltern Studies, the product of a highly influential school of colonial and post-colonial history which he initiated and led. (As I noted in Chapter 4 it had some correspondence with my grandfather Kshiti Mohan's giving precedence to those poems of Kabir which the poorer followers loved.) The school of Subaltern Studies comprehensively disputed elitist interpretations of history. In his introduction to its first volume, published in 1982, Guha is deeply critical of the fact that the historiography of Indian nationalism had been, for a long time, dominated by both colonialist elitism and 'bourgeois-nationalist' elitism – which Ranajitda did much to disestablish. This was a big move to liberate the writing of Indian history – and by implication history everywhere – from a debilitating concentration on elitist perspectives. Although Subaltern Studies had not yet been born when I first knew Ranajitda, our daily conversations made it clear that he was already thinking in terms of an anti-elitist reassessment of history.

Ranajitda and the circle around him were not only intellectually important for me; they also contributed greatly to my social life in Calcutta. Regular conversations with the group, which included Tapan Raychaudhuri, Jacques Sassoon, Mrinal Datta Chaudhuri, Paramesh and Chaya Ray, Rani Raychaudhuri and many others, were a huge addition to my life as a young teacher in Calcutta. When Dharma Kumar visited Calcutta and came with me to Ranajitda's *addas*, she expressed astonishment at the range of issues we managed to discuss in our evening gatherings. Even now, I feel that as academic discussions go, it would be hard to match those in the small unassuming apartment in Panditiya Road in the mid-1950s.

4

Once I had settled into my new job and got to know the new students, I did not of course neglect my old haunt – the coffee house on College Street, opposite Presidency College and not far away from the base of Calcutta University. It was the summer of 1956 and among the vigorous debates going on then were the immediate reactions to Nikita Khrushchev's revelations about Stalinist practices, in the Twentieth Congress of the Communist Party of the Soviet Union. The Congress had taken place in February 1956, a few months before I returned to Calcutta, and the implications of what had emerged were sinking in slowly in left-wing political circles there. When I asked one of the old loyalists I knew well what he thought, he told me immediately, 'I hate

Khrushchev more than any revolting little insect' and refused to have any further discussion. When I ventured that what Khrushchev had reported was shocking but completely unsurprising, I got a blast of political rebuke.

My own awakening to the tyranny of the Soviet system had come a decade earlier (as I mentioned in Chapter 12) with my reading about the 'show trials' and the Stalinist purges, including the treatment of Bukharin, the leading Leninist philosopher of his time, whose writings I knew well. So I did not see a sudden break in what was happening – only a change in what was being officially admitted. When one of the faithful followers, angry with me, referred to the American writer John Gunther's observation that he (Gunther) had been present at the trial of Bukharin and others, and they all looked very healthy and unmolested – so they really could not have been tortured or restrained – I was truly astonished by the political naivety on display.

I liked Khrushchev's story, told by him a few years later, about visiting a school and asking the students there a friendly question, 'Tell me, who wrote *War and Peace*?' There was silence first, and then one of the children replied with a terrified look, 'Believe me, Comrade Khrushchev, I did not do any such thing.' Khrushchev complained to the head of the secret service that this was an unacceptable state of public fear and the bullying must stop immediately. The story ends with the secret service commander telling Khrushchev a few days later 'You need not worry any more, Comrade Khrushchev – the boy has now confessed that he did write *War and Peace*.'

In October and November 1956, as the shock of the Twentieth Congress was being absorbed by left-wing circles, the Hungarian uprising against Soviet rule occurred and was brutally suppressed by the Soviet Army. The Communist Party of India failed to denounce Soviet authoritarianism in the way various other communist parties (the Italian party in particular) had and it was becoming increasingly clear that the days of a united Leninist Communist movement in the world were coming to an end. I was disturbed by the brutality of the Hungarian suppression as well as by the shocking revelations in Khrushchev's denunciation at the Twentieth Congress. The questions now being raised seemed to me to be issues that should have been addressed much earlier. While I was never in the Communist Party (nor ever tempted to join it), I did think that class-based militancy had a very positive role to play in India, plagued as the country had been by long-standing inequalities and inequities. In that context, I tried to argue that the ability of a Communist Party to be effective and constructive would be much enhanced if it took on seriously the kind of pro-democracy questions that were at last being aired in the 1950s.

The Communist movement in India did eventually take up the issue of its compatibility with India's political democracy, and, while the process of response was painfully slow, it was good that the shocks of 1956 and later remained present in the political debates in the country. However, unlike the Communist parties in China, Vietnam and Cuba, the Indian party never became powerful enough to be a decisive political force, and it split several times, first in 1964.

5

While I was a dedicated teacher in Calcutta, enjoying my classes at Jadavpur, but waiting for two years to pass before I could submit my doctoral dissertation in Cambridge, there was a development in Trinity College which put me into some confusion. The College has a small number of Prize Fellowships – four in my time – given on the basis of competitive assessment of the research work of postgraduate students. (You could have more than one go, within a time limit.) A Prize Fellow is, in fact, a full Fellow of the College and receives emoluments for four years, without having to do any pre-specified work – in other words, free to work on any subject he or she chooses.

As I left Trinity for India in the summer of 1956, Piero Sraffa had remarked, 'Why not submit your thesis for the competition for the Prize Fellowship? You won't get it so soon, but you could improve your thesis with any comments that you might receive, and you might have a serious chance the year after.' So without much thought I had sent in a copy of my thesis-in-waiting from Calcutta and forgotten all about it.

The results of the Fellowship Elections were announced in the first week of October and, since I was not expecting to be elected, I paid no attention to the timing of the announcement. Instead, since there was a break in teaching in Jadavpur University for what is called Puja vacation in Calcutta, I went off to Delhi without leaving any forwarding address. I had a great time in Delhi, meeting for the first time remarkable economists such as K. N. Raj, who would later be my colleague at the Delhi School of Economics, I. G. Patel (who was married to Alakananda – or Bibi – the daughter of Amiyakaka, who was like a sister to me) and Dharm Narain, an outstanding empirical economist whom I came to know well, along with his wife Shakuntala Mehra. There was also a lively young woman, Devaki Sreenivasan, visiting Delhi from Chennai (Madras), who would later become Devaki Jain after her marriage to Lakshmi Jain, a stalwart in the old Congress tradition, while she herself became a leading figure in the global feminist movement. I met Devaki for the first time at a friend's house: at that meeting she seemed most amused by my traditional Bengali attire, which presumably she had never seen before – over the years she would become a close friend. So I was having a sequence of jolly talkative evenings in Delhi, far away from Jadavpur University, which was meanwhile receiving a cluster of communications from Trinity telling me that quite unexpectedly I had been elected to a Prize Fellowship.

Since Jadavpur had no knowledge of where to reach me, Trinity received no response – or acknowledgement – to the telegrams they (and my teachers – Sraffa, Dobb and Robertson) sent me. However, Trinity decided to elect me formally as a Fellow anyway, without waiting for me to sign in. By the time I saw all the accumulated communications in Calcutta, I had been a Fellow of the College for a few weeks already, without being aware of it. But then I had to do something I had not planned, since I now had two full-time jobs which I was unintentionally holding simultaneously. I had to choose between continuing in Calcutta and going back to Cambridge. After talking with both Trinity and Jadavpur, I split the time and returned to Cambridge earlier than I had intended, in the spring of 1958.

6

I greatly enjoyed the four years of my Prize Fellowship. Since I had decided not to do any further work on my doctoral topic – the choice of techniques – I thought I should use the opportunity to learn some serious philosophy. The open-shelved library of Cambridge University makes the hunt for one book lead to another on any subject, which is most rewarding. But I also attended lectures on mathematical logic and recursive function theory as a mathematical discipline, and hung around in philosophy seminars and discussions.

I approached C. D. Broad, a fine philosopher at Trinity whose *The Mind and Its Place in Nature* had much impressed me. I asked him whether he could advise me on what to read and also perhaps look at some essays I was planning to write. Broad readily agreed and countered by asking whether I would like to listen to some poetry he wanted to recite for me (he had a prodigious memory). Both the philosophy and the poetry turned out to be very enjoyable.

I grew in confidence when some essays I wrote were accepted for publication in the standard philosophy journals, and gradually I became more and more involved in philosophical disputations. I discussed in an earlier chapter my attempt to use game theory to comment, in a meeting of the Apostles, on philosophical problems raised by John Rawls. Another very valuable part of my early philosophical education was through Isaiah Berlin, the great social philosopher and historian of ideas. I learned a lot from Berlin's writings (as I had from Rawls's) and became strongly influenced by his idea that the value of an argument lies not merely in the victorious perspective that the winning side provides, but also in the relevance and contingent enlightenment that a defeated argument may continue to yield.

As a young, apprentice philosopher, I decided to dispute the view expounded in Berlin's book *Historical Inevitability* that causal determinism must entail fatalism. Berlin argued that since determinism makes things predictable (we can anticipate what you will choose), it makes people lose their freedom of choice and – most importantly – lose the freedom to bring about valued changes in the world. This fatalism is one of the problems of Marxism, Berlin claimed, and to restore human freedom Marxists should abandon their deterministic approach. In disputing this line of reasoning, I presented the argument that being able to predict what I would choose does not make my choice go away. In a choice over x, y and z, I might rank x the best, y the second, and z the last, and your knowing my ranking need not reduce, in any way, my freedom to choose. So I may freely choose x (the option I have best reasons to choose), and you may be able to predict that. That predictability is the result of your working out what I would choose, rather than my having no choice. So 'historical inevitability' does not confine people in a fatalistic world.

My criticism – in an essay entitled 'Determinism and Historical Predictions' – was published in 1959 in a new journal published in Delhi called *Enquiry*. I did not know Isaiah Berlin then, but as a brash young man I took the liberty of sending him my critique of his arguments. To my astonishment I received a very reasonable and friendly reply. Even more astonishingly, in the 'Introduction' he wrote to his next book, *Four Essays on Liberty* (1969), there were four references to my argument. This was very satisfactory for my youthful pride. I was particularly pleased when, as a part of his argument, Berlin said that he had to disagree with 'Spinoza and Sen'. (I thought I could perhaps put up Isaiah Berlin's remark, in an enlarged form, on the walls of my office!) More seriously, I was immensely impressed – this was indeed a part of his greatness – by the way Berlin paid real attention to arguments coming from anywhere, in this case a young author completely unknown to him, in an article published in a totally obscure magazine in Delhi that had just been started by some young Indian scholars. That was the beginning of my long friendship with Isaiah, from whom I went on to learn so many things.

7

While I was becoming more and more involved with philosophy, Piero Sraffa reminded me that I had to submit my Ph.D. thesis – I had now completed more than three years. It was essentially the same as my fellowship dissertation for Trinity (except for the Indian examples). Lord Adrian, who was then Master of Trinity and had chaired the election meeting at which I had been elected to a Prize Fellowship, expressed some surprise after hearing about my plan to take a Ph.D. 'Do you really need it when you have your Prize Fellowship already? Or are you thinking about going to America?' I told him I was interested in visiting American universities at some stage, but had no immediate plans. I am not sure what Adrian made of my considering a trip to the USA. He was, in general, very kind to me, and I understood from a member of the Prize Fellowship Committee that he had strongly backed my election.

I was happy to hear that David Champernowne and Nicholas Kaldor, who had been referees consulted by the College in judging my fellowship thesis, were also going to be my Ph.D. examiners. I expected an easy time, which is indeed what happened. However, what I had not anticipated was that Champernowne and Kaldor would disagree with each other throughout the oral examination about what I had said in my thesis. I am not sure which of the two won, but I was happy that this was the focus of their debate in my oral examination.

The week after my thesis was approved for a Ph.D., Henry Schollick, one of the directors of Blackwell Publishing, the firm in Oxford, paid me a surprise visit and gave me a fully written-up contract to sign for the publication of my thesis as a book. I was impressed by his trust since he had not read – or even seen – the thesis yet. Of course I accepted, but there was work to be done. Piero Sraffa was happy about the Blackwell offer, but told me, 'Now you must change the title.' Sraffa had allowed 'Choice of Capital Intensity in Development Planning' as the registered title of my Ph.D. topic ('for university officialdom'), but 'now your work will face the world'. When I asked him whether it was really necessary to change the title, he responded:

> Let's think how the public will understand the subject matter of your book from its title, 'Choice of Capital Intensity in Development Planning'. Capital is the seat of governance of a country, like London, and development is understood to be the setting up of new buildings and townships. So, let's see, the thesis is about what proportion of the new buildings in Britain should be located in London. Have I got it right?

I went back to my study immediately and wrote to Mr Schollick that the title must be changed to 'Choice of Techniques' (as Sraffa had originally suggested).

I was lucky with the interest the book aroused – I think mostly because of the subject matter. When I told Blackwell to stop further reprints of what I knew was only a moderately good thesis on a very limited subject (it was by then in the third reprint of the third edition), I wondered whether it would have sold at all had it retained the original title. I recognized that in Piero Sraffa, besides his many other qualities, I had a friend I could rely on to persuade me out of my idiocies.

8

The Prize Fellowship gave me the opportunity to enjoy high table at Trinity at lunch and dinner. Many of the conversations there were quite general but a few underlined the extraordinary opportunities I had by being at the College. A good example was my attempt to understand basic methods of reasoning in fluid dynamics from talking to Geoffrey Taylor, a pioneering contributor to – almost the founder of – the subject, who also regaled me with fascinating accounts of his boating experiences. Another was my trying to become more clued up on the history of nuclear fission by chatting with Otto Frisch, another pioneer in his field – who also shared with me his theory about how much extra sleep you need the following night to make up for 'lost sleep the night before, perhaps because of all-night dancing parties'. Armed with diverse bits of knowledge coming to me from many different directions, I felt confident I was receiving quite a balanced education.

I also made use of the freedom that the Fellowship gave me to visit friends in London, particularly at the London School of Economics, and in Oxford, including visiting old friends such as Devaki Sreenivasan. There was also Jasodhara (Ratna) Sengupta who was studying English literature at Oxford, and she was a cousin through her father being my mother's cousin. She became involved with Amiya Bagchi, a brilliant economics student at Trinity who had also come from Presidency College, and she would later marry him; we often all met up in Oxford or Cambridge.

Through Jasodhara I came to know Priya Adarkar, who was the sister of my friend Dilip Adarkar from Cambridge. Priya was a remarkably intelligent, creative and charming young woman with a sharp intuition about relationships, which I lacked, and her company enriched me in many different ways. Ved Mehta, who first made his name as a *New Yorker* columnist, wrote in an autobiographical account that when, at Oxford, he was in love with Priya, he saw me as a barrier (even quoting Priya herself to that effect). When it became clear that she and I should distance ourselves because of the ambiguity of our relationship, it might have been the right decision, but it was a substantial loss for me. In later life, Priya worked together with the great playwright Vijay Tendulkar, including translating his plays. Her many-sided talents found expression through different channels – in publishing, translating and writing plays.

9

I feel I should record here an account of my first – and so far only – brush with the College regulations, which taught me something about styles of reprimand that I found quite educative. Not long after moving back from Calcutta to Trinity, I had to face a difficult choice involving a conflict between my social responsibilities and the regulations of the College. My friend Michael Nicholson's girlfriend Christine arrived unexpectedly late one evening to see him in Cambridge – they were, I believe, working out the details of their wedding. Despite many efforts, Michael could not find a hotel room for Christine in Cambridge, but College regulations specified firmly that no one (except the Master) could allow a woman to sleep in his College room, in what was still an all-male college.

Michael was a research student then, and even though being a Fellow made no legal difference to the rules involved, we decided that the penalties in the event of discovery would not be quite as severe for me as for him. We thought that if Christine were to sleep in the spare room downstairs in my apartment in New Court, I would get into far less trouble if she were discovered than Michael would if she were spotted in his room. So Christine was duly placed in the billiard room in my set (so called because it housed the great mathematician G. H. Hardy's billiard table). The plan was that as soon as Trinity's back gates opened at dawn, Christine would slip away quietly through the avenue across the river to the back gate. When I went to sleep upstairs, I could hear Michael and Christine chatting away animatedly and I felt more and more pessimistic about Christine's ability to be up in time to leave without provoking any crisis.

The bed-maker alas did discover her – I don't think Michael was still with her – and when, some hours later, I awoke, she informed me sternly that she had already reported this serious breach of Trinity rules to the authorities. So I consulted my friend and adviser, the historian Jack Gallagher, a very experienced Fellow, and asked him what he thought would happen next. He said he thought that the Vice Master, Sir James Butler, would scold me severely. So I prepared for the worst.

For weeks and weeks absolutely nothing happened. One day, when I had nearly forgotten the episode, Butler asked me after lunch at Trinity whether I would like to have a walk with him in the Fellows' Garden. I told him that normally I would like nothing better, but that afternoon I was planning to go to the library, and asked him whether I could take the walk with him on another day. Sir James looked very firmly at me and said, 'Sen, I would regard it as a great personal favour if you would walk with me now in the Fellows' Garden.' So I said, 'In that case, of course.' As we walked along the avenue across the river, Butler asked me whether I knew how old the tall trees around us were. I did not, so he told me. In the Fellows' Garden, he asked me about various plants, and whether I knew what they were. I did not, so he told me.

As we were approaching the College on our return journey, Butler told me about a Fellow who had lived in the College, while his wife had a flat nearby in Portugal Place. When this elderly Fellow was dying and it was clear he had at most a couple of days left, he asked for permission for his wife to be with him in College for his last day or two. Sir James then asked me, 'What do you think, Sen, the College decided about his request?' I said, 'I suppose it had to agree.' 'Nonsense,' said Butler, 'the request had to be turned down – of course.' Then he changed the topic, and as we walked back through the avenue, with Butler giving me further instruction about the trees, I knew I had been severely reprimanded. Education, I decided, comes in many different forms.

22

Dobb, Sraffa and Robertson

I

As a Prize Fellow at Trinity, my duties involved only research of my own choosing. But, partly because of my experience at Jadavpur University, I had come to understand that teaching can not only be very enjoyable in itself, but a wonderful way of supplementing one's research. So I readily accepted Trinity's suggestion that I should supervise the work of a number of College students doing economics.

I was also asked whether I wanted to do any lecturing. I was attracted by this too, so applied for – and got – an Assistant Lectureship in economics. I gave some elementary lectures on economic principles, and also teamed up with Professor James Meade, a splendid mainstream economist with a strikingly insightful mind, who in 1957 had moved from the London School of Economics to Cambridge to become Professor of Political Economy after Dennis Robertson. I held joint classes with Meade which followed his general lectures in economic theory. We discussed many of the analytical complications that standard mainstream economics produces, and of course also addressed students' queries, which were often very engaging.

I also gave some lectures on investment planning, which linked up with my research on choice of techniques. I was privileged to have James Mirrlees, a recent arrival at Trinity from Scotland, sitting in on those lectures. Mirrlees's coming to Cambridge was a big event, since the sharpness of his mind left people in no doubt that he would one day be a leader in academic economics – as he later became – first in Oxford and then in Cambridge. Not only did he produce work that changed our understanding of what optimal policy demands, he also trained a great many of the leading economists in Britain.

Another uplifting presence at my lectures was that of Stephen Marglin from Harvard. I was very impressed by him, sitting in the first row and asking me questions with such powerful insight and originality that it was hard to believe he had only just completed his undergraduate education. He had produced a masterful senior thesis as a part of his Bachelor's degree at Harvard, which overturned some well-established procedures in making investment decisions, particularly those concerned with the sequencing of investments. He also became a close friend.

2

As a young lecturer, I was thrilled to be teaching in Trinity in collaboration with Dennis Robertson, Maurice Dobb and Piero Sraffa. I talked a little about them earlier – they were my teachers – but it was when I became their colleague that I really got to know them well.

Dennis was less close to my own work than Dobb or Sraffa, but I had known him reasonably well from my first year in Cambridge, not only because he was at Trinity, but because he was always friendly and eager to talk. Dennis particularly aroused my curiosity because – unlike most economists of his generation – he had an unquestioning loyalty to utilitarian ethics. He thought the virtue of precision was overrated and that we can make perfectly sensible judgements about social welfare even if we have difficulty in putting different people's utilities in sharp one-to-one correspondence with each other. He had some instinctive sympathy for the poor, but I could not persuade him of the overwhelming importance of public policy in radically reducing economic inequality.

Robertson did accept, on good utilitarian grounds, that securing extra income for the very poor – for example, for the chronically unemployed – should be an important aim of public policy, but there was little passion in him to pursue egalitarianism as a major social objective. Such an objective could have followed from greater use of his own beliefs in interpersonal comparison of utilities (by which more and more income is less and less effective in adding to a person's total utility), but he did not seem particularly keen on going deeply into possible policy moves for equity and justice. While it was easy to make him talk about Alfred Marshall, I found it harder to draw him into a discussion of the ideas of a more radical Trinity thinker – Henry Sidgwick – despite sharing with him his utilitarian concerns.

It is possible that Dennis's lack of interest in the economics of social justice – on which Sidgwick had so much to say – related to his very deep interest in what we might call the engineering side of macro-economics. Indeed, his fame as an economist related mainly to a number of contributions he had made in practical macroeconomics, dealing with the determination of aggregate economic magnitudes such as national income, investment, savings and total employment in the economy. His fellowship dissertation at Trinity on 'A Study of Industrial Fluctuation', written just as he was agitating over what role – if any – he should play in the First World War (he was a pacifist, but did ultimately join up), was a brilliant contribution to the analysis of economic processes that lead to booms and slumps.

Robertson's work explored a number of ideas that John Maynard Keynes would also pursue. They were socially close as well, and both were active as Apostles. Since they were not only working on similar problems and exploring similar economic connections and exchanging ideas with each other all the time, Robertson understandably observed that he 'had so many discussions' with Keynes that 'neither of us now knows how much of the ideas therein contained is his and how much is mine'. That closeness did make personal relations between Robertson and Keynes quite problematic. Keynes, of course, became extremely well known in a way that Robertson did not and, given the overlap of their work, Dennis might have found that a little unjust. As a student I spent some time trying to ascertain in their respective works which of them had priority. But this proved very difficult, and I eventually acknowledged that Dennis was right that attempting to separate them would be hopeless.

3

In the way that economists are categorized, Dennis was certainly a conservative. He did not like revolutions – he would leave that to

Maurice Dobb. But in fact he doubted that Dobb would like revolutions either – 'Maurice, you know, likes a peaceful world without turmoil,' he told me. He might well have been right too in identifying Dobb's instinctive tastes, but not, I believe, his *reflected* political preferences.

I remember my last dinner with Dennis, which was at David Champernowne's house. I was going to India for a month in two days' time. Dennis said, 'Do you know, Amartya, no one knows the right tune for "The Owl and the Pussycat"? My great-grandmother taught it to me, and I try hard not to forget any of it.' I replied, 'I want to hear it,' and David joined me in this request. And so Dennis sang. At the end, he said, 'When I'm dead, no one will know the correct tune of "The Owl and the Pussycat".' Two days later I went to India – and Dennis's last words to me were 'When you come back, we will continue our argument.' I think he was referring to our disagreement on what to me was the huge importance of reducing inequality – about which we had argued from time to time over several years.

On my way back from the airport a month later, I nearly missed my train to Cambridge at King's Cross and had to run along the platform. I was still puffing when I spotted an old friend, Michael Posner, another economics teacher at Cambridge, in the same compartment. He asked me immediately whether I knew that Dennis Robertson had just died. I felt total grief. Even now, sixty years later, I continue to miss Dennis – and feel very nostalgic when I think about the owl and the pussycat.

4

Maurice Dobb was a hero of mine from the time I started doing economics in Calcutta. His Marxism made him particularly alluring, as I was also strongly interested in Marx's ideas. He was a member of the Communist Party until his death in 1976 and was loyal to it even when reports of events in the Soviet Union and Eastern Europe disturbed him. He did think that the Party was often too dogmatic, and I learned from another member of the University branch that he spoke along those lines quite regularly at their meetings. Dennis Robertson was right that Dobb was not keen on disorder, and my friend Jack Gallagher did an amusing imitation of Maurice giving a speech in Red Square in October 1917. It began with Dobb saying, 'Comrades, the time is not ripe.'

I described in Chapter 13 how I was bowled over when I first read, in Calcutta, Dobb's 1937 classic, *Political Economy and Capitalism*, in particular by one of the essays there called 'The Requirements of a Theory of Value'. There he argued for the importance of theories of value, as distinct from a theory of price determination. Both the labour theory of value and utility theory were great examples of theories of value, which must not be seen, Dobb argued, simply as intermediate products on the way to a theory of prices (as mainstream economists tended to see them) but as rich descriptions which we have reason to be interested in for their own distinct importance.

The crucial thing I derived from those early readings of Dobb was the importance of closely scrutinized descriptive economics, which could enlighten us in our basic interest in human society, and go well beyond helping us to predict prices. I was frustrated that economics seemed to be moving steadily towards a very narrow range of issues, concentrating primarily on how easily certain economic magnitudes, not always very important, can be predicted. Maurice Dobb seemed to me to stand firmly against that trend. Even though I only became one of Dobb's students in my second year as an undergraduate, I had started visiting him regularly well before that for long conversations.

When, after Calcutta, I came back to Trinity as a Prize Fellow in 1957, we continued our regular chats. I was struck that, in addition to his great insights in economics, he was always a very kind person – always going out of his way to help others. He typically made a pot of tea for us when we were talking, using an old teapot with a broken lid which he had not bothered to replace. He told me later that when the teapot itself broke, his bed-maker kindly bought a new teapot for him as a present, and gave it to him, saying, 'I know, Mr Dobb, that you don't like lids, and so I have thrown the lid away.' I asked Maurice whether he had explained the history of his lidless teapot to the bed-maker, to which he replied, 'No, of course not.' So he continued to have tea from a lidless pot for as long as I can remember.

5

I was lucky to have Piero Sraffa as my Director of Studies throughout my undergraduate years in Trinity. He duly dispatched me to my supervisors – Maurice Dobb, Joan Robinson, Kenneth Berrill and Aubrey Silberston at different stages – but encouraged me to come and talk with him whenever I wanted. And so I did, as I have discussed earlier (in Chapter 16), treating him as a kind of an extra supervisor. It soon became clear to me that Sraffa enjoyed chatting about a huge variety of subjects – from economics and European political traditions to coffee-making. I also learned that this extraordinarily original and questioning intellectual enjoyed working with others in ambitious joint enterprises.

After I became a Prize Fellow and then a lecturer at the College, I had a much greater opportunity to spend time with Sraffa, and between 1958 and 1963 we had long walks after lunch nearly every day, often out to Coton, a few miles from Cambridge. Among other things I came to recognize how important his student days in Italy had been to him, working with Antonio Gramsci and others in the circle around *L'Ordine Nuovo*, a left-wing journal aimed at resisting the threat of fascism and achieving radical social changes in Italy. Gramsci founded the journal in 1919 – and became its editor. Sraffa wrote regularly in its pages and joined its editorial board in 1921 before he had to leave Italy in the late 1920s because of fascist persecution. By the time he moved to Britain in 1927, he had become a substantial figure in Italian leftist intellectual circles, and was close to – but not a member of – the Italian Communist Party.

6

Piero published very little, and yet he had a profound influence on a number of different areas of intellectual investigation. There were various stories around his reluctance to write. When I arrived in Cambridge, I was told that Nicholas Kaldor, who was always rather sedate, had complained to his doctor that he was afraid that he was developing 'athlete's foot'; the doctor (who knew his patients well) had observed that this would be 'as unlikely as Mr Sraffa developing writer's cramp'.

In fact, Sraffa actually had what could be called 'publication cramp', for he wrote a great many notes, mostly in Italian, on different subjects in economics, philosophy and politics. They sometimes came up in our conversation and I formed the impression that the idea of converting a selection of them – after serious editing – into a publication had occurred to him. On one occasion, when I had asked Sraffa why he liked David Hume so much, he had told me that, aside from an early anonymous publication on this, he had a long note on the subject among his papers. These unpublished writings are preserved in Trinity's Wren Library.

As well as his tremendous contribution to both economics and philosophy (of which more in a moment), Sraffa, together with Maurice Dobb, was responsible for an important contribution to editorial work – the definitive edition of the collected works of David Ricardo, eleven volumes which started to appear in 1951 and which were already being much discussed when I arrived in Cambridge in 1953. The last volume, the 'General Index', came out in 1973. The index itself, which is extraordinarily detailed and annotated, took Piero and Maurice one year to produce. I remember Kenneth Arrow telling me of his frustration when he tried to see Piero on a visit to Cambridge and was told that he was not seeing anyone as he was very busy preparing the index to Ricardo. Arrow asked me, 'Aren't you amazed? Isn't an index something you do on a rainy Sunday when you don't have to go anywhere?' I tried to defend Piero by explaining that it was not that kind of an index, but I don't think Ken was at all convinced.

7

In economics specifically, there are *at least* three major insights or ideas that have emanated from Sraffa's work. The first was his demonstration in the 1920s that interpreting market outcomes as resulting from a perfectly competitive equilibrium, as was standard practice in mainstream economics, may involve a serious internal contradiction. This was because in the presence of constant (or increasing) returns to scale a perfectly competitive equilibrium was impossible. A competitive market ensures that a firm can go on increasing its sales indefinitely as long as the price of the good sold does not start going up, and constant or increasing returns to scale ensure that unit costs of producing a good will go down, if it changes at all. So there is nothing to stop expansion. This pointed to the inescapable need to acknowledge the presence of elements of monopoly amidst market competition – a consideration not accommodated in the ongoing grand theory of mainstream economics, led by Alfred Marshall (the leader of the then-dominant 'Cambridge School') and his followers (Dennis Robertson among them).

Sraffa thus demonstrated that the foundations of the established price theory were incurably defective. His essay first came out in Italian, but an English version of it appeared in the *Economic Journal* in 1926 and had an immediate impact. Dennis Robertson attempted a defence of the Marshallian theory, but eventually accepted that Sraffa had won the argument. Sraffa's diagnosis was followed by a large and new literature, led particularly by Joan Robinson and Edward Chamberlin, which explored the properties of 'imperfect competition' and 'monopolistic competition'.

The second significant contribution, which involves more technical reasoning, relates to Sraffa's demonstration that the commonly used notion of capital as a factor of production, with a numerical value, is deeply illusory and generates contradictions of its own (unless very special assumptions are made). Techniques of production cannot be ranked in terms of being more or less 'capital intensive', since capital intensities, which are dependent on interest rates, can repeatedly reverse their relative ranking as interest rates are systematically raised. This demonstration goes by the fetching name 'multiple switching'. The idea of 'more' or 'less' capital thus becomes muddled, which makes it difficult to treat capital as a factor of production. And this is quite different from the way factors of production are meant to behave in mainstream economics. Correspondingly, there is a deep incongruity in a substantial part of mainstream economics because it treats capital as a factor of production.

A third contribution, which is more constructive, is Sraffa's demonstration that a comprehensive description of all production activities that are going on (with all the inputs and outputs), along with a given interest rate (or, alternatively, a given wage rate), will be mathematically adequate to tell us what the market prices of all commodities are. We don't need the demand conditions of the commodities involved to identify all the prices. This was neatly and very elegantly demonstrated, among other propositions, in a short book Sraffa published in 1960, called *Production of Commodities by Means of Commodities*.

This is a remarkable analytical result, but we need to be careful not to see in this third contribution more than Sraffa had claimed. There has been a strong temptation by critics of neoclassical economic theory to take Sraffa's demonstration as showing the redundancy of demand conditions in the *causal* determination of prices. Joan Robinson has not been the only commentator to take this unjustified leap, but she made the most of it:

> . . . when we are provided with a set of technical equations for production and a real wage rate which is uniform throughout the economy, there is no room for demand equations in the determination of equilibrium prices.

This, I fear, is not true. Since the entire calculation in the Sraffa system is made for a given and observed picture of production (with inputs and outputs all fixed, as in a snapshot of production operations in the economy), the question as to what would happen if demand conditions change – which could of course lead to differing levels of production of the commodities involved – is one that is not at all addressed in this exercise. The tendency to interpret mathematical determination (that is, what we can *calculate*) as causal determination (that is, what *fixes* what) can thus lead to a major confusion.

What we get from Sraffa is grand enough. From production relations we come to a theory of prices, once the wage rate (or alternatively the profit rate or interest rate) is specified. For a given configuration of production – indeed, of production of commodities by means of commodities – there is a clearly calculable relation, in fact a direct relation, between the profit rate and the wage rate. If you specify one, you get the other from it. This is almost a graphic depiction of a class war and, as Maurice Dobb would put it, a remarkably insightful description of the economics of class relations.

Sraffa's book has a subtitle: *Prelude to a Critique of Economic Theory*. Clearly there may have been some expectation on his part that it would lead to a fuller critique of mainstream economic theory. But I do not believe Piero was seriously planning to produce such a critique. He was certainly very interested in how others would extend what he had already done. I was privileged to read the manuscript of the book, well before it was published – in fact Maurice Dobb and I read it as it was being written. I was allowed to do this only in his rooms in Trinity after dinner, while Piero (wearing green eye shades to protect his vision from overhead lights) would read *Le Monde* or *Corriere della Sera*. Whenever I took my eyes away from his text, he would immediately ask me, 'Why did you pause? Are you worried about something I said?' It was both an exciting and an exacting experience for me – harrowing and thrilling at the same time.

Sraffa's little book is very illuminating in itself, not simply as a prelude to a possible later critique – if we interpret clearly what he is saying. However, others have taken Sraffa's ideas to explore further issues, particularly Luigi Pasinetti and Pierangelo Garegnani, but also Heinz Kurz, Krishna Bharadwaj, Geoffrey Harcourt, Richard Davies, Alessandro Roncaglia and Ajit Sinha, among others. Pasinetti has also written a far-reaching account of the relation between Sraffa's work and that of the Cambridge Keynesians.

8

Sraffa's economic ideas greatly interested me, but I was even more captivated by his philosophical ideas. By the time I met him, he had already helped to bring about one of the most critical developments in contemporary philosophy, particularly in Anglo-American philosophy, namely Ludwig Wittgenstein's momentous rejection of his early position in his path-breaking book *Tractatus Logico-Philosophicus* and the development instead of his later philosophy published in *Philosophical Investigations*.

Early in his life, Wittgenstein had been a student of Bertrand Russell, and when he left Trinity and Cambridge in 1913, he had already established his reputation as one of the foremost philosophers in the world. By the time he returned in January 1929 (shortly after Sraffa himself had arrived in Cambridge), he had become much celebrated. The formidable demands of the logical structure of statements on which the *Tractatus* insisted were widely known and immensely influential across the philosophical world.

Given Wittgenstein's extraordinary reputation, his return was quite an event in Cambridge. John Maynard Keynes wrote immediately to his wife, Lydia Lopokova, about the return of the genius philosopher: 'Well, God has arrived. I met him on the 5.15 train.' Cambridge was excited. The last sentence of the *Tractatus* was a famous imperative, exacting enough to stop informal speech in its tracks: 'Whereof one cannot speak, thereof one must be silent.' Sraffa had no disagreement with the demand made by Wittgenstein's imperative, but argued that we could speak and communicate perfectly well without following Wittgenstein's austere rules.

In the *Tractatus*, Wittgenstein used an approach that is sometimes called 'the picture theory of meaning', which sees a sentence as representing a state of affairs by being a kind of picture of it. There is an insistence here – it can be said at the risk of some over-simplification – that a proposition and what it describes must have the same logical form. Sraffa found this philosophical position to be altogether erroneous, indeed absurd, and in their frequent conversations tried to convince Wittgenstein of the mistake. That is not how people communicate with each other, he argued, and there was no reason why they should. We speak according to rules of communication, mostly implicit, that others know, and these rules need not have the logical form on which Wittgenstein insisted.

According to a widely told anecdote, Sraffa conveyed his scepticism of Wittgenstein's insistence on a strictly specified logical form for meaningful communication by brushing his chin with his fingertips. That Neapolitan gesture of scepticism was understood clearly enough by Wittgenstein, so Sraffa asked, 'What is the logical form of this communication?' When I asked Piero about this event, he insisted that the story, if not entirely apocryphal ('I can't remember any such specific occasion'), was more of a morality tale than an actual occurrence. 'I argued with Wittgenstein so often and so much', he said, 'that my fingertips did not need to do much talking.' But the story does illustrate graphically the force of Sraffa's questioning and the nature of his scepticism of the philosophy in the *Tractatus*. (Of course it also helps us to understand how social conventions, with regard to both words and expressions, facilitate communication.)

Wittgenstein would later describe to Georg Henrik von Wright, the distinguished Finnish philosopher who was also at Trinity, how these conversations made him feel 'like a tree from which all branches have been cut'. They were evidently momentous for him. Sraffa's criticisms were not, in fact, the only critiques that Wittgenstein faced around that time. Frank Ramsey, the young mathematical prodigy in Cambridge, offered others. Wittgenstein thanked Ramsey in the Preface to his *Philosophical Investigations*, but recorded that he was 'even more' indebted to the criticism that 'a teacher of this university, Mr P. Sraffa, for many years unceasingly practised on my thoughts', adding that he was 'indebted to *this* stimulus for the most consequential ideas of this book'. In explaining Sraffa's critique, Wittgenstein told a friend (Rush Rhees, another Cambridge philosopher) that the most important thing Sraffa taught him was an 'anthropological way' of seeing philosophical problems.

It is conventional to divide Wittgenstein's work between the 'early Wittgenstein' and the 'later Wittgenstein,' with the year 1929 clearly the dividing line between the two phases. While the *Tractatus* tried to see language in isolation from the social circumstances in which it is used, the *Philosophical Investigations* emphasizes the conventions and rules that give utterances particular meaning. The association of this perspective with what came to be known as 'ordinary language philosophy', which would flourish in the period that followed Wittgenstein's changed understanding of communication, is easy to see.

The scepticism that is conveyed by the Neapolitan habit of brushing the chin with the fingertips (even when the brushing is done by a Tuscan from Pisa, born in Turin) might be seen as part of the rules and conventions – the 'stream of life' – in the Neapolitan world. In *Philosophical Investigations*, Wittgenstein used the expression 'language-game' to illustrate how people learn how to use language and the meaning of words and gestures (even though, of course, there is much more to any actual language than this).

9

Was Sraffa thrilled by the impact that his ideas had on, arguably, the leading philosopher of our times? When I asked him that question more than once in our regular afternoon walks, he said, no, he was not. When pressed, he explained that the point he was making was 'rather obvious'.

When I arrived in Trinity in 1953, not long after Wittgenstein's death, I was aware that there had been something of a rift between the two friends. In response to my questions, Sraffa was most reluctant to go into what actually happened. 'I had to stop our regular conversations – I was somewhat bored' was the closest I ever got. However, the events have been described by Ray Monk in his biography of Wittgenstein:

> In May 1946 Piero Sraffa decided he no longer wished to have conversations with Wittgenstein, saying that he could no longer give his time and attention to the matters Wittgenstein wished to discuss. This came as a great blow to Wittgenstein. He pleaded with Sraffa to continue their weekly conversations, even if it meant staying away from philosophical subjects. 'I'll talk about anything,' he told him. 'Yes,' Sraffa replied, 'but in *your* way.'

There are many puzzling features in Sraffa's friendship with Wittgenstein. How could Sraffa, who loved dialogue and argument (I was lucky to be a beneficiary of this), become so reluctant to talk with one of the finest minds of the twentieth century? Furthermore, how could those conversations, which were so important for Wittgenstein and which proved to have such momentous implications for contemporary philosophy, seem 'rather obvious' to this young economist from Tuscany?

I doubt that we shall ever be sure of knowing the answers to these questions. There is also a related question: why was Sraffa so reserved about the depth and novelty of his conversations with Wittgenstein? I think at least part of the answer lies in the fact that what appeared to Wittgenstein as new wisdom was a common subject of discussion in the intellectual circle in Italy clustered around *L'Ordine Nuovo*. This included, I surmise, the so-called 'anthropological' aspects of rules of communication. Yet the impact of the scepticism that Sraffa conveyed to Wittgenstein would end up generating a huge new departure of analytical thinking in mainstream philosophy and reviving the so-called 'ordinary language philosophy'. It would, I believe, be hard to overestimate the creativity resulting from Sraffa's critique.

10

Reading Sraffa, and my conversations with him, led me to Antonio Gramsci's foundational contributions to philosophy. When John Maynard Keynes wrote to Sraffa in January 1927, communicating the willingness of Cambridge University to offer him a lecturing position, Gramsci had just been arrested (on 8 November 1926). After some harrowing experiences in prison, not least in Milan, Gramsci went on trial, along with a number of other political prisoners, in Rome in the summer of 1928. He received a sentence of twenty years ('for twenty years we must stop this brain from functioning,' said the Public Prosecutor in a statement that achieved some fame of its own), and was sent to a prison in Turi, about twenty miles from Bari. There, from February 1929, Gramsci was engaged in writing the essays and notes that would later become famous as his *Prison Notebooks* (published in Italy in the 1950s and translated into English in 1971).

Gramsci's notes brilliantly open a window on what Gramsci, Sraffa and their circle of friends were interested in. They had an immediate and strong involvement in practical politics, but the conceptual world beyond immediate politics was also much in their focus. Sraffa was very keen that Gramsci should write down his thoughts while in prison, and opened an account for him with a Milan bookshop (Sperling & Kupfer) to supply unlimited quantities of books and writing materials, the cost of which Sraffa would settle himself.

In an essay in the *Prison Notebooks* on 'the study of philosophy', Gramsci discusses 'some preliminary points of reference', which include the bold claim that 'It is essential to destroy the widespread prejudice that philosophy is a strange and difficult thing just because it is the specific intellectual activity of a particular category of specialists or of professional and systematic philosophers.' Rather, argued Gramsci, 'It must first be shown that all men are "philosophers", by defining the limits and characteristics of the "spontaneous philosophy" which is proper to everybody.'

What kind of an object is this 'spontaneous philosophy'? The first item that Gramsci lists under this heading is 'language itself, which is a totality of determined notions and concepts and not just of words grammatically devoid of content'. The role of conventions and rules, including what Wittgenstein came to call 'language-games', and the relevance of 'the anthropological way' which Sraffa championed to him, all figure prominently in Gramsci's understanding of the world – an understanding that he and Sraffa shared.

Sraffa and Gramsci remained in close communication until Gramsci's death in 1937, and it is not hard to see that he had a profound influence on Sraffa, particularly on his Marxian thinking. There was, however, discussion in the circle around *L'Ordine Nuovo* that, despite their good relations, Sraffa was not a completely loyal follower and disagreed with Gramsci on some crucial subjects. My understanding of the Gramsci–Sraffa relationship developed further in the late 1950s and early 1960s when I had long conversations with Sraffa (as I will relate in Chapter 24) and then again in the 1970s when I came to know Altiero Spinelli, the great Italian statesman and my father-in-law. Both men widened my perspective on the intellectual concerns of the Italian left and were essential to my own understanding of the world.

23

American Encounters

I

In 1959, I became engaged to Nabaneeta Dev, a poet, novelist and literary scholar, and we were married in June 1960. I had known Nabaneeta since 1956 when I was teaching at Jadavpur University, Calcutta, where she was studying comparative literature. Not long afterwards, she was awarded a Fellowship by Indiana University in America to do a Ph.D. there, beginning in the autumn of 1959, and on her way there she stopped in England. In addition to visiting Oxford as well as Cambridge together, we had a very pleasant trip to Wales. The wedding took place in Calcutta a year after that.

Nabaneeta was already a successful young poet, and would later become one of the most well-known creative writers in Bengali literature; she also became a renowned university professor at Jadavpur University. Our marriage sadly ended in divorce in 1973, but we had two wonderful daughters, Antara and Nandana. Nabaneeta's parents were famous poets as well, and she carried her celebrity status – and the many accolades that came her way – with unaffected approachability and warmth.

When we were living together, she had visits from an unending stream of literary fans keen to consult her and show her their work. When she was not at home, I had to entertain them as well as I could. For someone specializing in economics, mathematics and philosophy, this could be a challenge. On one occasion, a poet arrived with a substantial collection of his poems, wanting to read them aloud to Nabaneeta and to receive her critical judgement. But since she was not at home, the poet said he would settle instead for reading his several hundred poems to me. When I pleaded that I altogether lacked literary sophistication, I was assured by him: 'But that is absolutely perfect. I am especially interested in seeing how the common man – the unsophisticated common man – reacts to my poetry.' I am happy to report that the common man reacted with dignity and self-control.

2

In 1960–61, Nabaneeta and I both thought that spending a year at an American university was an attractive idea. Nabaneeta was heavily involved in what was then the new discipline of comparative literature, while I was keen to spend some time with American economists, away from the tussle in Cambridge between neo-Keynesian and the neoclassical schools. I was pleased therefore when a letter arrived, quite coincidentally, from MIT, offering me a one-year position as a visiting assistant professor in the Department of Economics. Additionally, I was told that my teaching load would be cut to half the standard requirement if I would also accept a research Fellowship at the Center for International Studies led by two well-known development experts, Max Millikan and Paul Rosenstein-Rodan. My friend Solomon Adler – a brilliant scholar and a stateless American, who had found a refuge in Cambridge, England, because of the intolerance of the left in America – advised me unhesitatingly, 'Do go and visit them! You will have fun in MIT.' He added, 'There is no better place for economics in the world.'

The appointment was to begin in the autumn of 1960, when Nabaneeta was taking a year at Harvard (located in Cambridge, Massachusetts, like MIT), on leave from Indiana University. At Harvard she worked in particular on oral epic poetry, under the guidance of Professor A. B. Lord, the leading collaborator of Milman Parry, who had established the discipline.

We flew to Boston just before the start of the academic year 1960–61. Nabaneeta plunged into oral epic poetry, but she was also busy with other aspects of comparative literature, including the study of Sanskrit with the great Sanskritist Daniel H. H. Ingalls. In her orbit I found myself spending a lot of time in the company of epics from different parts of the world, such as *Gilgamesh*, the *Iliad* and *Odyssey*, the *Song of Roland*, the *Nibelungenlied*, *Kalevala* and others. While I was having fun with grand stories and sharing the joys of epic narrative, Nabaneeta was doing the hard work of examining the details of linguistic composition from which (for example, from the tendency to repeat frequently a few chosen phrases) it could be surmised that a particular composition had oral rather than written origins.

At that time I was engaged in a different kind of literary work – editing my grandfather Kshiti Mohan's manuscript on Hinduism (as I described in Chapter 4), while he had been, distressingly for me, growing older and more feeble (he died on 12 March 1960). The book was so short – Kshiti Mohan had a passion for brevity and concision – that on the editorial advice of Penguin Books we were planning to add selections from the classics of Hindu literature, beginning with the wonderfully agnostic verse from the *Rig Veda* – the 'Song of Creation' from Mandala X – to which I referred earlier.

Despite my reasonably solid grounding in Sanskrit, I decided that I could do with some advice on subtler aspects of the textual remarks made by my grandfather as well as on the selection of Hindu literary texts to be included at the end of the book. Who better to seek advice from, I thought, than Daniel Ingalls? But Ingalls had the reputation of living a secluded life in his well-concealed office inside the Widener Library, where he was hard to find and harder to draw into conversation. Some friends I consulted before I dared to approach the reclusive Ingalls communicated their serious scepticism about the likelihood of success in getting help from him.

However, I made an appointment and went to see Ingalls in his Widener Library hideaway. To my delight, the meeting was a total success. After hearing my concerns, as well as my request for help, he asked me how Fridays at 3 p.m. might suit me. I hesitantly asked him how many times I could come and see him. He evidently thought that this was a dumb question. 'Until, of course, our work is finished,' was his reply.

What Ingalls gave me was strikingly wise advice. His knowledge of the literature was of course beyond compare, but what I did not anticipate was his remarkable ability to judge what would be appropriate for a presentation on Hinduism that would be both popular as well as engaging for readers seeking insight, without wanting to be overwhelmed by details. He was like a sculptor with a huge mass of clay who knew exactly how to shape what he wanted to create.

3

One of the nicest aspects of being at MIT was that my close friend Sukhamoy Chakravarty from Presidency College was also teaching there, with a visiting appointment. He and his wife Lalita had an apartment on Prentiss Street in Cambridge, as we did. Both the apartments had been arranged by our always helpful and immensely efficient friend Ramesh Gangolli, who was completing his Ph.D. in mathematics at MIT. He and his wife Shanta, and Sukhamoy, Lalita, Nabaneeta and I frequently had dinner together at one of our homes in turn. Other than the enjoyable nature of those evenings because of our conversations, our get-togethers also helped to keep us all in touch with news from India.

My teaching load at MIT was quite slight and I soon discovered that lecturing on basic economics to engineering students who knew some maths was not an exacting task. The students were agreeable, eager to listen and to talk. The research on development problems which I had undertaken to do for the Center for International Studies was not very time-consuming either. So I had free time, which was both pleasing and useful.

The two economists from whom I expected to learn most – Paul Samuelson and Robert Solow – were easy to approach and talk with, though Solow spent most of his time in Washington DC advising the newly elected President Kennedy. Despite that, I could catch him often enough when he came back to Cambridge, and I did not hesitate to invade his privacy.

Bob Solow may not have been aware how much I was learning from him through our intermittent conversations. Of course I was familiar with a fair number of his writings before I had come to MIT, but I had no idea how interesting and often gripping his conversation would be on any topic. On the first day we talked, he asked me what

I was working on at that time. I was, in fact, looking at a question posed to me by Maurice Dobb, on the way relative prices of old and new machines depended on interest rates and wages, and how this affected the relative merits of using older or newer machines respectively in high-interest and low-interest economies. I had just sent a letter to Maurice about a general rule that it is better economic value to buy older machines than newer ones in a country with lower wage and higher interest rates, compared with high-wage, low-interest countries. It is easy to show that the return the people of a country with a high-interest economy would get from older machines would be higher at prevailing prices.

This is an analytical relation and yielded a general rule, but I had not meant the example to be more than a matter of some curiosity (when eventually published – in the *Review of Economics and Statistics* – the result appeared in a paper called 'On the Usefulness of Used Machines'). Solow asked me, 'Are you sure? Can you show it to me?' He took my scribbles home and told me next morning, 'You know, you are right.' I told him that I was now certain I was, since he had just checked the proof. But I also asked him whether he always did that whenever something even slightly new came in front of him – no matter how far from his own interests it was. Bob answered: 'What's the point of being a teacher if you don't like to check it out?' What he did not say was that commitments of this kind made him one of the greatest of all teachers of economics. This I knew not only from his students, many of whom rose to dizzying heights, but also from my own experience in the brief year I spent at MIT, learning economics faster than I had ever done before.

4

One of the most agreeable features of the Economics Department at MIT at that time was the fact that the economists generally lunched together in the Faculty Club every weekday, sitting around a circular table. Aside from Samuelson and Solow, others normally present included Franco Modigliani, Evsey Domar, Frank Fisher, Edwin Kuh, Louis Lefeber, Richard Eckaus and many others with whom I much enjoyed talking. There was a lot of levity, but the striking difference from the get-together of economists at the older Cambridge was an almost total absence of sectarianism between members of different schools of thought. I have never been uninterested in arguing (and there was plenty of that at the lunch table at MIT), but the weariness I felt in the old Cambridge from hearing well-rehearsed attacks on sharply delineated schools of thought was splendidly absent.

The combination of intellectual stimulation and relaxed time at MIT gave me an opportunity to reflect on my understanding of economics as a whole. It was a pleasure to move away from seeing economics in terms of fights-to-win between different schools of thought. I came to see economics as an integrated subject that had room for different approaches, of varying importance depending on the context, which could make productive use of distinct tools of analysis (with or without mathematical reasoning of particular types) to do justice to questions of many kinds. Since I have been, from my very early days, involved in different approaches to economics and have always liked exploring writers with diverse interests and commitments (from Adam Smith, Condorcet, Mary Wollstonecraft, Karl Marx and John Stuart Mill to John Maynard Keynes, John Hicks, Paul Samuelson, Kenneth Arrow, Piero Sraffa, Maurice Dobb and Gérard Debreu), I wanted to examine how they could be made to talk to each other. This proved to be not only educational for me but also a great deal of fun, and the conviction that economics was a greater subject than it first appears also emerged firmly in my mind. It was an incredibly constructive time – and a rather unexpected one.

5

MIT had a number of excellent economists, but there would have been a consensus that Paul Samuelson was its leading light – indeed, he was already well known as one of the greatest economists in the world, and had written definitive treatises on almost every part of the subject. I had first started reading his work in my room at the YMCA in Calcutta and now found myself able to go to his classes, learning both from his economics and from his style of reasoning and exposition.

When Samuelson asked me to give one of his regular lectures in economic theory, as he had to go to Washington DC for a meeting, I felt challenged as well as honoured. 'It is meant to be on welfare economics,' he said, 'which I have been told you know something about.' I agreed to take on the job of substitute teaching, but told myself that it is one thing to lecture on welfare economics from what I knew (particularly from Samuelson's own writings) and quite another to try to replace Paul Samuelson as a lecturer.

I enjoyed giving the two-hour lecture on welfare economics, and it was quite exciting for me to have outstanding students (such as Peter Diamond, who would flower later as one of the most original thinkers among economists). I lectured along Samuelsonian lines (Chapter 8 of his *Foundations of Economic Analysis* was dedicated to the subject, as I had known since my days at Presidency College), but in the process I also convinced myself that despite the astonishing greatness of Samuelson, his approach to welfare economics was not perfect. One serious problem was how to capture the idea and exact formulation of interpersonal comparisons of different people's utilities (or – for that matter – interpersonal comparisons of any index of individual advantages). Besides the obvious difficulty of obtaining empirical evidence about utilities (already a much-discussed problem), we needed a robust analytical framework for comparing – in various ways – the utilities of different people. There are no common units between one person's utility and that of another.

In the class I taught, I made only a brief reference to the analytical problems of interpersonal comparison and mostly followed Samuelson's lead (though I did not believe he had really taken the challenges of interpersonal comparisons seriously enough). Trying to fill the gap motivated me to attempt to develop a solid analytical foundation for systematic interpersonal comparisons of utilities. When in 1970 I published what I argued was a more satisfactory way of establishing an analytical framework for interpersonal comparisons, by making use of what mathematicians call 'invariance conditions', it was essentially a continuation of the debate I'd had with Samuelson when I was doing substitute teaching for him.

The use of invariance conditions to characterize interpersonal comparisons seemed unusual to many at the time, but there soon developed quite a large literature in social choice theory adopting the approach. Samuelson was always kind about our disagreement, but it was only years later that he seemed to accept the framework I was using. The style of arguing with Samuelson, in contrast with arguments in old Cambridge, was also interesting to me. He remained entirely focused on the truth that could emerge from the argument, rather than being concerned with winning the debate, which he could have done easily enough, given his dominant standing in economics.

6

When I was busy at MIT, I suddenly received a letter from the Economics Department of Stanford University, inviting me to teach a course on development economics in the summer semester. Since I was becoming more and more interested in social choice theory, of which the undoubted pioneer, Kenneth Arrow, was a Stanford professor, the idea of visiting there had an immediate appeal. On enquiry, it turned out that Arrow was going to be away from Stanford then, but he wrote me a very kind letter saying he hoped to catch up with me before long. Over the years we did get together – and indeed worked together – often (teaching at Harvard when we were both there in 1968–9, and producing three joint books, working alongside Kotaro Suzumura, a great Japanese social choice theorist).

The immediate reason behind Stanford's proposal about getting me to come there was that their leading – indeed, only – Marxian economist, Paul Baran, who taught a regular summer course, had just had a heart attack and had suggested my name as a possible substitute. I had met Baran a few times when he had visited the English Cambridge, and had much enjoyed chatting with him. He told me how much he enjoyed visiting Piero Sraffa in his college set in Trinity. As he was examining the bookshelves in Sraffa's outer room, his host told him, 'Oh, ignore these – the really important books I keep in the inner study – let me take you there. The books here are all rubbish.' As he was moving from one room to another, Baran noticed, with some amusement, that all his own books had been firmly placed by Sraffa among the designated rubbish.

The time – a little more than two months – that we spent in Stanford was wonderful. The classes were enjoyable; my colleagues tremendously nice to chat with; the evenings in Stanford and the neighbourhood full of interest; and there was always San Francisco to visit to see a play. My old friend Dilip Adarkar and his wife Chitra were there (Dilip was finishing his Ph.D at Stanford) and fixed us up with comfortable accommodation and gave us their delightful company over those months. There were some excellent students who were planning to learn from Paul Baran and (sadly for them) got me instead – but several of them became lifelong friends. Nabaneeta and I greatly enjoyed what the Bay Area had to offer, and toured California from Big Sur to Los Angeles.

7

Then the summer came to an end. We returned to England on the *Queen Elizabeth II* from New York to London. In New York we stayed with Ved Mehta, deepening our friendship and being guided by him on what to do in the big city while waiting for our departure. The crossing of the Atlantic began with a big storm – the *Queen Elizabeth II* was the only passenger ship that decided to sail despite the weather. There is remarkable beauty in a turbulent sea, which you can enjoy if you feel absolutely safe – as we did on that gigantic ship.

The experiences in America made me academically quite greedy. From the point of view of work, MIT and Stanford seemed perfect. I told myself that a mixed life, if well organized between India and a good American or British university, could be both enjoyable and productive. After being at MIT in 1960–61, I was lucky enough to be able to arrange every fourth year a visit to an agreeable American university (coinciding, each time, with the US presidential elections). I was a visiting professor at the University of California at Berkeley in 1964–5 and then at Harvard in 1968–9. My social choice work, which proceeded steadily after I returned to Delhi, took great leaps during the years in America, both because I learned about what was emerging abroad, but also because I could present the results of my own work and get the reactions of people who were involved in the field.

At Berkeley I made good use of the opportunity to talk with Peter Diamond, John Harsanyi, Dale Jorgenson, Daniel McFadden, Carl Riskin, Tibor Scitovsky, Benjamin Ward, Roy Radner, Oliver Williamson, Meghnad Dessai and Dipak Banerji, among many others with a direct or indirect interest in subjects that attracted me, including social choice theory. At Harvard, I had the tremendous company of Kenneth Arrow and the great philosopher John Rawls (we did joint classes), but also of Samuel Bowles, Franklin Fisher, Thomas Schelling, Charles Fried, Allan Gibbard, Stephen Marglin, Howard Raiffa and Jerome Rothenberg, among others.

Oddly enough, my presence in America also coincided with radical political developments there. I was fortunate to see at close quarters the development of the free speech movement in Berkeley in 1964–5 and the students' occupation of the University Hall at Harvard in 1969. As it happened, I was also present at Columbia University in the spring of 1968, and had an eventful visit to Paris in the early summer of 1968. Thanks to all these coincidences, classical factor analysis might even have identified me as the 'root cause' of the disturbances!

8

Even though I had participated in student protests in Calcutta, I had not seen anything like the sudden, but systematic, development of student agitation that occurred with the free speech movement in Berkeley in 1964. The cause – free speech in the broadest sense – also resonated strongly with me, as did the underlying concerns, which related to the Civil Rights movement and resistance to the Vietnam War. I was teaching full-time, in particular a course in social choice theory that attracted quite a sizeable and enthusiastic audience. The classes were never disrupted and we had excellent discussion on how the issues involved in the free speech movement were relevant to social choice debates and procedures.

I was learning a lot, while trying to teach how reasoning in social choice proceeds and makes a difference. Since choice of leadership and of policies were being widely discussed among the leaders of the free speech movement – I received regular reports on them from friends – there was an uncanny proximity between things happening in the world outside and issues discussed inside our class. Even when I missed some important connection, I could rely on being corrected by one bright student or another who embraced both action and theory.

Even though I was a visiting professor, both Nabaneeta and I were not that much older than most of the graduate students; in addition to friendships with my colleagues, we also made friends with many of them. Carl and Myra Riskin were among the closest, but there were others, including Shyamala Gopalan (from India), who was doing much admired cancer research, and her husband Donald Harris (from Jamaica), a talented economist, on whose doctoral examination committee I sat. Shyamala and Don lived in Oakland, and Nabaneeta's and my apartment off Telegraph Avenue was almost halfway between Oakland and Berkeley, so it was easy for us to visit them. I first met their daughter Kamala when she was only a few days old and I remember how she protested when her parents' friends made too much noise. When she grew up, she earned a tremendous and justified reputation as a young political leader. As I write, she has just been elected the first female Vice President of the United States of America – an extraordinary achievement.

If I try to contrast the America I saw in my four-yearly visits with the America of today, I must recognize that some of the big difference owes much to the processes of change I was lucky enough to witness over the decades. The power of money may not have diminished, but protests about it have a solid footing now in a way that they did not have when I first visited. The word 'socialism' may still cause panic, but what makes the 'socialist parties' in Europe identifiably socialist (such as concern for public health, social security, minimum wages) can today get a hearing even in America – if they come without the dreaded socialist label. Public debates and radical movements have made a significant contribution to this change.

24
Cambridge Re-examined

I

On my return to Cambridge in September 1961, Trinity offered me a flat across the street from the College. Number 15 Trinity Street was at the centre of the town, just a minute's walk away. I was very pleased to be back.

The day after we arrived in Cambridge, Joan Robinson paid us a visit. She was very keen to meet Nabaneeta and was extremely welcoming to her. Even as I was thinking about how fond I was of Joan, she told me she hoped that I had not forgotten my Cambridge economics under the influence of MIT and Stanford. She also told me that the 'neoclassical poison' could easily be removed from economics if I would just take more interest in the big battle that was going on in the subject. She was, of course, half-joking, but I could see her old concerns had not disappeared.

Towards the end of the week, we went to see Maurice Dobb and had lunch with him and his wife Barbara in their family home in Fulbourn, not far from Cambridge. Here there was no talk of economic battles and we had a wonderful afternoon. I remember thinking that, while the big influence in drawing me to Trinity as an undergraduate was Maurice's economics, it was his personality and friendliness that now made me such a devotee of his.

2

As I was resettling in Cambridge, I heard about the turmoil surrounding the arrival of Frank Hahn, which had happened during my year

368

away. Hahn, a great mathematical economist and a hugely effective teacher and communicator, already justifiably famous, had been at Birmingham University, which he was persuaded to leave in order to move to Cambridge. He came with a Fellowship at Churchill College, and settled down remarkably quickly and well. His wife Dorothy – also an economist – became a senior figure at Newnham College. Frank rapidly became a close friend, and I came to rely on his and Dorothy's advice on many things.

Nicholas Kaldor had been very impressed by Frank after meeting him at a seminar exactly once, and had subsequently played a leading part both in persuading Cambridge to make a good offer and in persuading Frank to come to Cambridge. I told Nicky I was very pleased that he had taken that initiative, since Frank was a splendid economist and had great leadership qualities – and also (teasing him slightly) that it was very good that he – Kaldor – could form such a strong opinion about a person on the basis of only one meeting. Nicky replied that I was vastly underestimating him and he would usually need one meeting less than that to form a definitive opinion.

I was a strong admirer of Hahn's work, particularly of the way he handled complicated analytical problems. However, a number of mainstream Cambridge figures, Joan included, fumed about his influence, particularly the role he gave to mathematical economics. The dominant Cambridge orthodoxy had not been happy either with James Meade's appointment in 1957 as Professor of Political Economy (the senior economics chair in Cambridge, originally held by Alfred Marshall). There had been a strong local belief that either Joan or Nicky would be offered the post. However, while Meade differed firmly from the Cambridge orthodoxy, he tended at first to be rather quiet and non-combative. This was certainly the case when he and I taught classes together in 1958.

With the arrival of Frank Hahn, things began to change. There was a public battle going on between the orthodox and the rebels. Of the latter, Frank was the leader, and he was not reluctant to use his voice to dismiss the alleged centrality of neo-Keynesian ways of looking at the economic world. When I got back from America, I noted a new combativeness in James Meade, directed particularly against the unwillingness of the orthodox to listen to anyone else. He gave the

clear impression that he had at last decided that he had had enough –
on one occasion raising his voice sky-high to drown out what Joan
Robinson was saying after she had treated him similarly. The episode
might have been entertaining – as a shouting match between two famous people can sometimes be – but it was also depressing.

The fights seem to go on endlessly. There was a weekly seminar for
a small number of strictly chosen economists who formed a 'secret'
club called the Tuesday Club, though it met on Monday evenings (or
perhaps it was the Monday Club and met on Tuesdays). The discussions there were occasionally interesting, but mostly reflected the
differing loyalties of members to distinct schools of thought and were
often simply tribal. I did not offer to make a presentation at the club,
but sometimes enjoyed the discussions and invariably relished the
pre-meeting dinner at the restaurant above the Arts Theatre to which
Richard Kahn and Joan Robinson used to take us (Kahn was one of
the most generous hosts I have known).

I was also having my own battle at that time: to be permitted to
teach welfare economics and social choice theory. I had a lecturing
job at the University and a commitment to deliver two lectures a
week. I taught development economics and investment planning, and
also gave a set of lectures on general economic principles in the third
term of the final year – as a kind of supplement to the teaching offered
earlier in the academic year. I was happy enough to give these lectures
to very full classes – students generally flock to lectures when exams
are on the horizon. The faculty establishment was, however, as
strongly resistant to allowing me to teach a course in welfare economics as it had been to my learning the subject at all when I was a
graduate student. My proposal to start such a course was put before
the Faculty Board of Economics, chaired by Richard Kahn, but the
proposal was promptly rejected. After blocking it for a couple of years
('welfare economics is not a real subject,' a powerful member of the
faculty told me), I was eventually permitted to offer a short course of
just eight lectures. This was regarded as an indulgence to me rather
than an acknowledgement of the relevance of welfare economics as
part of the curriculum. When James Mirrlees was appointed to my
old post at Trinity after I left for Delhi, he too offered to teach a
course on welfare economics. Yet again this was not allowed, and he

was told by the faculty leaders, 'That little course was a special concession to Sen; it does not count as a normal part of economics teaching. Think of something else.'

3

My appreciation of Cambridge was thus becoming increasingly bifurcated. I enjoyed college life and talking with most of my colleagues, yet the priorities of the Faculty of Economics seemed calculated to keep me away from what I liked most. I came to terms with it, but it was not easy, and I had to create room for fruitful work. Although I was not being encouraged to think about social choice, there were other subjects towards which I could enjoyably turn and of course I was still learning much from Dobb and Sraffa.

Trinity was the main base of other intellectual encounters, going well beyond economics. It had a great record of bringing students – or young academics – from places far away and helping them to become something quite different. The person about whom I was asked most often when I was a young Fellow at Trinity was, unsurprisingly, Ramanujan, the mathematical genius from India. But there was also Chandrashekhar, one of the most original and influential of modern astronomers, who after Trinity went on to work at the University of Chicago. There were many others – from Jawaharlal Nehru to Muhammad Iqbal, the visionary poet – who had been at Trinity well before my time, but whose associations with the College were clearly important for their work and who came often into our conversations.

In a special lecture I had to give at Trinity many years later, I mentioned the time I joined the College, when I was still recovering from the high-dose radiation treatment for my oral cancer administered the year before. Michael Atiyah, a superb mathematician and an immensely likeable person, who was awarded the first Abel Prize (the highest distinction in mathematics), and who had been Master of the College immediately before me, read the text of my speech which Trinity had published and told me something about himself which I did not know:

I have just been reading the Trinity Annual Record and enjoyed both your article on Sraffa (& Wittgenstein) and your 80th birthday speech. I discovered that Trinity nearly lost two consecutive Masters at an early age. While you endured oral cancer at the age of 15, which hung over you for many years, I had cerebro-spinal meningitis in Cairo at the age of 13. This can kill within a few days and I was just saved by the new sulfonamide drug (M&B 693) that had recently appeared and which my schoolmaster and my uncle managed to find.

Michael often talked about his Sudanese ancestry and his Egyptian childhood, but that did not weaken in any way his strong identity as a British mathematician. His Sudanese identity merged seamlessly with his Trinity identity.

Reasons to reflect upon our varying identities seemed omnipresent in my college life and became increasingly clear to me in my years at Cambridge. The men who had fallen in wartime and been commemorated in Trinity Chapel were indubitably British, yet their kinship with Trinity members of later years – from all over the world, from Sudan to India – had a reality that coexisted with their respective nationalities. The social analysts who tend to think of identity as a unique – and sharply divisive – classificatory device miss the richness of the multiple identities we all have. Our geographic origins, citizenship, residence, language, profession, religion, political predispositions and many other aspects of our identity can happily coexist, making us, together, the people that we are.

Of course, identity can also be a source of conflict, especially if its multiple aspects are not properly understood. Divisions can suddenly appear and be encouraged to inflame hostilities, as they were in India in the 1940s to fan the violence in pre-Partition politics. The quiet Indians of the 1930s were suddenly persuaded to start seeing themselves as either belligerent Hindus or battle-ready Muslims. There was a similar fostering of violence in Ireland, particularly in the north, exploiting the vulnerability of the Catholic–Protestant division. As I reflected on the complexity of identity problems, I began to see more clearly how they could be hugely important – and potentially inflammable – even when they survive in a concealed rather than a clearly visible form.

4

The mischief and the violence that can result from confused thinking about a supposedly unique dominant identity is accompanied by a different kind of identity problem – one that can lead to a misunderstanding of the way that social organization works. I came to consider it because of some conversations I had with the world-renowned economist Oskar Lange, when I was just beginning my doctoral research.

As a pioneering analyst of market socialism, Lange not only clarified the different forms that a socialist economy can take, but in the process also threw light on how a competitive market economy operates, and how decentralized information can be cogently put together by a smoothly operating market system under both socialism and capitalism.

As a professor at the University of Chicago, Lange became a naturalized American citizen in 1943. But shortly thereafter he began to question his own earlier work. By the time the Second World War came to an end, Lange had accepted (to the considerable surprise of his colleagues and other economists) the superiority of the Soviet type of centralized resource allocation, and had rejected the merits of decentralization through markets – including the idea of market socialism, which was so much a creation of his own economic thinking. He also renounced his American citizenship and began writing a series of monographs championing Joseph Stalin's ideas, including – I have to hold my breath here – 'Stalin's economic theories'.

Lange's name had come up often in the political and economic discussions at the coffee house in College Street in Calcutta during my days at Presidency College around 1952. Sukhamoy Chakravarty was fascinated by Lange's political journey and, after Lange's sudden turn towards Stalinist theory, Sukhamoy told me that he was bewildered. Lange's conversion to Soviet-style economics was often mentioned by the communist faithful, while of course being denounced as misguided nonsense by those critical of the communist system. Among professional economists, the stellar quality of Lange's early work continued to be admired – Ken Arrow was particularly vocal in his praise – though his later ideas were typically treated with scepticism.

When I talked about Lange, Maurice Dobb also expressed much admiration for his early work, and that he was unable to understand the direction in which Lange was now heading. Sraffa was more explicit, and described Lange as a very smart and kind man who had badly confused the demands of economic reasoning and ideological politics. Sraffa remained in touch with Lange, and it was he who told me, sometime in early 1956, that Lange was about to visit Cambridge and had expressed a particular interest in meeting me.

It turned out that Lange had heard from Maurice Dobb about my current area of research (I was just getting into my work on 'choice of techniques') and he wanted to give me some advice. When I met Lange, he was enormously friendly. He said he would like to see what kind of theory I ended up developing, but also felt that economic decisions of this kind were so dominated by political priorities that any work in pure economic theory, such as my attempted exercise in choice of techniques, was bound to miss out important dimensions of the decision-making involved.

'Let me illustrate,' he said, and went on to describe how the Polish government had built a big industrial complex with a huge steel mill – and a related industrial unit (called the Vladimir Lenin Steelworks) – in Nowa Huta, next to the old city of Krakow. 'In terms of pure economic analysis, it is hard to justify the decision to put it there, usurping prime agricultural land and dependent on bringing from a distance many of the ingredients of production, including coal and iron ore,' Lange said. The question was, why did they go for such a gigantic industrial investment in what seemed like an unsuitable location? Why there?

I couldn't guess what the answer might be, and asked, 'Why indeed?' 'It is because', Lange replied, 'Krakow has been a very reactionary city, with a long right-wing history – they didn't even fight the Nazis properly.' Therefore the decision was taken that a modern industrial town 'with a large proletariat' was just what Krakow needed. 'People in Krakow are already beginning to become less reactionary,' Lange said confidently. 'You would never get an answer to this question by digging deeper and deeper into cloistered economic reasoning. The reasoning in this case was entirely political.'

Lange had to go to another appointment, and so he left, asking me very cordially to visit him in Poland. I was grateful that he had taken the trouble to come and see me and explain the need to highlight the relevant political considerations in economic decision-making.

After he had gone, I kept wondering whether he really was right. He must have been correct to point to the relevance of political considerations in economic decisions, but the Nowa Huta example was much too neat and formulaic. Would things indeed develop as expected by Lange and his friends? I did not know the answer then, but I found out later. It turned out that the anti-communist Solidarity Movement, which was prominent by the early 1980s, had a strong base within the Vladimir Lenin Steelworks at Nowa Huta, and gradually the former expectations of the Polish government were completely overturned. The steelworks became a bastion of the new Catholic labour movement. Rather than Nowa Huta reforming Krakow, it was Krakow that overwhelmed Nowa Huta. Lange was right in that politics are certainly important in economic decisions, but events can also move in the opposite way to that planned by the political leaders.

Identities may not be immune to change, but they cannot be easily subjected to planned manipulation. Over the years, the Solidarity Movement expanded and matured, and I would have welcomed the opportunity to discuss the issue again with Lange in the light of his original expectations and what actually happened in Nowa Huta. Sadly he died in 1965, well before Solidarity became a force to be reckoned with. In thinking about the changeability and manipulability of identity, I became increasingly convinced that we must consider much more carefully how our identities adjust to circumstances, often in unpredictable ways.

5

Since I had time in hand after fulfilling my teaching and research duties in Cambridge, I decided, after some hesitation, to explore social choice theory anyway. As Kenneth Arrow's work was becoming somewhat better known and understood, many people across the world were beginning to take an interest in social choice and it seemed to me that there were some prominent issues in the field needing urgent exploration. James M. Buchanan, a very agreeable but rather conservative economist, asked the wonderfully foundational question – whether the idea of social preference, used by Arrow and many social choice theorists, actually made any sense. Society is not a person so how can we sensibly think of something as the 'preference of a society'? In particular Buchanan asked, not unreasonably, whether it made sense to talk about consistency properties of social choice (what Arrow called 'collective rationality') since a society could not engage in integrated reflections in the way an individual does.

On this and related themes Buchanan published two extremely interesting papers in 1954, when I was still an undergraduate in Cambridge. As I was then preparing for my BA examination, I could not go much beyond noting the relevance of Buchanan's questions and his broad line of reasoning. Why should a cluster of social choices have any kind of regularity, such as transitivity (demanding that if x is socially preferred to y and y to z, then x must be socially preferred to z)? And going on from there, would Arrow's impossibility theorem collapse if we stopped demanding such coherence or – going further – if we were to abandon the very idea of social preference?

I had no one around me to talk about these concerns, and in the busy years that followed Buchanan's publications in 1954 (with my research on other subjects and my teaching at Jadavpur University) the Buchananite questions went on the back burner. However, in my year at MIT in 1960–61, and in particular during my substitute teaching for Samuelson on welfare economics, I was reminded that there was unfinished business in exploring the idea of social preference to which I would, sooner or later, have to return. I even took the liberty of asking Samuelson whether he had thought about Buchanan's questions. He clearly had, but my way of asking the question made him laugh. 'We will do it together some day,' he said kindly.

Sometime after returning to Cambridge from America, I decided to look properly at Buchanan's scepticism of Arrow's framework and his dismissal of Arrow's impossibility theorem. There was still no one in Cambridge to discuss this with, and I remembered one of Tagore's invigorating songs from the days of India's struggle for independence: 'If no one responds to your call, you must go alone.' Solitary progress was not impossible and after some work I concluded, tentatively, that Buchanan's scepticism about social preference made a lot of sense – at least, for certain types of social choice.

Consider, for example, voting systems. It could be hugely problematic to ascribe some kind of a social preference as the basis of voting decisions that would emerge, in one way or another, from the established institutions. If you find that candidate x can beat y, and y can beat z, that need not give any kind of guarantee that x would be able to beat z. It may be tempting to think that x is better than y, and y better than z, so x should be better than z, but voting results are best seen just as procedural outcomes without any immediately cogent valuational implications. Buchanan therefore seemed to me to be right in his scepticism about social preferences – if they were to be extrapolated from voting results.

However, our understanding would be quite different if the social choice were to reflect social welfare judgements rather than voting outcomes. Any necessary coherence of social welfare rankings would make the values of social welfare chime together. If, for example, social policy a would yield more social welfare than policy b, and policy b more social welfare than policy c, then we should be able to presume that policy a would offer more social welfare than policy c, because of valuational congruity. In that case, ideas of collective rationality should make sense for social welfare judgements in a way that they would not for purely institutional outcomes. Thus, in the case of welfare judgements, demands such as transitivity of social preference would make sense. This would be Arrow's world – not Buchanan's.

What do we conclude, then, about Arrow's impossibility theorem? In the case of social welfare assessment, the theory would continue to be relevant – armed with the coherence needed for collective rationality – on Arrow's own line. But there is a genuine difficulty in the other case – in trying to ascertain social preference from voting and elections. If collective rationality was a problematic demand in voting decisions, we could not get Arrow's impossibility result – at least not by using Arrow's mathematical reasoning, since Arrow made crucial use of collective rationality in proving the impossibility. Is that, then, the end of the impossibility result for procedural cases such as voting (though not for social welfare judgements)? Or is there some way in which we could drop collective rationality and still get Arrow's impossibility result?

I thought a fair amount about this question and continued to do so among other ongoing work in my year after graduation (even as I was getting into working on 'choice of techniques'), but could not fully resolve it. Eventually, after many years, I did develop a proof of Arrow's impossibility without the requirement of collective rationality, a somewhat complicated mathematical theorem which (decades later) served as the backbone of my presidential address for the Econometric Society. I sent this new theorem and its proof to Arrow in the late 1970s, and he told me he was convinced that there must be an error somewhere. He promised to send me a correction, but that never came, and to my great comfort he eventually accepted the validity of the theorem and its proof. There are happy moments too in social choice theory.

6

Aside from Buchanan's concerns, I explored a few other analytical questions in social choice theory, but I missed having others around me interested in these issues. Maurice Dobb had presciently warned me about the loneliness of working on a subject in which there was little interest among colleagues, students, teachers or friends. As always, however, the broad range of Piero Sraffa's interests provided a relief from this severe isolation. Piero used to do serious philosophy without calling it philosophy, and he did social choice too without acknowledging that it was social choice he was doing.

On one particular subject, Sraffa's disagreement with Gramsci was very significant – both on its own and in the way it related to social choice theory. This concerned the extent of the importance to be attached to individual liberty among other human values, and whether it should have a place of its own among the basic demands reflected in the axiomatic structure of social choice theory. The latter question was of particular interest to me since the accommodation of liberty in social choice was one of the major problems I wanted to explore in trying to extend normative social choice theory beyond the classic Arrow framework (which had no room for liberty in the basic axioms for social choice). It was Sraffa's investigation of the importance of liberty that helped me to start thinking about the subject after my return from MIT, during my last two academic years (1961–3) in the old Cambridge.

What was Sraffa concerned with in discussing the place of liberty in social and political arrangements? He criticized the Communist Party's inclination to ignore the importance of personal liberty, and he was particularly critical of the neglect of what the Party tended to call, rather dismissively, 'bourgeois liberty'. I had myself encountered a similarly dismissive attitude from the official Left towards the idea of liberty (described by them also as 'bourgeois liberty') in my student days in the early 1950s at Presidency College. As a student in Calcutta, I knew nothing about the Gramsci–Sraffa debate of the 1920s, but came to it while talking with Piero in the course of one of our afternoon walks.

After I had returned from MIT I was struck by the persistence of essentially the same debate, as in Calcutta, about the place of personal liberty in left-wing political theory. Sraffa did not doubt that the rhetoric of liberty could be misused as a reactionary attack on the pursuit of economic equity and other egalitarian values – as Gramsci had evidently also feared. It was certainly possible to find this kind of anti-egalitarian use, which tended to set the idea of liberty against that of equity (despite the famous championing of both in the early years of the French Revolution). However, Sraffa argued that such misuse could be avoided without neglecting the real importance of liberty in human life. We need liberty to do anything significant, and it is possible to accept its importance without being afraid that it can operate as a barrier to achieving other important social objectives. As Sraffa put it, it is a mistake:

> ... to pour too much scorn on bourgeois 'liberty' (as is done, for example, by *L'Unità* [the main newspaper affiliated with the Italian Communist Party]): whether it is thought to be beautiful or ugly, this is what the workers need most at the moment and it is an indispensable condition of all further conquests.

Sraffa had considerable influence in making Gramsci rethink the significance of liberty, even though Gramsci's ultimate endorsement of its importance remained, as far as I could see, significantly less enthusiastic than Sraffa's.

One of the interesting issues here is that, although Karl Marx himself had a very strong interest in the central role of liberty for advancing the quality of human life, the communist movement itself has always been far less sympathetic to individual liberty. This was the case not only in Italy but almost everywhere it came to power (from the Soviet Union and China to Cuba and Vietnam). As a young man, Marx wrote a great deal in favour of the liberty of the press and strongly defended free speech. His advocacy applied also to his writings on the liberty of social cooperation and industrial unionization – his sympathies in this respect were contradicted by the effective abolition of trade union movements that occurred in most communist countries in the world. Altogether, Marx wanted to expand the domain of liberty in social decisions. He was keen, as we saw earlier, to emphasize the role that liberty could play in enriching human life through expanding room for choice, by making it 'possible for me to do one thing to-day and another tomorrow, to hunt in the morning, fish in the afternoon, rear cattle in the evening, criticize after dinner, just as I have in mind, without ever becoming hunter, fisherman, shepherd or critic'.

In my initial speculations on liberty in my first year of research at Cambridge (fleeing from the dry discipline of capital theory), I enjoyed considering various consistency problems that occurred to me in accommodating liberty in social choice. I hoped to engage Piero during our walks by sharing some of the more interesting ones with him and greatly benefited from the interest he took in them. I published one of the results a few years later in a paper in the *Journal of Political Economy* ('The Impossibility of a Paretian Liberal', 1970), which has probably been read more than any other paper I have written.

7

Another social choice problem that Piero and I often discussed (though we did not call it anything as formal as 'social choice') concerned the role of discussion and debate in enhancing the reach of what happens in a society. This discussion too had a particularly practical context. Sraffa was wholeheartedly involved in the battle against fascism and was close to the Italian Communist Party, which was the principal opposition to the fascists in Italy. But he was also strongly opposed to one of the major policy decisions that his friend Gramsci, as the leader of the Communist Party, had taken – namely, a refusal to join hands with the other anti-fascist parties in Italy. Gramsci was concerned that they should not be deflected from their well-defined political objectives, but Sraffa argued that this was a mistake.

In 1924, in a powerful critique of the party's unilateralism, Sraffa made a statement on the importance of having a united 'democratic opposition'. It was critically important, he argued, for the various parts of the anti-fascist movement to work together in combined opposition to Mussolini's fascism. Talking with each other could help to make the movements more clear-headed and, furthermore, joining together could add strength to the resistance to fascism. Gramsci was initially not at all persuaded by Sraffa's arguments and attributed Sraffa's disagreement to his being still under the spell of 'bourgeois thinking'. However, later on, Gramsci had to change his mind. The Italian Communist Party did ultimately link up with the other anti-fascist parties and groups, producing a strong resistance movement to Italian fascism.

In our afternoon walks, Piero told me that the differences he had with Gramsci were far less important than what he had learned from him. I expect he was right in this, since the influence of Gramsci's ideas on Sraffa, I could easily see, was very profound. And yet, as someone whose interests were at that time strongly turning to social choice theory (including to liberty and persuasion), I could not help feeling that the arguments Sraffa was trying to present to Gramsci were tremendously important as well. They also indicated Sraffa's interest in the philosophy underlying social choice, even though he did not believe that social choice theory was a discipline that could stand on its own.

PART FIVE

25

Persuasion and Cooperation

I

When I arrived in England in the autumn of 1953, the immediate memory of the First World War had mostly gone, but that of the Second was very fresh all over Europe. The agonizing concerns that preceded the war were also strong. The mood was well captured by W. H. Auden's poem 'In Memory of W. B. Yeats', written in early 1939:

> All the dogs of Europe bark,
> And the living nations wait,
> Each sequestered in its hate.

The events that followed only confirmed Auden's worst expectations.

I heard a lot in my early years in Britain about how worrying the period before the war had been. The terrible possibility of a repeat of the world war haunted a great many Europeans and the birth of the movement for European unification was motivated strongly by the desire for political unity – free from self-destructive wars. The hope of achieving such an outcome is brought out clearly by the two pioneering documents that launched the movement: the Ventotene Declaration of 1941 and the Milan Manifesto of 1943, prepared by four outspoken Italian intellectuals who staunchly argued for European unity – Altiero Spinelli, Ernesto Rossi, Eugenio Colorni and Ursula Hirschmann.

The merits of economic integration were well understood by the supporters of the Ventotene and Milan declarations. Even the case for financial union in the long term had been clearly presented by people close to them (particularly by Luigi Einaudi, who would later become the President of Italy). The immediate concern underlying the need for European unification was not considerations of trade and business, nor of integrated banking and monetary arrangements (those would come later), but the necessity of political unity for the sake of European peace.

I have had the opportunity to watch the process of European unification stretching over seventy years. As I recounted earlier, the ease with which in my youthful hitch-hiking days I met – and interacted closely with – people in different European countries, who had similar behaviour and priorities, gave me a sense of being in a place that was coming together as 'Europe'. My primary motivation then was not so much the development of political wisdom, but to become acquainted with Europe and to enjoy my travels. But it gradually became clear to me that I was also watching the unfolding of European integration.

The formation of a united Europe was an old dream, which had gone through successive waves of cultural and political integration, greatly helped by the spread of Christianity. King George of Poděbrady in Bohemia was talking about pan-European unity even in 1464. He was followed by many others in the subsequent period. In the eighteenth century, from across the Atlantic, George Washington wrote to the Marquis de la Fayette that 'one day, on the model of the United States of America, a United States of Europe will come into being'. Over time, it began to look as if we might see the realization of George Washington's vision.

As I write in 2021, the mood is changing – in Hungary and Poland and to some extent even in France and Italy – as public opinion turns against European unity and even against some of the demands of the European democratic tradition. This backward-looking attitude has of course been very prevalent in Britain too, and in the 2016 referendum on the so-called Brexit a narrow majority voted in favour of leaving the European Union. There is now a strong sense of Ventotene-in-reverse.

2

However, over the intervening eighty years, there have been some amazing achievements in Europe – on the rule of law, on human rights, on participatory democracy, on economic cooperation – none of which could have been confidently anticipated when I landed at Tilbury docks in 1953. Perhaps the most impressive thing I saw was the positive manifestation of the development of the welfare state, including the National Health Service. This radical change was clearly related to new social thinking – I remember reading a lot of William Beveridge (and his rousing battle against 'want, disease, ignorance, squalor and idleness') as I was settling down in Britain. As I searched for its roots, the change also seemed to be connected, rather dialectically, with the war that had just ended, and in particular with an appreciation of shared experiences which made people better realize the importance of cooperation.

I was fortunate to be able to share my questions and my speculations with Piero Sraffa, who had thought about these issues a great deal. I was also struck by the fact that, in addition to invoking Gramsci's ideas (not an unusual thing for Sraffa to do), he was very keen that I should read John Maynard Keynes on the formation – and importance – of public opinion and its role in social transformation, in particular his *Essays in Persuasion* (1931). Sraffa greatly admired Keynes – his old friend – for emphasizing the central role of persuasion in changing human society. Among other things, Keynes was eager to show how crucial it was for different sides to work together for the realization of their respective goals. This is the case even when their goals do not fully coincide, but share something of a common objective.

In the period between the two world wars Keynes was much concerned with reducing hostility between the European countries. This applied especially to governmental policies after the end of the First World War, and the serious harm that was done by the Versailles Treaty of 1919, by which the victors, including Britain, France and the United States, imposed harsh reparations on a defeated Germany. The ruthlessness of the reparations, Keynes thought, was hugely misconceived, since it would ruin Germany and badly affect other European economies; and it would also leave Germany with a strong sense of grievance about the treatment it had received.

Keynes knew that punishing a defeated Germany and ruining its prosperity were popular thoughts in Britain, but he wanted the British public to understand that imposing such severe penalties and forced austerity on Germany was not in the interest of Germany, Britain or France. In *The Economic Consequences of the Peace*, he argued that public education and public reasoning were critically important, and he expressed, with some passion, his aim of 'setting in motion those forces of instruction and imagination which change *opinion*'. Indeed, he dedicated his book to 'the formation of the general opinion of the future'.

Keynes's efforts to sway contemporary government policy were not immediately successful (his recommendations were mostly overruled), but he contributed a great deal to the 'general opinion of the future' about what went wrong then and led to the economic decline in the 1930s. Keynes died at the age of sixty-six in 1946, having been enormously influential in the establishment of a framework of international institutions. His biggest contribution to economics was the so-called 'general theory', set out in his classic book, *The General Theory of Employment, Interest and Money* (1936), which changed the understanding of the causes of unemployment and economic depression.

Even though the lessons from Keynes's far-reaching economic analysis are often forgotten (as evidenced spectacularly in the severe imposition of austerity in Europe, including Britain, following the financial crisis of 2008 – a deeply counterproductive move), we really cannot afford to ignore the economic wisdom that came with the so-called 'Keynesian revolution'. Nor can we forget the major changes that Keynes brought about constructively in the realm of enlightened 'opinion'. In terms of relations between different nations, the institutions established – very much inspired by Keynes's ideas – through the Bretton Woods agreement in 1944, including the International Monetary Fund and the World Bank, have been shaping the world ever since.

3

The positive effects of cooperation between countries have parallels in the constructive outcomes of cooperation among individuals, within each country. The most striking development – the birth of the welfare state – was clearly, in one respect, connected with the legacy of wartime, and in particular with the shared experiences and efforts that made people better realize the importance of working together.

Surprisingly, in the difficult years of food shortage during the Second World War there was actually a sharp reduction in the incidence of undernourishment in Britain. Faced with the prospect of a diminution in total food supplies in the 1940s (partly because of transport difficulties and dangers during the war), the government put in place a system for more equal sharing out of what was available – through rationing and price control. The result was that suddenly the chronically undernourished could afford to buy enough food for their needs – more than they had ever been able to before. Rationing at low, controlled prices may have been aimed initially only at countering mass hunger, but by making food available at affordable prices to all, Britain took a huge step forward in advancing nourishment for the poor. In fact, the incidence of severe and extreme undernourishment disappeared almost entirely in Britain just when the total availability of food per head was at its lowest point. Similar things happened with the better allocation of medical care.

The results of better sharing were astounding. During the war decade of the 1940s, life expectancy at birth in England and Wales jumped up by 6.5 years for men, compared with 1.2 years in the preceding decade. For women it went up by 7 years, far exceeding the rise of 1.5 years in the pre-war decade. Britain had faced shortages – of food, medicine and other things – in previous times as well, but something really radical happened during the Second World War. Perhaps it was the cluster of shared misfortunes connected with the war, combined with the understanding of the need to fight together, shoulder to shoulder, that generated such a cooperative perspective and a dialogue of integration. Indeed, as the study of food distribution during the war years by Richard Hammond shows, the British developed a new conviction – a shared persuasion – that they could not leave others behind to starve. 'There was a revolution in the attitude of the British state towards the feeding of its citizens.' And once the sharing culture, especially under the aegis of the National Health Service, had become established and was clearly flourishing, there was no real temptation to drop it all and return to the pre-war health asymmetries of a seriously unequal society. Aneurin Bevan, a strong advocate of greater equity during and after the war, inaugurated the first National Health Service hospital in Britain – the Park Hospital in Manchester – in 1948, which was thus only five years old when I landed in England.

4

Something special was emerging from post-war Europe in general and from Britain in particular from which the world had a lot to learn. Not long after arriving in Cambridge, I remember sitting on one of the metal chairs near the river at the back of my college and asking myself, 'why has nothing like the NHS happened in India?' Whereas the British political process, much inspired by the new Labour leadership, had been trying out new ideas on cooperation, the imperial tradition of keeping the colonies unchanged continued without much of a break all the way to India's independence. The differences in the process and reach of persuasion were critically important here. The Raj had little interest in communicating the experience of sharing with its colonial subjects, and there was not much practice, nor any serious learning, that its subjects could derive from the social success of the newly radicalizing post-war Britain.

In fact, the British in India went in a very different direction from the British in Britain. Rabindranath Tagore was particularly eloquent on this contrast. In his last public lecture – the 'Crisis in Civilization' – he discussed this and similar contrasts:

> I cannot help contrasting the two systems of governments, one based on co-operation, the other on exploitation, which have made such contrary conditions possible.

Indeed, just when serious undernourishment was being successfully eradicated in Britain, India suffered a gigantic famine – the Bengal famine of 1943 – which killed nearly 3 million people. How could a country ruled by the foremost democracy in Europe allow such a famine to develop? The answer to this question leads us back to the analysis in Chapter 7 and the disastrous role played by the embargo on communication, until it was partially broken by a courageous journalist.

The famine occurred, as I have described, during the Second World War when the British were in retreat, chased by the advancing Japanese military forces. The British were very afraid of the demoralization that could arise from the free flow of information about the retreat of their forces. So the Raj rulers decided to restrict the flow of information, censoring the Bengali newspapers and severely restricting their freedom to publish. However, it did not formally censor the best-known English paper, the British-owned *Statesman*. Instead, as we have seen, the government appealed to its sense of patriotism – requesting that it should not do anything that would be detrimental to the British war efforts.

The Statesman agreed to that censorship for a long time, taking care that nothing about the famine was discussed in the paper. However, in the summer of 1943, Ian Stephens, its English editor, who was becoming increasingly enraged by the government's suppression of catastrophic news, decided to publish photographs of people suffering from destitution in Bengal. The photographs were presented *without* discussion or critique.

One day – I can even guess that it was 13 October 1943 – Stephens decided he could not suppress his growing moral doubts about the unacceptability of silence and the absence of criticism of the Raj. He saw clearly that he was betraying his profession; he was a journalist, but was writing nothing about the most important calamity around him. So, on 14 October and again on 16 October, *The Statesman* published vitriolic attacks on the British policy regarding the famine, with news coverage providing the evidence. India did not have a parliament then, but Britain did. The British Parliament had not discussed the man-made disaster before Stephens spoke. All that changed immediately after *The Statesman*'s reporting.

Indeed, after the *Statesman* editorials, the gravity of the situation could not but be discussed in London, and it received wide attention in the British papers. Within a few days there was a resolution for government intervention to stop the famine and within a few weeks official famine relief was instituted for the first time in the 1943 famine. Because the famine had been going on for nine months, more than a million people had already died. Eventually, public persuasion resulted in a major change in policy.

Many years after his crucial intervention, I had the opportunity to meet Ian Stephens in Cambridge. It was Morgan Forster who had told me – I think at a meeting of the Apostles – that Stephens had become a Senior Research Fellow at King's College after his retirement from India, and he actually had rooms there. Forster said that he would be happy to introduce me, but I could also go and knock on his door, since he was a welcoming person. So I went and knocked, but there was no reply. As the door was unlocked, I went in. Stephens was on his head – a habit he had picked up in India – doing yoga in a corner of the room, looking like an ancient statue. My appearance brought him down and upside-up, and then we chatted. I must have had six or seven meetings with him in all, when we talked about what had happened in Calcutta. He was very proud of that period of his life.

Forster had told me when we first talked, 'Remember, Ian Stephens is no friend of India.' What he had meant was that after India's independence and partition the British residents there who did not immediately return to Britain divided themselves into different camps, and Stephens was definitely in the Pakistani camp. He had a (rather British) view that Muslims were less hostile to the Empire, unlike the Hindu rebels, which is not exactly true. (In Forster's *A Passage to India* (1924), Aziz, the Indian protagonist, is clearly a Muslim.) Stephens was very critical of Indian policies, particularly concerning Kashmir – and after he left *The Statesman* in 1951 he went to Pakistan, a move that was connected with his disapproval of what was happening politically in India. The fact that Stephens was on the Pakistani side didn't worry me in the least. The lives that he had saved in Bengal were of both Hindus and Muslims, and the great benefits that humanity derived from his role as a responsible editor were not specific to any one religion.

5

I learnt several things from my conversations with Ian Stephens, most profoundly why the suppression of public discussion can be disastrous for a population, even helping to usher in a famine. A government that generates a calamity like this may have some chance of escaping public anger if the news of it is effectively suppressed, so that it doesn't have to face criticism of its policy failure. That is what the British achieved, to some extent, in the case of the Bengal famine. It was only after Stephens blew the whistle that the Parliament in Westminster had to discuss the famine and the British press demanded that it be stopped immediately. It was only then that the Raj had to take action.

Public discussion clearly has an important role in determining how a society performs. Keynes's emphasis on persuasion aligns very well with John Stuart Mill's advocacy of public reasoning in good policy-making. Mill's characterizations of democracy as 'government by discussion' belongs to the same territory. Those, incidentally, are not Mill's exact words, but those of Walter Bagehot (mentioned earlier) – though Mill had done the most for the idea to be understood.

Public reasoning in pursuit of better decision-making has been used not just in the post-Enlightenment Western world, but in other societies and at other times too. While the Athenian origins of voting procedures are often remembered, it is important to note that the Athenians also engaged in discussion as a source of enlightenment. The idea received a good deal of attention in India too, particularly in Buddhist traditions. As we saw in Chapter 6, in the third century BC, Emperor Ashoka, the Buddhist emperor who ruled over nearly all of the Indian subcontinent (and well into what is now Afghanistan), hosted the third – and largest – Buddhist Council in his capital city of Patna (then called Pataliputra) to settle disputes in the same way. He emphasized the contribution that open discussions could make to a better understanding of what society needed. He tried to popularize the idea by placing easily readable inscriptions on stone pillars across the country and beyond, advocating peace and tolerance and regular and orderly public discussion to resolve differences.

Similarly, when in early seventh-century Japan the Buddhist Prince Shotoku produced the so-called 'constitution of seventeen articles' in AD 604 (this was six centuries before Magna Carta), he argued for the need to be better informed through consultation: 'Decisions on important matters should not be made by one person alone. They should be discussed with many.' The idea that democracy is 'government by discussion' – and not just about voting – remains extremely relevant today. Many of the large failures of democratic governance in recent years have arisen, I would argue, precisely from inadequate public discussion, rather than from any obvious institutional barrier.

I have been interested in this question since my schooldays when my grandfather Kshiti Mohan drew my attention to Emperor Ashoka's edicts on public arguments, but Mill and Keynes offered me a new clarity about the role of public discussion in social choice. This was not an aspect of social choice that had particular prominence in Kenneth Arrow's thinking about the subject, which influenced me so much in other ways, but I was happy that it was another of the many topics in social choice theory that Piero Sraffa and I could discuss during our afternoon walks. Despite Piero's reluctance to use the term 'social choice theory' (which he found disagreeably technical), he was influential in teaching me that discussion and persuasion are just as much a part of social choice as voting.

26

Near and Far

I

By the early 1960s, I was hearing a lot about a new centre of economics in India, the Delhi School of Economics, and about the leadership of Professor K. N. Raj there. I had come to know Raj a little when I met him during my short visit to Delhi in 1957. We had kept in touch and in one of his letters of 1961, he suddenly asked me, 'Do you want a job at the Delhi School?' In response I asked, 'Do you actually have a job to offer?' He replied, 'We don't know. The famous old professor here, V. K. R. V. Rao, who held this chair, has retired, and he says that he will let the post be filled only when he finds a suitable successor.' 'Can he do that?' I asked with some amazement. 'Can he really decide when the chair from which he has retired is to be filled?' The short answer was, I gathered, 'Yes'.

Soon after my correspondence with K. N. Raj, Madhav Rao, the son of V. K. R. V. Rao, who was an undergraduate student of economics in Cambridge, told me that his father wanted to have lunch with me – 'a good South Indian lunch', he added – when I next visited Delhi. Madhav was smarting that morning from his unsuccessful attempt to visit A. C. Pigou, the great Cambridge economist, who had been V. K. R. V.'s doctoral supervisor a long time earlier in Cambridge. Madhav had made an appointment, but when he arrived at Pigou's college rooms on the third floor, Pigou asked, 'Welcome to you, but why have you come here?' Madhav replied, 'My father, V. K. R. V. Rao, did his Ph.D. under you, and he has asked me to pay you his respects – and of course mine too.' 'Very well,' said Pigou, 'you have now paid them.' After this Pigou went to look out of a window and Madhav went down the staircase, sixty seconds after he had arrived. Although it was well known that Pigou was seriously afraid of catching infections from visitors (long before any global pandemic), Madhav was saddened by his experience and told me so. He added, 'My father will give you a very good *long* South Indian lunch.'

The following year, in the spring of 1962, when I visited Delhi, the lunch at Rao's was indeed long and relaxed, and the vegetarian food was totally delicious. After that, as I was leaving, Rao asked me, 'Why don't you apply for my chair?' I asked myself, 'Is this it, then?' Could it be that the difficult bit, involving a job interview, was over?

It proved to be so. The formal selection process went almost as quickly as Madhav's visit to Pigou. There was a short formal interview (with Darjeeling tea) chaired by the Vice Chancellor, and questions from Professors A. K. Dasgupta and I. G. Patel. After that a job offer came rapidly. Nabaneeta and I had already talked about the possibility, which she liked a great deal, so I was able to accept straightaway.

In June 1963, we packed our things and left for Delhi. Our first child, Antara, was expected in late September or early October, and Nabaneeta was very keen that our daughter be born in India. As we were packing up our Cambridge apartment, we were helped by a couple of our kindly English friends – we were all quite sad to leave each other. I noticed that one of our friends was examining very carefully a print of a picture by Gauguin of a graceful Polynesian family which we had on the wall, a favourite of mine. 'Do you like the picture?' I asked her. 'Yes,' she said, 'very much. But I'm mainly looking at the people you have in your family picture.' She wanted to make sure – 'They are your relations, aren't they?' I had to take a gulp, but looking again at Gauguin's Polynesian friends, said, 'Yes, indeed they are, but I have not met them yet.'

2

We can have close friendships far beyond our own immediate circles. In addition, many real possibilities for friendship never develop because of barriers of geography. Perhaps that was what the young German woman I met at the wine festival on the Rhine in Rüdesheim was trying to make me understand. On the eve of my departure, while

I had grumbles about Cambridge economics, I knew I must give Cambridge enormous credit for expanding the reach of my acquaintance. Many encounters in university life and outside it had given me plentiful opportunities for meeting people whom I would never otherwise have known.

There can be something highly constructive about work that takes us into the orbits of those who live at a distance. Even though globalization gets a lot of blame for allegedly causing problems, we can view it more positively if we regard the extension of our relationships as something of value. The Industrial Revolution and the expansion of networks of world trade may appear to some as disruptive forces but, apart from any impact on overall living standards, such global developments generate connections with people who, in the absence of activities that take us into unfamiliar territory, we would never have known – indeed, of whose existence we might have remained thoroughly ignorant. Knowing others can have profound implications for how we think about the world, including what we see as our own moral universe.

In an article entitled 'Of Justice', which was included in *An Enquiry Concerning the Principles of Morals* (1777), the great philosopher David Hume noted how the expansion of global trade, and of economic relations with others, can extend our moral concerns, including our sense of justice:

> ... again suppose that several distinct societies maintain a kind of intercourse for mutual convenience and advantage, the boundaries of justice still grow larger, in proportion to the largeness of men's views, and the force of their mutual connexions.

The reach of our sense of justice may depend on who we come to know and with whom we become familiar, and this can be facilitated by our encounters, including those of trade and exchange. In contrast, a lack of familiarity can keep other people away from our thoughts and excluded from our concern about justice in relation to them: contact offers the possibility of moral thinking on a larger scale. This is true not only between different communities but within them too. It is hard to avoid the thought – mentioned earlier – that the striking reduction in under-nutrition in Britain during the Second World War and the subsequent establishment of the National Health Service resulted, at least to some extent, from a new closeness in human relations brought about by the exigencies of war. Attitudinal change, by which British society accepted greater responsibility for the well-being of its people, helped to facilitate institutional reform. In a strongly stratified society, we can also look in the opposite direction and ask whether the divisions of caste and class may actually generate a lack of shared purpose.

I knew I would have to think about these contrasts and work on them as an economics teacher in India. One of the great social and political analysts, Dr B. R. Ambedkar, who played a leading role in the making of independent India's democratic constitution, had urged us never to forget the penalties of divisiveness. His revulsion against caste-based inequality and against the continued hold of untouchability in many parts of India made Ambedkar – himself belonging to an 'untouchable' caste – convert to Buddhism, which rejects caste divisions, shortly before his death in 1956. In my last couple of years in Cambridge I read Ambedkar's insightful investigations into the history of inequality, especially in India, which made a very strong impression on me.

3

As the day of moving permanently back to India approached, I became seriously concerned about losing my close links with my friends from Pakistan – friendships that I knew would be hard to maintain once I settled down in the capital city of what they would perhaps see as an enemy country. While I was making arrangements to move to Delhi early in 1963 (as a first run – the final move would come that summer), India suddenly became involved in a war with China. It did not last long, but the incident drew the attention of all of us to the possibility that wars can suddenly erupt between neighbours. I was aware, of course, that there was quite enough political tinder to engulf India in a flaming war with Pakistan. Since I very much wanted to visit Pakistan to see my friends before tanks and aeroplanes interfered, I decided to take an unusual route back to India: first to Lahore in Pakistan (the home of my friend Arif Iftekhar, to which he had returned after his studies in Cambridge) and then from Lahore to Karachi (where Mahbub ul Haq then lived) and, finally, to Delhi. Arif was in Islamabad for work when I arrived in Lahore, so I had a day on my own while he tried to get back quickly to join me. That 'free day' I spent seeing beautiful mosques, guided by Arif's mother's advice, in that extraordinarily gracious city. Arif returned the same evening and, since the Iftekhars were both very left-wing and immensely rich, the next day we roamed the city visiting trade union headquarters as well as palaces. There were so many wonderful things to see in Lahore, which I explored over a few days.

On one of our evenings, Arif's car broke down right at the exit gate of the Lahore Club after a sumptuous dinner there. Dozens of the occupants of other cars stuck behind us came out in loud protest. Some of the young men, who evidently knew Arif well, surrounded his car and started chanting something very loudly, which sounded to me like a threatening incantation. It was an ominous scene, especially since I could not at first hear what they were saying. When comprehension returned, I was reassured to find that the chants were nothing more incendiary than the repetition of a rhyme in the form of a slogan: 'Move the car, Iftekhar, Iftekhar!' As Arif was fixing something under the bonnet, I stepped out and introduced myself, and there followed what seemed like a hundred warm handshakes, combined with the firm instruction: 'Enjoy Pakistan!' I promised to do my best to carry out the command of my newly acquired friends.

Lahore is a city that is hard not to enjoy, with its beautiful mosques and other elegant buildings, and of course the greatest garden in the world, the Shalimar gardens, where the Mughal emperors and nobility used to rest on their way to Kashmir. The Iftekhars, who were old landlords in the city – in sharp contrast with Arif's fiery left-wing politics – had been the official keepers of the Shalimar gardens for many centuries, and Arif's mother told me about the letters they had from the ever-polite Mughal kings, requesting permission to have use of the garden on their way to Kashmir in the summer. While walking in that extraordinary garden, Arif told me how frustrated he was to be unable to be politically active. The barriers were both the demands of Arif's family business (which, though large, he said he was ready to abandon if he could) and the strict policing of left-wing politics by an intolerant government (which was rather harder to overcome). Arif was the best speaker in our time at the Cambridge Union and was also one of the finest and warmest human beings I have known. I was sure he would do what he could to help people without turning his familiar life upside down.

A close friend of ours, Shireen Qadir, also lived in Lahore. When I told Arif I would like to visit her, Arif said that he had heard good things about her, but under no circumstances would he drive me to the 'reactionary' house of Manzur Qadir, Shireen's father, an enormously famous lawyer whose politics Arif evidently disagreed with. So Arif chucked his car keys to me and said, 'Drive yourself! Lawrence Road is not far and my car is just outside.' Shireen was quite surprised to see me driving a very large car into the compound of their home.

When I arrived at Karachi airport from Lahore, Mahbub and another mutual Cambridge friend, Khalid Ikram (who would later marry Shireen), were waiting. Khalid made an innocuous joke – he was worried because the plane was delayed, thinking I was coming from India on an Indian plane ('that can be very dangerous, you know'). But he had meanwhile been reassured that I was only coming from Lahore on a Pakistani plane. In those days, jocular elements in the Indo-Pakistani war of words tended to dominate over manifestations of actual dislike.

I had many long conversations with Mahbub and his wife Bani in Karachi, and I could not help feeling that Mahbub was basically frustrated, despite the high office he occupied as the economic head of Pakistan's Planning Commission (later he would be elevated even further when he became the Finance Minister of Pakistan). He explained to me what he had learned through his attempts at invigorating economic planning in Pakistan. There were good things that could easily be made to happen, but the barriers to progress – coming from narrow-minded politics and the prevailing feudal structure – were hard to overcome.

As the sun set on a magically bewitching Karachi, Mahbub's voice rose, mixing analysis with deeply rebellious passion. He knew how to confront Pakistan's old problems, but was sceptical of finding any immediate possibility of progress. He knew he wanted to achieve many things – and not just for Pakistan – but he had to find a different base from which to do them. Some years later he would get such an opportunity with the UNDP (the United Nations Development Programme), where he would pioneer the human development approach by which nations are assessed in terms of the quality of life of their populations (including their education, nutrition and access to other resources). As the Human Development Office was being set up in New York in the summer of 1989, Mahbub repeatedly telephoned me and insisted, 'Amartya, drop everything and come here. We will make sense of the world!' And through the 1990s, he would go a considerable distance in doing just that through his very influential annual *Human Development Report* (on which I was privileged to help him, as a kind of lieutenant).

4

I travelled to Delhi from Pakistan just in time to start teaching at the Delhi School of Economics, which the students called D-School. Among my identities, that of teacher has always been the strongest, going back all the way to the time when I was teaching tribal children in makeshift night schools when I was myself a student in Santiniketan. The thrill I experienced from teaching my astonishingly talented

Reading in the garden of Santiniketan, c. 1964.

students in Delhi is hard to describe. I expected them to be of high quality, but they turned out to be much more than that.

I lectured on economic theory at different levels, but over the years also taught game theory, welfare economics, social choice theory and economic planning; and also epistemology and philosophy of science (for postgraduate students of philosophy) and mathematical logic (for anyone who wanted to learn something about it). As at Jadavpur University, through working to teach others I ended up learning a good deal myself.

I had started teaching at the D-School in March 1963, but the summer vacation came quite soon after in the calendar of Delhi University – at the beginning of April – and since this meant a recess of two months, I went back to Cambridge and joined Nabaneeta there. But then the time for the final departure to Delhi did actually come and Nabaneeta and I took a long air journey with many stops – including Athens and Istanbul – to Delhi.

We had a marvellous couple of weeks in Greece, where I had some lecturing obligations. This was at a research institution led by Andreas Papandreou, a brilliant economist and an extremely talented political leader who was fighting for the democratic rights of Greek citizens. The military rulers in Greece did not like Papandreou at all. Soon after our visit, he was arrested and victimized by the military regime, and left the country. However, popular agitation and legal challenges eventually led to the fall of the military junta and Papandreou's triumphant return. He went on to become the Prime Minister. Meanwhile, he and his wife Margaret had become close friends of ours, and we remained in touch through their political ups and downs. Their son, also called Andreas, would later do a Ph.D. with me at Oxford, writing a brilliant thesis on externalities, especially analysing environmental policies.

Nabaneeta and I greatly enjoyed the fabulous sites of ancient Greece, including seeing some enactments of ancient plays. Nabaneeta knew some Attic, which helped from time to time. It was on the advice of the Papandreous that we fitted in a visit to Crete and saw the stunning remnants of the Minoan civilization and the breathtaking old palace at Knossos. Seeing these extraordinary sites helped me to understand the achievements of the ancient world in the development of human civilization. Even as I was plunging into the history of ancient Greece in Crete, I wanted to get back quickly to my students in the D-School.

5

Aside from greatly enjoying the opportunity to teach at the D-School, I benefited from the fact that many research students there and some young teachers were becoming interested in social choice theory. Maurice Dobb had advised me to work on some different subject until I found myself in the company of other social choice theorists. He was right, but it turned out that it was possible to generate quite rapidly a community of students with social choice expertise. The D-School students had mostly not heard of the subject at all, but, from the very first lecture about it, I could sense a determination on the part of many to make it their own. To my surprise a community of social choice theorists emerged in Delhi with remarkable speed – indeed, some of them started breaking fresh ground, extending the theory as well as coming up with new applications. Very soon after he came to the D-School, one of my first students, Prasanta Pattanaik, was producing powerful – and difficult – social choice results, which garnered recognition across the world. It was an unusual pleasure for me to lecture on what were being celebrated across the world as 'Pattanaik theorems', with Prasanta himself sitting modestly on his bench as one of the students in the class.

One of the interesting features in the treatment of social choice theory in our seminars was that we tried to incorporate ideas and distinctions that have been useful in other approaches to moral philosophy, for example those from Hume, Smith and Kant. We also discussed the moral principles carefully proposed and scrutinized by Hobbes, Rousseau and Locke in the concept of the 'social contract' – an interpersonal contract in which each person undertakes to do (or *not* to do) certain things for the sake of others, provided the others make similar promises in return. In constructive social choice reasoning the idea of social contracts can have considerable use, for example in assessing the fairness of tax systems, or people's willingness to accept the rationing of food to meet situations of shortage (as in the

Second World War – discussed earlier). We also examined how a set of contractual obligations, with penalties for violation, compared with reasoned obligations that people accept as their duty without an insistence on reciprocity (*shartaheen kartavya*). (This was discussed in Chapter 6, following a line of argument advanced by Gautama Buddha in *Sutta Nipata* and elsewhere.) In fact, both reciprocal and non-reciprocal obligations to others can be easily scrutinized through social choice arguments, as Smith's work illustrates.

Being a social choice theorist gives you certain analytical capabilities, but the kind of social aggregation problem we take up depends also on what we think is important and interesting. I was proud of the seriousness with which some of my students applied the social choice approach to practical concerns related to policy-making. I also had students doing subjects very different from social choice, and some of those were exceptionally talented in their chosen fields (including Prabhat Patnaik, who became a leading development economist). It is hard to describe how joyful it is when the performance of your students draws global attention – no matter what you yourself are doing.

6

While the satisfaction of teaching in Delhi was high, it was impossible to escape the reality of widespread deprivation in India. The problem was not only that of poverty, but also the lack of crucial public services, including school education and basic health care. This was not because people had no interest in expanding these facilities, but largely because the public resources devoted to school education and basic health care were astonishingly small. The extraordinary neglect of these public facilities received very little social attention in the making of public policy and planning the economy. Sure enough, famines had been conquered in independent democratic India, but endemic under-nutrition remained widespread and elementary medical care for all was persistently absent. This paucity of educational and health services was closely connected with India's persistent social and economic iniquities. Neglected people of the lowest social strata in India were often assumed to have little use for education and health care (unlike the privileged), and such monstrous misconceptions have often helped to harden traditional asymmetries even further.

As I tried to investigate the nature of the social neglect, working together with some of my students (such as Anuradha Luther and Prabhat Patnaik), it was useful to examine the relationship between a general deficiency in the country in aggregate terms and the severe deprivation of the poorer and more disadvantaged sections of the population.

The presence of inequality stretches back a long time in India, and historically it seems to have been more severe there than in most other countries in the world. The deficiencies have included not only large asymmetries in income and wealth (separating the poor and the very poor from the comfortable and the rich), but also huge social inequities, such as the low status and terrible social standing of the underdogs of society, of which untouchability is the extreme end. Already in the sixth century BC, Gautama Buddha had argued against tolerating social barriers that divide and segregate human beings from each other. In fact, Buddhism as a movement was no less a protest against social inequity than it was a radical departure in epistemology and metaphysics concerning the nature of the world.

7

I decided to use the example of inequality reduction in war-affected and post-war Britain in my teaching at the D-School as something from which India could definitely learn, and looked for appropriate readings. From Britain came not only Marx (straight from the British Museum), but also the pioneering voice of Adam Smith, the founder of English – and Scottish – political economy. I had encountered little of Smith's work in my economics curriculum at Cambridge – but rather more, earlier on, at Presidency College, and even more in conversations in the coffee house across the road in College Street. While assembling my teaching materials for classes at D-School, I could see how very relevant Smith was to the understanding of inequality and its remedies in India.

Smith had a serious interest in supplementing market processes through the use of non-market institutions, for example by state intervention to expand public services such as government-supported education and health care. It was helpful to discuss in class how a combination of institutions might have clear advantages in over-coming divisiveness and deficiencies, especially for the seriously deprived parts of the population.

A powerful component of Smithian moral reasoning is the use of what he called 'the impartial spectator': paying attention to the lack of bias and divisiveness that we should try to utilize by imagining how someone from outside, devoid of personal or local prejudices, would assess a particular situation, including ongoing inequalities. In class discussions we used the research findings put together by Hammond, Titmuss and other social investigators, particularly on the degree to which Britain's post-war constructions drew on the lessons of the cooperative features of the country's war-time experience.

Our class discussions also included the fact that Smith – with his deep sympathy for the poor and the disadvantaged – always stood up against the claimed 'superiority' of the better placed. One example we considered was from Smith's *Theory of Moral Sentiments*, published in 1759, which described the anti-Irish prejudices of the upper-class Eng-lish. Another, also from the *Theory of Moral Sentiments*, concerned the continuing tolerance of the terrible practice of slavery by substantial sections of the upper classes in America and Europe. Students in my class brilliantly investigated how some of the institutions of inequality in India, which forced members of the lowest caste to do dreadfully demeaning work, came close to generating the moral degradation of slavery.

Smith's uncompromising rejection of terrible institutions such as slavery can be compared with the position that his friend David Hume took on the same subject. Hume, as we have seen, believed that human relations should be as broad-ranging as possible. However, while being generally critical of slavery, Hume showed some weakness in his opposition to it. Smith, on the other hand, was resolutely firm in his total hatred of racism and in declaring the complete unacceptability of slavery in any form. He was furious about the slave-owners' attrib-ution of a lower form of life to the slaves.

In making his point, Smith pronounced that those forcibly taken away from Africa as slaves were not only not inferior to white people, but, compared to the white slave-owners, they were in important ways superior human beings. In a resounding declaration he asserted:

> There is not a negro from the coast of Africa who does not, in this respect, possess a degree of magnanimity which the soul of his sordid master is too often scarce capable of conceiving.

When I read aloud that passage from Smith in a lecture at the D-School, I remember the relief – and indeed the thrill – that could be detected in the class. My students in Delhi may not have known much about people from the coast of Africa, but there was an immediate solidarity with ill-treated human beings from far away as well as nearby. They were not only persuaded by Smith's words; they took pride in them.

Our reasoned sympathy, across the borders of geography and time, may come from the strength of our spontaneous affections or from the power of argument, as it did for Smith. Rabindranath Tagore, whose ideas I have discussed often in this book, was right to see the overwhelming importance both of instinctive sympathy and of persuasion by reasoning. He was shocked by the exclusion of so many people from the concern of the world because of their race or location. In his last public lecture in 1941, shortly before his death, Tagore expressed horror at the treatment received by some parts of humanity, much as Smith had found the enslavement of people intolerable. As Tagore put it,

> The best and noblest gifts of humanity cannot be the monopoly of a particular race or country; its scope may not be limited nor may it be regarded as the miser's hoard buried underground.

It was reassuring to find that the fundamental respect and understanding of people for which Smith and Tagore argued was so clearly recognized by the students. This must surely be a strong source of hope for the world.

Notes

1. DHAKA AND MANDALAY

p. 10 *Mentally you are still in Mandalay*: George Orwell discusses this contrast in his *Homage to Catalonia* (1938) (London: Penguin Books, 1989, 2013), p. 87.

p. 14 *they are 'constantly laughing'*: For an engaging account of the dedicated – and highly courageous – work of the 'backpack doctors' from Johns Hopkins, see Dale Keiger, 'Medicines Where They Need It Most,' *Johns Hopkins Magazine*, 57 (April 2005), p. 49.

p. 15 *The military won that propaganda war*: One of the active participants in that nasty propaganda war was Facebook. The pliable use by the Burmese military of Facebook's communication channels against the Rohingyas to deadly effect has been well investigated in recent years, including by the *New York Times*. Facebook has confirmed many of the details about this shadowy, military-driven campaign. The company's head of cybersecurity, Nathaniel Gleicher, agreed that it had found 'clear and deliberate attempts to covertly spread propaganda that were directly linked to the Myanmar military'. See 'A Genocide Incited on Facebook, with Posts from Myanmar's Military,' *The New York Times*, 15 October 2018.

2. THE RIVERS OF BENGAL

p. 25 *'the paradise of nations'*: Adam Smith, *The Nature and Causes of the Wealth of Nations*, in *The Works of Adam Smith* (London, 1812), Book I, On the Causes of Improvement in the Productive Powers. On Labour, and on the Order According to Which its Produce is Naturally Distributed Among the Different Ranks of the People, Chapter

III, 'That the Division of Labour is limited by the Extent of the Market'.

p. 25 *'those great inlets, such as the Baltic'*: Smith, *The Nature and Causes of the Wealth of Nations*.

p. 26 *'The sea of Tartary is the frozen ocean'*: Smith, *The Nature and Causes of the Wealth of Nations*.

p. 27 *Ganga has had a tendency to spill out of its riverbed*: See Richard E. Eaton, *Essays on Islam and Indian History* (Oxford: Oxford University Press, 2000), p. 259.

p. 33 *'We are men of the river'*: Raihan Raza, 'Humayun Kabir's "Men and Rivers",' *Indian Literature*, 51, no. 4 (240) (2007), pp. 162–77; http://www.jstor.org/stable/23346133. The quotes are to be found in *Men and Rivers* (Bombay: Hind Kitabs Ltd,1945), p. 183.

3. SCHOOL WITHOUT WALLS

p. 40 *'I consider the three years I spent'*: Satyajit Ray has discussed his debt to Santiniketan on several occasions, but a particularly clear statement can be found in his book *Our Films, Their Films* (1976) (Hyderabad: Orient BlackSwan Private Ltd, 3rd edn, 1993). I have tried to discuss these issues in my Satyajit Ray Memorial Lecture, 'Our Culture, Their Culture', *New Republic*, 1 April 1996.

p. 40 *The group included many excellent teachers*: Sylvain Lévi was a famous historian and Indologist who taught mainly in Paris and authored, among other works, the widely acclaimed *The Theatre of India*. Charles Freer Andrews, a close friend of Gandhi and Tagore, was an English priest who was an activist for India's independence. Leonard Elmhirst was an agronomist and a philanthropist as well as the founder of Dartington Hall, a famous progressive school and also an institution for the cultivation of rare music. My first visit outside Cambridge – this was in December 1953 (two months after I had joined Cambridge) – was to Dartington Hall, where I vastly enjoyed the hospitality of the Elmhirsts.

p. 41 *'It was there, sitting at the feet of "Master-Mashai" [Nandalal Bose]'*: On this, see Dinkar Kowshik's fine biography, *Nandalal Bose, the Doyen of Indian Art* (New Delhi: National Book Trust, 1985, 2nd edn, 2001), p. 115.

p. 41 *Kenduli, where a great Indian poet*: This is only one of the possible locations of old Kenduli – Kendubilva in Sanskrit. There are other claimants, including a particularly strong one from Odisha. As

Jayadeva wrote entirely in Sanskrit, not in Oriya or Bengali – his *Gita Govinda* is one of the most celebrated later writings in classical Sanskrit – the dispute cannot be resolved by examining the texts of his writings.

p. 42 *'The principle of his method of teaching'*: I am grateful to Megan Marshall, the distinguished author of the prize-winning biography of the famous Peabody sisters (*The Peabody Sisters: Three Women Who Ignited American Romanticism*, Boston: Houghton Mifflin, 2005), for letting me see her grandfather Joe Marshall's unpublished 'Santiniketan Journal'.

p. 45 *Another was singing*: Since my son Kabir teaches music at a distinguished school in Boston, and is a successful composer and vocalist, I have to guess that he must have got the genes for it from his mother, my late wife, Eva Colorni, who was very musical indeed.

p. 49 *'The music of life'*: See *Visva-Bharati News*, Vol. XIV, 7 (July 1945–June 1946).

p. 54 *My advocacy of impatience*: The need for impatience is one of the principal themes of my book *Development as Freedom* (New York: Knopf; Oxford: Oxford University Press,1999) and also of my joint book with Jean Drèze, *An Uncertain Glory: India and Its Contradictions* (2013) (London: Penguin Books, 2nd edn, 2020).

p. 56 *'the imposing tower of misery'*: From an interview with *Izvestia* in 1930. See Krishna Dutta and Andrew Robinson, *Rabindranath Tagore: The Myriad-Minded Man* (London: Bloomsbury Publishing, 1995), which is a beautifully researched biography.

4. THE COMPANY OF GRANDPARENTS

p. 59 *Didima said that she felt sad*: I heard the account of that morning from Didima, but this incident, along with a great many others from the lives of my grandparents, can be found in the admirably researched Bengali book of Pranati Mukhopadhyay, *Kshiti Mohan Sen O Ardha Satabdir Santiniketan* ('Kshiti Mohan Sen and Half a Century of Santiniketan') (Calcutta: West Bengal Academy, 1999), p. 223. I have drawn frequently on this wonderful book to check and authenticate some of my personal memories of events I experienced, and I am extremely appreciative of the quality of Mukhopadhyay's painstaking research.

p. 64 *Who really knows?*: The poem is from *Rig Veda*, Mandala X, verse 10.129. The English translation here is from Wendy Doniger, *The Rig Veda: An Anthology* (London: Penguin Books, 1981), pp. 25–6.

p. 65 *Even though he is very well versed*: Taken from Pranati Mukhopadhyay's biography of Kshiti Mohan (in Bengali), *Kshiti Mohan Sen O Ardha Satabdir Santiniketan*, pp. 42–3.

p. 65 *'I am not yet ready to abandon hope'*: *Selected Letters of Rabindranath Tagore*, edited by Krishna Dutta and Andrew Robinson (Cambridge: Cambridge University Press, 1997), p. 69.

p. 67 *To keep me in the conservative [Hindu] fold*: Translated from a citation of Kshiti Mohan Sen in Mukhopadhyay, *Kshiti Mohan Sen O Ardha Satabdir Santiniketan*, p. 17.

pp. 67–8 *There were huge territories to visit*: It is estimated that the current number of Kabir Panthis is close to 10 million, and the size of this group would have already been very substantial in the last decade of the nineteenth century. They were also already spread out over a large territory.

p. 68 *Syed Mujtaba Ali*: See Syed Mujtaba Ali, 'Acharya Kshiti Mohan Sen', in a Bengali volume of essays, *Gurudev O Santiniketan*, cited by Mukhopadhayay, *Kshiti Mohan Sen O Ardha Satabdir Santiniketan*, p. 466.

p. 72 *His four-volume compendium*: The original version was published in 1910–11. A later Bengali version has been reissued more recently, with a helpful Introduction by the distinguished historian Sabyasachi Bhattacharya, in one volume, *Kabir* (Calcutta: Ananda Publishers, 1995). Some excellent translations of Kabir's poems and illuminating commentary can be found in Arvind Krishna Mehrotra, *Songs of Kabir* (New York Review Books, 2011).

p. 73 *English translations of 'one hundred poems of Kabir'*: This collection was published as *One Hundred Poems of Kabir*, translated by Rabindranath Tagore, with the assistance of Evelyn Underhill (London: Macmillan, 1915). In the Introduction to the volume, tribute is paid to Kshiti Mohan's 'painstaking labours' which had 'made the present undertaking possible', p. xliii.

p. 73 *Even though some of these translations were published*: See Ezra Pound, 'Kabir: Certain Poems', *Modern Review*, June 1913; reprinted in Hugh Kenner, *The Translations of Ezra Pound* (New York: New Directions, 1953; London: Faber, 1953).

p. 73 *the fuller and more ambitious work*: The proofs of parts of *Kabir: Poesie*, translations by Ezra Pound, can, however, be found at Yale, in the Yale Collection of American Literature: Beinecke Rare Book and Manuscript Library, Ezra Pound Papers Addition, YCAL MSS 53

Series II Writings 700 (I am very grateful to Craig Jamieson for drawing my attention to the availability of this unpublished document). Pound, who did not know any Hindi or Bengali, was being assisted in his attempt at translation by Kali Mohan Ghosh (see *Selected Letters of Rabindranath Tagore*, edited by Krishna Dutta and Andrew Robinson (Cambridge: Cambridge University Press, 1997), p. 116). There was also an earlier manuscript of translations, by Ajit Kumar Chakravarty, of Kshiti Mohan's collection of Kabir's poems.

p. 74 *From my childhood the 'Sants'*: This is a translation from Kshiti Mohan Sen's Bengali introduction to his collection of Kabir's poems. He was always very keen on appropriate acknowledgement and named the people who had helped him most: 'Among the people from whom I got most help, from the songs they sung and from their handwritten notes, are: Dakshin Baba of Varuna Adikeshhab, Jhulan Baba of Gaibi, Nirbhay Das of Chuachua Tal, Dindev of Chaukandee, and [also from there] the blind sadhu Surshyamadas.' He also listed twelve published works which he had seen and taken into account, including one, *Kabir Shhabdabali* by Prasad, that is now often cited as a kind of rival to Sen's collection, but that collection, like the other printed works, were not the last words for Kshiti Mohan, who had to check the extent to which each of them tallied with 'what were being sung by the practitioners and which they and I judged to be true to the tradition'.

p. 75 *pioneering subaltern theorists*: See Ranajit Guha (ed.), *Writings on South Asian History and Society*, Subaltern Studies series I (Delhi and Oxford: Oxford University Press, 1982). I came to know Ranajitda, as I called him, in 1956, and my interactions with him will figure in a later chapter.

p. 75 *'that wonderful Dadu, whose personality attracts me'*: See Pranati Mukhopadhyay, *Kshiti Mohan Sen O Ardha Satabdir Santiniketan* (Calcutta: West Bengal Academy, 1999), pp. 199, 516.

p. 75 *There was certainly an elitist tendency*: There were similar questions raised, on much the same elitist grounds, about Kshiti Mohan Sen's collection of Bengali Bauli poems as well.

p. 76 Kabir Ke Pad, *edited by Kshiti Mohan Sen*: *Kabir* [Hindi] (Delhi: Rajkamal Prakashan, 1942; reissued 2016).

p. 77 *This thesis, certainly heterodox*: K. M. Sen, *Hinduism* (1961), reissued with a new Foreword by Amartya Sen (London: Penguin Books, 2005; reprinted 2020).

5. A WORLD OF ARGUMENTS

p. 80 'Though we cannot point out': Selected Letters of Rabindranath Tagore, edited by Krishna Dutta and Andrew Robinson (Cambridge: Cambridge University Press, 1997), p. 990.

p. 81 'I am not affected by posers': See The Oxford India Gandhi: Essential Writings, compiled and edited by Gopalkrishna Gandhi (New Delhi: Oxford University Press, 2008), p. 372.

p. 81 'My remarks on the Bihar calamity': This sad letter can also be found in The Oxford India Gandhi: Essential Writings, p. 372.

p. 84 'In stepping on the soil of Russia': See Rabindranath Tagore, Letters from Russia, translated from Bengali by Sasadhar Sinha (Calcutta: VisvaBharati, 1960), p. 108.

p. 85 interview to Izvestia in 1930: This episode in Tagore's life, among many others, is well discussed by Krishna Dutta and Andrew Robinson in Rabindranath Tagore: The Myriad-Minded Man (London: Bloomsbury, 1995), p. 297.

p. 85 'I must ask you': Quoted in Dutta and Robinson, Rabindranath Tagore: The Myriad-Minded Man, p. 297.

p. 86 an advocate of blind faith: Nabaneeta Dev Sen has discussed well how exactly this metamorphosis occurred. See her article, 'The Foreign Reincarnation of Rabindranath Tagore', Journal of Asian Studies, 25 (1966), reprinted in her Counterpoints: Essays in Comparative Literature (Calcutta: Prajna, 1985).

p. 86 letters that Bertrand Russell wrote to Nimai: Nimai Chatterji was very amused when he got these letters; he showed them to me, knowing that I admired Russell a great deal. I had to explain that I greatly admired Russell as a philosopher (particularly of mathematics), but not so much as a historian of thought.

p. 87 In a second letter . . . Russell: Nimai Chatterji died suddenly in January 2011. His collection of literary and cultural objects are in the Tate Modern in 'the Nimai Chatterji collection', but his exchange of letters on Tagore's reception in the West have not yet been published. They belong to the Bangla Academy in Calcutta (Kolkata), and the collection is intended for publication after editing. I am grateful to Nimai Chatterji for having shared some of his letters with me.

p. 87 Nietzsche, who was peculiarly caricatured: See Bertrand Russell, A History of Western Philosophy (New York: Simon & Schuster, 1945; London: Allen & Unwin, 1946).

p. 88 *'last night I dined with one of the poets here'*: Tagore's letter to Kshiti Mohan, 28 June 1912, in *Selected Letters of Rabindranath Tagore*, edited by Krishna Dutta and Andrew Robinson, p. 90.

p. 88 *His Western promoters left no room*: I have discussed this issue in 'Tagore and His India' in *The New York Review of Books*, 26 June 1997, and also in *The Argumentative Indian* (London: Penguin; New York: FSG, 2005), Chapter 5.

p. 90 *'Leave this chanting and singing'*: I have edited the standard translation to get rid of the archaic language.

p. 90 *'Stupendranath Begorr'*: See George Bernard Shaw, *Back to Methuselah (A Metabiological Pentateuch)* (London: Constable; New York: Brentano's, 1921).

p. 92 *Rabindranath's criticism of nationalism*: Different types of reaction to Tagore's criticism of nationalism, particularly in his novel *The Home and the World,* have been well scrutinized by Dutta and Robinson in *Rabindranath Tagore: The Myriad-Minded Man* (1995).

6. THE PRESENCE OF THE PAST

p. 94 *Sanskrit became something of a lingua franca*: Sheldon Pollock, 'India in the Vernacular Millennium: Literary Culture and Polity, 1000–1500', *Daedalus*, 127 (2) (Summer 1998), pp. 41–74.

p. 97 *Buddha and Jesus ultimately arrive at the same conclusion*: For further discussion, see Amartya Sen, *The Idea of Justice* (London: Allen Lane, 2009), pp. 170–73.

p. 98 *The elegance and reach of analytical reasoning*: I wrote something along these lines during my college days, but lost it. I am immensely grateful to my dear musician friend T. M. Krisha for recovering this idea from what I tried to say in a public discussion.

p. 102 *'Nowhere in our European past do we find'*: Joseph Wood Krutch, *The Nation*, 69 (12 May 1924).

pp. 103–4 *Gyan Chaupar*: The game Snakes and Ladders appears to have been patented in London in 1892 by Frederick Henry Ayres, a famous toymaker.

p. 104 *'The trembling hazelnut eardrops'*: *The Rig Veda*, translated by Wendy Doniger (London: Penguin Books, 1981), p. 241.

p. 106 *As the excavations of the old ruins have revealed*: It can be questioned whether Nalanda was really the oldest university in the world. What about the justly famous Buddhist educational centre in Takshashila (or Taxila) at the western end of ancient India (now in Pakistan), next to neighbouring Afghanistan, which started functioning around 500 BC, not long after Buddha's death (and long before Nalanda was established)? But the institution in Taxila was really a religious school, albeit a very distinguished one for a rather narrower engagement in Buddhist education. There was certainly no dearth of scholarship at the eastern edge of Afghanistan and adjacent ancient India (they were culturally integrated), and even the greatest – and the earliest – Indian grammarian, the redoubtable Panini in the fourth century BC, came from the border of Afghanistan. However, Taxila did not try to offer systematic instruction on different branches of advanced learning (particularly on secular subjects), as Nalanda and its followers in Bihar – Vikramshila, Odantapuri and others – did, in what can be broadly described as the Nalanda-inspired world of higher education. It does not diminish the glory of Taxila, in its own context, to recognize Nalanda as the oldest university in the world.

8. BENGAL AND THE IDEA OF BANGLADESH

p. 122 *had been stabbed on the street by communal thugs* . . . : The use of the word 'communal' for sectarian religious hostility towards members of other religions is quite well established in India and in the rest of the subcontinent, and this usage was already common in the 1940s. The term can sometimes be confusing, but it cannot be readily replaced by words such as 'religious', since the hostilities involved often come from people who are not particularly religious, but are firmly hostile to people born in rival religious communities. I will continue to use the term 'communal' in the way that it is used in the subcontinent, but with the warning, just noted, to avoid confusion with communities other than those defined by religion.

p. 122 *All that mattered to these dedicated murderers* . . . : For an analysis of the role of identity in violence, see my *Identity and Violence: The Illusion of Destiny* (New York: Norton, and London: Penguin, 2006).

p. 125 *It was the Muslim League, led by Muhammad Ali Jinnah* . . . : In this context it is important to note that Ayesha Jalal has convincingly argued that Jinnah's insistence on partition was at least partly presented as a bargaining demand for getting a more prominent role for Muslims in an undivided but independent India; see her *The Sole Spokesman: Jinnah, the Muslim League and the Demand for Partition* (Cambridge: Cambridge University Press, 1985).

p. 126 *The extent to which the privileged parts of the Hindu middle and upper classes ... :* Joya Chatterji, *Bengal Divided: Hindu Communalism and Partition, 1932–1947* (Cambridge: Cambridge University Press, 1994).

p. 128 *There are striking descriptions of swearing-in ceremonies in the Mughal army ... :* See Richard M. Eaton, 'Who Are the Bengali Muslims?' in *Essays on Islam and Indian History* (Oxford: Oxford University Press, 2000).

p. 130 *'In his early youth the author ... grew up in the shadow of the Permanent Settlement ... ':* See Ranajit Guha, *A Rule of Property for Bengal: An Essay on the Idea of Permanent Settlement* (1963) (Durham, NC, and London: Duke University Press, 1996), Preface to First edition, p. xv. I shall come back to Guha later in the book.

p. 130 *'Being zamindar [landowner] meant being treated as royalty ... ':* See Tapan Raychaudhuri, 'Preface' to *The World in Our Time: A Memoir* (Noida, Uttar Pradesh: HarperCollins Publishers India, 2011).

p. 131 *But Huq continued to pursue his own priorities as the leader of Bengali Muslims ... :* On these issues, see Sana Aiyar's important paper, 'Fazlul Huq, Region and Religion in Bengal: The Forgotten Alternative of 1940–43', *Modern Asian Studies*, 42(6) (November 2008), and the other studies to which Aiyar refers.

p. 134 *'From the West came Zafar Mian ... ':* Translated by Richard M. Eaton in his book *The Rise of Islam and the Bengal Frontier, 1204–1760* (Berkeley, CA: University of California Press, 1993), pp. 214–15.

9. RESISTANCE AND DIVISION

p. 146 *'There is no power on earth ... ':* For an illuminating history of Subhas Chandra Bose's life, see Sugata Bose, *His Majesty's Opponent: Subhas Chandra Bose and India's Struggle Against Empire* (Cambridge, MA: Belknap Press of Harvard University Press, 2011).

p. 148 *Jinnah propounded his 'pernicious Two-Nation theory':* Rafiq Zakaria, *The Man Who Divided India* (Mumbai: Popular Prakashan, 2001), p. 79.

p. 149 *'There was no concerted rational approach on the part of the Congress ... ':* Zakaria, *The Man Who Divided India*, p. 84.

p. 149 *'how did a Pakistan come about ... ?':* Ayesha Jalal, *The Sole Spokesman: Jinnah, the Muslim League and the Demand for Pakistan* (Cambridge: Cambridge University Press, 1985), p. 4.

p. 151 *Ashutosh remained an eternal optimist, with great faith* ... : We never discussed this issue – in fact I was not even aware of his voting dilemmas until they emerged from the study of letters between Amiya Dasgupta and my father, through the research of Alaknanda Patel (Amiya Dasgupta's daughter).

p. 153 *I spoke on the subject of economic inequality'*: Amartya Sen, *On Economic Inequality* (Oxford: Oxford University Press, 1973; expanded edition, with James Foster, 1997).

10. BRITAIN AND INDIA

p. 156 *'Jagat Seth, Raja Mohan Lal . . .'*: Quoted in Michael Edwardes, *Plassey: The Founding of an Empire* (London: Hamish Hamilton, 1969), p. 131.

p. 157 *'the biggest Empire ever, bar none'*: Niall Ferguson, *Empire: How Britain Made the Modern World* (London: Allen Lane, 2003) p. xi. For a more critical assessment of the achievements and failures of the empire, see Shashi Tharoor, *Inglorious Empire: What the British Did to India* (London: C. Hurst & Co. and Penguin Books, 2017).

p. 159 *'made in two decades an astonishing leap . . .'*: C. A. Bayly, *The Birth of the Modern World, 1780–1914* (Oxford: Blackwell Publishing, 2004), p. 293.

p. 165 *'mercantile company which oppresses . . .'*: Adam Smith, *The Wealth of Nations, Books I–III* (1776) (London: Penguin Books, 1986), Book I, Ch. VIII, 'Of the Wages of Labour', p. 176.

p. 165 *'The economic figures speak for themselves'*: William Dalrymple, 'Robert Clive was a vicious asset-stripper. His statue has no place on Whitehall', *The Guardian*, 11 June 2020; <https://www.theguardian.com/commentisfree/2020/jun/11/robert-clive-statue-whitehall-british-imperial> (Accessed 3 December 2020).

p. 166 *'altogether unfit to govern its territorial possessions'*: Adam Smith, *The Wealth of Nations, Books IV–V* (1776) (London: Penguin Books, 1999), Book V, Ch. 1, Part I, 'Of the Expense of Defence', p. 343.

p. 166 *The British claimed a huge set of achievements*: William Dalrymple, *Anarchy: The Relentless Rise of the East India Company* (London: Bloomsbury Publishing, 2019), p. 394.

p. 167 *'Take up the White Man's burden'*: Rudyard Kipling, 'The White Man's Burden' (1899).

p. 169 *The tragedy, he said in this last lecture*: Rabindranath Tagore, *Crisis in Civilization* (Calcutta: Visva-Bharati, 1941).

11. THE URBANITY OF CALCUTTA

p. 174 '*Where the cholera, the cyclone, and the crow*': Rudyard Kipling, *The Collected Poems of Rudyard Kipling* (Ware, Herts: Wordsworth Editions, 1994), 'A Tale of Two Cities' (1922), pp. 80–81.

p. 174 '*an idiotic decision*': Geoffrey Moorhouse, *Calcutta: The City Revealed* (London: Penguin Books, 1994), p. 26.

p. 177 '*I stood a wondering stranger*': James Atkinson, *The City of Palaces; a Fragment and Other Poems*, 'The City of Palaces' (Calcutta: The Government Gazette, 1824), p. 7.

p. 177 '*when not that of an imperialist*': Ved Mehta, *The Craft of the Essay: A Reader* (London: Yale University Press, 1998), p. 210.

p. 178 '*For the Englishman, both Indian modernity*': Amit Chaudhuri, *Calcutta: Two Years in the City* (New Delhi: Penguin Books, 2013), pp. 266–7.

p. 179 *Job Charnock was also better placed to challenge land-based armies*: Most of these concerns not only made sense and had been written about quite extensively, there is some evidence that they were explicitly in the minds of Charnock and his associates. See the enlightening collection of writings – old and new – on the subject: P. Thankappan Nair, *Job Charnock: The Founder of Calcutta: An Anthology* (Calcutta: Calcutta Old Book Stall, 1977).

p. 180 '*In Indo-European history there is not, undoubtedly*': J. J. A. Campos, *History of the Portuguese in Bengal* (Calcutta and London: Butterworth, 1919), p. 43.

p. 188 *his notes from that time were studied by his grandson, Gopal Gandhi*: Gopalkrishna Gandhi, *A Frank Friendship: Gandhi and Bengal. A Descriptive Chronology* (Calcutta: Seagull Books, 2007).

p. 189 '*I knew immediately that if I ever made* Pather Panchali': Satyajit Ray, *Our Films, Their Films* (1976) (Hyderabad: Orient BlackSwan Private Ltd, 3rd edn, 1993), p. 9.

p. 189 '*What should you put in your films?*': Satyajit Ray, *Our Films, Their Films*, 3rd edn, pp. 160–61.

12. COLLEGE STREET

p. 194 *it was from Calcutta University*: The University had strict rules about attendance, and partly because of serious illness, but also because of my political activities and frequent willingness to cut classes to do some reading in the library, or chat in the coffee house, I fell short of the attendance requirement necessary for being counted as a regular student from Presidency College. I was told that I would have to take the exams as a *non-collegiate* student on my own – not as part of Presidency. Since I was seen as a good student (having come first in earlier university exams), the College, too, was unhappy about this. Somehow it was arranged that I could sit the exam as a 'collegiate' student from Presidency College after all, and I imagine that the books were fiddled.

p. 195 '*My country! In thy day of glory past*': Henry Louis Vivian Derozio, 'To India – My Native Land', *Anglophone Poetry in Colonial India, 1780–1913: A Critical Anthology*, edited by Mary Ellis Gibson (Athens, OH: Ohio University Press, 2011), p. 185.

p. 200 '*Some of us got all our education from our fellow students*': Tapan Raychaudhuri, *The World in Our Time* (Noida, Uttar Pradesh: HarperCollins Publishers India, 2011), p. 154.

13. WHAT TO MAKE OF MARX

p. 209 *Why not drop the labour theory altogether*: Dobb quotes this cogent remark of Samuelson as the point to which he – Dobb – must respond, which he goes on to do, distinguishing between the *closeness* of approximation and the *relevance* of approximation in thinking about the nature of the problem. I have discussed in some detail the significance of the distinction to which Dobb is drawing our attention in my commentary, 'On the Labour Theory of Value: Some Methodological Issues', *Cambridge Journal of Economics*, 2(2) (June 1978), pp. 175–90.

p. 209 *an essay entitled 'The Requirements of a Theory of Value'*: Maurice Dobb, *Political Economy and Capitalism: Some Essays in Economic Tradition* (1937) (Abingdon and New York: Routledge, 2012), pp. 1–33.

pp. 212–13 '*the conditions for the free development*': Karl Marx and Friedrich Engels, *The German Ideology* (1932) (New York: International Publishers, 1947), p. 22.

p. 215 '*no society can legitimately call itself civilised*': in Aneurin Bevan's powerful book *In Place of Fear* (London: Heinemann, 1952), p. 100.

p. 219 '*In the pre-Namier days Marxists regarded it*': Eric Hobsbawm, 'Where are British Historians Going?', *Marxist Quarterly*, 2 (1) (January 1955), p. 22.

p. 221 '*The figure that had emerged*': Gareth Stedman Jones, *Karl Marx: Greatness and Illusion* (London: Allen Lane, 2016), p. 5.

14. AN EARLY BATTLE

p. 235 *John Gunther, the American journalist*: John Gunther, *Inside Europe* (London: Hamish Hamilton, 1936).

15. TO ENGLAND

p. 240 *That library*: In those days, the British Council and its library were on a street in Calcutta called Theatre Road, which was soon to be renamed by the city authorities 'Shakespeare Sarani' (or Shakespeare Street). The British colonialists received a much better deal in this respect from the city administration than the United States: at the height of the Vietnam War, Harrington Street, on which the US Consulate was located, was renamed 'Ho Chi Minh Sarani'.

18. WHAT ECONOMICS?

p. 287 *'It is not wonder, but rather the social enthusiasm'*: A. C. Pigou, *The Economics of Welfare* (1920) (Basingstoke: Palgrave Macmillan, 4th edn, 1932), p. 5.

p. 289 *Veblen was a productive thinker*: Thorstein Veblen, *The Theory of the Leisure Class* (1899) (Abingdon: Routledge, 1992).

p. 292 *the brilliant South African economist*: J. de V. Graaff, *Theoretical Welfare Economics* (London: Cambridge University Press, 1957).

20. CONVERSATION AND POLITICS

p. 313 *He discusses his priorities beautifully*: Tam Dalyell, *The Importance of Being Awkward: The Autobiography* (Edinburgh: Birlinn Ltd, 2011).

pp. 314–15 *A. C. Pigou had already written*: A. C. Pigou, *The Economics of Welfare* (1920) (Basingstoke: Palgrave Macmillan, 4th edn, 1932).

pp. 319–29 *The story had a happy ending*: W. G. Runciman, Amartya K. Sen, 'Games, Justice and the General Will', *Mind*, LXXIV (296) (October 1965), pp. 554–62.

p. 320 *I addressed it further in my book*: Amartya Sen, *The Idea of Justice* (London: Allen Lane, 2009).

21. BETWEEN CAMBRIDGE AND CALCUTTA

p. 331 *The book investigates*: Ranajit Guha, *A Rule of Property for Bengal* was originally published in 1963 by Mouton and the École Pratique des Hautes Études and republished by Orient Longman in 1982, and later – in 1996 – was reprinted by Duke University Press (for which I had the privilege of writing a longish Foreword). Since secure airmail for precious packages used to be quite expensive (in relation to an Indian teacher's salary), I was given the pleasant job of carrying the final manuscript to Europe in my briefcase, to send it to the publishers – Mouton and the École Pratique.

22. DOBB, SRAFFA AND ROBERTSON

p. 344 *'neither of us now knows how much'*: D. H. Robertson, 'Preface to 1949 Edition', *Banking Policy and the Price Level* (1926) (New York: Augustus M. Kelley 1949), p. 5.

p. 348 *he had a long note on the subject*: I have been trying to persuade Trinity College to spend a little money to undertake translations of the papers – in Italian – that Sraffa left behind. I have, I fear, not succeeded in getting my college to allocate this relatively small sum, even though Trinity had received from Sraffa on his death in 1983 an inheritance of more than $1 million. Had we obtained the subvention for translation, I would have worked with Professor Cheryl Misak (the author of a brilliant book on Frank Ramsey), with the assistance of two Italian scholars. Seeing my inability to get even a small amount of research support, Cheryl asked my philosophy colleague at Trinity, Huw Richards, 'Doesn't a former Master have any influence in this college?' Huw explained, 'You should know, Cheryl, that a Master has zero influence in the college, and a former Master has something less than that.'

p. 350 *a short book Sraffa published*: Piero Sraffa, *Production of Commodities by Means of Commodities: Prelude to a Critique of Economic Theory* (Cambridge: Cambridge University Press, 1960).

p. 350 *'when we are provided'*: Joan Robinson, 'Prelude to a Critique of Economic Theory', *Oxford Economic Papers*, New Series, 13(1) (February 1961), pp. 53–8.

p. 354 *'In May 1946 Piero Sraffa'*: Ray Monk, *Ludwig Wittgenstein: The Duty of Genius* (London: Jonathan Cape, 1990), p. 487.

p. 355 *Gramsci was engaged in writing*: Gramsci's *Prison Notebooks*, which (along with *The Modern Prince and Other Writings*, London: Lawrence and Wishart, 1957), help us to have a fuller understanding of Gramsci's perspective.

p. 356 '*It must first be shown that all men are "philosophers"*': Antonio Gramsci, *Selections from the Prison Notebooks*, edited and translated by Quintin Hoare and Geoffrey Nowell Smith (London: Lawrence and Wishart, 1971), 'The Study of Philosophy (Some Preliminary Points of Reference)', p. 323.

23. AMERICAN ENCOUNTERS

p. 361 *the result appeared in a paper*: Amartya Sen, 'On the Usefulness of Used Machines', *Review of Economics and Statistics*, 44(3) (August 1962), pp. 346–8.

p. 363 *I lectured along Samuelsonian lines*: Paul A. Samuelson, *Foundations of Economic Analysis* (Cambridge, MA: Harvard University Press, 1947).

p. 363 '*invariance conditions*': My paper was entitled 'Interpersonal Aggregation and Partial Comparability', *Econometrica*, 38 (3) (May 1970), pp. 393–409. For a fuller exploration of the approach, see my *Collective Choice and Social Welfare* (1970) (republished Amsterdam: North-Holland, 1979; expanded edition, London: Penguin Books, 2017).

24. CAMBRIDGE RE-EXAMINED

p. 376 *two extremely interesting papers*: James M. Buchanan, 'Social Choice, Democracy, and Free Markets,' *Journal of Political Economy*, 62 (2) (April 1954), pp. 114–23; and 'Individual Choice in Voting and the Market,' *Journal of Political Economy*, 62 (3) (August 1954), pp. 334–43.

p. 377 *reflect social welfare judgements rather than voting outcomes*: A critical examination of this contrast and some related distinctions was later included in my presidential address to the American Economic Association: 'Rationality and Social Choice', *American Economic Review*, 85 (1) (1995), pp. 1–24.

p. 378 *presidential address for the Econometric Society*: The lecture was published as 'Internal Consistency of Choice', *Econometrica*, 61 (3) (1993), pp. 495–521.

p. 379 '*to pour too much scorn*': For the source of the citation and its translation, and also for related views of Sraffa and Gramsci, see Jean-Pierre Potier, *Piero Sraffa – Unorthodox Economist (1898–1983): A Biographical Essay* (1991) (Abingdon: Routledge, 2015), pp. 23–7.

p. 380 '*possible for me to do one thing today*': Karl Marx and Friedrich Engels, *The German Ideology* (1845) (New York: International Publishers, 1947), p. 22.

25. PERSUASION AND COOPERATION

p. 385 *the Milan Manifesto*: Three of these four pioneers became relations of mine in the 1970s, when Eva Colorni and I were married (she was daughter of Ursula and Eugenio and stepdaughter of Altiero). I had many opportunities to talk about the motivation behind the two declarations with Altiero and Ursula in the 1970s. Eugenio had been killed by the fascists in May 1944, two days before the Americans liberated Rome. I also had illuminating conversations on the history of these developments with Eva and her sisters Renata and Barbara.

p. 388 '*setting in motion those forces of instruction*': John Maynard Keynes, *The Economic Consequences of the Peace* (London: Macmillan, 1919; New York: Harcourt, Brace and Howe, 1920; republished with an Introduction by Robert Lekachman, New York: Penguin Classics, 1995).

p. 389 *better allocation of medical care*: R. J. Hammond, *History of the Second World War: Food*, Vol. II, *Studies in Administration and Control* (London: HMSO, 1956) and Brian Abel-Smith and Richard M. Titmuss, *The Cost of the National Health Service in England and Wales*, NIESR Occasional Papers, XVIII (Cambridge University Press, 1956).

p. 389 '*There was a revolution in the attitude*': R. J. Hammond, *History of the Second World War: Food*, Vol. I, *The Growth of Policy* (London: HMSO, 1951). See also Richard M. Titmuss, *History of the Second World War: Problems of Social Policy* (London: HMSO, 1950).

p. 390 '*I cannot help contrasting the two systems*': Rabindranath Tagore, *Crisis in Civilization* (Calcutta: Visva-Bharati, 1941).

p. 391 *more than a million people had already died*: Ian Stephens wrote a book called *Monsoon Morning* (London: Ernest Benn, 1966), which is about his experiences, his growing doubts and his ultimate revolt. He was naturally rather proud of the change he brought about. The only time I have written an obituary in *The Times* in London was when I found that Stephens's official obituary in the paper didn't even mention his role in stopping the Bengal famine and saving perhaps a million lives. I was happy that *The Times* did carry my supplementary obituary and I was allowed to give Stephens the credit that he so strongly deserved.

26. NEAR AND FAR

p. 397 *'again suppose that several distinct societies'*: David Hume, *An Enquiry Concerning the Principles of Morals* (1777) (LaSalle, IL: Open Court, 1966), p. 25. The open-minded liberality of this remark would seem to be in conflict with other remarks Hume did also make, about the superiority of the 'whites'. Unlike Adam Smith, who never came even close to saying anything that betrayed racial or ethnic prejudice, Hume evidently allowed himself some inconsistency.

p. 403 *the idea of social contracts*: For a discussion of the extensive need for different types of social contracts for a good society, see Minouche Shafik, *What We Owe Each Other: A New Social Contract* (London: The Bodley Head, 2021).

p. 404 *Being a social choice theorist*: Tapas Majumdar, who was a very young teacher at Presidency College when I was an undergraduate there (I have talked about him – and his influence on me – in an earlier chapter), later on became very interested in applying social choice theory to educational problems – both in India and throughout the world. Working at his academic base at the Jawaharlal Nehru University in Delhi, he greatly added to the reach and relevance of the discipline of social choice.

p. 406 *research findings put together by Hammond, Titmuss*: See Richard Titmuss, *Essays on 'The Welfare State'* (1958) (Bristol: Policy Press, 2019). See also R. J. Hammond, *History of the Second World War: Food*, Vol. I, *The Growth of Policy* (London: HMSO, 1951), and Richard M. Titmuss, *History of the Second World War: Problems of Social Policy* (London: HMSO, 1950).

p. 406 *One example we considered*: Adam Smith, *The Theory of Moral Sentiments* (1759). See also its anniversary edition, edited by Ryan Hanley (London: Penguin Books, 2009), with an Introduction by Amartya Sen.

p. 407 *'There is not a negro'*: Adam Smith, *The Theory of Moral Sentiments* (1759), Vol. 2, Chapter II, 'Of the Influence of Custom and Fashion upon Moral Sentiments'.

p. 407 *The best and noblest gifts of humanity*: Rabindranath Tagore, *Crisis in Civilization* (Calcutta: Visva-Bharati, 1941).

Name Index

Abbas, Khwaja Ahmad, 188
Abbott, George, 277
Abe, Shinzo, 268
Abel-Smith, Brian, 424n
Abul Faz'l (adviser to Akbar), 100
Adarkar, Chitra, 273, 365
Adarkar, Dilip, 273, 323, 339, 365
Adarkar, Priya, 339–40
Adler, Solomon, 358
Adrian, Lord Edward Douglas, 1st
    Baron, 337–8
Ahmad, Muzaffar, 124, 135, 139,
    140–41
Aiyar, Sana, 417n
Akbar (Indian emperor), 100, 128,
    136–7
Alauddin Khalji, 163
Al-Biruni (Iranian mathematician,
    10th–11th century), xv
Ali, Syed Mujtaba (Bengali writer),
    50, 68, 412n
Ambedkar, Bhimrao Ramji
    (Babasaheb), 107, 398
Andreatta, Giana, 271–2
Andreatta, Nino (Beniamino),
    271–2
Andrews, Charles Freer, 40, 89, 410n
Angelico, Fra, 295
Annan, Noel, 318

Antara (daughter of AS: Antara Dev
    Sen), ix, 61, 357, 396
Aris, Michael (Oxford scholar,
    married to Aung San Suu
    Kyi), 13
Aristotle, 213
Arrow, Kenneth, 203–6, 291–2, 320,
    348, 364, 366, 374, 394;
    'impossibility theorem', 204,
    205–6, 291, 292, 293, 376,
    377–8; *Social Choice and
    Individual Values* (1951), 203,
    205, 291, 292, 293, 294
Aryabhata (ancient mathematician),
    98, 99, 102–3
Ashoka (Indian emperor), 59, 109,
    163, 393, 394
Atiyah, Michael (mathematician),
    371-2
Atkinson, James, 177, 419n
Auden, W. H., 385
Aung San Suu Kyi (Burmese
    political leader), 12–14, 15–16
Aurangzeb (Indian emperor), 128
Ayres, Frederick Henry, 415n
Azad, Maulana Abul Kalam, 33, 148

Baba, Dakshin, 413n
Baba, Jhulan, 413n, 240, 258

Babua (cousin: Amit Kumar Sen), 5
Bachchuda (maternal cousin: Som
    Shankar Dasgupta), 57, 127,
    304–5
Bacon, Francis (philosopher), 240, 258
Badamashi (maternal aunt: Renu), 60
Bagchi, Amiya, 339
Bagehot, Walter, 109, 393
Baij, Ramkinkar 40
Balasubramanian, Aditya, ix
Bana (Sanskrit playwright), 94
Bandopadhyay, Kanika (Mohordi), 45
Banerjee, Rishikesh, 329
Banerjee, Surendranath, 184
Banerji, Anita, 329
Banerji, Dipak, 366
Baran, Paul, 364–5
Barenda (maternal cousin: Barendra
    Mohan Sen), 37, 58, 282
Basu, Prahlad, 220–21, 272, 321
Bauer, Lord Peter, 286, 289–90
Bayly, Christopher, 159, 418n
Bentham, Jeremy, 196, 290
Berlin, Isaiah, 301, 336–7
Berlusconi, Silvio, 271
Berrill, Kenneth, 260, 289, 347
Besley, Tim, ix–x
Béteille, André, 200
Bevan, Aneurin, 215, 389, 390, 420n
Beveridge, William, 387
Bharadwaj, Krishna, 351
Bhattacharya, Bijon, 188
Bhattacharya, Dhiresh (professor at
    Presidency College), 196
Bhattacharya, Nikhilesh, 198
Bhattacharya, Reba, 329
Bhattacharya, Sabyasachi, 412n
Bhattacharya, Sourin, 329
Bheltu (school friend: Subrata Roy),
    54, 192

Bhose, Suniti, 198, 241
Bhulu-da (school friend: Subhomoy
    Ghosh), 55
Bhuri Singh, king of Chamba, 65–6
Bhusuku, Siddhacharja (Buddhist
    poet in early Bengal), 29–30
Bhutan, King of (Jigme Khesar
    Namgyel Wangchuck), 71
Bickford-Smith, Coralie, x
Bipradas (author of *Manasamangal*),
    28–9, 180
Biswajit-da (school friend: Biswajit
    Ray), 55
Blair, Tony, UK prime minster, 312
Bloch, Marc, 210, 211, 289
Blunt, Anthony, 317
Bose, Buddhadeb, 32, 150, 176, 330
Bose, Minakshi, 198, 241, 330
Bose, Nandalal, 40, 41, 71, 410n
Bose, Satyendra Nath, 150, 190–91,
    193, 234
Bose, Sisir, 145
Bose, Netaji Subhas Chandra, 116,
    119, 145–7, 184, 268, 417n
Bose, Sugata, ix, 417n
Botticelli, Sandro, 295
Bowles, Samuel, 366
Bradfield, John, 277
Brahmagupta (ancient
    mathematician), 98, 102–3
Braithwaite, Richard (philosopher),
    316
Bratherton, Dr David (oncologist),
    280–81
Brecht, Bertolt, 92
Brittan, Samuel, 313–15
Broad, C. D. (philosopher), 336
Brown, Aldrich (Ricky), 308, 310
Brownlie, Ian, 309–10
Bruno, Giordano, 128

Bruno, Michael, 265–6
Buchanan, James M., 376–7, 378, 423n
Buck, Pearl, 118
Buddha, Gautama, 87, 95–7, 99–100, 107, 405; *Sutta Nipata*, 96–7, 403–4
Bukharin, Nikolai, 235, 245, 333
Burgess, Guy, 317
Burke, Edmund, 166, 219–20
Burnyeat, Myles, 318
Butler, Sir James, 341
Butterworth, John Blackstock, 154
Byron, Lord, 169, 240

Campos, J. J, 180,
Canova, Antonio, 288
Chakraborti, Dhirendra, 329
Chakravarty (Hindu priest in Sonarang), 136
Chakravarty, Ajit Kumar, 413n
Chakravarty, Lalita, 360
Chakravarty, Narayan, 250
Chakravarty, Sukhamoy, 192, 198, 200, 203, 205, 241, 360, 373
Chaltu (school friend: Supriya Roy), 54, 192
Champernowne, David, 338, 345
Chanda, Anil, 251
Chandidas (fifteenth-century Bengali poet), 135
Chandragupta Maurya, Indian emperor, 162–3
Chandrasekhar, Subrahmanyan (astrophysicist), 371
Charnock, Job, 174, 179, 180, 419n
Chatterjee, Dipankar, 54, 173
Chatterji, Joya (school friend), 126, 417n

Chatterji, Nimai, 86–7, 414n
Chattopadhyay, Anirban, x
Chattopadhyay (Chatterjee), Bankim Chandra, 176, 178
Chaudhuri, Amit, 178, 419n
Chaudhuri, Binay, 198
Chowdhury, Dr Abhijit, x
Chiang Kai-shek, Generalissimo, 48
Chiang Kai-shek, Madame, 48
Chinikaka (paternal uncle: Ashoke Kumar Sen), 5, 227
Chitta (school friend: Chitta Ranjan Das), 54
Chotokaka (paternal uncle: Arun Kumar Sen), 5
Choudhury, Rezwana (Bannya) (singer and musician), 45
Churchill, Winston, 118, 144, 162
Clive, Robert, 156–7, 162, 166, 174, 181, 220, 418n
Cole, Max (W. A.), 310
Colorni, Eugenio, 385, 424n
Colorni, Eva (wife of AS), 54, 68, 411n, 424n
Condorcet, Marquis de, 203, 204–5, 291, 362
Conrad, Joseph, 50
Cornwallis, Lord, 129–30, 131–2, 134, 331
Cory, William, 316
Cripps, Sir Stafford, 143–4
Curie, Marie, 229, 230
Curzon, Lord, 126–7

Dadu (sant, oral poet), 67, 72, 73, 75, 76, 413n
Dalrymple, William, 165, 418n
Dalyell, Tam, 312–13, 421n
Das, Nirbhay, 413n

Das Gupta (Calcutta bookshop), owner of, 200, 203, 205

Dasgupta, Ajit, 329

Dasgupta, Alakananda (daughter of Amiyakaka: Bibi), 335

Dasgupta, Alokeranjan (school friend and poet), 53

Dasgupta, Amiya Kumar (Amiyakaka), 150, 151, 193, 239, 327, 335, 396, 418n

Dasgupta, Ilina (maternal cousin), 58, 127

Dasgupta, Mamata (maternal aunt: Labumashi), 127

Dasgupta, Sailen, 127

Dasgupta, Sumona (maternal cousin), 58, 127

Datta, Bhabatosh (professor at Presidency College), 196–7

Datta, Jyotirmoy, 198, 235, 241, 330

Datta, Manjula (school friend), 52, 54

Datta Chaudhuri, Mrinal, 54, 173, 191–2, 241, 329, 332

David, Jacques-Louis, 288

Davies, Richard, 351

De, Barun, 198, 241

De, Shyam Sundar, 300–301

Deaton, Angus, ix–x

Deb, Radhakanta, 194

Debreu, Gérard, 362

Derozio, Henry, 195–6, 238, 420n

Desai, Meghnad, 366

Dev, Nabaneeta (wife of AS), 273, 303, 357–9, 360, 365, 367, 368, 396, 402; 'The Foreign Reincarnation of Rabindranath Tagore', 414n

Devaki (friend from Delhi and Oxford: Devaki Sreenivasan, later Jain), 335, 339

Dey, Bishnu, 176

Dey, Mukul, 192

Dey, Sushil, 330

Dhar, Bithi (school friend), 52, 54

Diamond, Peter, 363, 366

Dickinson, Lowes, 86–7

Digby, Simon, 266, 283–4

Digby, William, 266

Dindev of Chaukandee, 413n

Dirac, Paul, 190

Dobb, Barbara, 368

Dobb, Maurice, 260, 335, 343, 347, 350, 351, 361, 362, 371; Marxism, 209–10, 211, 217, 221, 240, 261–2, 269, 285, 286, 287, 289, 345–6; and 'objective illusion' concept, 217; and AS's choice of Trinity, 240, 247, 260, 368; and welfare economics, 289, 293, 294, 378; and AS's doctoral thesis, 294, 327, 378, 403; Dennis Robertson on, 344–5; kindness of, 346, 368; indexes of works of Ricardo, 348; and Oscar Lange, 374; *Political Economy and Capitalism*, 209–10, 346, 420n; 'The Requirements of a Theory of Value', 209, 211, 346, 420n

Domar, Evsey, 361

Doniger, Wendy, 411n, 415n

Drèze, Jean, ix, 411n

Dryden, John, 240

Duguid, Richard, x

Dula (maternal cousin: Chitra Sen, later, Basu), 58, 185

Dunn, John, 318

Durlabh, Rai, 156

Dutt, Michael Madhusudan (poet), 160, 176, 178

Dutta, Krishna, 85, 411n, 412n,
    413n, 414n, 415n
Dwivedi, Hazari Prasad, 75–6

East, Edward Hyde, 194
Eaton, Richard M., 410n, 417n
Eckaus, Richard, 361
Edwardes, Michael, *Plassey: The
    Founding of an Empire*, 418n
Einaudi, Luigi, 385–6
Eliot, T. S., 86
Elmhirst, Leonard, 40, 410n
Eltis, Walter, 315
Engels, Friedrich, 212–13, 424n
Epstein, David (mathematician),
    266
Euclid, 98

Farouk, King of Egypt, 248
Farrell, Michael, 286
Faxian (Chinese scholar), 26
Feinstein, Charles, 309
Ferguson, Niall, 157
Fisher, Franklin, 361, 366
Forster, E. M., 54, 220–21, 320–22,
    391–2
Freud, Sigmund, 140
Fried, Charles, 366
Frisch, Otto, 339
Fuller, Sandra, x

Gablu (maternal cousin), 58
Galbraith, John Kenneth, 212
Gallagher, Jack, 341, 346
Gandhi, Gopal, 181, 188, 414n,
    419n
Gandhi, Mahatma: non-violent
    strategy of, 46, 139, 145, 252;
    1945 visit to Santiniketan,
    48–9, 83; differences/disputes
    with Tagore, 49, 79–82, 83–4,
    86, 88, 91–2; and critical
    reasoning, 79–81, 82–3, 86;
    and the *charka*, 81–2, 83–4;
    and technology, 81–2, 83–4;
    and Indian nationalism, 91, 92;
    witticism on British civilization,
    92; and Cripps Mission (March
    1942), 144; Quit India
    movement, 144, 145; and
    exclusion of Bose (1939), 145;
    Gopal Gandhi as grandson of,
    181, 419n; attitude to Calcutta
    theatre, 187–8; *The Oxford
    India Gandhi: Essential
    Writings* (compiled/edited
    Gopal Gandhi), 414n
Gangolli, Ramesh, 323–4, 360
Gangolli, Shanta, 324, 360
Garegnani, Pierangelo, 270, 287,
    309, 351
Garibaldi, Giuseppe, 159
George of Poděbrady (king of
    Bohemia), 386
Ghosal, Upendranath (professor at
    Presidency College), 196
Ghosh, Dipankar, 272–3
Ghosh, Dwarkanath, 272
Ghosh, Kali Mohan, 65, 413n
Ghosh, Ramesh (professor at
    Presidency College), 196
Ghosh, Shanti Deb (singer and
    musician), 45
Ghosh, Sisir Kumar, 77
Ghosh, Tanayendra Nath, 43
Ghosh, Tushar, 198
Gibbard, Allan, 366
Gibson, Mary Ellis, 420n
Giotto, 295
Gleicher, Nathaniel, 409n

Golwalkar, Madhav Sadashiv (Hindutva theorist), 149
Goodwin, Richard, 289
Gopalan, Shyamala (cancer researcher), 367
Gorbachev, Mikhail (Soviet political leader), 85
Gordon, Ania, x
Gorky, Maxim, 135, 244
Goswami, Nityananda Binod, 39, 43
Graaff, Jan de, 292, 421n
Gray, Victoria, ix
Gramsci, Antonio, 240, 261, 270, 293, 309, 381, 387, 424n; and *L'Ordine Nuovo*, 347, 356; political persecution of, 355; and concept of liberty, 378, 379–80; *Prison Notebooks*, 355–6, 423n; *The Modern Prince and Other Writings*, 423n
Greene, Graham, 90
Guha, Marta, 331
Guha, Ramachandra, 414
Guha, Ranajit, 75, 130, 330–32, 413n; *A Rule of Property for Bengal*, 331, 417n, 422n
Gunther, John, 235, 333
Gupta, Ajay (maternal uncle: Ajaymama), 242, 243
Gupta, Jean, 243
Gupta, Partha, 198, 235, 241, 245, 246, 308
Gwalior, Maharaja of, 284–5

Hacking, Ian (philosopher), 266
Hahn, Dorothy, 369
Hahn, Frank, 318, 368–70
Haldane, J. B. S., 61, 202, 236–7, 238
Hamied, Khwaja Abdul, 242, 243
Hamied, Yusuf, 243

Hammond, Richard, 389, 406, 424n, 425n
Hanger, Mrs (Cambridge landlady), 256–7, 259, 282–3
Hanley, Ryan, 425
Haq, Khadija ul (Bani), 265, 400
Haq, Mahbub ul, 264–5, 273, 313, 315, 323, 398, 400–401
Harcourt, Geoffrey, 351
Hardy, G. (mathematician), 240, 340
Hare, David (Scottish watchmaker in Calcutta), 194
Harris, Donald, 367
Harris, Kamala (now Vice-President of the United States), 367
Harsanyi, John, 366
Haskell, Francis, 318
Hastings, Warren, 166, 175–6, 219–20
Hayes, Allan, 266
Hegel, G. W. F., 206, 218, 219
Henry VIII, King of England, 257
Hicks, John, 193, 362
Hirschmann, Ursula, 385, 424n
Hoare, Quintin, 423n
Hobbes, Thomas, 96, 403
Hobsbawm, Eric, 220–21, 222, 232, 286, 303–4, 309, 310, 311; 'Where Are British Historians Going?' 218–19, 220, 420n
Homer, 95, 196, 359
Hossain, Hameeda, 275
Hossain, Kamal, 16, 274
Housman, A. E., 240
Hume, David, 196, 348, 397, 403, 406, 425n
Hunt, Winifred, 251–2
Huntington, Samuel, 137
Huq, Fazlul, 131, 417n
Huld Markan, Inga, x

Hutchinson, Matt, x

Iftekhar, Arif, 273, 398–400
Ikram, Khalid, 400
Indrani (daughter of AS: Indrani Sen) ix, 61
Ingalls, Daniel H. H., 358, 359–60
Iqbal, Muhammad, 371

Jafar, Mir, 156–7
Jaffé, Michael, 318
Jagabandhuda (mathematics teacher), 43–4
Jahan, Rounaq, ix
Jain, Lakshmi, 335
Jalal, Ayesha, 149, 416n, 417n
Jamieson, Craig, 413n
Jasimuddin (Bengali poet), 176
Jayadeva (Sanskrit poet, 12th century), 41, 100, 410–11n
Jayawardena, Kumari, 276
Jayawardena, Lal, 265, 276, 318, 323
Jinnah, Muhammad Ali, 125, 131, 147–8, 149–50, 416n
Joggeshwar, 60, 115
Johnson, Harry, 286, 289
Joliot-Curie, Irene, 229
Jorgenson, Dale, 366
Jude, Brother (head of St Gregory's School in Dhaka), 16, 17

Kabir (fifteenth century poet), 67–8, 72–7, 100, 331, 412–13n
Kabir, Humayun, writer and political leader, 32–4
Kabir (son of AS: Kabir Sen), ix, 61, 68, 411n
Kahn, Richard, 286, 292, 320, 370

Kaldor, Nicholas, 286, 292–3, 338, 347–8, 369
Kalidasa (Sanskrit playwright), 94, 321–2; *Meghaduta*, 98
Kalyan-da (husband of Mejdi), 58
Kamal, Sultana, 275
Kankarmama (maternal uncle: Kshemendra Mohan Sen), 57, 85, 115, 118, 124, 141–2, 144, 145, 232
Kant, Immanuel, 301, 403
Kar, Shib Krishna, 54, 173, 304–5
Karim (AS's father's laboratory assistant), 5
Kashinathda (geography teacher: Kashinath Bhattacharya), 43, 54
Keiger, Dale, 409n
Kennedy, John F., 360
Kenner, Hugh, 412n
Keynes, John Maynard, 286, 317, 344, 352, 355, 362; emphasis on persuasion, 387–8, 393, 394; and inter-war hostilities, 387–8; and Bretton Woods institutions, 388; *Essays in Persuasion* (1931), 387; *The Economic Consequences of the Peace*, 388; *The General Theory of Employment, Interest and Money* (1936), 388; see also Keynesian economics *in subject index*
Khan, Yar Latif, 156
Khilji, Bakhtiar, 107
Khokonda (maternal cousin: Kalyan Dasgupta), 57, 118
Khrushchev, Nikita, 202, 308, 332–3
Khyapa Jyatha ('mad uncle' – nick name), 250

Kipling, Rudyard: on Calcutta, 173, 174, 177, 178, 189; as blind to 'Bengal renaissance', 178; 'Mandalay', 10, 22; 'The White Man's burden', 166–7; 'A Tale of Two Cities', 177
Kowshik, Dinkar, 410n
Krishna, T. M. (musician and political thinker), 415n
Krutch, Joseph Wood, 102, 415n
Kuh, Edwin, 361
Kumar, Dharma, 324–5, 332
Kumar, Radha, 325
Kundu, Madhusudan, 53
Kurz, Heinz, 351

La Fayette, Marquis de, 386
Lal, Mohan, 156
Lalitda (school teacher at Santiniketan: Lalit Majumdar), 44–5
Lange, Oscar, 373–5
Lawrence, T. E., 248
Layard, Richard, 71
Lebedef, Herasim, 186
Lefeber, Louis, 361
Lekachman, Robert, 424n
Lenin, V. I., 53, 202
Leonardo da Vinci, 295
Letta, Enrico (Italian political leader), 271
Lévi, Sylvain, 40, 410n
Levison, Dr (oncologist), 280
Lily (student from Odisha in Strathnaver), 247
Linlithgow, Lord (Viceroy of India, 1936–43), 143
Littlewood, J. E. (mathematician), 240
Lloyd, Geoffrey, 318
Locke, John, 403

Lopokova, Lydia, 352
Lord, A. B. (Harvard professor with expertise in oral epic poetry), 358
Lukács, Georg, 92
Luther, Anuradha, 405

Macaulay, Thomas, 258
Madan, Mir, 156
Madhavacharya (14th century Sanskrit philosopher), 100; Sarvadarshana Samgraha, 64
Mahafizuddin (Muslim priest in Sonarang), 136
Mahalanobis, Prasanta Chandra, 191
Maitra, Heramba (principal of City College in Calcutta) 187
Mashima (Tapas Majumdar's mother), 198
Mohitda (school teacher at Santiniketan – Mohit Majumdar), 44
Majumdar, Nani Gopal, 198
Majumdar, Tapas (professor at Presidency College), 196, 197–8, 425n
Mandela, Nelson, 269
Mangano, Silvana, 242
Manju (sister of AS: Supurna Sen, later Datta), childhood of, 4–5, 9, 12, 18, 22, 35, 58; in Burma, 9, 12; death of (February 2011), 35; moves to Calcutta (1952), 227; and AS's cancer diagnosis, 227, 234; at AS's degree ceremony (1955), 323
Mansoor (school friend), 54
Manto, Saadat Hasan, 150
Mantu-da (friend and part of the Santiniketan circle), 55

Mao Tse-tung, 214
Marglin, Stephen, 343 366
Marris, Robin, 289
Marshall, Alfred, 344, 349, 369
Marshall, Joe, 42, 411n
Marshall, Megan, 411n
Marvell, Andrew, 199, 240
Marx, Karl, 135, 140, 203, 308, 362, 405; focus on human beings, 55, 215–19, 220–21, 222; on British rule in India, 159, 160; standing/stature of in 1950s Calcutta, 207–9; 'labour theory of value', 207–10, 211, 213; idiosyncrasies in work of, 211–12; and concept of liberty, 212–13, 380; and authoritarianism of later communist regimes, 212, 380; and the 'needs principle', 213–15; 'objective illusion' concept, 216–18, 222; 'false consciousness' concept, 216; two-way relations between ideas and material conditions, 218–19, 222; pedagogy about human behaviour, 220; nineteenth-century surroundings of, 221–2; *The German Ideology* (with Engels), 212–13, 220, 424n; *The Critique of Gotha Programme*, 213–14, 215–16, 220; *Communist Manifesto* (with Engels), 216; *see also* Marxist thinking *in subject index*
Maskin, Eric, 44
Matthews, Robin, 289
Mazumdar, Dipak (Hapan), 272
Mazumdar, Pauline, 272

Mazur, Barry, 44
McFadden, Daniel, 366
Meade, James, 342, 369–70
Mehra, Shakuntala, 335
Mehrotra, Arvind Krishna (poet and writer), *Songs of Kabir*, 412n
Mehta, Aparna (later Basu), 272
Mehta, Ved, 177, 339–40, 365, 419n
Mejda (paternal cousin: Amal Kumar Sen), 5
Merkel, Angela, 307
Mia, Kader (riot victim), 122–4
Michael (Trinity College porter), 322–3
Michelangelo, 210–11, 295
Miliband, David, 311
Miliband, Ed, 311
Miliband, Marion, 311
Miliband, Ralph, 311
Mill, John Stuart, 109, 213, 362, 393, 394
Miller, Henry, 86
Miller, Jonathan, 318
Millikan, Max, 358
Miradi (cousin: Mira Ray), ix, 18
Mirrlees, James, 318, 342–3, 370–71
Misak, Cheryl, 422n
Mitchell, J. S., 280
Mitra, Amit (school friend), 52, 54–5, 173
Mitra, Haridas, 52
Mitra, Sombhu, 188
Mitra, Subodh, 228–9
Mitra, Suchitra, 45
Modigliani, Franco, 361
Monk, Ray, 354, 422n
Moore, G. E., 240, 316, 317
Moore, Thomas, ix
Moorhouse, Geoffrey, 174, 419n

Morrison, John (AS's tutor in Trinity College, later Master of Churchill Collge, Cambridge), 259

Mountbatten, Lord, 150

Mujibur Rahman, Sheikh (Bangabandhu), 132

Mujumdar, Shailaja (music teacher), 45

Mukherjee, Mr (Warden of YMCA), 183

Mukherjee, Buddinnath, 194

Mukherjee, Dr Kamakhya, 235–6

Mukherjee, Jaya, 52, 54

Mukherjee, Prabir , 273

Mukherjee, Samir, 273

Mukhopadhyay, Binodbehari, 40

Mukhopadhyay, Pranati, 71, 411n, 412n, 413n

Mukundaram, *Chandimangal*, 133–4

Murshed, K. G., 246–7

Murshed, Kaiser, 246, 247

Nabokov, Vladimir, 50

Naguib (president of Egypt), 248

Nair, P. Thankappan, 419n

Namier, Lewis, 219, 220

Nandana (daughter of AS: Nandana Dev Sen), ix, 61, 251, 357

Nandy, Arabinda, x, 60–61

Narain, Dharam, 335

Nash, John, 319

Nasser, Gamal Abdel, 248

Nazrul Islam, Kazi (Bengali poet), 91, 135, 176; 'Kandari Hushiyar', 135–6

Nehru, Jawaharlal, 54, 81, 144, 148, 150, 271; 'tryst with destiny' speech, 157; at Trinity,

371; *Glimpses of World History*, 284

Nesbit, Lynn, ix

Neumann, John von, 319

Newton, Isaac, 258

Nicholson, Christine 340–41

Nicholson, Michael, 269–70, 275, 340–41

Nietzsche, Friedrich, 87, 414n

Okazaki, Hisahiko, 266, 267–8

Orwell, George (Eric Arthur Blair), 10, 11, 409n

Owen, Susan, 89

Owen, Wilfred, 89

Paine, Thomas, 196

Pal, Prasanta, 268

Pal, Radhabinod, 267–8

Panini (Sanskrit grammarian, 4th century BC, 93–4, 329, 416n

Panyarachun, Anand (former prime minister of Thailand), 266

Papandreou, Andreas, (prime minister of Greece), 402

Papandreou, Andreas (son of Greek prime minister), 402

Papandreou, Margaret, 402

Parry, Milman (pioneer in the study of oral epic poetry), 358

Pasinetti, Luigi, 270–71, 287, 351

Patel, Alaknanda, 418n

Patel, I. G., 335, 396

Patel, Sardar Vallabhbhai, 144

Patnaik, Prabhat, 404, 405

Pattanaik, Prasanta, 403–4

Pearson, William, 40

Perry, Commodore Matthew, 158, 161

Pigou, A. C., 287, 314–15, 395–6, 421n
Piyali (maternal cousin: Piyali Sen, later Ray), 58, 185
Pliny the Elder, 28
Pollak, Ken, 276
Pollock, Sheldon, 415n
Pollock, William Frederick, 317
Pooley, Bev, 276
Posner, Michael, 345
Potier, Jean-Pierre, 424n
Pound, Ezra, 42, 73, 90, 412–13n
Prabuddha (school friend: Prabuddha Ghosh), 54
Prasad Malviya, Mahaveer, *Kabir Shhabdabali*, 413n
Prodi, Romano (prime minister of Italy), 271
Proffitt, Stuart, ix
Ptolemy, 27–8

Qadir, Manzur, 400
Qadir, Shireen, 400

Radcliffe, Sir Cyril, 153–4
Radhakrishnan, Sarvepalli, 77
Radner, Roy, 366
Rahman, Fazlur, 151
Rahman, Shamsur (Bengali writer), 176
Raiffa, Howard, 366
Raj, K. N., 335, 395
Rajagopalachari, C., 181
Rama Rau, Santha, 320–21
Ramanujan, Srinivasa, 240, 371
Rana, Kumar, ix
Ramsey, Frank, 316, 318, 353, 422n
Rao, Madhav, 395–6
Rao, V. K. R. V., 395, 396
Rashed, Zafar Ahmad, 33

Ratnamala (cousin: Ratnamala Sen), ix
Rawls, John, 290–91, 319, 320, 336, 366
Ray, Buddha (maternal cousin), 43, 240
Ray, Chaya, 332
Ray, Paramesh, 329, 332
Ray, Samir, 198, 234
Ray, Satyajit, 40, 41, 92; and Calcutta, 173–4, 189; *The Chess Players* (1977), 128; *Mahanagar* (The Big City, 1963), 173–4; *Pather Panchali* (1955), 189, 419n; *Our Films, Their Films* (book, 1976), 410n, 419n
Raychaudhuri, Rani, 332
Raychaudhuri, Tapan, 130, 131–2, 200, 241–2, 245–6, 332, 417n, 420n
Raza, Raihan, 410n
Reba (Didi, maternal cousin: Reba Gupta), 57
Reddaway, Brian, 289
Rhees, Rush (philosopher), 353
Ri, Chie, x
Ricardo, David, 348
Richards, Adam, 14
Richards, Huw, 422n
Riskin, Carl, 366, 367
Riskin, Mayra, 367
Robert (student of Modern Literature at Cambridge), 296, 297, 298
Robertson, Jane, x
Robertson, Dennis, 261–2, 286, 287, 293, 314, 335, 342, 343–5, 349; *Banking Policy and the Price Level*, 422n

Robinson, Andrew, 85, 411n, 412n, 413n, 414n, 415n

Robinson, Austin, 284–5

Robinson, Joan, 320, 347, 349, 369, 370; strong ties with India, 284–5; rejection of neoclassical economics, 285, 286, 294, 350, 368; and growth maximization approach, 287–8; hostility to welfare economics, 292; *The Economics of Imperfect Competition* (1933), 264; *The Accumulation of Capital* (1956), 284, 285–6; 'Prelude to a Critique of Economic Theory', 422n

Rolland, Romain, 75

Romero, Jose, 266–7

Roncaglia, Alessandro, 351

Roosevelt, Eleanor, 49–50

Rosenstein-Rodan, Paul, 358

Rossellini, Roberto (film director), 189

Rossi, Ernesto, 385

Rothenberg, Jerome, 366

Rothschild, Emma, x

Rousseau, Jean-Jacques, 96, 319–20, 403

Roy, Ram Mohan, 159–60, 176, 194, 196

Royce, Claire, 275–6, 277, 278

Royce, Diana, 276, 277

Royce, Eleanor, 276

Royce, Henry, 276

Rudra, Ashok, 54

Runciman, Garry, 318, 319–20, 421n

Russell, Bertrand, 86–7, 240, 316, 317, 414n

Ryle, Gilbert, 319–20

Sadhan (school friend: Sadhan Gupta), 54

Saha, Meghnad, 137

Saint-Simon, Henri de, 159

Salgado, Ranji, 315–16

Salma (Cambridge friend: Salma Ikramullah, later Sobhan), 274-5

Salvesen, Salve, 266, 268–9

Salvesen, Sylvia, 268–9

Samuelson, Paul, 209, 315, 360, 361, 362–4, 376, 420n

Sarkar, Sushobhan (professor at Presidency College and later at Jadavpur University) 175, 196, 329–30

Sassoon, Jacques, 332

Savarkar, Vinayak Damodar, 148–9

Schelling, Thomas, 366

Schenkl, Emilie, 145

Schollick, Henry, 338

Schwartz, Marlene, 304

Scitovsky, Tibor, 366

Sedley, Stephen, 309

Sen, Abanimohan (Kshiti Mohan's older brother), 65, 67, 136

Sen, Amita (mother of AS), 22–3, 36–7, 69, 70, 123, 150, 151, 226–7; surname of, 6–7; as skilled stage dancer, 7–8, 36, 187; and death of Tagore, 35–6; settles in Pratichi (1964), 60–61; helps Joggeshwar, 60; death of (2005), 61; literary work, 61; and left-wing politics, 124, 129; and AS's cancer diagnosis, 227, 234, 236; at AS's degree ceremony (1955), 323

Sen, Ashutosh (father of AS):
teaches chemistry at Dhaka
University, 4, 5, 6, 18, 60, 114,
150–51, 190; in Burma
(1936–9), xiii, 9, 10, 11–12;
visiting professor at Mandalay
Agricultural College, 9; and
AS's school education, 17,
36–7; and river journeys,
20–23; settles in Pratichi
(1964), 60–61; job in New
Delhi, 60; death of (1971), 61;
and communal violence in
1940s, 122–4; as sceptical of
nationalist politics, 124, 140;
moves to Calcutta (1945), 150,
151; brief business career,
151–2; as eternal optimist, 151,
418n; as Land Development
Commissioner in Delhi, 152–3;
trains in USA for project
management in, 152; moves to
Calcutta (1952), 226–7; works
for West Bengal Public Service
Commission, 226–7; and AS's
cancer diagnosis/treatment,
227, 228–9, 234, 235, 236,
278–9; does Ph.D at University
of London, 239, 244–5; and
fast motorbikes, 251; lectures
in London (1955), 323; at AS's
degree ceremony (1955), 323
Sen, Atul (brother of Kiran Bala), 69
Sen, Basu (paternal cousin:
Dadamani), 5
Sen, Bhubanmohan (Kshiti Mohan's
father), 66–7, 68
Sen, Binay Ranjan, 142
Sen, Biren (Kshiti Mohan's nephew),
65

Sen, Bratin (maternal cousin), 58
Sen, Dayamayi (Kshiti Mohan's
mother), 68–9
Sen, Dhiren (Kshiti Mohan's
nephew), 65
Sen, Dr Amiya (Amiyamama), 226,
227, 279
Sen, Indira (sister of Kiran Bala), 70
Sen, Jagatlakkhi (paternal
grandmother: Jagatlakshmi), 6
Sen, Jitendra Prasad (paternal uncle
of AS, father's elder brother), 5
Sen, Kajali (maternal cousin), 58
Sen, Kiranbala (maternal
grandmother: 'Didima'), 8–9,
21, 37, 59, 60, 61, 63, 78; as
skilled midwife, 8, 70; family
background, 69–70; marries
Kshiti Mohan, 69–70; close
relationship with Kshiti
Mohan, 70–71; and Bihar
earthquake (January 1934), 79;
and Bengal famine (1943), 115,
118, 121; prison visits by,
141–2
Sen, Kshiti Mohan (maternal
grandfather): Sanskrit
scholarship of, 6–7, 36, 58,
64–5, 66–7, 68, 71–2, 77;
teaches at Santiniketan, 7, 8,
36, 38, 40, 57, 63–4, 65–6,
71–2; cottage in Gurupalli, 8,
37, 57–9; house in Sripalli, 8,
60; family background, 21,
66–7, 68–9; expertise in rural
poetry/texts, 36, 68, 72–7, 331;
influence on Tagore, 36, 66,
72–3, 75; trip abroad with
Tagore (1927), 51; early
morning walks with AS, 58–9;

and theory of evolution, 61–2; weekly talks in the Mandir, 63–4; Tagore recruits for Santiniketan School, 65–6, 71–2; studies at Queen's College in Benares, 66; and 'Kabir Panth' pluralist tradition, 67–8, 72–7, 78, 125, 149, 412n; and the Bauls of Bengal, 68, 76, 413n; marries Kiran Bala, 69–70; close relationship with Kiran Bala, 70–71; scholarly books by, 72–8, 359–60; version of Kabir's poems, 72, 73–6, 331, 412n, 413n; English book on Hinduism (1961), 77–8, 359–60, 413n; death of (1960), 78, 359; on Tagore's reception in West, 88–9; Tagore's letter to KMS on Western misinterpretation, 88; cultural optimism of, 105; opposes the partition of India, 125, 126, 147, 149; rejects sectarian anti-Muslim history, 128; on narrowness of cultural separatists, 136; prison visits by, 141–2; and history of Calcutta, 178; and Ashoka's edicts on public arguments, 394

Sen, Madhusudan (father of Kiran Bala), 69

Sen, Mira (cousin: Miradi, later Mira Ray), 5, 18, 185

Sen, Nilima, 45

Sen, P. K., 329

Sen, Satyen (Lankarmama, 'uncle'), 124, 141, 144

Sen, Shebak (brother of Kiran Bala), 69

Sen, Sharada Prasad (paternal grandfather), 5, 6, 330

Sen, Shomi (maternal cousin), 58

Sengupta, Jasodhara (Ratna), 339

Sengupta, Jati, 198, 241

Sengupta, Jyotirmoy (paternal uncle: Shidhukaka), 124, 135, 138–41

Seth, Jagat, 156

Seth, Vikram, 54

Shafik, Minouche, 425n

Shahabuddin (law student in Cambridge), 255–6

Shakespeare, William, 43, 169, 232, 240, 297

Shankardass, Kumar, 273

Shanta (school friend: Shanta Ghosh), 54

Shastri, Bidhu Shekhar, 51

Shaw, George Bernard, 50, 90, 232–3

Shotoku (Japanese Buddhist prince), 393

Shudraka (Sanskrit playwright), 94; *Mricchakatika*, 98, 100–102

Shejd (maternal cousin: Shyamali Sen), 57

Sica, Vittorio de (film director), 188–9

Sidgwick, Henry, 316, 344

Silberston, Aubrey, 260, 289, 347

Simm, Paul, ix

Simpson, Dr (general practitioner – personal doctor), 279

Singh, Manmohan (prime minister of India), 324

Sinha, Ajit, 351

Sinha, Sasadhar, 414n

Sinha, Sitikanta, 41
Siraj-ud-Doula, Nawab, 155–7, 162, 163, 164, 174
Skinner, Alice, x
Skinner, Quentin, 317
Smith, Adam, 159, 213, 288, 362, 403, 404; and importance of rivers, 25 6, 28, 32; on East India Company, 165–6; and 'labour theory of value', 208; relevance to modern inequality, 405–6; hatred of slavery, 406–7; 'the impartial spectator', 406; *The Wealth of Nations*, 165–6, 409–10n; *Theory of Moral Sentiments*, 406
Smith, Geoffrey Nowell, 423n
Sobhan, Rehman, 273–4, 299–300, 323
Solow, Robert, 360–61
Spaventa, Luigi, 277–8
Spinelli, Altiero, 356, 385, 424n
Spurway, Helen, 236
Sraffa, Piero: care with language use, 50; and Wittgenstein, 83, 261, 351–5, 356; long walks with AS in Cambridge, 190, 347, 381, 394; and left-wing politics, 221, 261, 270, 271, 286, 293, 347, 356, 378–80, 381; and Gramsci, 240, 261, 293, 347, 355–6, 378, 379–80, 381, 387, 424n; and AS's choice of Trinity, 240, 260; as Director of Studies for AS, 259–61, 347; significant contributions to economics, 287, 348–51; and social choice theory, 293, 378–9, 380–81, 387, 394; and AS's doctoral

thesis, 294, 327–8, 334, 337, 338–9; and AS's Prize Fellowship, 334, 335; as colleague of AS at Trinity, 343, 347, 371, 374, 378–81; reluctance to write/publish, 347–8; student days in Italy, 347, 354–5, 381; edits/indexes works of Ricardo, 348; philosophical ideas, 351, 352–6, 378, 381; and Paul Baran, 364; and Oscar Lange, 374; and concept of liberty, 378–80; his papers stored in the Wren Library at Trinity, 422n; *Production of Commodities by Means of Commodities*, 350–51, 422n
Stalin, Joseph, 202–3, 245, 373
Stedman Jones, Gareth, *Karl Marx: Greatness and Illusion*, 221–2, 420n
Stephen, James Fitzjames, 317
Stephens, Ian, 119, 391–3; obituary in *The Times*, 424–5n; *Monsoon Morning*, 424n
Stone, Richard, 289
Stoppard, Tom, *Professional Foul*, 140
Strachey, Lytton, 316–17
Subrahmanyam, Sanjay, 325
Sunil-da (Santiniketan friend), 55
Sunipa (maternal cousin: Mejdi), 57, 58
Surshyamadas (blind sadhu), 413n
Sushima (maternal cousin: Chordi), 58
Suzumura, Kotaro, 364
Syed Mujtaba Ali, 50

Tagore, Debendranath, 41

Tagore, Rabindranath, xiv; AS family's friendship with, 7–8, 35–6, 59, 65–6, 71–5, 78, 411n; dance dramas, 7, 8, 36, 187; establishes Visva-Bharati school (1901), 7, 41–3, 65; and naming of AS, 8, 138; and importance of rivers, 24, 25; death of (1941), 35–6; 'Crisis in Civilization ' (last speech, April 1941), 36, 86, 169, 390, 407; emphasis on freedom and reasoning, 36, 39–40, 42–3, 55–6, 85–8, 91, 407; Kshiti Mohan's influence on, 36, 66, 72–3, 75; rejects religious hostility, 36, 91; views on education, 36, 38–43, 49, 55–6, 62–3, 84–5, 91; as fiercely critical of nationalism, 39, 91–2; widespread misunderstanding of in West, 42, 66, 86–90, 414–15n; Rabindra Sangeet (Tagore songs), 45, 52, 91, 126–7, 376; differences/disputes with Gandhi, 49, 79–82, 83–4, 86, 88, 91–2; and Cheena Bhavan at Santiniketan, 51; Nobel Prize for Literature (1913), 55, 73, 88, 89; recruits Kshiti Mohan for Santiniketan School, 65–6, 71–2; and Yeats' literary dinner (London, 1912), 66, 88; in Japan and China (1924), 71; view of technology, 81, 82, 83–4; *Izvestia* interview (1930), 85, 411n, 414n; alleged mysticism of, 86–90; religious beliefs, 88, 90; recognizes limits of knowledge, 90; authors two national anthems, 91, 126–7; Hibbert Lectures (Oxford, early 1930s), 132; and Nazrul Islam, 135; books banned under Raj, 168; and Calcutta, 176; Mahalanobis as academic secretary of, 191; E. M. Forster on, 321; 'Nadee', 24; *One Hundred Poems of Kabir* (English translations), 73, 412n; *Russiar Chithi* (Letters from Russia), 84–5, 414n; *Gitanjali*, 88; *The Home and the World* (novel), xiv, 92, 415n

Tan Chameli, 51

Tan Lee, 29–30, 50–51, 52, 53–4, 173

Tan Wen, 51

Tan Yun-Shan, 40, 51

Tapati (school friend), 54

Taylor, Geoffrey (mathematician), 339

Tendulkar, Vijay (playwright), 340

Tennyson, Alfred, 240, 317, 320

Teresa, Mother, 173

Thapar, Romila, 245

Tharoor, Shashi, *Inglorious Empire*, 418n

Thatcher, Margaret, 289, 312

Titian, 295

Titmuss, Richard M., 406, 424n, 425n

Tomlinson, George, 316, 320

Trevelyan, Robert, 87

Trevor-Roper, Hugh, 219

Trilling, Lionel, 86

Tuktuk (maternal cousin), 58

Tuludi (Kiranbala Sen's younger sister), 69, 242
Tutu, Desmond, 269

Umadi (history teacher: Uma Ghosh), 43
Underhill, Evelyn, 73, 412n

Veblen, Thorstein, 288–9, 421n
Vidyasagar, Ishwar Chandra (social reformer and educationist), 160, 176
Virgil, 28
Visconti, Luchino, 189
Voltaire, 196

Ward, Benjamin, 366
Washington, George, 386
Wedderburn, Bill, 310
Wedderburn, Dorothy (earlier Barnard, Cole), 310–11
Weil, Robert, ix
Whitehead, Alfred North, 240
Williamson, Oliver, 366

Wittgenstein, Ludwig, 240, 351–2; social sentiments 83–4; and Sraffa, 83, 261, 351, 352–3, 354—5, 356; and the rules of language, 261, 352–3, 354–5, 356; as an Apostle, 316, 317; return to Cambridge (1929), 352; *Tractatus Logico-Philosophicus*, 261, 351, 352, 353; *Philosophical Investigations*, 261, 351, 353, 355, 356
Wollstonecraft, Mary, 213, 362
Woolley, Leonard, 248
Wren, Sir Christopher, 258
Wright, Georg Henrik von, 353

Yeats, W. B., 42, 66, 88, 89, 90
Yi Jing (Chinese scholar), 26–7, 106

Zafar (Bahadur Shah II, Mughal monarch), 163–4
Zakaria, Rafiq, 148, 149, 417n

Subject Index

Achaogen (pharmaceutical firm), 242
Addenbrooke's Hospital,
    Cambridge, 277; Radio
    Therapy Centre (RTC), 279–81
Afghanistan, 26, 128, 133, 145,
    158, 393, 416n
Africa, 12, 25–6, 242, 269, 305,
    407; in Santiniketan's
    curriculum, 39, 40, 91
Agra (India), 20, 128, 137
Aix-en-Provence, 303–4
Ajay, river (Bengal), 23
All Souls College, Oxford, 193, 310
Allahabad University, 66
Alpbach (Austria), 303
al-Qaeda, 305
antisemitism, 305
Armenians, 161, 184
Asian Civilization Museum
    (Singapore), 108
Asiatic Society, Calcutta, 175, 176
Asutosh College, Calcutta, 175
Athens, ancient, 393
Australia, 243
Austria, 298, 303, 304

Baha'i (immigrant comunity from
    Iran, 161
Baharampur (Bengal), 235

Bangladesh, 4, 15, 16, 20, 27, 30,
    247, 274–5; Vanga (old
    sub-region), 29; commitment to
    secularism, 91, 132–3, 134,
    137; independence, 91, 274;
    national anthem of, 91, 126–7;
    Bengali identity, 132–7;
    'Language Movement Day' (21
    February 1952), 134–5
Bauls, 68, 76, 413n
Bedford College, London, 311
Benares (Varanasi, India), 19, 24,
    66–7, 77
Bengal: rivers of, 6, 19–24, 26–8,
    32–3, 161, 179; communal
    violence, emergence and
    expansion of, in 1940s, 33–4,
    36, 76, 91, 122–4, 125, 148,
    150, 184, 305–6, 372; partition
    of Bengal (1947), 18, 30, 33;
    Adam Smith on the economic
    importance of rivers, 25-26;
    pre-colonial history of, 26–30,
    128–9, 133–4, 136–7, 155–6,
    161, 180–82; cotton textiles
    made in, 27, 179; East India
    Company in, 27, 129–30, 160,
    161, 164–6; foreign trading
    firms 27, 161; and Mughal

Bengal – *cont'd*.
empire, 27, 128, 136–7, 155–7;
Vanga (old sub-region), 29, 30;
regional contrasts within, 30–32;
left- wing politics, 84–5, 129;
anxiety during Second World
War, 113, 115; famine (1769–
70), 119, 165–6, 168; British
attempt at partitioning, 126–7;
anti-British nationalism in, 126,
184; class-based Hindu elite in,
127, 128–9; proposal of a united
Bengal in a partitioned India,
127; pre-Mughal Muslim rules,
128–9, 133–4; Permanent
Settlement (Cornwallis Code,
1793), 129–30, 131–2, 134,
331; Buddhist Pala kings, 133;
the 'San'(calendar), 136–7;
'August rebellion' (1942), 144;
provincial elections (1946), 144,
148, 151; British dominance
after Plassey (June 1757), 155,
156, 158, 162, 163, 164, 174;
'financial bleeding of' by East
India Company, 164–6; 'Bengal
renaissance' in Calcutta, 175–6,
178; Young Bengal (radical
intellectual movement) in,
194–6; the importance of secular
politics in Bengal, 131, 132–7;
the *see also* Calcutta; Dhaka
Bengal Engineering College,
Calcutta, 175
Bengal famine (1943), 60, 99,
113–21, 142, 168; and Calcutta,
114–16, 117, 119, 120–21, 173,
391–3; censorship of newspapers
during, 118, 119, 167, 390–93,
424–5n; British public unaware
of, 119, 390–93, 424–5n; as
class-based calamity, 120, 201;
cultural depictions of, 188
Bengal Technical College, Calcutta,
175
Bengali language: emergence around
tenth century, 28; *Charjapad*
(early writings), 29–30; regional
accents, 30; Tagore's love of, 39;
Syed Mujtaba Ali's use of, 50; as
medium of instruction at
Santiniketan, 93; and early
Muslim kings, 133; and Bengali
identity, 134–6; and 'Bengal
renaissance' in Calcutta, 178;
common Bengali concept of
'home', 4; the Bengali-speaking
Rohingyas in Burma, 13
Bengali language movement (*bhasha
andolan*), 132, 134–6
Bengali literature: celebration of
rivers, 19, 24, 26, 28–9, 32–3;
Mangal Kavyas (narratives in
poetry), 28–9, 180; and
Bhusuku, 29–30; Humayun
Kabir's *Nadi O Nari*, 32–4; of
Kazi Nazrul Islam, 135–6, 176;
and Calcutta, 176, 178, 180, 1
Bankim Chandra
Chattopadhyay, 176, 178;
Michael Madhusadan Dutt,
160, 176–8; Buddhadeb Bose,
176, 330; Jasimuddin, 176;
Bishnu De, 176; Syed Mujtaba
Ali, 50; Shamsur Rahman, 176;
Nabaneeta Dev Sen, 357–8
Berkeley, University of California at,
365, 366; Free Speech
Movement (1964-5), 366–7
Bhagirathi, river, 19, 28

Bhaskaras (ancient mathematicians), 98

Bicycle Thieves (Vittorio de Sica film, 1948), 188–9

Bihar (Indian state): ancient university of Nalanda, 27, 44, 105–8, 109, 415–16n; earthquake (January 1934), 49, 79–81, 82; Mejdi moves to rural Bihar, 58; as original centre of Buddhism, 105–8, 109; love of rural Bihar, 58

Bijak (a selection of Kabir's poems, English translations), 73

Birmingham University, 369

Bitter Rice (*Riso Amaro*, Giuseppe De Santis film, 1949), 242

Blackwell Publishing, 338–9

Boko Haram, 305

Bologna university, 105

Bolpur (West Bengal), 41

Bombay (now called Mumbai), 6, 164, 179, 184, 241–3

Brahmaputra river, 20, 24–5

Bretton Woods institutions 388

Britain: AS's arrival in Britain in 1953, 249–52; early-setting sun in, 295; Versailles Treaty (1919), 387–8; post-war policies on inequality, 387, 389–90, 397–8, 406; misguided policy of austerity following 2008 crisis, 215, 388; leaves European Union, 386; *see also* British Raj; East India Company

British Council library, Calcutta, 239–40, 263, 421n

British Raj: inadequacy of public education policy, 84–5, 167; Tagore's criticism of, 84–5, 92, 169; failures over Bengal famine, 116–21, 142, 168, 390–93; imprisonment through 'preventive detention', 139, 141–2, 173, 232, 244; AS's relatives imprisoned, 124, 135, 138–42, 144, 173, 232, 244; Curzon's attempt at partition, 126–7; India's capital moved from Calcutta to Delhi, 126, 164; enhancing of Hindu-Muslim differences, 129–30; Permanent Settlement (Cornwallis Code, 1793), 129–30, 131–2, 134, 331; and Indian agriculture, 129, 130, 131–2, 134, 325, 331; Indian Civil Service (ICS), 142, 246; 'orderly culture' of, 142; Cripps Mission (March 1942), 143–4; Linlithgow declaration (1939), 143; Mutiny (1857), 153, 163; established Bitish rule after victory at Plassey (1757), 155–7, 158, 162, 164, 174; assessment of impact on India, 157–8, 159–69; Karl Marx on, 159, 160; claimed achievements of the Empire, 162–3, 166–7, 168–9; 'post-Plassey plunder', 164–6; classical imperialism phase, 165, 166–7; censorship by, 167, 168, 391, 392–3; absence of welfare systems, 390; *see also* East India Company

Buddhism: Faxian's *A Record of Buddhistic Kingdoms*, 26; Sahajiya thought, 29–30; defiance of caste, 29, 107, 398; Ashoka (emperor), 59, 109,

Buddhism – *cont'd.*
163, 393, 394; Sanskrit as
language of scholarship, 94;
Bihar as original centre of,
105–8, 109; first and third
Buddhist Councils, 109, 393;
Pala kings in Bengal, 133; in
Japan, 268, 394; and Ranji
Salgado, 315; school at
Takshashila (Taxila), 415–16n;
Buddhism in Burma, 13, 15
Budiganga, river, 20
Burma, 9–12; warmth and kindness
of Burmese people, 11, 14;
Aung San Suu Kyi's leadership,
12–14, 15–16; Japanese
military occupation (1941), 17,
37, 116, 143; Zafar's grave in,
163–4; military rule, 12–14,
15–16; brutality against
Rohingyas, 13–16, 409n;
persecution of different
minority groups, 11, 13–16.

Calcutta (also known as Kolkata):
theatre in, 7, 36, 186–8, 273;
AS's childhood visits, 17, 19,
20, 69, 120–21, 173; WW2
bombing of, 17, 37, 120, 173;
silting of Calcutta port, 19, 27;
YMCA hostel at Mechua
Bazar, 26, 182–3, 185, 199,
213, 223, 225–6, 362; mouth
of the Ganges near, 27–8, 161,
178–9; East India Company in,
27, 160, 161, 164–6, 174,
175–6, 178–80, 182; and
Ghoti–Bangal rivalry, 30, 31–2;
visiting during the Bengal
famine (1943), 114–16, 117,
119, 120–21, 173, 391–3;
Hindu–Muslim riots (1926),
125; British move their capital
to Delhi, 126, 164; absentee
Hindu landlords in, 130;
communal violence in 1940s,
148; AS's parents move to
(1945), 150, 151; militant trade
unions in, 152; 'Maratha ditch'
at, 164; image of, 173–4,
177–8, 185–6; Satyajit Ray on,
173–4, 189; Kipling on, 173,
174, 177, 178, 189; British
choice of Calcutta, 174,
178–80; origins of modern city,
174, 176–7, 178–80, 419n;
'Bengal renaissance' in, 175–6,
178; cultural and intellectual
richness of, 175–6, 178, 186–9;
the founding of the economics
department at Jadavpur, 175,
328–35, 342, 357; British
colonial heritage, 176–7,
184–5; and Bengali literature,
176, 178, 180, 186–8; Victoria
Memorial Hall, 177, 184–5;
Thornton's chart of the
Hooghly River, 179–80;
pre-colonial history of the
region, 180–82; underground
metro system, 181; bookshops
in, 183, 200, 203, 205, 238; as
a multicultural city, 184;
nationalist movements in, 184;
Town Hall, 184; *boi mela*
(annual book fair), 186; Young
Bengal (radical intellectual
movement) in, 194–6;
Carmichael Hospital, 224–5; R.
G. Kar Medical College and

Hospital, 224; AS's parents move to (1952), 226–7; Chittaranjan Cancer Hospital, 226, 227, 228–34, 235–6, 278–9; railway station (Howrah station), 241–2; anglicized part of, 246, 247; Bangla Academy in, 414n; absentee Hindu landlords in Calcutta earning land rent from east Bengal; *see also* Presidency College, Calcutta

Calcutta University, 175, 194, 200, 241, 419–20n

California, 365

Cambridge University: founding of (1209), 107; choice of Trinity (1953), 239–41; the Majlis, 273–5; Marshall Library, 275; resistance to social choice theory, 289, 292–3, 294, 370–71, 376–7, 378, 403; Socialist Club, 308–10, 311, 312; the Apostles, 316–21, 336, 344; Madhav Rao visits A.C. Pigou, 395–6; AS leaves (June 1963), 396–7, 402 *see also* Trinity College, Cambridge

caste system: Buddhist defiance of, 29, 107, 398; inequities of, 49, 71–2, 79–81, 398, 405, 406; tenuous scriptural basis of, 71–2; Gandhi and Bihar earthquake, 79–81, 82; Buddha protests against, 96, 100, 107, 405; powerful hold of, 99–100

Center for International Studies (MIT), 358, 360

Central Calcutta College (later Maulana Azad College), 200

Central Labour College, London, 215

Chamba, kingdom of, 65–6

Chandraketugarh (archaeological site), 180–81

Charjapad (old Bengali writings), 29–30

Chartres Cathedral, France, 302, 303

Chaturanga (Bengali journal), 32

chess, the game of, 103

Chicago, University of, 371, 373

China: ancient contacts with India, 26–7, 106, 108, 160; Cheena Bhavan at Santiniketan, 51; Tagore's voyage to (1924), 71; Kshiti Mohan's accompanying Tagore in visiting China and Japan, 71; Japanese war-time atrocities in, 92, 143, 267; Chinese students at the ancient Nalanda university in India (from the seventh century), 106, 108; Han Dynasty, 108; and the Silk Route, 108; Mao's policy experiments in, 214; Nanjing massacre, 267; and concept of liberty, 380; war with India (1963), 398

Christianity, 67, 97, 183, 195, 305, 386; Unitarianism, 41, 196; early Christians in India, 160–61; Christian humanity, 270, 313; Catholic–Protestant division in Ireland, 372

CIPLA (Indian pharmaceutical firm), 242–3

City College, Calcutta, 175, 187

Civil Rights movement, 366

Cochin, 'native kingdom' of, 167

Columbia University, 366

Communist Party, British, 261–2, 269, 309, 310, 345
Communist Party, Italian, 277, 347, 379, 381
Communist Party of India, 119, 124, 140–41, 144–5, 152, 183, 201, 333–4
Community-based categorization: hostility against minorities, 13–16, 409n; vulnerable minority groups in Burma, 13–16, 409n; carefully cultivated vilification, 14–16, 33–4, 76–7, 91, 184, 266, 305, 372; power of intense propaganda, 14–16, 409n; selective hatred emerging in today's world, 14–16, 78, 305; communal bloodshed at partition (1947), 18, 150; Muslim separatism, 33; violence/bloodshed preceding partition, 33–4, 36, 91, 122–4, 125, 148, 150, 184, 305–6, 372; Tagore's rejection of, 36, 39, 91; and Kshiti Mohan's demonstration of communal distortions of classical ancient texts, 67–8, 71–7, 78, 125; insular interpretations of Hinduism today, 78, 107; disruptive role of identity, 91, 122–3, 147, 182, 266, 305–6, 372; reduction of people to singular identities, 91, 100, 122–3, 132–3, 182, 216, 266, 305, 372; Buddha's arguments for equality, 96; and multiple human identities, 100–101, 123, 132–3, 263, 372; and ancient Sanskrit classics, 100–102; and Nalanda's Buddhist world vision, 107, 109; similarity of class-identity of victims of violence despite different religious backgrounds, 123–4, 125; Muslim League and India's partition, 125–6, 130–31, 147–8, 149–50, 151, 416n; sectarian anti-Muslim history writing, 128; British rule enhances Hindu-Muslim divergence, 129–30; narrowness of cultural separatists, 136; Huntington's thesis of 'clash of civilizations', 137; use of the word 'communal', 416n
comparative literature, 358–9
'Conshi' (a derogatory name for a 'conscientious objector'), 251–2
Conservative Party in Britain, 277, 312
Coventry, 258, 275–7
COVID-19 pandemic, 61
Crete, 402

Darjeeling, hill station of, 245, 308
Dartington Hall, 410n
decisional analysis, 98
Delhi, 20, 60, 126, 152–3, 164
Delhi School of Economics (also called D-School), 319, 335, 395–7, 401–2, 403–7
Delhi University, 51, 153
democracy: history of democratic thought, 109, 393–4; in Britain during last years of Raj, 119, 390; British claims over Raj's

achievements, 166, 168, 169; in post-independence India, 168, 169, 284, 334, 398, 404; constructive role of opposition/ dissent, 201–2; and left-wing politics of 1950s, 201–3, 245, 333–4; implications of Arrow's theorem, 205–6, 291; Galbraith's idea countervailing power, 212; Marx's treatment of democracy, 212; anti-fascist movement in Italy, 381; Europe's post-war achievements, 386–7; backward-looking attitudes in today's UK and Europe, 386; the role of public reasoning, 393–4; fall of military junta in Greece, 402

Denmark, 299–300

Desh (Bengali cultural magazine), 117–18

development economics: Adam Smith's integrated understanding of, 26, 28, 32, 288, 406–7; key role of education, 56, 84–5, 288; development research, 265, 276, 360; Human Development Reports, 265, 400–401; distorted thinking over growth, 287–8; and growth maximization approach, 287–8; Peter Bauer's developmental ideas, 290;.

Dhaka: Wari (part of the old, historic city), 4–5, 9, 150; Jagat Kutir (AS's family house in Dhaka), 5, 6, 18, 41, 122, 150; St Gregory's School in Lakshmi bazaar, 16–17, 35, 40, 93; during Second World War, 17, 18, 37, 113, 122; and the river Padda, 19–20; and Curzon's partition plan, 126–7; Muslim Nawabs in, 128; muslin (a type of refined textile), 134.

Dhaka University, 5, 6, 151, 193, 274–5, 330; Ashutosh Sen's teaching , 4, 5, 6, 18, 114, 150, 330; Ashutosh Sen's lack of sympathy for the land-dominated thinking of the Hindu rich and his attempts to encourage secular elements in the Muslim League,150–51; moves to Calcutta (1945), 60, 150–51, 190, 193

Dhaleshwari, river, 21, 23–4

Dharti Ke Lal (Khwaja Ahmad Abbas film, 1946), 188

Dolomites, 297–8

Dresden, 258

East Asia Summit, 105, 107

East Bengal (Calcutta football team), 31–2

East India Company, 129–30, 160, 161, 162; arrival in Calcutta (1690), 27, 174, 178–80, 182; 'the financial bleeding of Bengal', 164–6; spread of its rule, 164; Adam Smith's indictment of, 165–6; Edmund Burke's opposition to, 166, 219–20; governance by Warren Hastings, 166, 175–6, 219–20

East Pakistan, 18, 30, 124, 132, 134–5, 247

Econometric Society, 378

economic and social arguments: the importance of rivers, 25–6, 27–8, 32, 161, 179; impact of the Silk Route, 108, 109; deficiencies of the market mechanism, 114–20, 188, 217, 286, 314–15, 348–9, 406; economics at Presidency College, 192–3, 196–8, 207–9, 220; Marx's absence from curriculum in 1950s, 207–9; 'labour theory of value', 207–10, 211, 213, 289, 346, 420n; slogans of Cambridge economists, 260–61; imperfect competition, 264, 284, 349; neo-Keynesian schools, 270–71, 286, 287, 288, 289, 290, 369; capital theory, 270, 285, 286, 287, 294, 380; sectarianism between schools of thought at Cambridge, 285–90, 362, 364, 368, 369–70; main debates in Cambridge in 1950s, 287–90; use of 'aggregate capital' in modelling, 287; externalities, 314–15, 402; shared 'public goods', 315; classificatory devices in epistemology, 328–9; investment planning, 342–3, 370; relative prices of old and new machines, 361; Solow as a great teacher of economics, 361; Tuesday Club at Cambridge, 370; market socialism, 373; Keynes' 'general theory', 388; rationing and price control during the Second World War, 389

educational approaches at Santiniketan, 17–18, 36–40, 42–3, 65–6; in India, 20, 56, 94; physical punishment prohibited by Tagore, 36; Tagore's views on, 36, 38–43, 49, 55–6, 62–3, 84–5, 91;and social choice theory, 425n
Egypt, 248–9
English language and literature: poetry, 22, 169, 174, 177–8; teaching at Santiniketan, 43; and non-native English speakers, 50; Kshiti Mohan's book on Hinduism, translated into English 77–8; translation of Tagore's poems, 88
Enquiry (journal in Delhi), 337
European integration in early 1960s, 304; united Europe as an old dream, 38; Ventotene Declaration (1941), 385; Milan Manifesto (1943), 385, 424n; big achievements but growing scepticism, 386–8
evolution, theory of, 61–2

Facebook, 409n
Falklands War (1982), 312
famines: focus not just on food availability but on food entitlement, 98, 99, 115–21, 168–9; Bengal famine (1769–70), 119, 165–6, 168; as class-based calamities, 120, 201; prevention of, 121, 168–9
films and departures in cinema, 5, 92, 128, 173–4; Italian neorealist tradition, 188–9, 242, 295; in 1950s India, 188, 189

First World War: and Tagore's poetry, 89; fallen Trinity men, 258, 262–3, 305, 372; and Dennis Robertson, 344
Florence, 297
fluid dynamics, 339
football (soccer), 31–2, 46
France: trading companies in Bengal, 27, 156, 180; and social choice theory, 203, 204; student unrest in Paris (1968), 366; AS's visits to Paris, 302–3; to Aix-en-Provence, 303–4; European unity movement, 386; and Versailles Treaty (1919), 387–8
French Revolution, 195, 379
friendship, importance of, 54–5, 185, 396–7

gambling, discussion in the Rigvedas (2nd millennium BC), 103–5
game theory, 319–20, 336, 402
Ganga ('the Ganges'), river, 19–20, 24–5, 27–8, 161, 178–80
Gaur, ancient kingdom in Bengal, 30
gay communities, hatred and bigotry against, in Poland, 14
gender bias in Indian culture, 12, 52–3, 71–2
gender-related issues: agency of women, 7–8, 12, 52–3; women in theatre, 7–8, 36, 187; education at Tagore's school, 7, 52–3; maternal mortality, 8–9; gender bias in Indian culture, 52–3, 71–2; inequality, 52–3, 71, 98, 99, 217–18, 274–5; and 'objective illusion' concept, 217–18; ideas developed by

Salma Sobhan, 274–5; Ain O Salish Kendra (Centre for Law and Legal Redress), 275; conditions of women in prison, 311; names acquired through marriage, 311
General Belgrano, sinking of (1982), 312
Germany: AS's travel in Germany, 300–307; taking boats along the Rhine, 306–7; Nazi era, 4, 36, 143, 145–6, 251, 269; post-second-world-war global frame of mind, 306–7, 396; Allied fire-bombing of German cities during the war, 304–5
Gilgamesh (Mesopotamian epic), 359
globalization, 108–9, 158, 159–61, 397
Goalando (Bengal), 20
Gothic architecture, 302
Grantchester Meadows, 281, 325
Greece, 402
Gyan Chaupar (Snakes and Ladders), 103–4, 415n
Gypsies, hatred and bigotry against, 14

Harvard, 3, 13, 44, 320, 358–9, 364, 365, 366
health care/medicine: and child birth, 8–9; in Thailand, 11; in today's Burma, 11, 14; Yi Jing's comparative study between China and India, 27, 106; Ayurvedic system, 66; Gandhi's view of, 82; National Health Service (NHS), 215, 279–81, 387, 389, 390, 397–8; and the

health care/medicine *Cont.*
'needs principle', 215; in 1950s
Calcutta, 224–5, 226, 227,
228–34, 235–6, 278–9; medical
linear accelerators, 231; and
value of a positive attitude,
237–8; medicine for AIDS,
242; in Cambridge, 277,
279–81; RTC at
Addenbrooke's, 279–81
hiccups, remedy for, 6
Hindu Mahasabha (political party),
131
Hinduism: Lokayata/Charvaka
school, 5, 64, 95, 223; today's
aggressive political version, 14,
78, 107, 149; communal
violence in 1940s, 18, 33–4, 36,
76, 91, 122–4, 125, 148, 150,
184, 305–6, 372; epics
Ramayana and *Mahabharata*,
62, 64, 94–5, 133; Upanishads,
62; and atheistic philosophy,
64–5, 94, 95, 103; *Rig Veda*,
64–5, 103, 104–5, 359, 411n,
415n; the *Vedas*, 64–5, 102–3,
104–5, 359; 'Kabir Panth'
pluralist tradition, 67–8, 72–7,
78, 125, 149, 412n; Bhakti
movement, 67, 73; distorted
readings of texts, 71–2; Kshiti
Mohan's English book on
(1961), 77–8, 359–60, 413n;
Sanskrit as language of
scriptures, 94; *Bhagavadgeeta*,
95, 96; 'Hindutva' term, 107,
149; and demands for partition,
126; sectarian anti-Muslim
history writing; Hindu
majoritarianism, 148–9; the

Brahmo Samaj (reformist
society), 196; eating rules and
prohibitions, 299; and Bishop
of Edinburgh, 313
Hindusthan Standard (old, now
defunct, newspaper), 57
Hiroshima atomic bomb, 146, 232,
258, 267, 268
hockey, Indian women's team, 246
Hotel Select, Paris, 302–3
human rights activism, 274–5
Hungary, 14, 386; uprising (1956),
308, 333

Ichamati, river (Bengal), 23
identities: reduction of people to
singular identities, 91, 100,
122–3, 132–3, 182, 216, 266,
305, 372; disruptive role of
insistence on a single dominant
identity, 91, 122–3, 147, 182,
266, 305–6, 372; multiple
human identities, 100–101,
123, 132–3, 263, 372; class-
identity of victims of communal
violence, 123–4, 125; Bengali
identity, 132–7; Marx on
plurality of identities of human
beings, 215–16; and conflicts in
today's world, 305; national
identity, 305; planned political
manipulation of, 374–5
indexing, 348
Indian Association for the
Cultivation of Science,
Calcutta, 175
Indian Civil Service (ICS), 142,
246
Indian National Army (Azad Hind
Fauj), 116, 119, 146–7, 268

Indian National Congress, 33, 131, 149, 151, 183; socialist wing of, 119, 124, 141, 145; and Second World War, 143, 144, 145; Quit India movement, 144, 145; and Subhas Chandra Bose, 145, 146; and secular politics, 148, 149; first meeting (1885), 184

Indian People's Theatre Association (IPTA), 188

Indian Statistical Institute (ISI), Calcutta, 175, 191

Indiana University, 357, 358

Industrial Revolution, 397

inequality: and caste system in India, 49, 71–2, 79–81, 398, 405, 406; gender-related issues, 52–3, 71, 98, 99, 217–18, 274–5; and Soviet Union, 84; Buddha opposes, 96; AS's work on, 98, 99, 193, 217–18, 315, 404–6; and Shudraka's Mricchakatika, 100–102; class analysis of, 125; land inequality embedded under British rule, 129–30, 131–2, 134, 331; Nazrul's opposition to, 135–6; in post-independence India, 192, 193, 334, 398, 404–6; and labour theory of value, 209–10; Marx and the needs principle, 213–15; and Marx's objective illusion, 217–18; illiteracy and poverty in India, 234; roots of deprivation, 275; and Cambridge economics of 1950s, 287–8, 315, 343–4, 345; and growth maximization approach, 287–8; and Rawlsian

theory, 290–91; long history of in India, 334, 398, 404–6; and utilitarian ethics, 343–4; and Britain's post-war policies, 387, 389–90, 397–8, 406; results of better sharing in Britain during 1940s, 389, 390, 397–8, 405–6

Innsbruck, 298

International Bar Association, 273

International Economic Association, 265

International Monetary Fund, 315, 388

Iran, 161

Iraq War (from 2003), 312

Ireland, 372

Irrawaddy, river, 10, 22

Islam: communal violence in 1940s, 18, 33–4, 36, 76, 91, 122–4, 125, 148, 150, 184, 305–6, 372; in Kabir's novel Nadi O Nari, 33; Muslim separatism in Bengal, 33, 125–6, 130–31, 147–8, 149–50, 151; 'Kabir Panth' pluralist tradition, 67–8, 72–7, 78, 125, 149, 412n; Sufi tradition, 67, 73, 78; Muslim majority in Bengal, 126; Muslim elite in North India, 127–8; pre-Mughal Muslim rule in India/Bengal, 128–9, 133–4, 284; Nawabs in India, 128; Muslim 'Ashrafs' in Bengal, 129; Arab traders on Indian west coast, 161; eating rules and prohibitions, 299

Islamic State, 305

Islamic studies, 266

Islamophobia, 305

Israel, Central Bank of, 265

Israel–Palestine situation, 265–6
Italy: neorealist tradition in film,
    188–9, 242, 295; Marxism in,
    270, 347, 354–6, 381; political
    career of Nino Andreatta, 271;
    political career of Luigi
    Spaventa, 277–8; deprivation in
    Mezzogiorno, 277; CONSOB,
    278; anti-fascist movement,
    295, 347, 381; AS takes 'Fine
    Arts Tour' of (1954), 296–8;
    listed buildings in, 296;
    left-wing intellectual circles in
    1920/30s, 347, 354–6, 379–80,
    381; Neapolitan gesture of
    scepticism, 352–3; and
    European unity movement,
    385–6, 424n

Jadavpur University, Calcutta, 175,
    328–35, 342, 357
Jamuna, river (northern India), 20,
    179
Japan: military occupation of
    Burma (1941), 17, 37, 116,
    143; violence of WW2
    occupation forces, 36, 85–6,
    92, 267; education in, 56;
    Tagore's voyage to (1924), 71;
    atrocities in China, 143; and
    Netaji Subhas Chandra Bose,
    146; Meiji restoration (1868),
    158, 161, 162; and Perry's
    warships (1853), 158, 161;
    Okazaki Institute in Tokyo,
    266; Buddhism in, 268, 394;
    'constitution of seventeen
    articles' (AD 604), 393
Johns Hopkins Medical School, 11,
    14, 409n

Journal of Political Economy, 380
Jugabani (right-wing magazine),
    329
justice: Kshiti Mohan's sense of,
    71–2, 75; AS's work on, 98,
    101–2, 290–91, 319–20; and
    Shudraka's Mricchakatika,
    100–102; niti and nyaya
    (Sanskrit terms), 101–2; AS's
    The Idea of Justice (2009),
    101–2, 320, 415n, 422n;
    Burke's ideas of, 219–20;
    Justice Pal's dissenting
    statement, 267–8; Rawls'
    theory of, 290–91, 319–20;
    'Games, Justice and the General
    Will' (AS and Runciman),
    319–20, 422n; and Robertson's
    utlitarian ethics, 343–4; and
    human cconnections, 397; 'Of
    Justice' (David Hume), 397

Kabir Panth pluralist tradition,
    67–8, 72–7, 78, 125, 149,
    412n
Kalevala (Finnish epic), 359
Kanpur (India), 24
Karachi, 400
Karen people, 11
Kashmir, 392, 399
Kenduli (West Bengal), 41,
    410–11n
Keynesian economics, 215, 270–71,
    286, 287, 288, 289, 290, 369,
    388
King's College, Cambridge, 220–21,
    264, 265, 316
Krakow (Poland), 374–5
Krishak Praja Party, 131
Kushana period, 181

La Martinere College, Calcutta, 272
Labour Party, British, 143, 144,
    312–13, 314, 389–90
Lahore, 398–400
Lahore Resolution (1940), 33, 131,
    148
Langal ('Plough', literary magazine),
    135
language: non-native speakers, 50;
    Panini (grammarian), 93–4,
    329, 416n; and identity, 134–6;
    and Gramsci, 261, 356; and
    Wittgenstein, 261, 352–3,
    354–5, 356; 'the picture theory
    of meaning', 352–3; 'ordinary
    language philosophy', 353, 355,
    356
Latin America, 242
left-wing politics: in 1940s India/
    Bengal, 84–5, 119, 124–5, 129;
    influence of Soviet Union, 84–5,
    119, 141, 144–5, 202–3,
    332–4; Tagore's visit to USSR
    (1930), 84–5; and Bengal
    famine (1943), 119, 201;
    Congress Socialist Party, 119,
    124, 141, 145; and Nazrul
    Islam, 135–6; and uncle Shidhu
    (Jyotirmay Sengupta), 140–41;
    British Labour Party, 143, 144,
    312–13, 314, 389–90; in 1950s
    Calcutta, 188, 201, 207, 245,
    308, 331, 332–4, 379; and
    1950s democracy, 201–3, 245,
    333–4; authoritarian
    tendencies, 201–3, 212, 235,
    245, 308–9, 332–4, 379–80;
    and concept of liberty, 201,
    212–13, 332–4, 379–80;
    Student Federation in Calcutta,

201; denial over Soviet tyranny,
    235, 245, 308–9, 332–4;
    Cambridge economics of
    1950s, 240, 261–2, 269,
    270–71, 285, 286, 287–8,
    289–90, 293, 345–6; and
    international trade, 243; and
    Lal Jayawardena, 276; in
    post-war Italy, 277–8; and
    welfare economics, 293;
    Cambridge Left in 1950s,
    308–12; Oxford left in 1950s,
    309–10; and the Apostles at
    Cambridge, 317; and AS's job
    at Jadavpur, 329; Italian
    intellectual circles in 1920/30s,
    347, 354–6, 379–80, 381;
    intolerance of American Left,
    358; Oscar Lange's turn to
    Stalinism, 373–5; market
    socialism, 373; in 1960s
    Pakistan, 399–400 *see also*
    entries for Communist Parties
Liberal Party, British, 312, 314
Lokayata/Charvaka school of
    thought, 5, 64, 95, 223
London, 66, 215, 239, 244, 249–52,
    323, 325
London, University of, 239, 244
London School of Economics, 54,
    153, 239, 272, 339, 342
Lucknow, 127–8

Madhumati, river (Bengal), 23
Manas Sarovar (Himalayan lake), 24
Manashamangal Kavya (old Bengali
    poetic composition), 28–9, 180
Mandalay (Burma), 9–12
Mandalay Agricultural College, 9,
    11–12

Maratha warriors, 164, 179
maritime commerce, 25–6, 27–8, 32, 161
Marxist thinking: and 1940s India, 124–5; and Sushobhan Sarkar, 196; and 1950s India, 207–9; and Maurice Dobb, 209–10, 211, 217, 221, 240, 261–2, 269, 285, 286, 287, 289, 345–6; decadence of tradition by 1950s, 221; intellectual reach of, 221; applicability to today's world, 222; and Cambridge economics of 1950s, 240, 261–2, 269, 270–71, 285, 286, 289, 293, 345–6; world of Italian Marxism, 270, 347, 354–6, 381; Joan Robinson's rejection of, 285, 286; and Cambridge Socialist Club, 308, 309, 311; and problem of fatalism, 336
Massachusetts Institute of Technology (MIT), 324, 358–64, 365, 376
mathematics: AS's childhood enthusiasm for, 31, 69, 93; traditional Indian interest in, 41, 102–3, 159; reasoning, 43–4, 83, 98, 192, 203–6, 293, 377–8; teaching of at Visva-Bharati school, 43–4, 93, 97–8; foundations of, 43, 44, 83, 98; philosophy of, 44, 83, 98; in AS's teaching career, 44, 402; analytical reasoning, 97–8, 191–2, 197, 349–50, 361, 363–4, 369, 378, 404; and Sanskrit, 98, 99, 102–3; *Aryabhatiya*, 99; 'Vedic',

102–3; and global search for ideas, 108–9; AS studies with economics at Presidency College, 192–3, 194; mathematical logic, 203–6, 336, 402; and social choice theory, 203–6, 293, 363–4, 377–8; at Trinity, 240, 266, 336, 371–2; Lie groups in, 324; recursive function theory, 336; confusion of mathematical and causal determination, 350; invariance conditions, 363–4
Matto (AS's home village), 5–6, 12, 21
Maymyo (Burma), 10, 11–12
Mayurakkhi, river (Bengal), 23
media: censorship during WW2 and Bengal famine, 118, 119, 167, 390–93, 424–5n; in-post independence India, 167, 168, 169
Medical College, Calcutta, 175, 200, 225–6
Meghna, river, 20, 21, 22, 24
Mind (philosophy journal), 319–20
Miracle in Milan (Vittorio de Sica film, 1951), 188–9
Mohammedan Sporting (Calcutta football team), 31
Mohan Bagan (Calcutta football team), 31–2
Moulmein (Burma), 22
Mughal empire, 27, 107, 128–9, 136–7, 163–4, 179, 399
Murshidabad (Bengal), 155, 156, 174
music, 52, 157, 281, 320, 324, 410n, 411n; AS's ineptitude at singing, 45; Gandhi on, 48–9

Muslim League, 125–6, 130–31,
    147–8, 149–50, 151, 416n

Nagasaki atomic bomb, 146, 232,
    258, 267, 268
Nalanda, ancient Buddhist
    university, 27, 44, 105–8, 109,
    415–16n
National Cadet Corp (NCC), 46–8
National Health Service (NHS),
    215, 279–81, 387, 389, 390,
    397–8
National Union of Students, 296
nationalism: in AS's family, 6, 124–5,
    135, 138–42, 144;
    independence movements, 33,
    116, 119, 125–6, 130–31,
    143–51, 184, 268; Tagore as
    fiercely critical of, 39, 91–2;
    anti-British in Bengal, 126, 184;
    Indian Association, 184; and
    Henry Derozio, 195–6; and
    school of Subaltern Studies, 332
'neoclassical' economists, 269, 285,
    286, 287, 288–9, 294, 350, 368
Netherlands: trading companies in
    Bengal, 27, 179, 180; AS
    travels in (1955), 300
New York City, 365, 401
New York Times, 409n
Newnham College, Cambridge, 274
Nibelungenlied (German epic), 359
Nile, river, 25–6
night school run by AS and his
    classmates for tribal children at
    Santiniketan, 44–5, 99, 201,
    401; education of pre-
    agricultural tribal population, 59
Northern Ireland, 372
Norway, 269, 298–9

Notting Hill (London), 323
nuclear disarmament campaign, 309
nuclear fission, 339

The Observer, 313–14
Odantapuri university (Bihar), 416n
Odisha (Indian state), 247, 410–11n
oral epic poetry, 94–5, 358–9
L'Ordine Nuovo (Italian journal),
    347, 354–5, 356
Oxford University, 107, 193, 245,
    247, 339–40, 402; the Majlis
    at, 274; Socialist Club, 309–10

Padda, river, 19–21, 22, 23, 29,
    32–3
Padma, river (branch of old Ganga),
    27
Pakistan, 12, 149, 150, 392, 398–401
Pali texts, 71, 94
Paris, 302–3, 366
Park Hospital, Manchester, 389, 390
Parsees, 161
Past & Present (history journal), 232
Pathans from Afghanistan, 128–9,
    133
Patna (India), 19, 24, 26, 105, 109,
    179, 393
Penguin Books, 77–8, 359
Persian language, 67
Perugia, 297
pharmaceutical industry, 242–3
Philippines, 267
philosophical thought: and
    mathematics, 44, 83, 98;
    atheistic, 64–5, 94, 95, 103;
    'Song of Creation' from Rig
    Veda, 64–5, 103, 359, 411n; of
    Guatama Buddha, 95–7; ethics
    of 'unconditional onus', 96–7,

philosophical thought – *cont'd.*
403–4; 'social contract'
concept, 96, 97, 403, 425n;
Western ethics, 96; story of the
Good Samaritan in Gospel
according to Luke, 97, 307;
and the Apostles at Cambridge,
316, 318–20, 336; Rawlsian,
319, 320, 336; determinism,
336–7; and AS's Prize
Fellowship, 336–7;
Wittgenstein's extraordinary
reputation, 351–5; of Sraffa,
351, 352–6; and Gramsci,
355–6; AS teaches at Delhi
School of Economics, 402
Pitti Palace, Florence, 297
Plassey, Battle of (23 June 1757),
155, 156–7, 158, 162, 163,
164, 174
Poland, 14, 300, 374–5, 386
polonium, 230
Portugal, trading companies in
Bengal, 27, 179, 180
poverty: and communal violence in
1940s, 123–4, 125; in Calcutta,
178, 183, 185–6; and crime,
186; in post-independence
India, 234, 404–5; roots of
deprivation, 275; and
Cambridge economics of
1950s, 287–8, 343–4; and
growth maximization
approach, 287–8; and
utilitarian ethics, 343
Prabashi (Bengali cultural
magazine), 118
Presidency College, Calcutta: AS as
student of, 25–6, 49–50, 93,
175, 182–6, 190–206, 207–9,

219–20, 234–8, 329–30, 373,
379, 405–6, 419–20n; AS's
wish to study at, 173;
Sushobhan Sarkar's teaching,
175, 329–30; Satyajit Ray as
student at, 189; record of
exceptional students, 190–92;
economics teaching at, 192–3,
196–8, 207–9, 220;
mathematics teaching at,
192–3; history of, 193–6; and
emergence of Young Bengal,
194–6; radical tradition of,
195–6, 238; poetry circle at,
198–9, 234–5; fellow students
of AS, 198–200; coffee house
conversations, 199–200, 203,
205, 222, 238, 267–8, 332,
373, 405–6; as co-educational,
199; AS returns to after cancer
treatment, 234–5, 238
prison system, Indian, 138–9,
141–2

Quakers, 251–2
Quarterly Journal of Economics,
326
Queen Elizabeth II (ocean liner),
365
Quit India movement, 144, 145

racism: growth of intolerance in
today's world, 13–16, 305,
409n; role of propaganda,
14–16, 409n; cultivated
hostility to refugees, 305; Adam
Smith's hatred of, 406–7
Rajgir, old town in Bihar, location of
the first Buddhist Council in the
sixth century BC, 109

Rakhine (Burma), 15
Rangoon, 163–4
Ravensbrück concentration camp, 269
religion: religious extremism, 14–16, 150; 'intelligent creation' idea, 55; and natural selection, 62; weekly assemblies at Santiniketan, 63–4; atheism, 64–5, 94, 95, 103; Hindu–Muslim interaction, 67–8, 72–7, 78; 'Kabir Panth' pluralist tradition, 67–8, 72–7, 78, 125, 149, 412n; Tagore-Gandhi dispute over Bihar earthquake, 79–81, 82; Tagore's beliefs, 88, 90; Mughal plurality policy, 128–9; counter-reformation in Europe, 128; intolerance in sixteenth-century Europe, 128; reformism in nineteenth-century Calcutta, 196; identity conflicts in today's world, 305 *see also* Christianity; Hinduism; Islam
Renaissance painting, 295
Reserve Bank of India, 325
rivers, 6, 10, 19–29, 32–4, 106, 161, 179
road transport in Bengal, 181
Rohingya community in Burma, 13–16, 409n
Rome, University of (La Sapienza), 277
Rothamsted Research (Harpenden), 239
Royal Asiatic Society of Bengal (Asiatic Society, Calcutta), 175, 176
Royal Holloway College, 311

Rüdesheim wine festival, 306–7, 396
Rupnarayan, river (Bengal), 23

Saha Institute of Nuclear Physics, Calcutta, 175
saltpetre trade, 179
sampling theory, 191
Sanskrit: AS's love of, 5, 31, 64, 93–5, 98; Kshiti Mohan's scholarship, 6–7, 36, 58, 64–5, 66–7, 68, 71–2, 77; and AS's name, 8; literature, 24, 62, 64–5, 93, 94–5, 98, 100–105; Yi Jing learns, 26–7, 106; Bengali's descent from, 28; teaching at Visva-Bharati, 39, 51, 72, 93–5, 97; Devanagari (common script of), 49; epics *Ramayana* and *Mahabharata*, 62, 64, 94–5, 133; atheistic and agnostic treatises in, 64–5, 94, 95, 103; 'Chatushpathis' at Benares, 66, 77; varieties of, 93; as language of Buddha/Buddhist scholarship, 94, 95; as language of Hindu scriptures, 94; and mathematics, 98, 99, 102–3; *niti* and *nyaya* (concepts of justice), 101–2; 'mother-in-law' anxieties in 'gambler's lament', 104–5; and Daniel Ingalls, 358, 359–60
Sanskrit College, Calcutta, 200
Santiniketan (West Bengal): AS born in (1933), 4, 8, 57; Gurupalli ('the village of teachers'), 8–9, 57–60, 78; Sripalli area, 8–9, 60–62; Pratichi (house in), 8, 60–61; AS moves to (1941), 17–18, 23, 30–31, 36–7, 57,

Santiniketan – *cont'd.*
78; AS's family's base shifts to (1947), 18, 151; on Ajay river, 23; and Bihar earthquake (January 1934), 79

Santiniketan, Visva-Bharati School: as co-educational, 7, 39, 52–3, 199; higher education/advanced research facilities at, 7, 40–41, 51; Kshiti Mohan teaches at, 7, 8, 36, 38, 40, 57, 63–4, 65–6, 71–2; AS's mother studies at, 7, 36; Tagore establishes (1901), 7, 41–3; teachers at, 7, 24–5, 38–9, 40–41, 43–5, 54, 57, 65–6; broad and inclusive curriculum, 17–18, 39–40, 91; freedom/relaxed atmosphere at, 17–18, 24–5, 37–9, 42–3, 52, 91, 113; and global history, 17–18, 39, 91, 161–2; AS moves to (1941), 17–18, 23, 30–31, 36–7, 57, 78; open-shelved library, 18, 161–2, 178, 181–2; AS's classmates and friends, 29–30, 50–55, 173, 192; sport at, 37, 46; classes held outdoors, 38–9, 42; prohibition of physical punishment, 38; Sanskrit teaching at, 39, 51, 72, 93–5, 97, 101–2; Kala Bhavan (school of fine arts), 40–41; mathematics teaching at, 43–4, 93, 97–8; English teaching at, 43; National Cadet Corp (NCC) at, 46–8; visiting speakers, 48–50, 83; school magazines, 53–4; Tagore at weekly assemblies, 62–3; the Mandir at, 62–4; referred to as 'ashram', 62; Tagore recruits Kshiti Mohan for, 65–6, 71–2; and Tagore-Gandhi disputes, 82–4; excursions to Rajgir and Nalanda 109; and Bengal famine (1943), 113–15; experience of Second World War at, 146–7; medical care at, 225

scientific knowledge: AS's father teaches chemistry, 4, 5, 6, 18, 60, 114, 150–51, 190; theory of evolution, 61–2; Tagore-Gandhi dispute over Bihar earthquake, 79–81, 82; AS's study of physics, 93; 'Bose–Einstein statistics', 150, 190; AS studies 'Intermediate Science' at Santiniketan, 173; education in Calcutta, 175, 190–91, 200

Scotland, 'West Lothian Question', 312–13

Scottish Church College, Calcutta, 175, 200

Second International Economic History Conference (1962), 303–4

Second World War: bombing of Calcutta, 17, 37, 120, 173; Dhaka during, 17, 18, 37, 113, 122; Japanese military occupation of Burma (1941), 17, 37, 116; Nazi atrocities, 36, 251, 269; and Tagore's last speech (April 1941), 36, 86; eastern front moves closer to India, 113; rising food prices during, 113, 114, 115–17, 120; Indian National Army (anti-British), 116, 119, 146–7, 268; censorship of Bengali newspapers during, 118, 119, 167, 390–93; Linlithgow declaration (1939), 143; civilian casualties, 258; Japanese war crimes, 267–8; Nazi occupation of Norway, 269; Allied fire bombings of German cities, 304–5; liberation of Auschwitz, 309; period before in Britain, 385; undernourishment in UK reduced during, 389, 390, 397–8, 405

Shalimar gardens (Lahore), 399

Shreyashi (Bengali magazine edited by AS's mother), 61

Silk Route, 108, 109

Singapore, 51, 108

Sino-Indian Cultural Society (Nanjing), 51

Sipra, river (Ujjain), 321

slavery, 406–7

social choice theory: and AS's Nobel Prize (1998), 98–9; and Tapas Majumdar, 197, 425n; AS introduced to, 203–6; and mathematics, 203–6, 293, 363–4, 377–8; AS's strong interest in, 203–6, 290, 291–2, 294, 364, 375–81; Arrow's work on, 203, 204, 205, 291, 292, 293, 294, 375–6, 377–8, 394; initiated in eighteenth-century France, 203, 204; de Condorcet and majority rule, 204–5, 291; majority vote, 204–5, 291; voting mechanisms, 204–5, 291,

377–8; Arrow's 'impossibility theorem', 204, 205–6, 291, 292, 293, 376, 377–8; description of, 204; and concept of liberty, 212–13, 378–80; and Marx, 212; resistance to at Cambridge, 289, 292–3, 294, 370–71, 376–7, 378, 403; social welfare judgements, 290–91, 343, 377–8; and nature of social communication, 293; and AS's time in USA, 365–7; AS's research at Trinity (1961-3), 375–81; Buchanan's work on, 376–7, 378, 423n; Arrow's 'collective rationality', 376, 377, 378; role of persuasion/discussion, 380–81, 387, 388, 390, 394; AS teaches at Delhi School of Economics, 402, 403–4; and other approaches to moral philosophy, 403–4; 'Pattanaik theorems', 403

sociology, 311

Solidarity Movement in Poland, 375

Sonarang (Bikrampur District of Dhaka), 21, 66

Song of Roland (French epic), 359

Sorbonne (Paris), 303

South Africa, post-apartheid, 269

Soviet Union: education in, 84–5; and Indian left-wing politics, 84–5, 119, 141, 144–5, 202–3, 245; and Second World War, 119; German invasion of (June 1941), 144; influence of in 1950s Calcutta, 202–3, 245, 332–4; purges and show trials, 202–3, 235, 245, 308, 333;

Soviet Union – *cont'd.*
   treatment of Eastern Europe,
   235, 301, 373–5; Twentieth
   Congress of Communist Party
   (1956), 308, 332–3; invasion of
   Czechoslovakia (1968), 310;
   Samuel Brittan visits, 314; and
   concept of liberty, 332–4, 380
Sperling & Kupfer (Milan
   bookshop), 355
Sphulinga (school magazine at
   Santiniketan), 53
spying, 317
Sri Lanka, 24, 25, 26, 276, 288
Sri Vijaya (now Sumatra), 26
St John's College, Cambridge, 316
St John's College, Oxford, 13
St Pancras station, London, 250
St Thomas the Apostle, 161
St Xavier's College, Calcutta, 175,
   200, 247
Stanford University, 273, 364–5
The Statesman (English newspaer,
   Calcutta), 119, 391–3,
   424–5n
statistics, 191–2
stochastic programming, 198
SS *Strathnaver*, 241, 243–7, 263,
   295
Stromboli (volcano), 249, 295
subaltern studies, 75, 331–2, 413n
Suez Canal, 248, 249
Sufi tradition, Islamic, 67, 73, 78
Sumatra (Sri Vijaya), 26, 106
Sunga period, 181
the supernatural on American TV,
   28–9
Supreme Court of India (Delhi), 273
Sweden, 298–9
Switzerland, 298

Takshashila (Taxila), religious
   school at, 415–16n
Tamralipta, ancient city of (Bengal),
   26, 27, 106
Tarikh-ilahi (Akbar's calendar),
   136–7
Tate Modern, 'the Nimai Chatterji
   collection', 414n
technology: and Kiran Bala's family,
   69; Gandhi and the *charka*,
   81–2, 83–4; Tagore's view of,
   81, 82, 83–4
Tennessee Valley Authority, 152
textiles industry in Bengal, 134, 179
Thailand, 11, 158, 266
theatre: women on stage in Calcutta,
   7–8, 36, 187; in Calcutta, 7, 36,
   186–8, 273; Rama Rau's *A
   Passage to India*, 320–21; West
   End in London, 325
The Times, 424–5n
tolerance and plurality, values of,
   67, 78, 90, 128, 201–2, 393
trade union movements, 140–41,
   152, 380, 399
Travancore, 'native kingdom' of,
   167
Trinity College, Cambridge: AS as
   undergraduate, 43, 44, 50,
   220–21, 257–62, 264–78,
   282–93, 308–16, 321–3, 347;
   Wittgenstein at, 83, 351–5;
   college regulations, 185,
   340–41; as single-sex college,
   199; AS rejected then accepted
   (1953), 240–41; students in
   digs, 255, 256–7; porters at,
   257–8, 322–3; AS arrives at
   (1953), 257–9; Great Gate,
   257, 262; history of, 257, 258;

Wren Library, 258–9, 348;
Nevile's Court, 258, 259–60;
AS as Prize Fellow, 261, 262,
277, 281, 334–8, 339–41, 342,
346, 347; AS as research
student at, 262, 293–4, 326–8,
337–9, 373–5; AS's Assistant
Lectureship at, 262, 342–5,
347, 370–71; AS's rooms in
New Court, 278; AS's rooms in
Whewell's Court, 282–4; AS as
Senior Scholar at, 296; and the
Apostles, 316; AS receives
degree in Senate Hall, 323; AS
returns to (September 1961),
368–9; AS as Master of the
College, 3, 13, 262–3, 281, 323,
422n; AS gives 80th birthday
lecture, 371–2; record with
overseas students/academics,
371–2; AS's research in social
choice theory (1961-3),
375–81; inheritance from
Sraffa, 422n
Tunisia, 265

Udayer Pathe (Bimal Roy film,
1944), 188
Uffizi Gallery, Florence, 297
Ujjain (Kalidasa's home town), 321–2
United Nations, 49–50, 56; 'Mother
Language Day', 134–5; Food
and Agriculture Organization
(FAO), 142; Development
Programme (UNDP), 400–401
United Nations University, Helsinki,
265, 276
United States: AS teaches at
Harvard, 3, 13, 44, 320, 364,
365, 366; television in, 28–9;

AS's father trains for project
management in, 152; as
pre-eminent imperial power,
157; Perry's warships in Japan
(1853), 158, 161; AS teaches at
MIT, 324, 358–64, 365, 376;
AS teaches at Stanford, 364–5;
AS teaches at Berkeley, 365,
366–7; Civil Rights movement,
366; public debates and radical
movements, 367; and Versailles
Treaty (1919), 387–8
Universal Declaration of Human
Rights, 49–50
universities: Nalanda as world's
oldest, 105–8, 109, 415–16n;
Bologna as oldest in Europe,
105; Nalanda re-established
(2014), 105, 107, 108, 109;
and egalitarian vision, 107;
under the Mughals, 107; in
today's India, 107; dialectical
method at Nalanda, 108
University College of Science,
Calcutta, 200
utilitarian economic thought, 240,
343–4; and Rawls' theory of
justice, 290–91; social
aggregation, 290; and theory of
value, 346; interpersonal
comparisons, 363–4

vaidyas (the medical caste), 11
Vanga, ancient kingdom of, 29, 30
Vatican Museums, 297
Venice, 297
Verona, 297
Versailles Treaty (1919), 387–8
Vietnam, 380
Vietnam War, 366, 421n

Vikramshila University (Bihar), 106, 416n
Vladimir Lenin Steelworks (near Krakow), 374–5

war crimes, 267–8
Warsaw, 300, 301
Warwick University, 153–4
welfare economics: resistance to at Cambridge, 289, 292–3, 294, 370–71, 376–7, 378, 403; need for aggregation, 290–91; interpersonal comparisons, 363–4; and Samuelson, 363–4; AS's lecture at MIT, 363, 376; AS teaches at Delhi School of Economics, 402 *see also* social choice theory

welfare systems: European welfare state, 215, 387, 388–9, 390, 397–8; and legacy of Second World War, 387, 388–90, 397–8
Welwyn Garden City, 315–16
wildlife: in Burma, 10; seen on river journeys, 21–2; Kiran Bala and stray animals, 70
World Bank, 56, 388
World Institute for Development Economics Research (UNU-WIDER), 265, 276

Yale, 323
Yemen, 248

Zemdri (antibiotic), 242

More from
AMARTYA SEN

IDENTITY AND VIOLENCE:
The Illusion of Destiny

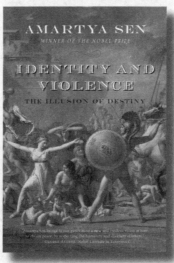

"*Identity and Violence* is a moving, powerful essay about the mischief of bad ideas." —*Economist* (UK)

"Impassioned, eloquent and often moving, *Identity and Violence* is a sustained attack on the 'solitarist' theory which says that human identities are formed by membership of a single social group."
—Joy Gray, *Guardian* (UK)

In this sweeping philosophical work, Amartya Sen proposes that the murderous violence that has riven our society is driven as much by confusion as by inescapable hatred. Challenging the reductionist division of people by race, religion, and class, Sen presents an inspiring vision of a world that can be made to move toward peace as firmly as it has spiraled in recent years toward brutality and war.

LIVERIGHT